Perspectives on Verbal and Psychological Abuse

Roland D. Maiuro
Editor

SPRINGER / PUBLISHING COMPANY

NEW YORK

Springer Publishing Company, LLC
11 West 42nd Street
New York, NY 10036
www.springerpub.com

ISBN: 978-0-8261-9465-7
e-book ISBN: 978-0-8261-9467-1

15 16 17 18 / 5 4 3 2 1

Content herein was selected from *Violence and Victims* (ISSN: 08866708; eISSN: 19457073) published bimonthly by © Springer Publishing Company, LLC. For more information, visit www.springerpub.com/journals/violence-and-victims.html

The author and the publisher of this Work have made every effort to use sources believed to be reliable to provide information that is accurate and compatible with the standards generally accepted at the time of publication. The author and publisher shall not be liable for any special, consequential, or exemplary damages resulting, in whole or in part, from the readers' use of, or reliance on, the information contained in this book. The publisher has no responsibility for the persistence or accuracy of URLs for external or third-party Internet websites referred to in this publication and does not guarantee that any content on such websites is, or will remain, accurate or appropriate.

Printed in the United States of America.

Contents

Introduction

Unlike physical abuse, which is often easily visible, psychological and verbal abuse can be subtle, elusive, and difficult to pinpoint. Yet every day in America, nearly one in two teenagers who are in a relationship feel they are being threatened or pressured to act in ways they don't wish to. According to a recent study, nearly 50% of both men and women have experienced some form of psychological abuse by their intimate partners. In some respects, emotional abuse is more devastating than physical abuse because victims are more likely to blame themselves. This interdisciplinary collection of authoritative research articles, published in the peer-reviewed journal *Violence and Victims,* provides comprehensive coverage of issues related to psychological and verbal abuse in intimate relationships—a topic on which there has been a paucity of research. These articles address how psychological aggression can be reliably measured as well as some of the challenges inherent in proving that these non-physical violent acts have occurred. Authors from a variety of professional disciplines—psychology, psychiatry, sociology, criminology, counseling, and social work—present research related to perpetrators of psychological abuse, victims of this abuse, and effective interventions.

Until recently, little was known about the complexity and degree of severity of psychological abuse. "The Nature and Prevalence of Partner Psychological Abuse in a National Sample of Adults" is a detailed analysis of the occurrence of serious psychological abuse in a person's "worst relationship" from a sample of adults in the United States. "Psychological Abuse: A Variable Deserving Critical Attention in Domestic Violence" focuses on the fact that psychological abuse almost always precedes physical abuse, necessitating prevention and treatment efforts directed toward psychological abuse before it escalates. The study "Perceived Verbal Conflict Behaviors Associated With Physical Aggression and Sexual Coercion in Dating Relationships: A Gender-Sensitive Analysis" concludes that gender-sensitive approaches are necessary to understand and prevent verbal conflict patterns with physical aggression and sexual coercion in intimate partnerships. "Stalking and Psychological Abuse: Common Factors and Relationship-Specific Characteristics" is a study of college students conducted to expand the models of personality characteristics in perpetrators of stalking and psychological abuse. Harsh parental discipline, anxious attachment, and need for control were all common factors in predicting these behaviors.

Psychological abuse can lead to a multitude of unfavorable repercussions for both women and men in their personal and professional lives. "Psychological Intimate Partner Violence During Pregnancy and Birth Outcomes: Threat of Violence Versus Other Verbal and Emotional Abuse" examines how physical abuse is linked to poor birth outcomes, but acknowledges that the effects of psychological abuse are less well understood. A survey was conducted in women with no history of physical abuse who were, however, threatened by an intimate partner during pregnancy. This scenario resulted in lower birth weight and other injurious effects.

"Measuring Interference With Employment and Education Reported by Women With Abusive Partners: Preliminary Data" evaluates the reliability of the Work/School Abuse Scale. The Work/School Abuse Scale is a useful measure of how physical abuse and other harmful influences in women's lives isolate them from activities that provide income, social contacts, and a sense of accomplishment. "Effects of Men's Subtle and Overt Psychological Abuse on Low-Income Women" is a study of over 800 low-income women in long-term heterosexual relationships. Men's overt psychological abuse, violent behavior, and sexual aggression were examined along with subtle psychological abuse as they relate to women's psychological and emotional states. In general, subtle psychological abuse was more strongly correlated with women's adverse emotional state. "The Impact of Different Forms of Psychological Abuse on Battered Women" describes a study including interviews with battered women receiving shelter or non-shelter services from a domestic violence agency. These women were interviewed about psychological abuse and its effects. The study demonstrated that both psychological and physical abuse leads to depression and low self-esteem. Additionally, the fear of being physically abused was predicted by the experience of psychological abuse. "The Development of a Measure of Psychological Maltreatment of Women by Their Male Partners" describes how the scale of measurement was developed and the results of a study comprised of reports by both male and female participants.

Research indicates that men are typically rated as having greater pathology and being more dangerous than women. In the article "Psychologists' Judgments of Psychologically Aggressive Actions When Perpetrated by a Husband Versus a Wife," the results of a study indicated that those surveyed rated the husband's behavior as more likely to be psychologically abusive and more severe in nature than when the wife used the same actions. "Abused Women or Abused Men? An Examination of the Context and Outcomes of Dating Violence" is a study that examines the issue of whether women or men are equally abused in dating relationships. The study indicates that women are more likely to experience sexual victimization and men are more often victims of psychological abuse. Rates of physical violence were shown to be similar across genders. "Psychological Abuse: Implications for Adjustment and Commitment to Leave Violent Partners" studies the contribution of psychological abuse to battered women's decisions to terminate their abusive relationships. The results suggest that psychological abuse and PTSD symptoms are important factors to assess among battered women. "Psychological and Physical Dating Violence Perpetrated by Pregnant and Parenting Latina Adolescents" examines predictors of such violence among 126 individuals in this group. Latina teenagers who engaged in negative communication patterns with their parents and those who were both the victim and perpetrator of physical abuse within their dating relationships were more likely to perpetrate psychological abuse.

While most psychological abuse occurs in intimate relationships, it can also happen in less intimate relationships, such as those in the workplace. "Interpersonal and Systemic Aspects of Emotional Abuse at Work: The Target's Perspective" evaluates people who "felt abused" or had difficulties with a boss or co-worker. The study found that work is a critical source of achievement and self-esteem. Workers expect the workplace to be supportive and challenging for their development and believe that the organization for which they work should provide acknowledgement and encouragement to help them develop professionally and personally. The study determined that research and organizational attention needs to be focused on identifying and clarifying the roles that the organization plays in emotional abuse at work.

This collection of distinguished articles contributes greatly to the understanding of an insidious form of violence—verbal and psychological abuse—that can be extremely destructive and is experienced by nearly half the population. Presenting perspectives from an interdisciplinary group of experts on the topic, this book provides a foundation for reliable measurement of psychological aggression, strategies for determining that non-physical acts of violence have occurred, and guidelines for effective treatment.

Violence and Victims, Volume 29, Number 1, 2014

The Nature and Prevalence of Partner Psychological Abuse in a National Sample of Adults

Diane R. Follingstad, PhD

Center for Research on Violence Against Women Department of Psychiatry, University of Kentucky Medical College, Lexington, KY

M. Jill Rogers, MS

Department of Educational, School and Counseling Psychology, University of Kentucky, Lexington, KY

A detailed analysis of the occurrence of serious psychological abuse (PSYAB) in one's "worst relationship" was solicited from a nationwide sample of adults in the United States. To designate that they experienced any of the psychologically abusive behaviors, respondents had to have perceived malignant intent by the perpetrator. Respondents reported significant rates of the presence and frequency for 14 specified categories of serious PSYAB as well as for the 42 individual behaviors constituting these categories (i.e., 3 per category). The 3 behaviors within each category frequently co-occurred even though they represented distinct manifestations and increasing levels of severity for that type of PSYAB. Only some of the behaviors demonstrated a relationship between frequency of that behavior in a relationship and subsequent emotional and behavioral impact. Neither demographics nor social desirability were strongly related to report of partner PSYAB.

Keywords: intimate partner violence; psychological aggression; couple psychological abuse; couple interactions

The significance of investigating psychological abuse (PSYAB) arises from the concern that this form of intimate partner violence (IPV) is likely to produce debilitating effects on its recipients. Tolman and Bhosley (1991) asserted that PSYAB was more strongly associated with psychosocial problems for female victims than threats of, or actual, physical abuse. Researchers have linked this form of abuse within a relationship to everything from mental disorders (e.g., Sackett & Saunders, 2001) to problematic traits (e.g., low self-esteem; Aguilar & Nightingale, 1994), to lifestyles reminiscent of hostages (e.g., Romero, 1985), and to effects on one's attitudes and beliefs (e.g., Marshall, 2001). PSYAB within an intimate relationship has also been associated with marital dissatisfaction (Stuart & Holtzworth-Munroe, 2005), the subsequent onset of physical violence (Murphy & O'Leary, 1989), and a negative impact on children whose parents engage in PSYAB (O'Leary & Jouriles, 1994). Although it is likely that devastating impacts occur, especially from long-standing and/or severe PSYAB, Follingstad's

(2009) review of the literature suggested that problematic measurement of the concept often results in contradictory results or results requiring more corroboration for even the most commonly assessed outcome variables. In light of the seriousness of the potential impacts, we must know more about the nature and prevalence of serious PSYAB.

As a field of study, PSYAB received its impetus from researchers and advocates who reported on the seemingly ever-present coexistence between IPV and nonphysical manifestations of domination and intimidation (e.g., Follingstad, Rutledge, Berg, Hause, & Polek, 1990; Murphy & O'Leary, 1989; Pence & Paymar, 1993). However, the phenomenon of PSYAB has long been recognized as also occurring in relationships without physical abuse (e.g., O'Leary & Cascardi, 1998). Because of the importance of understanding the role and function of PSYAB within populations experiencing physical abuse, much of the research to date has been conducted on battered women (e.g., Sackett & Saunders, 2001). Dating populations in colleges or high schools (e.g., Katz & Arias, 1999; Murphy & Hoover, 2001; Pipes & LeBov-Keeler, 1997) have been targeted as populations of interest because community samples of marital/cohabiting relationships have been more difficult to obtain (e.g., Russell & Hulson, 1992; Taft et al., 2006). In addition, community samples have often been fairly circumscribed and localized, thus preventing broad generalization of the results. The experience of female recipients of PSYAB has been studied more extensively than the experience of male recipients, although Russell and Hulson (1992) and Simonelli and Ingram (1998) investigated men's reactions to experiencing physical and emotional abuse. Thus, the study of PSYAB within the broader adult population in the United States is seriously lacking.

Just identifying a national sample for investigation will not solve the conceptual, definitional, and measurement problems that have existed since the inception of research in this field. (For a thorough discussion, see Follingstad, 2007.) A major hindrance for the designation of PSYAB (defined here as those tactics representing the egregious end of the psychological aggression continuum) has been the inclusion of less harmful relationship conflict behaviors along with the most severe forms of psychological maltreatment. Thus, the measures that have been developed, used, and modified across studies (O'Leary, 2001) have not been definitive for determining that truly *abusive* actions have occurred, and it is not surprising then that various measures are differentially related to outcome variables. For example, one measure may be heavily weighted with items assessing verbal abuse (i.e., criticism, name-calling, ridicule, and screaming) but another measure may tap behaviors indicative of threatening and intimidating behavior, such that only the second measure would correlate with a measure of fear/terror. Some current measures lack a context for "abuse" behaviors so that whether the occurrence of a behavior was perceived as negative/problematic or not, whether the recipient deemed the action to arise out of malevolent intent, whether any reactions were experienced by the recipient of the action, and whether the behavior is generally perceived as serious are all unknown.

When Maiuro (2001) concluded that "we are far from developing reliable 'norms' regarding these behaviors (p. xvi)," he stressed concerns regarding measures that are overly inclusive (and therefore not distinctive for determining abuse) and that lack the ability to assess the *impact* of PSYAB on recipients. To date, our knowledge of the prevalence of psychologically abusive behaviors in the greater population is limited (Leeper, 2009). The purpose of this study was to determine the prevalence of PSYAB engaged in by U.S. citizens' partners in their "worst" cohabiting relationship as well as its frequency and subjectively perceived emotional impact (EI) and behavioral impact (BI). Frequency was hypothesized to be related to stronger impacts across PSYAB categories and specific behaviors. Social desirability was assessed to determine whether this response set influenced reporting PSYAB that would require it be used as a covariate. The establishment of attachment as salient in individuals' internal working models of their self-view (i.e., anxiety) and their view of others (i.e., avoidance) in intimate relationships (e.g., Crowell, Fraley, & Shaver, 2003; Mikulincer & Shaver, 2003) resulted in these dimensions being assessed as potential covariates as well. The relationship of respondents' demographics to reporting of partner PSYAB was also assessed.

METHOD

Participants

Volunteers ($N = 971$) who were at least 18 years of age logged on to an Internet site where the questionnaire was located. Screening eliminated those who were not U.S. citizens ($n = 36$) and those who had never cohabited for at least one year with a romantic partner ($n = 231$). Of those consenting to participate, only 55 did not finish the questionnaire. Because of no variability in their ratings (e.g., all attitude items were scored as 1), 35 additional participants were eliminated.

The final sample before eliminating the nonresponsive participants ($n = 649$) included 332 males (51%) and 317 females (49%). Twenty-three respondents were between 18 and 21 years of age (4%), 108 between 22 and 30 years (17%), 142 between 31 and 40 years (22%), 164 between 41 and 50 years (25%), 106 between 51 and 60 years (16%), 69 between 61 and 70 years (11%), and 37 more than the age of 71 years (6%). Although the highest percentage of participants were White ($n = 490$; 76%), the composition of the sample was within reasonable percentages of national census indicators of race except for Hispanics and included 70 African Americans (11%), 12 Asian Americans or Pacific Islanders (2%), 49 Hispanic respondents (8%), 4 Native Americans (1%), 9 Biracial or Multiracial respondents (1%), and 15 "other" (2%). Most participants reported their primary sexual orientation to be heterosexual ($n = 592$; 91%), with 57 individuals reporting primarily bisexual (6%) or homosexual (3%) orientation. Categories of family income indicated that 241 reported a family income of less than $30,000 (38%), 162 reported $30,000–$50,000 (25%), 118 reported income in the range of $51,000–$71,000 (18%), and 121 reported an income more than $75,000 (19%). Participants designated the environment of their youth—150 reported growing up mostly in urban areas (23%), 199 in suburban areas (31%), 199 in small towns (31%), and 100 in rural areas (15%). Education categories demonstrated a reasonable spread with 28 participants having less than a high school education (4%), 179 receiving a high school diploma or a general equivalency diploma (GED; 28%), 265 receiving some college education (41%), 119 completing a 4-year college degree (18%), and 57 receiving a postbaccalaureate degree (9%). There were fewer individuals with less than a high school education and an overrepresentation of individuals with "some" college in the sample than would be expected from census data. (See Follingstad, 2011 for comparison of all sample statistics with U.S. Census data.)

Measures

Measure of Psychologically Abusive Behaviors (MPAB). The MPAB (Follingstad, 2011) was a 42-item self-report measure designed to focus on the more extreme end of the continuum of psychological aggression (based on findings from Follingstad, Coyne, &

Gambone, 2005 and Leeper, 2009). To ensure that items would be perceived as seriously abusive, the likely malevolent *intent* of each behavior was included as part of the definition. For example, an item asking whether one's partner had ever thrown a temper tantrum included the language "in order to frighten you," thus requiring the respondent to decide whether he/she *perceived* the occurrence as including that negative intention/outcome rather than viewing the temper tantrum as childish, or laughable, or just something to be ignored. The scale demonstrated good psychometric properties for documenting the existence and extent of psychologically abusive behaviors in problematic adult intimate relationships.

Building upon the concept of a prior scale of psychological *aggression* (Follingstad et al., 2005), the MPAB was organized to contain three behaviors of increasing severity within each of 14 categories of PSYAB. The 14 categories appear to be basically non-overlapping types of PSYAB in terms of severity ratings (i.e., except for several categories at the midrange of the ratings, the categories demonstrated statistical differences; see rankings in Table 1). The categories include the following: Sadistic Behavior, Threats to Intimidate, Isolation, Manipulation, Public Humiliation, Verbal Abuse, Wounding Regarding Sexuality, Treatment as an Inferior, Monitoring, Creating a Hostile Environment, Wounding Regarding Fidelity, Jealousy, Withholding Emotionally and Physically, and Controlling Partner's Personal Decisions. The 42 behaviors (i.e., 14 categories with three items each) were all rated as strongly in violation of intimate partner behavior, with many of the behaviors rated at the highest end of the scale (i.e., from 7 to 10 on a 10-point scale; Follingstad, 2011). Within each of the 14 categories, contrasts among the three behaviors yielded significantly different severity ratings for all but one of the categories (Follingstad, 2011). The Cronbach's alpha for the entire scale was .979, with the average range of individual item correlations with the overall score being .72. Split-half reliability produced internal consistency correlations of .96. Females rated items higher than males, but no other demographics were associated with ratings. Social desirability only accounted for 1%–2% of the variance.

To maximize the likelihood that participants would report on the existence of PSYAB in their lifetime, participants were asked to report on their subjectively perceived worst relationship. Specifically, they indicated whether that partner ever engaged (PRESENCE) in each of the 42 behaviors on the MPAB. If a behavior was indicated as present, respondents rated its yearly frequency (FREQ; 10 categories ranging from "less than once a year" to "more than 100 times a year") and the extent to which the occurrence of that behavior impacted them emotionally (EI) and behaviorally (BI), each being rated on a 5-point Likert scale from *not at all* to *a lot*. The EI specified for each of the 42 items varied, such that if a particular emotional intention was part of the description of the abusive behavior (see Table 2), that wording was used to assess EI. For example, if the partner threatened to harm others close to the person to intimidate him/her, then the EI item asked the extent to which the person was intimidated by that behavior occurring. Otherwise, the generic EI item asked the extent that the behavior "upset" him/her. BI items were structured similarly such that abuse items having implicit behavioral consequences reflected that consequence in the impact question, but the generic BI item asked to what extent the person changed his/her behavior in negative ways for themselves (e.g., did what the partner wanted, became more passive) so that their partner would not engage further in that behavior. To understand participants' subjective view of their partner and willingness to label that person as "psychologically abusive," participants provided a rating on a Likert scale from 1 (*not at all*) to 6 (*a lot*). This rating was used to understand which dimensions of the reported abuse (presence, types, frequency, EI, BI) were related to participants' labeling of their partners.

TABLE 1. Means and Rankings of the 14 Categories of Psychological Abuse

Categories of Psychologically Abusive Behaviors	Percentage of Relationships in Which Category Is Present	Rank of Presence	Mean Frequency Rating	Rank of Frequency	Mean Emotional Impact (EI)	Rank of Emotional Impact	Mean Behavioral Impact (BI)	Rank of Behavioral Impact
Sadistic Behavior	21	14	4.10	14	3.21	8	2.91	2
Threats to Intimidate	46	5	4.21	13	2.84	14	2.68	9
Isolation	34	12	5.18	5	3.57	4	2.80	7
Manipulation	47	4	4.55	10	3.26	6	2.79	8
Public Humiliation	35	11	4.67	8	3.82	1	2.83	4
Verbal Abuse	53	3	5.51	2	3.10	11	2.81	6
Wounding Regarding Sexuality	37	10	5.35	3	3.73	2	3.15	1
Treatment as Inferior	41	9	5.53	1	3.21	8	2.61	11
Monitoring	42	8	5.30	4	3.23	7	2.68	9
Creating a Hostile Environment	45	7	5.07	6	3.65	3	2.83	4
Wounding Regarding Fidelity	32	13	4.39	12	3.29	5	2.88	3
Jealousy	46	5	4.48	11	3.04	13	2.61	11
Withholding Emotionally and Physically	60	1	4.57	9	3.06	12	2.32	14
Controlling Partner's Personal Decisions	60	1	4.84	7	3.14	10	2.61	11

Note. Frequency data rated on a 1–10 scale; EI rated on a Likert scale of 1–5; BI rated on a Likert scale of 1–5.

TABLE 2.   Rankings of 42 Behaviors on the Measure of Psychologically Abusive Behaviors

Items From the Measure of Psychologically Abusive Behaviors	Presence in % of Relationships	Ranking of Presence	Rank of Frequency	Rank of EI	Rank of BI
1a. Harmed or destroyed your personal things of value (e.g., pictures, keepsakes, clothes) as a way to intimidate you.	17	29	37	35	25
1b. Threatened to harm others (e.g., your family, your children, your close friends) around you to intimidate you.	9	38	26	7	3
1c. Harmed pets as a way to intimidate you.	4	42	41	6	7
2a. Threw a temper tantrum (e.g., breaking objects, acting in a rage) as a way to frighten you.	44	3	32	40	32
2b. Verbally threatened to physically harm you or made a gesture that seemed physically threatening as a way to frighten you.	22	22	23	21	9
2c. Threaten to kill you as a way to frighten you.	9	38	38	1	1
3a. Acted rude toward, gossiped about, or told lies about your family and friends to discourage you from spending time with them?	27	15	14	8	22
3b. Tried to keep you from socializing with family or friends without him/her being present.	18	28	9	25	11
3c. Tried to forbid you from socializing with family or friends to keep you separate from them.	16	30	4	20	15

(Continued)

TABLE 2. Rankings of 42 Behaviors on the Measure of Psychologically Abusive Behaviors (Continued)

Items From the Measure of Psychologically Abusive Behaviors	Presence in % of Relationships	Ranking of Presence	Rank of Frequency	Rank of EI	Rank of BI
4a. Continued to act very upset (e.g., pouted, stayed angry, gave you the silent treatment) until you did what he/she wanted you to do.	37	7	17	34	31
4b. Threatened to end the relationship as a way to get you to do what he/she wanted.	25	18	31	26	18
4c. Threatened to commit suicide as a way to get you to do what he/she wanted.	11	34	42	10	12
5a. Threatened to reveal an embarrassing secret as a way to hurt or manipulate you.	7	41	34	2	19
5b. Revealed important secrets to others that you had told him/her as a way to embarrass you.	14	32	33	3	6
5c. Insulted or ridiculed you in front of others.	30	12	21	11	34
6a. Criticized and belittled you as a way to make you feel bad about yourself.	42	4	8	22	8
6b. Yelled and screamed as a way to intimidate you.	38	6	3	41	33
6c. Called you a derogatory name as a way to make you feel bad about yourself.	28	14	5	30	23
7a. Criticized your physical looks/sexual performance to humiliate you.	20	26	13	9	2
7b. Refused to have sex to make you feel insecure or inadequate.	26	16	10	18	13

(Continued)

TABLE 2. Rankings of 42 Behaviors on the Measure of Psychologically Abusive Behaviors (Continued)

Items From the Measure of Psychologically Abusive Behaviors	Presence in % of Relationships	Ranking of Presence	Rank of Frequency	Rank of EI	Rank of BI
7c. Insisted on sex with him/her in belittling or humiliating ways.	9	38	20	5	5
8a. Tried to make you think he/she was more competent and intelligent than you as a way of making you feel inferior?	32	9	6	33	41
8b. Treated you as useless/ stupid as a way to make you feel inferior.	23	21	11	19	10
8c. Tried to demand obedience to orders that he/she gave as a way of establishing their authority over you.	15	31	1	23	16
9a. Intentionally turned a neutral interaction into an argument or disagreed as a way to create conflict.	22	22	18	29	28
9b. Treated an argument as though he/she had to "drive you into the ground" and make you feel bad when making their points.	25	18	7	12	14
9c. Treated you with strong hatred and contempt to make you feel bad.	32	9	22	4	17
10a. Tried to make you report on the details of where you went and what you did when not with him/her as a way to check on you.	36	8	2	32	21
10b. Lisrtened in on phone conversations, read your e-mail, or went through your belongings without your permission as a way to check on you.	21	25	19	13	39

(Continued)

TABLE 2.   Rankings of 42 Behaviors on the Measure of Psychologically Abusive Behaviors (Continued)

Items From the Measure of Psychologically Abusive Behaviors	Presence in % of Relationships	Ranking of Presence	Rank of Frequency	Rank of EI	Rank of BI
10c. Followed or had you followed by someone else as a way of checking up on your activities.	11	34	35	27	29
11a. Pointed out others as attractive as a way of making you feel insecure.	12	33	28	38	24
11b. Flirted with others in front of you as a way to make you jealous and insecure.	26	16	24	28	26
11c. Implied he/she was having an affair as a way to make you feel insecure and worried.	11	34	39	16	4
12a. Acted very upset because he/she felt jealous if you spoke to or looked at any person to keep you from contact with others.	40	5	25	37	28
12b. Falsely accused you of trying to have an affair or actually having an affair to have you restrict your behavior as proof you were not.	24	20	29	24	36
12c. Tried to prevent you from speaking to or looking at any person who could be a potential romantic partner for you.	19	27	27	36	20
13a. Ignored important holidays and events as a way to punish or hurt you.	11	34	40	17	40
13b. Refused to speak to you as a way to punish or hurt you.	53	1	30	39	42
13c. Withheld physical or verbal affection as a way to punish or hurt you.	31	11	40	15	35

(Continued)

TABLE 2. Rankings of 42 Behaviors on the Measure of Psychologically Abusive Behaviors (Continued)

Items From the Measure of Psychologically Abusive Behaviors	Presence in % of Relationships	Ranking of Presence	Rank of Frequency	Rank of EI	Rank of BI
14a. Acted very upset when he/she didn't get to make small decisions, such as programs on television or restaurant choices, to control you.	22	22	15	42	27
14b. Tried to make personal choices that should have been left up to you (e.g., which clothes to wear, whether you should smoke/drink, what you eat) to control you.	49	2	16	31	30
14c. Tried to make major decisions that affected you without consulting with you to control you.	29	13	36	14	29

Note. EI = emotional impact; BI = behavioral impact; a = milder items; b = moderate items; c = severe items; 1 = Sadistic Behavior; 2 = Threats to Intimidate; 3 = Isolation; 4 = Manipulation; 5 = Public Humiliation; 6 = Verbal Abuse; 7 = Wounding Regarding Sexuality; 8 = Treating as an Inferior; 9 = Creating a Hostile Environment; 10 = Monitoring; 11 = Wounding Regarding Fidelity; 12 = Jealousy; 13 = Withholding Emotionally and Physically; 14 = Controlling Partner's Personal Decisions.

Balanced Inventory of Desirable Responding (BIDR). The BIDR, a 40-item measure by Paulhus (1988), expanded the concept of social desirability from a conscious approach to life situations, represented by the impression management (IM) subscale, to include self-deception (SD) to assess less conscious aspects of presenting oneself in overly positive ways. Response options range from 1 (*not true*) to 7 (*very true*), but a score is registered only if the respondent chooses 6 or 7, indicating that the trait is highly representative of him/her. Thus, for each subscale, scores range from 1 to 20. Internal consistency of the subscales has been reported as ranging from .68 to .86, and test–retest reliability as .69 and .65 for SD and IM, respectively. The subscales have demonstrated reasonable discrimination from each other (although they were highly correlated in this study), and concurrent and convergent validity have been demonstrated. Cronbach's alpha for the overall BIDR in this study was .87.

Experiences in Close Relationships—Revised (ECR-R). The ECR-R (Brennan, Clark, & Shaver, 1998) was an attachment measure that focuses on the two dimensions of anxiety about relationships and avoidance of them. Fraley, Waller, and Brennan (2000) compared the ECR-R to three other inventories of attachment using item response theory analysis and concluded that the ECR-R possessed the best psychometric properties (e.g., test–retest correlations of the subscales were .93 and .95, respectively). Both subscales demonstrated adequate construct validity (Sibley, Fischer, & Liu, 2005). In this study, anxiety and avoidance subscales demonstrated excellent internal consistency (.94 and .93, respectively).

Procedure

A national sample was solicited through the Online survey site of Zoomerang.com that links with MarketTools.com to provide samples designated by the customer. MarketTools uses census information to direct surveys to individuals on their volunteer site who fit the sample requirements. Participants are potentially any person with access to a computer who volunteers to take surveys at ZoomPanel.com for which they receive incentive points that can be redeemed for a wide range of products such as donations to charity, electronics and appliances, entertainment, health and personal care products, jewelry and accessories, sports equipment, tools, and so forth.

Screening questions ruled out anyone under 18 years of age, persons who were not U.S. citizens, and those who had not cohabited with a romantic partner for at least one year. Individuals read the informed consent document and indicated their consent by choosing the option to proceed to the questionnaire. Those not wishing to participate were electronically exited from the study and individuals could exit the study at any time by closing out the Website. Only completed questionnaires were retained.

The survey ended with debriefing information (including potential referral sources) and the option of commenting on the study. Of those individuals availing themselves of this option, reactions were almost unanimously positive, and the only negative comments focused on the length of the survey.

RESULTS

General Prevalence Data

Interestingly, a sizeable portion of participants' worst relationships were in actuality their *only* cohabiting relationship ($n = 129$; 21%). These individuals were significantly different from the rest of the sample in terms of the following: (a) more likely to be married to the partner about whom they were reporting ($F[1, 612] = 74.15, p < .0001$); (b) having lived with that partner three times as long as other respondents ($F[1, 612] = 126.19, p < .0001$); and (c) being significantly happier in that worst relationship ($F[1, 612] = 49.10, p < .0001$). Several of the main analyses were rerun after removing these participants, and although stronger correlations or higher significance levels were evident, rarely did the results change from significant to nonsignificant or vice versa. Therefore, they were included in all analyses.

Categories of Psychological Abuse. The mean number of PSYAB categories that were reported in one's worst relationship was 5.96 ($SD = 4.5$; Median $= 10$). The distribution of the number of categories that were ever present was fairly flat and the mode for this variable was 0 (i.e., 16% of the respondents reported none of the 14 types were ever present). The four quartiles for this variable were Q1 $= 0–2$; Q2 $= 3–6$; Q3 $= 7–10$; and Q4 5 11–14. Percentages of the 14 types of PSYAB that were ever present in respondents' worst relationships are reported in Table 1, that is, if any one of the three behaviors in a category was ever present, that category was scored as PRESENT. Percentages ranged from 60% to 21%, with Withholding Emotionally and Physically and Controlling Partner's Personal Decisions tied for the highest percentage. Sadistic Behavior was present less often than all other categories. Table 1 ranks the percentages from the most to least prevalent types.

A dummy variable (CATAMT) was created for each PSYAB category summing how many of the three behaviors in that category were reported as present. Thus, a participant's score for each category could range from 0 to 3, and mean scores for each PSYAB type were calculated. Results indicated that, in respondents' worst relationships, the Verbal Abuse category had the highest mean score, whereas Sadistic Behaviors had the lowest mean score. The relative rankings of these data, compared with the PRESENCE data earlier were very similar, suggesting that these two ways of scoring the presence of PSYAB categories appear redundant and do not independently contribute unique information.

Individual Behaviors. The mean number of PSYAB behaviors which persons claimed were present in their worst relationship was 9.96 (SD = 9.57; Median = 7). Only 96 respondents (16%) reported that the partner in their worst relationship had done none of the 42 psychologically abusive behaviors. Forty persons (7%) stated that only one behavior occurred and 34 (6%) reported only 2 behaviors occurred. Scores of 0, 1, or 2 comprises the first quartile of the total number of PSYAB behaviors that were present, whereas the second quartile consisted of individuals reporting 3–7 behaviors by their partner. Experiencing 8–15 different abusive behaviors placed an individual in the third quartile, such that the final quartile had a very wide range of 16–42 behaviors present within one's worst relationship. Only a very small portion of individuals reported that their partner engaged in a large proportion of the 42 behaviors, that is, 31 respondents (5%) reported 30 or more behaviors were present and 5 individuals reported that all 42 had taken place.

The most commonly reported abusive behavior, "refusing to speak as a way to punish or hurt you," was present in 53% of individuals' worst relationships (see Table 2 for percentages for all behaviors). The most commonly occurring abusive behaviors (i.e., top third) were present in 28%–53% of these worst relationships and the overall average for the 42 behaviors to occur was 23.7%. Only 5 of the 42 behaviors were present in fewer than 10% of people's worst relationships.

Frequency and Impact of PSYAB

Categories of PSYAB. To investigate the frequency of PSYAB by category type, the mean frequency of the three items within an abuse category was calculated. In addition, the mean EI and BI scores were also calculated across the behaviors that occurred within a category of abuse. Treatment as an Inferior was ranked as the most frequently occurring category when it was present (see Table 1) with Verbal Abuse as the second most frequent type (approximately 11–20 times per year), Wounding Regarding Sexuality ranking third in frequency, and Monitoring ranking fourth. Not surprisingly, Sadistic Behavior was the least frequent type of PSYAB when it was present in a relationship.

Table 1 also ranks the mean EI and BI that respondents assigned to the 14 categories of PSYAB they experienced. Mean EI ratings did not vary much across categories such that the difference on a 5-point scale between the highest and lowest mean was .98. The numerical means reflect ratings mostly in the range of producing "somewhat" to "quite a bit" of an impact on the person. Mean ratings of the BI across the 14 categories also did not vary greatly, with the difference between the highest and lowest means being .47. Respondents consistently reported lower means for experiencing BI (M = 2.75) from abuse categories than EI (M = 3.30). The categories rated as producing the worst EI were Public Humiliation and Wounding Regarding Sexuality, whereas the relatively least harmful ones were Jealousy and Threats to Intimidate. The two categories producing the worst BI were Wounding Regarding Sexuality and Sadistic Behavior, whereas the relatively least harmful ones were Withholding Emotionally and Physically, Controlling Partner's Personal Decisions, Jealousy, and Treatment as an Inferior.

Individual Items. The most *frequently* occurring PSYAB behaviors were not necessarily the same as those abusive actions that were present more often in respondents' worst relationships (see Table 2). For example, having one's partner demand obedience ranked 31st in terms of being present in people's worst relationships, but when it was present, it had the highest mean frequency of all the behaviors. Average frequencies of the specific behaviors ranged from 11 to 20 times a year down to twice a year. The psychologically abusive behaviors that were rated as relatively milder in nature (see Follingstad, 2011) were spread throughout the frequency distribution such that there was not a direct match between a behavior being considered a "lesser evil" and that behavior always ranking as one of the more frequently experienced abusive actions. Therefore, some of the moderate and severe items were reported as occurring rather frequently. For example, screaming, name-calling, refusing sex, treating one's partner as stupid, withholding affection, insisting on belittling sex, insulting publicly, and invading privacy were all within the upper half of items in terms of frequency. Several items that were previously rated (Follingstad, 2011) as the worst violations of relationship behavior (e.g., threatening suicide as manipulation, harming a pet, threatening to kill, destroying things of value, and following the partner) demonstrated frequency rates of at least 2–4 times a year if that behavior was present within a respondent's worst relationship. The percentages of persons' worst relationships in which specific severe behaviors happened more frequently than 21 times per year were as follows: threatening to kill (2%), threatening to physically harm (6%), destroying things of value (3%), threatening to harm others (2%), severe name-calling (11%), forcing into belittling sex (3%), treating with hatred (8%), following (2%), and preventing partner from looking at opposite sex (4%).

Table 2 also provides rankings for the 42 items regarding the level of EI and BI reported by respondents when abusive behaviors occurred. "Threatened to kill you as a way to frighten you" was rated highest by respondents for both EI and BI. In contrast, throwing a temper tantrum to frighten you, acting upset to manipulate, emotionally manipulating you in order to make small decisions, and yelling and screaming were rated as having the lowest (relative) EI. Refusing to speak to punish or hurt you, "partner acting more intelligent to make you feel inferior," and "ignoring important events to punish or hurt you" were rated by respondents as having the least BI.

Relationship of Frequency of PSYAB, Emotional Impact, and Behavioral Impact

Frequency, EI, and BI were significantly intercorrelated (at the Bonferroni correction of the alpha level of .0004 for 126 correlations) for approximately two-thirds of the individual abusive behaviors (see Table 2). Correlations for these dimensions of the abusive actions ranged from .26 to .85, with many of the correlations demonstrating strong relationships. Among these 26 items, the correlations between EI and BI were often higher than the correlations of these components with the frequency rating, suggesting that EI and BI are similarly rated and appear to be more strongly associated with each other than with frequency. Some other patterns emerged with the remaining 16 behaviors. For example, some of the PSYAB actions demonstrated a significant correlation between EI and BI, but *neither* was associated with frequency. A review of these behaviors suggests that only one occurrence of them could easily produce a significant impact (e.g., threaten to kill you; threaten suicide to manipulate you; threaten to harm others you care about; and partner implies he/she is having an affair). Three other abusive actions demonstrated significance of the BI with both EI and frequency, but EI and frequency were not significantly associated. Perusal of these items suggests again that the abusive behaviors would not have to happen very often to produce negative emotional reactions (e.g., "pointing to others as attractive to make you worry about the relationship," "threatening to end the relationship," and "revealing a humiliating secret of yours"). Only two behaviors ("harming a pet to intimidate you" and "insisting on belittling sex") did not demonstrate significance for any of the correlations among frequency, EI, and BI, although they demonstrated trends toward significance. Thus, although increased frequency of a psychologically abusive action often seems to be associated with worsening impacts on the recipient, higher frequency does not seem to be a *necessary* component to produce stronger impacts for some of the PSYAB actions, and often the relationship between the EI and BI is much stronger.

Internal Consistency of PSYAB Categories

To determine the coexistence of behaviors within a category, correlations were conducted among the three items of each category using a Bonferroni correction for the alpha level at .0012. Even though the three items within categories represent distinct behaviors and increasing levels of severity of that type of abuse, all intercorrelations were significant at the .0001 level (ranging from .16 to .63). The strongest correlations among items were in the categories of Threats to Intimidate, Isolation, Treatment as an Inferior, Creating a Hostile Environment, Verbal Abuse, Jealousy, and Monitoring. Moderate correlations were found among items in categories of Wounding Regarding Fidelity, Withholding Emotionally and Physically, Public Humiliation, and Sadistic Behaviors. The weakest correlations, although still significant because of the sample size, were among items reflecting Controlling Partner's Personal Decisions, Wounding Regarding Sexuality, and Manipulation.

Relationship of Reporting Partner PSYAB With Social Desirability and Attachment

The four total scores representing presence of PSYAB, frequency, EI, and BI were correlated with social desirability (BIDR) and two dimensions of attachment (Anxiety and Avoidance). The BIDR was significantly, although weakly, correlated with all four total scores ($-.15$, $-.12$, $-.13$, and $-.14$, respectively), suggesting higher social desirability to be related to lower reports of partner PSYAB. However, the correlations accounted for only 1%–2% of the variance, suggesting that social desirability does not play a major role in influencing reporting of this form of abuse. Anxiety and Avoidance both showed low to moderate correlations with the four total scores. Anxiety was correlated with the four total scores with correlations ranging from .38 to .42, and Avoidance demonstrated correlations ranging from .29 to .31. The Anxiety correlations accounted for 14%–18% of the variance in the associations and Avoidance correlations accounted for 8%–10% of the variance.

Labeling Partners as Psychologically Abusive

To understand factors related to individuals' labeling a partner as psychologically abusive, respondents reported the degree to which they would label their worst partner as such. The mean rating by respondents, including those who had only one cohabiting relationship in their lives, fell into the "somewhat" range. Only 31% chose the option that their partner was not psychologically abusive at all, and the other five options ranging from "a little" to "a lot" had a flat distribution, with percentages of respondents evenly distributed across them. Higher ratings of one's partner as psychologically abusive were associated with all of the total scores (presence and means of FREQ, EI, and BI) as well as with the presence of each category of PSYAB (i.e., all correlations significant at $p < .0001$ ranging from .33 to .61). Thus, an increase in any of these overall dimensions was related to a person's labeling the partner. The degree to which respondents' labeled their partner was used as the criterion variable in a regression analysis that incorporated the four total scores as predictor variables. That statistic resulted in 37% of the variance explained by the mean EI score, with the other scores only contributing a negligible amount.

Another regression used the presence or absence of the 14 categories of PSYAB as the predictor variables for labeling one's partner as abusive. The presence of the category of Threats to Intimidate was most predictive ($R^2 = .368$), with Treatment as an Inferior contributing 6% and Creating a Hostile Environment contributing 2%. The total variance explained by this analysis was 41%.

A third regression involved the 42 PSYAB behaviors as predictor variables to explain the extent to which a partner was labeled psychologically abusive. Although 45% of the variance was accounted for, only six specific items contributed at least 1%. Temper tantrums designed to intimidate explained 25% of the variance, with rudeness to partner's family to discourage contact (9%), expressing hatred and contempt (4%), threatening to harm the partner (2%), acting more intelligent to make one's partner feel badly (1%), and threatening suicide to manipulate the partner (1%) contributing smaller amounts.

Demographics Related to Reporting Partner PSYAB

The gender of the respondent was the independent variable (IV) in a MANOVA for which the four total scores representing the dimensions of PSYAB were the dependent variables (DV). The overall MANOVA was significant ($F[4, 609] = 12.27, p < .0001$). Univariate analyses indicated that the genders did not report differences in the presence or frequency of PSYAB, but females ($M = 37.54, SD = 42.0$) reported greater EI than males ($M = 29.98, SD = 32.8$) as well as greater BI than males (females, $M = 31.54$, $SD = 39.2$; males, $M = 25.32, SD = 29.5$). Three MANOVAs used different contrasts of race categories as the IV and the four total scores as the DVs. None of the analyses between White participants versus all other racial groups—White versus African American participants or White versus Hispanic participants—resulted in significant differences, suggesting that racial groups completing the measure were not differentially reporting PSYAB. Additional racial groups had too few numbers for individual analysis.

A MANOVA using four levels of income as the IV and the four total scores as DVs was significant, $F(12, 1,590) = 4.07, p < .0001$. Univariate analyses suggested that the lowest income group reported greater amounts of PSYAB than the other three groups. For total occurrence of the 42 behaviors, $F(3, 604) = 10.67, p < .0001$, and for the EI of the behaviors, $F(3, 604) = 12.84, p < .0001$, the second lowest income group also reported significantly more PSYAB than the highest income group. Level of religious activity, growing up in an urban versus rural environment, and education were not significantly related to reported PSYAB by one's partner in the worst relationship. Because the numbers of individuals claiming their sexual orientation was primarily homosexual or bisexual was small, sexual orientation was not included in the MANOVA with the major demographics. However, using the GLM procedure in SAS, a separate MANOVA was conducted using sexual orientation as the IV and the four total scores as the DVs, but it was not significant ($F[8, 1,216] = .96, p = $ n.s.). In addition, a gender comparison for same-sex relationships did not indicate that homosexual females reported the presence, frequency, EI, or BI related to PSYAB differently from homosexual males ($F[4, 29] = .39, p = $ n.s.).

DISCUSSION

This study portrays, in a systematic way, a detailed analysis of the occurrence of serious PSYAB as reported by adults in the United States about their worst relationship. Because respondents were asked to consider their most problematic cohabiting relationship, the data from this study represents occurrences of PSYAB under that parameter rather than current experience.

Prevalence

Even though respondents reported on their worst relationship, it was fairly surprising that the average number of PSYAB *categories* that occurred was approximately six. It is important to remember that this score could have been obtained by a person's partner literally doing six different types of PSYAB only once, but this finding suggests that these serious violations of intimate relationship behavior are not uncommon occurrences when relationships are problematic. The fairly flat distribution implies that the mean number of PSYAB categories occurring in worst relationships was not a function of averaging relationships with no abuse with relationships with many kinds of abuse, but rather that the distribution was fairly consistent across the spectrum.

In line with general expectations, withholding emotionally/physically and controlling personal decisions were the most commonly reported categories and sadistic actions were least common. However, the rankings of intimidating threats, creating a hostile environment, and serious monitoring suggested these categories were not that uncommon, and they ranked as being present in problematic relationships higher than seemingly less malignant types, such as treating a partner as inferior. It is possible that monitoring a partner's activities may be present more often by virtue of being associated with jealousy, a category that lay persons viewed as more tolerable and possibly even as expected in romantic relationships (Follingstad, Helff, Binford, Runge, & White, 2004). The most frequently reported categories, with the exceptions of verbal abuse and intimidating threats, were those that a national sample ranked as *relatively* lower in terms of "violating" relationship behavior (Follingstad, 2011). Thus, the forms of PSYAB most likely to occur in respondents' worst relationships are generally those considered to be relatively lesser, although still serious, violations of the ways in which intimates are expected to treat each other.

The average number of the 42 psychologically abusive behaviors perpetrated by one's partner in the worst relationship was not much higher than the number of categories experienced. Also, three-fourths of the respondents reported no more than 15 total behaviors as ever being present. There were, however, a small proportion of relationships for which 30 or more behaviors were present, suggesting that some individuals are reporting being the recipient of an extremely wide range of these actions. Even including individuals who had only *one* cohabiting relationship (that seemed more committed and happier), it is important to note that some of the 42 behaviors were present in fairly large percentages of worst relationships. Refusing to speak as a way to punish/hurt you (53%), trying to make your personal choices (49%), throwing a temper tantrum to frighten you (44%), and criticizing and belittling you as a way to make you feel badly about yourself (42%) appear quite commonplace, even though the recipient had to believe that their partner intended deliberate psychological harm to count it as occurring. These specific behaviors were ranked at the lower end on the EI scale, although the mean ratings still indicated they produced somewhat of an EI.

Frequency, Emotional, and Behavioral Impact of Psychological Abuse

When "Treatment as an Inferior" was present in respondents' worst relationship, it occurred at the highest average yearly rate of all of the categories. As a ploy for attempting to gain control, this form of PSYAB may arise in relationships that would not automatically be labeled "abusive" on that basis, especially when considering that the EI and BI of treating one's partner as inferior ranked lower than many other forms. However, once it is present in a problematic relationship, treating one's partner as inferior unfortunately seems to be a fairly common occurrence. Sadistic Behavior, even though it was the least frequent type when it was present, was still reported as having a very negative impact on *behavior*. Surprisingly, the EI ratings for sadistic behaviors were midrange among the types of PSYAB, although this would still reflect the impact as somewhat intimidating. This may be because of a statistical artifact, because within the category of Sadistic Behavior, most ratings of EI were in response to the "mildest" item in which the partner destroyed things of value. The other two behaviors were present in only a small number of relationships (i.e., harming a pet and threatening to harm others important to you), resulting in the ratings reflecting mostly the impact of destroyed property rather than the two more serious actions. A similar artifact is likely also responsible for the lowest ranking category in terms of EI arising from Threats to Intimidate in that 59% of the ratings were regarding one's partner having a temper tantrum. The ratings for the other two behaviors in that category (i.e., threats to physically harm you and threats to kill you) were significantly higher than the temper tantrum item that made up the bulk of the ratings. Another possibility is that these ratings include men's *and* women's assessment, and men may not be particularly frightened by women's threats. It is interesting to note that similar to Follingstad et al.'s (2004) findings, the most negative EIs were associated with behaviors designed to produce hurt feelings (e.g., public humiliation, wounding regarding sexuality, and creating a hostile environment) as opposed to intimidating tactics (e.g., sadistic behavior or threats). However, all EIs and BIs were rated at the more negative end of the scale and did not differ much between categories, suggesting that even the "lower" scores were not perceived as low impact experiences for recipients.

Individuals consistently rated EI as more severe than BI. It is unknown whether this is a form of bravado (e.g., "It really hurt, but I managed to handle it"), evidence that PSYAB creates emotional reactions more than it actually changes people, an indication that emotional reactivity occurs at greater levels than behavioral changes, or evidence that behavioral changes are less subject to self-awareness than a person's sense of their emotions. The consistent association between the two impacts across abusive behaviors as well as their independence at times, from the dimension of frequency, suggests that these two concepts may not be distinct. Abusive behaviors for which frequency was *not* associated with ensuing impacts seem identifiable as severe actions for which one incident would prove devastating (e.g., threats to kill; implying that he/she is having an affair).

The fairly solid relationship between increased frequency of abusive behaviors and more negative ratings of impact appears to support the contentions of prior researchers that a pattern of abusive actions or the continuation of them may be an important dimension for defining PSYAB (e.g., Loring, 1994; Tolman, 1992). However, the frequency, EI, and BI of individual behaviors did not consistently demonstrate predictable patterns. Although one might predict that the relatively "milder" actions (see Follingstad, 2011) might constitute the behaviors that demonstrate higher frequency when they are present, some moderate and severe behaviors were among the higher frequency actions. Because the sample was deliberately chosen to *not* constitute a clinical population, the presence and frequency of severe PSYAB was startling, especially considering the relationships in which severe behaviors were present at a fairly high frequency level.

Individuals in the study reported that their partners seemed quite likely to engage in all three behaviors within a particular category of PSYAB, suggesting that people using a particular psychological strategy with specific intent may be likely to use variants on that strategy. Unfortunately, those categories with the strongest associations among the three behaviors were often the more severe ones. Possibly, a person using a pathological strategy on their partner has lost inhibition to prevent such behavior, such that they will adapt any number of similar behaviors within those categories for their use.

Respondents' ratings of their worst partner as psychologically abusive resulted in a very high percentage indicating at least some level of abusiveness. Stronger labeling was not surprisingly related to the presence of more types of abuse, higher ratings of impact, and the presence of more severe categories (e.g., creating a hostile environment, threats to intimidate). Thus, the degree to which adults place this label on a partner appears consistent with reported increases of dimensions of PSYAB.

Demographics

Because psychological conflict and aggression occur in many relationships, particular demographics were not expected to be associated with reports of partner PSYAB. However, because this field emerged from domestic violence studies in which battered women experienced PSYAB as well, the expectation has been that men are the perpetrators and females are the recipients. The interesting finding regarding gender in this study was that males and females were not different regarding the total number of abusive behaviors reported by their partners or the frequency of them, but that females report greater impact from the PSYAB. It is possible that the *quality* of the same behavior directed toward females by males is different from that directed toward males by females, thus resulting in more perceived harm. Because of the limitations of self-report, we do not know whether these differences reflect artifacts of self-reporting or role expectations by gender. The lack of gender differences in reports by homosexual and bisexual individuals regarding experienced PSYAB or its impact is an interesting contrast to heterosexual couples' data, but because of the small number of participants in this category, further research is needed.

The lack of differences when comparing racial groups suggests that we have no basis at this time for believing that African Americans, Whites, or Hispanics are more likely to use psychologically abusive actions in intimate relationships. People in the lowest income level were distinct from the other three levels in reporting greater amounts of PSYAB. This demographic has been associated with increased partner *physical* violence (e.g., O'Donnell, Smith, & Madison, 2002), and IPV may be a function of factors (e.g., more stressors, fewer resources) more prevalent in lower SES groups.

The weak relationship between social desirability and reporting PSYAB suggests that this trait does not appear to impact reporting to any great degree. More difficult to interpret are the moderate associations of the two dimensions of attachment with reports of PSYAB. Without a path model, we cannot determine whether anxiety about intimate relationships and avoidance of them are *precursors* that serve to influence relationship patterns and interpretations of events or whether they are *outcomes* of having experienced PSYAB in an intimate relationship. Follingstad, Bradley, Helff, and Laughlin (2002) suggested that anxious attachment was a precursor associated with angry temperament for physical violence in dating relationships, but explanatory path models and longitudinal studies will be required to answer this question about psychological maltreatment.

Limitations

One limitation of this study is the self-report nature of the data from one member of a couple. Because this study inquired about a person's worst relationship and collected data anonymously, it was not possible to identify what would be many participants' ex-partners. Although researchers have suggested that social desirability is not related to reports of one's own victimization (Arias & Beach, 1987), the potential filters of level of self-awareness and one's desired view of self may serve to decrease accuracy in reporting interpersonal behaviors that are considered violations of decency in intimate relationships. The anonymous nature of the survey was expected to counter that problem to some degree, although it cannot influence less conscious presentations of one's ideal self.

Another potential limitation of self-report data in this study was that some individuals reported on relationships that took place in the past because of the instructions to report on one's worst relationship. Although faulty memory might be implicated, salient negative events are more likely to be encoded and recalled, and all memory, current or historical, is subject to distortions. Therefore, data are reported as the *perceptions* of the respondents rather than assuming that reporting on past events is necessarily accurate.

Another potential limitation of the study is that participation in the study was reliant upon persons having computer skills to the extent that they could volunteer to complete surveys on the Website providing the sample. Even so, the sample was reasonably similar to census data, except for education, which unfortunately is frequently the case with volunteer samples of any kind.

Future Research

This research project has served to establish some basic information about what kinds of PSYAB appear to be present in problematic relationships, how frequently these behaviors are reported, and whether recipients feel negatively impacted by them. Knowledge would be served by further investigations with national samples to elucidate gender differences, to determine whether PSYAB is more reciprocal or unilateral in nature, to investigate how individuals report on their own use of psychologically abusive actions, to identify clusters of individuals with particular patterns of PSYAB, and to investigate whether outliers constitute a unique group.

REFERENCES

Aguilar, R. J., & Nightingale, N. N. (1994). The impact of specific battering experiences on the self-esteem of abused women. *Journal of Family Violence, 9*(1), 35–45.

Arias, I., & Beach, S. R. H. (1987). Validity of self-reports of marital violence. *Journal of Family Violence, 2*(2), 139–149.

Brennan, K. A., Clark, C. L., & Shaver, P. R. (1998). Self-report measurement of adult attachment: An integrative overview. In J. A. Simpson & W. S. Rholes (Eds.), *Attachment theory and close relationships.* New York, NY: Guilford.

Crowell, J. A., Fraley, R. C., & Shaver, P. R. (1999). Measurement of individual differences in adolescent and adult attachment. In J. Cassidy & P. R. Shaver (Eds.), *Handbook of attachment: Theory, research, and clinical applications* (pp. 434–465). New York, NY: Guilford.

Follingstad, D. R. (2007). Rethinking current approaches to psychological abuse: Conceptual and methodological issues. *Aggression and Violent Behavior, 12*(4), 439–458.

Follingstad, D. R. (2009). The impact of psychological aggression and women's mental health and behavior: The status of the field. *Trauma, Violence, & Abuse, 10*(3), 271–289.

Follingstad, D. R. (2011). A measure of severe psychological abuse normed on a nationally representative sample of adults. *Journal of Interpersonal Violence, 26*, 1194–1214.

Follingstad, D. R., Bradley, R. G., Helff, C. M., & Laughlin, J. E. (2002). A model for predicting dating violence: Anxious attachment, angry temperament, and need for relationship control. *Violence and Victims, 17*(1), 35–47.

Follingstad, D. R., Coyne, S., & Gambone, L. (2005). A representative measure of psychological aggression and its severity. *Violence and Victims, 20*(1), 25–38.

Follingstad, D. R., Helff, C. M., Binford, R. V., Runge, M. M., & White, J. D. (2004). Lay persons' versus psychologists' judgments of psychologically aggressive actions by a husband and wife. *Journal of Interpersonal Violence, 19*(8), 916–942.

Follingstad, D. R., Rutledge, L. L., Berg, B. J., Hause, E. S., & Polek, D. S. (1990). The role of emotional abuse in physically abusive relationships. *Journal of Family Violence, 5*, 107–120.

Fraley, R. C., Waller, N. G., & Brennan, K. A. (2000). An item-response theory analysis of self-report measures of adult attachment. *Journal of Personality and Social Psychology, 78*(2), 350–365.

Katz, J., & Arias, I. (1999). Psychological abuse and depressive symptoms in dating women: Do different types of abuse have differential effects? *Journal of Family Violence, 14*(3), 281–295.

Leeper, A. (2009). *Normative psychological aggression in intimate interpersonal relationships* (Unpublished doctoral dissertation). University of South Carolina, Columbia, SC.

Loring, M. T. (1994). *Emotional abuse*. New York, NY: Lexington Books.

Maiuro, R. D. (2001). Sticks and stones may break my bones, but names will also hurt me: Psychological abuse in domestically violent relationships. In K. D. O'Leary & R. D. Maiuro (Eds.), *Psychological abuse in violent domestic relations*. New York, NY: Springer Publishing.

Marshall, L. L. (2001). Effects of men's subtle and overt psychological abuse on low-income women. In K. D. O'Leary & R. D. Maiuro (Eds.), *Psychological abuse in violent domestic relations*. New York, NY: Springer Publishing.

Mikulincer, M., & Shaver, P. R. (2003). The attachment behavioral system in adulthood: Activation, psychodynamics, and interpersonal processes. In M. P. Zanna (Ed.), *Advances in experimental social psychology* (Vol. 35, pp. 53–152). New York, NY: Academic Press.

Murphy, C. M., & Hoover, S. A. (2001). Measuring emotional abuse in dating relationships as a multifactorial construct. In K. D. Leary & R. D. Maiuro (Eds.), *Psychological abuse in violent relations*. New York, NY: Springer Publishing.

Murphy, C. M., & O'Leary, K. D. (1989). Psychological aggression predicts physical aggression in early marriage. *Journal of Consulting and Clinical Psychology, 57*, 579–582.

O'Donnell, C. J., Smith, J., & Madison, J. R. (2002). Using demographic risk factors to explain variations in the incidence of violence against women. *Journal of Interpersonal Violence, 17*, 1239–1262.

O'Leary, K. D. (2001). Psychological abuse: A variable deserving critical attention in domestic violence. In K. D. O'Leary & R. D. Maiuro (Eds.), *Psychological abuse in violent relations*. New York, NY: Springer Publishing.

O'Leary, K. D., & Cascardi, M. (1998). Physical aggression in marriage: A developmental analysis. In T. N. Bradbury (Ed.), *The developmental course of marital dysfunction* (pp. 343–374). New York, NY: Cambridge University Press.

O'Leary, K. D., & Jouriles, E. N. (1994). Psychological abuse between adult partners. In L. L'Abate (Ed.), *Handbook of developmental family psychology and psychopathology* (pp. 330–349). New York, NY: Wiley.

Paulhus, D. L. (1988). *Assessing self-deception and impression management in self-reports: The Balanced Inventory of Desirable Responding*. Vancouver, Canada: University of British Columbia.

Pence, E., & Paymar, M. (1993). *Education groups for men who batter: The Duluth model.* New York, NY: Springer Publishing.

Pipes, R. B., & LeBov-Keeler, K. (1997). Psychological abuse among college women in exclusive heterosexual dating relationships. *Sex Roles, 36*(9/10), 585–603.

Romero, M. (1985). A comparison between strategies used on prisoners of war and battered wives. *Sex Roles, 13*(9/10), 537–547.

Russell, R. J. H., & Hulson, B. (1992). Physical and psychological abuse of heterosexual partners. *Personality and Individual Differences, 13*(4), 457–473.

Sackett, L. A., & Saunders, D. G. (2001). The impact of different forms of psychological abuse on battered women. In K. D. O'Leary & R. D. Maiuro (Eds.), *Psychological abuse in violent domestic relations.* New York, NY: Springer Publishing.

Sibley, C. G., Fischer, R., & Liu, J. H. (2005). Reliability and validity of the Revised Experiences in Close Relationships (ECR-R) self-report measure of adult romantic attachment. *Personality and Social Psychology Bulletin, 31*(11), 1524–1536.

Simonelli, C. J., & Ingram, K. M. (1998). Psychological distress among men experiencing physical and emotional abuse in heterosexual dating relationships. *Journal of Interpersonal Violence, 13*(6), 667–681.

Stuart, G. L., & Holtzworth-Munroe, A. (2005). Testing a theoretical model of the relationship between impulsivity, mediating variables, and husband violence. *Journal of Family Violence, 20*(5), 291–303.

Taft, C. T., O'Farrell, T. J., Torres, S. E., Panuzio, J., Monson, C. M., Murphy, M., & Murphy, C. M. (2006). Examining the correlates of psychological aggression among a community sample of couples. *Journal of Family Psychology, 20*(4), 581–588.

Tolman, R. M. (1992). Psychological abuse of women. In R. T. Ammerman & M. Hersen (Eds.), *Assessment of family violence: A clinical and legal sourcebook* (pp. 291–312). New York, NY: Wiley.

Tolman, R. M., & Bhosley, G. (1991). The outcome of participation in a shelter-sponsored program for men who batter. In D. Knudsen & J. Miller (Eds.), *Abused and battered: Social and legal responses to family violence* (pp. 113–122). New York, NY: Aldine de Gruyter.

Correspondence regarding this article should be directed to Diane R. Follingstad, PhD, Center for Research on Violence Against Women, Deptartment of Psychiatry/UK, 245 Fountain Court, Lexington, KY 40509. E-mail: Follingstad@uky.edu

Violence and Victims, Volume 14, Number 1, 1999

Psychological Abuse: A Variable Deserving Critical Attention in Domestic Violence

K. Daniel O'Leary

State University of New York at Stony Brook, NY

Policy makers and researchers give psychological abuse considerably less attention than physical abuse in the partner abuse area. One reason for the relative neglect of psychological abuse is that there are difficulties in arriving at a common definition of psychological abuse that might be useful to both the mental health and legal professions. Another reason for the relative neglect of psychological abuse has been an implicit assumption that physical abuse exacts a greater psychological toll on victims than does psychological abuse. At the extreme level of physical abuse, this assumption seems defensible, but at levels of physical aggression that are most common in marriage and long-term relationships, psychological abuse appears to have as great an impact as physical abuse. Even direct ratings of psychological and physical abuse by women in physically abusive relationships indicate that psychological abuse has a greater adverse effect on them than physical abuse. Retrospective reports, longitudinal research, and treatment dropout research all provide evidence that psychological abuse can exact a negative effect on relationships that is as great as that of physical abuse. Finally, psychological abuse almost always precedes physical abuse, so that prevention and treatment efforts clearly need to address psychological abuse. Eight measures of various forms of psychological abuse that have reasonable psychometric properties and considerable construct validity are reviewed and a definition of psychological abuse in intimate relations is provided.

In the domestic violence field there has been general agreement that research and public policy should focus on reduction of physical aggression. That focus has been reasonable since fear of physical abuse and the injury resulting therefrom has been presumed to be greater than the effects of psychological abuse. Since 1979, when the seminal books of Walker (1979) and Straus, Gelles, and Steinmetz (1979) appeared, the focus in domestic violence has been on physical aggression. Yet in 1979 Walker wrote as follows in *The Battered Woman:* "Most of the women in this project describe incidents involving psychological humiliation and verbal harassment as their worst battering experiences, whether or not they have been physically abused." (pxv.) The sample used by Walker was "a self-referred volunteer one." As depicted in the introduction to the book, the sample came from the New Brunswick, New Jersey, area, from Denver, and from England, where Walker visited "refuges for battered women." Walker went on to state that "the women were not randomly selected, and they cannot be considered a legitimate data base from which to make specific generalizations." Consequently, Walker attempted not to use any statistics throughout the book to analyze any of the data. Nonetheless, her book was one of the first descriptive analyses of domestic violence, and Walker portrayed the psychological aggression in a manner that was as important as the physical aggression.

In a now classic book on domestic violence, *Behind Closed Doors* (1979), Straus, Gelles and Steinmetz reported on their interviews with 2,143 individuals and their domestic violence experiences. As Straus and colleagues stated, when they began their work in the late 1970s, there was no book on physical violence between spouses. The book was written to be understood by the general public and therefore technical presentation and methodological details were avoided. With that caveat, the thrust of the text was on physical violence.

"Drive down any street in America. More than one household in six has been the scene of a spouse striking his or her partner last year. Three American households in five (which have children living at home), have reverberated with the sounds of parents hitting their children. Where there is more than one child in the home, three in five are the scenes of violence between siblings. Overall, every other house in America is the scene of family violence at least once a year." (p. 3).

Physical abuse was documented in this book in a fashion that it had never been portrayed before. Straus and his colleagues had a randomly selected sample of individuals who were in intact families. Interviews were completed with 65% of the individuals identified. Moreover, a measure of a number of specifically physically aggressive behaviors that might be engaged in by husbands and wives was utilized to determine the prevalence of physical aggression. Approximately 12 % of men and 12 % of women reported that they had engaged in physically aggressive behaviors against their partners in the past year. Verbal aggression also was addressed in the book (p 167–169, 173), but it was addressed largely in the context of the then popular theory of catharsis. (At that time, foam rubber baseball bats were advertised in the American Psychological Association's *Monitor* and in *Human Behavior* for getting rid of aggressive impulses.)

The book by Straus and his colleagues has certainly been one of the most influential in the field of family violence. By providing a measure of physical aggression in intimate relations, it gave others a means of conducting research on heretofore ignored subjects. The Conflict Tactics Scales also contained a measure of psychological aggression, but it received less emphasis—as it probably should have at the time, given the neglect of partner assault as a bonafide form of assault by the criminal justice system. At this point, however, it is time to recognize the importance of psychological aggression in its own right, and fortunately, several recent chapters have begun to address psychological abuse in marriage (e.g., Murphy & Cascardi, 1993; O'Leary & Jouriles, 1994). In this manuscript, data will be presented to provide documentation for the reliability and validity of the construct of psychological aggression. In doing so, I will provide evidence for the following positions:

1. Psychological aggression can be measured reliably.
2. When physical aggression occurs, it often is preceded by psychological aggression.
3. Psychological aggression often has effects that are as deleterious as those of physical aggression.
4. Psychological aggression can be defined in a manner that allows for reliable assessment and use of this construct in both mental health and legal settings.

PSYCHOLOGICAL AGGRESSION CAN BE MEASURED RELIABLY

There are a number of measures of psychological aggression that have reasonable internal consistency and that have important correlates with other variables of interest to researchers and clinicians addressing problems of partner abuse. Those measures of psychological aggression will be reviewed herein in the order in which they were published.

Conflict Tactics Scale. In 1979, Straus developed the Conflict Tactics Scale designed to evaluate the different tactics that might be used by partners in resolving a conflict. As noted earlier, the major thrust of the research using the CTS has been about physical violence, and, indeed, the most recent major text about that work was titled *Physical Violence in American Families* (Straus & Gelles, 1992). Included in the CTS, however, was a six-item psychological aggression scale. The internal consistency of the psychological aggression scale was .80 for husband to wife aggression and .79 for wife to husband aggression (Straus, 1990). Items on the psychological aggression scale include both verbal and non-verbal acts. Items of that scale are the following: (1) insulted or swore at her/him; (2) sulked or refused to talk about an issue; (3) stomped out of the room or house or yard; (4) did or said something to spite her/him; (5) threatened to hit or throw something at him or her; and (6) threw, smashed, hit or kicked something. As Straus (1990) noted, the items on this scale include verbal and nonverbal acts which symbolically hurt the other or the use of threats to hurt the other. Thus, the scale certainly is a measure of psychological aggression, and the revised CTS uses the label psychological aggression for this construct (Straus, Hamby, Boney-McCoy, & Sugarman, 1995).

Although the primary focus was initially on physical violence in families, Straus and his colleagues also showed that the more psychologically aggressive partners are to one another, the more likely they are to be physically aggressive (Straus, 1974; Straus & Smith, 1990). Moreover, the more psychologically aggressive parents are toward their children, the more likely they were to be physically abusive to the children. Such findings argued against the then popular catharsis model of coping with family problems (Berkowitz, 1973). Moreover, Suitor, Pillemer, and Straus (1990) reported that verbal aggression declines monotonically across the life course.

Index of Spouse Abuse. Hudson and McIntosh (1981) published one of the first measures of partner abuse called the Index of Spouse Abuse (ISA), which was intended to assess both psychological and physical abuse of women. The measure was developed using both undergraduate and graduate female college students at the University of Hawaii as well as a comparison group of abused and nonabused women. The ISA is a 30-item scale in which the respondent rates the extent to which a partner engages in the various behaviors (from 1 [never] to 5 [very frequently]). A severity of physical abuse index and a severity of psychological abuse index are obtained. The psychological and physical abuse scales of the ISA had internal consistencies greater than .90 (Campbell, Campbell, King, Parker, & Ryan, 1994; Hudson & McIntosh, 1981) and, as would be expected, the correlations of psychological and physical abuse were high ($r = .66$; Campbell et al., 1994; Hudson & McIntosh, 1981, $r = .86$). Factor analyses by Campbell et al. suggest different loadings of the ISA items of the physical aggression factor than the original Hudson and McIntosh (1981) analyses. The factor analyses also revealed a psychological abuse factor and a new factor that essentially comprised a second psychological abuse scale that Campbell and colleagues felt was a measure of domination and control.

In 1990, Hudson further developed the ISA with two separate scales, a psychological and a physical abuse scale. Each scale comprises 25 items with scores that range from 0–100. In 1994, Alta, Hudson, and McSweeney partly validated the scales and determined cutoff scores for determination of probable abuse. In brief, the ISA is a measure of psychological abuse that is internally consistent and factorially sound. Research by Campbell et al. (1994) indicates that measures developed with one racial group (unspecified Hawaiian sample) may not have the same psychometric properties in another population (African American). Nonetheless, the ISA has been given some validation support from clinical interviews by McFarlane, Parker, Soeken, and Bullock (1992). More specifically, physical abuse and psychological abuse were assessed with the ISA in a population of women identified as abused in a brief 5-item questionnaire used in an interview format. Moreover, the ISA physical abuse scale was found to correlate .77 with a dangerousness measure, and the psychological abuse scale was found to correlate .66 with a dangerousness measure (Campbell et al., 1994).

Spouse Specific Aggression and Assertion. In 1986, O'Leary and Curley published the Spouse Specific Aggression Scale (SSAgg) and the Spouse Specific Assertion Scale (SSAss). In line with the Zeitgeist of the times, the scales were developed to differentially assess psychological aggression and assertion. In the mid-1970s, assertion books were so popular that the there was a guide to the selection of assertion books (Landau, 1976), and assertion training had been recommended for abused women though we had expressed concern that assertion training, if not very carefully implemented, could place abused women at risk (O'Leary, Curley, Rosenbaum, & Clark, 1985). There are 12 items that assess psychological aggression, and 9 of those items were adapted from the Buss-Durkee Hostility Inventpry to reflect spouse-specific aggression (Buss & Durkee, 1957). In addition, 17 items were developed to assess assertion toward a partner (either male or female). The initial pool of items was rated by a panel of eight graduate-student judges who classified the items as describing an assertive response, an aggressive response, or neither. Interrater reliability of .86 was obtained on the final version of the scale. Internal consistency as measured by alpha was .82 for the spouse specific psychological aggression scale and .87 for the spouse specific assertion scale. In comparisons of groups of men and women hypothesized to have different levels of psychological aggression, physically abusive men reported more psychological aggression toward their partners than happily married men and than discordant nonphysically abusive men. In addition, the abusive men had lower spouse specific assertion scores than the happily married men but not than discordant nonabusive men. Women in physically abusive relationships reported more spouse-specific psychological aggression toward their spouses than the satisfactorily married women, but the discordant women did not report more spouse-specific aggression than the satisfactorily married women (O'Leary & Curley, 1986). More recently, spouse specific psychological aggression has been shown to characterize physically abusive men who were mandated to treatment as well as male volunteers who were not physically abusive (Rathus, O'Leary, & Meyer, 1997). Further, spouse specific aggression was one of the best differentiators of physically aggressive, discordant men from nonphysically aggressive discordant men (Boyle & Vivian, 1996).

Psychological Maltreatment of Women Inventory. In 1989 Tolman developed a scale called Psychological Maltreatment of Women Inventory (PMWI), an instrument to assess the manner in which a male partner controls a female partner. Participants are asked to indicate how often certain behaviors occurred within the last 2 years. The scale was developed with 407 batterers and 207 women at intake for a domestic violence program (though the men and women were generally not related). As a consequence of the context of the subject acquisition, the PMWI contains items that reflect quite controlling behaviors. For example, the dominance-isolation scale includes the following items: limited her access to telephone; prevented or limited her use of the car; limited her access to money; asked her to account for her time and report where she had been. The emotional verbal scale includes items such as the following: yelled and screamed; called her names; told partner that her feelings were crazy; insulted or shamed her in front of others. The PMWI was developed to be compatible with the Conflict Tactics Scale by Straus (1979) and the Index of Spouse Abuse (ISA) by Hudson and McIntosh (1981). Tolman wanted to have a measure that could be used to obtain men's reports of their own psychological aggression and he wanted to sample a broader range of psychologically abusive behaviors, especially of the monitoring and isolation qualities. Indeed some of the items in the PMWI were modified from the nonphysical abuse scale of the ISA of Hudson and McIntosh. Tolman excluded items that would assess behaviors described as psychological maltreatment, if those items had a direct physical component (such as interrupting sleep, forcing sex) or items that included threats of harm, since such items are covered in measures such as the CTS.

Factor analyses of an original pool of 58 items yielded a Psychological Maltreatment of Women Inventory with two factors whether using reports by men or women: an emotional-verbal abuse factor and a dominance-isolation factor. The first factor contains 28 items; the second has 20 items. As might be expected, the factors were highly correlated for both men ($r = .73$) and women ($r = .74$). While the men's and women's reports are not directly comparable as the men and women were from different relationships, in the populations used by Tolman the women's reports of the extent of maltreatment were considerably higher on both the dominance-isolation and the emotional-verbal subscales. Internal consistency of the dominance-isolation scale was reported for male respondents to be .91; it was .93 for the emotional-verbal abuse scale. For women reporting about their husbands dominance/isolation, the alpha was .94; for women reporting about their emotional-verbal abuse, the alpha was .92.

Another study compared violent men, using the two scales of the PMWI, to men in discordant nonviolent relationships, and happily married men. The two clinical groups had higher scores on the emotional/verbal abuse scale than the happily married men, but, contrary to predictions, they did not differ from one another (Rathus, O'Leary, & Meyer, 1997). Similarly, the two clinical groups had higher scores on the dominance/isolation scale than the happily married group, but they did not differ from one another. Physically abusive men in this study had to have at least two mild acts or one severe act of husband-to-wife physical aggression within the past year. They had an average of 7.5 acts in the year ($SD = 5.3$). The modal number of physically aggressive acts was three. With this sample of men who were physically aggressive toward their partners but had been volunteers for treatment or mandated to treatment, the levels of dominance and isolation differed from those of Tolman's sample of men in a group for batterers. The mean score of the men in the Tolman sample on dominance-isolation subscale was 43.3 ($SD = 15.8$) out of a possible range of 20 to 100. In contrast, the mean of the distressed, violent group on this scale was 29.6 ($SD = 5.5$). The sample differences on this variable are clearly a matter of importance, and, in accord with suggestions by a number of researchers in this area, it may be necessary to delineate types of men (and women) in different kinds of aggressive relationships (Hamberger & Hastings, 1986; Holtzworth-Munroe & Stuart, 1994; O'Leary, 1993).

A brief version of the PMWI contains two 7-item scales of dominance-isolation and verbal-emotional abuse (Tolman, in press). Both of these scales successfully discriminated between three groups: (1) battered, maritally distressed, (2) maritally distressed but not physically abused, (3) maritally satisfied and not physically abused. Women were recruited for this study from an agency for battered women and from newspaper announcements. The dominance-isolation scale had an internal consistency of .88 and the verbal-emotional abuse scale had an internal consistency of .92. Factor loadings of the abbreviated scale showed that the factor structure was consistent with the factor structure of the larger scale (PMWI). Moreover, the battered women scored significantly higher on the two abbreviated scales than the women in the other two groups: the maritally distressed but not physically abused women and the maritally satisfied women.

Additional analyses of the battered women who sought services from an agency for battered women and those who were not treatment seeking revealed that it was the women seeking help from an agency for battered women who differed on the maltreatment scales from the women in the relationships that were distressed but nonviolent. However, women in physically abusive relationships that were not treatment-seeking differed only on one of four measures, the short dominance scale, from the women in distressed nonviolent relationships. These findings seem to echo the need to distinguish between people in different types of physically abusive relationships, a point made by Hamberger and Hastings (1986), Holtzworth-Munroe and Stuart (1994), and O'Leary, (1993).

Index of Psychological Abuse. In 1991, Sullivan, Parisian, and Davidson presented a poster at the American Psychological Association in which they presented material on the development of a measure of psychological abuse. The 33-item scale was designed to measure the amount of ridicule, harassment, isolation, and control a woman experienced. Women indicated on a 4-point scale how frequently they experienced a particular form of abuse. The scale was intended to be used in both dating and marital relationships, and it was piloted in two research projects, one involving dating aggression in college students and one involving the follow-up of women who had utilized a battered women's shelter. Items were subjected to a principal components factor analysis which yielded six subscales with varied numbers of items listed in brackets: (1) Criticism & Ridicule [9], (2) Social Isolation and Control [5], (3) Threats and Violence [4], (4) Emotional Withdrawal [3], (5) Manipulation [3], and (6) Emotional Callousness [3]. The six scales were then developed with the dating population and later used with women from domestic violence shelters. Alphas for the six scales ranged from .68 to .93, and correlations among the measures ranged from .52 to .83, with 9 of the 15 correlations being higher than .70. While the correlations suggest strong overlap among the types of psychological abuse, there was some evidence that certain types of psychological abuse had greater associations with some dependent measures than others. For example, Criticism and Ridicule had the strongest associations with physical abuse, namely .61. All six scales had relatively low but significant correlations with depressive symptomatology, namely, all about .30 to .35. In brief, the Index of Psychological Abuse is a scale that could be used as is or developed further, depending upon the type of psychological abuse one wishes to assess.

The Abusive Behavior Inventory (ABI). In 1992, Shepard and Campbell used feminist theory to assess a wide range of abusive behaviors. Psychological abuse was seen as a means of establishing power and control over the victim. One hundred men and 78 women were divided equally into groups of abusers/abused and nonabusers/nonabused (the method of differentiating the criterion groups was not specified). All men were part of a chemical dependency program located in a Veteran's Administration hospital; the women were married to these men. The ABI is a 30-item inventory using a 5-point Likert scale (1 = no psychological abuse to 5 = very frequent psychological abuse) to measure the frequency of 20 psychologically abusive behaviors and 10 physically abusive behaviors during a 30-month period. The scale was developed for the purpose of evaluating a domestic abuse program.

Alpha coefficients for the four groups ranged from .70 to .92. As predicted, the men in the abuse group had higher scores on the psychological and physical abuse items than the nonabusive men. Physical abuse items had more consistent correlations with the total physical subscale than psychological abuse items had with their total psychological abuse subscale score. More specifically, 7 of the 20 psychological abuse items for men had higher correlations with the physical abuse subscale than with the psychological abuse subscale (e.g., items reflecting economic abuse, isolation, threats of force, and reckless driving). As the authors note, these results point to the need for replication and extension of measurement models with diverse populations. This is especially important because the way in which one should score psychological and physical aggression factors is often unclear when the items load on a factor other than the one hypothesized.

This study by Shepard and Campbell had one feature which is especially laudatory, namely, the use of the clinician's assessment of psychological abuse and the client's assessment of abuse. While details of the specific means of obtaining such ratings were not described, the need for clinical validation such as this is important. The correlations of the clinicians ratings with the Psychological Abuse Subscale were .20 for men's reports of the behavior and .25 for women's reports of the behavior. Unfortunately, the correlations were not reported for the four groups, and even the reported correlations are very modest. However, this is the only attempt to provide clinician's ratings of abuse in any of the psychological abuse measurement studies reported herein. Finally, it was a surprise to me that the mean ratings of psychological abuse were so low for the abuse group, namely 2.1 as reported by men and 2.8 as reported by women on a 5-point Likert scale for 20 psychological abuse items (range of scores could be from 1 to 5). Such data suggest that even when using the women's reports, men are seen as rarely engaging in the behaviors described. However, even the women's reports of the men's physical abuse were only 1.8. Since it is unclear how often these psychologically abusive behaviors are engaged in by men in various samples, especially highly controlling behaviors, it will be helpful for all investigators to describe the frequencies of all of the specific items in the scale.

Severity of Violence Against Women. In 1992(a), Marshall published her Severity of Violence Against Women Scales. The scales were developed with college females ($N = 707$) who rated 46 various acts of aggression in terms of seriousness, abusiveness, violence and threatening nature. The acts were to be rated "if a man carried out these acts with a women." Community women ($N = 208$) also rated the acts in terms of seriousness, aggressiveness, and abusiveness. When the students rated the violence, nine factors emerged ranging from symbolic violence and threats of mild violence to serious violence, and sexual violence. Because of problems of very low response rates of community women (16%), community women were not asked to evaluate the acts of aggression using the same descriptors as the students, and thus the factor analyses based on the community sample are not comparable to those of the students. However, a second order factor analysis revealed two factors that basically represented a psychological aggression factor and a physical/sexual violence factor. The acts represented in the Marshall scales represent detailed behaviors of different levels of psychological and physical aggression, and the use of the items and/or scales with populations of abused and maritally discordant populations would be valuable. Basically, the scales represent a beginning point for researchers interested in mapping the typologies of psychological abuse. Marshall extended her research on the assessment of psychological abuse of women by men to include a measure of psychological abuse by women of men (Marshall, 1992b). The types of violence measured were threats of mild violence, threats of moderate violence, and threats of severe violence. As was the case with the development of the violence against women scales, a college student sample and community sample of males rated acts of violence as if a woman engaged in the acts of violence against a man. That is, the acts represent behaviors that might be engaged in by women. Thus, replication and extension of this work with clinical populations is certainly in order.

The Measurement of Wife Abuse (MWA). Rodenburg and Fantuzzo (1993) published The Measurement of Wife Abuse, a measure "developed to improve upon previously constructed instruments, mainly by using empirical methods of construction." The sub-jects in the study were abused women, most of whom came from an outpatient clinic or a battered women's shelter. There were also some women who responded to radio and newspaper announcements about the study. To be included, a woman had be physically abused at least three times, as assessed by the Conflict Tactics Scale. The measure was a revision of an unpublished master's thesis (Lambert & Fantuzzo, 1988). The MWA exam-ines frequency of different kinds of abuse based on number of acts within a 6-month period as well as the emotional consequences experienced by the victim. Items for the scale were taken from Rhodes (1985) who compiled the items from over 250 restraining orders or legal documents which contained descriptions of abuse by partners. Card-sorting proce-dures were used initially to sort items into categories: (1) psychological abuse, (2) physical abuse, (3) sexual abuse, and (4) verbal abuse. Because the focus in this manuscript is on psychological abuse, that 15-item measure will be discussed here. Severity ratings based on a 4-point scale were subject to a confirmatory factor analysis. Concurrent validity was assessed by measures of association with the CTS. The psychological abuse measure con-tained 15 items that involved restriction (disabled car, locked in, electricity off) whereas the verbal abuse items were about verbal denigration (told ugly, told stupid, called bitch). Contrary to the author's expectations, the four factors of the MWA were all significantly intercorrelated, at approximately equal rates (all between .41 and .56). The psychological abuse measure and the verbal abuse measure correlated .46. Seventy-five percent of the items met a correlation criterion of .30 with its hypothesized factor. One item, attempted suicide, had a loading of less than .20. Thus, the psychological abuse scale has 14 items that have reasonable loadings. The correlations of the psychological abuse scale of the MWA with the Psychological Abuse and the Physical Aggression Scale of the CTS were .23 and .22, respectively. These correlations, while significant ($N = 132$), indicate rela-tively little overlap in the variance accounted for in the measures. Thus, while there is some evidence of convergence of measures, the validity of the psychological abuse scale of the MWA needs to be better established, or it would be important to provide evidence about why the MWA should not be associated with measures of abuse developed by others.

The Dominance Scale. In 1996, Hamby published The Dominance Scale, which appears to measure three different forms of dominance: Authority, Restrictiveness, and Disparagement. Each of these forms of dominance were seen as one kind of deviation from an egalitarian relationship. Hamby conceptualized the above three forms of dominance as "causes of violence, including physical and psychological aggression, not as violence in and of itself." The scale was developed with a college student population of whom only 14% were married, and thus the population was essentially about dating relationships. There were 51 males and 80 females attending one of two colleges in the Northeast. Participants were recruited through sociology and justice studies courses. Because of the small sample, factor analyses were not conducted on the full Dominance item pool. Instead, separate factor analyses were conducted for each theoretical scale to assess com-munalities. A one factor solution was obtained in each case. Restrictiveness and dispar-agement were uncorrelated ($r = .03$); authority and restrictiveness had a correlation of .38; authority and disparagement had a correlation of .58. According to Hamby, the pattern of correlations was not significantly different for males and females. Restrictiveness was significantly correlated with physical aggression and injury, but authority and disparage-ment were not. All three components of the Dominance Scale were significantly correlated with reports of one's own psychological aggression. As noted by Hamby, the results of stud-ies using authority or decisionmaking measures as a means of assessing dominance, may not be very closely related to partner violence. Based on her work, restrictive control may be more closely related to partner violence than authoritarian control. While the Hamby Dominance Scale is based on a relatively small college sample, the work raises important questions about dominance and the need to separate components of this construct.

Hamby argued that the Dominance Scale was not a measure of psychological aggression but instead a predictor of such aggression. However, the three dominance constructs all correlated, albeit moderately, with self-reported and partner-reported psychological aggression as measured by the revised Conflict Tactics Scale. Thus, the Dominance Scale can be interpreted as one form of psychological aggression, or at least a construct whose components are all significantly related to psychological aggression.

In summary, there are eight measures of psychological aggression that have both internal consistency and demonstrable construct validity. The following investigators all have measures of psychological abuse: Hamby (1996); Hudson & McIntosh (1981); Marshall (1992); O'Leary & Curley, (1986); Rodenberg & Fantuzzo (1993); Shepard & Campbell (1992); Straus (1979); Tolman (1989). Each of the measures was designed for a somewhat different purpose, and thus each assesses psychological abuse somewhat differently. As data are presented on the three other major issues in this paper, i.e., the temporal precedence of psychological to physical aggression, the impact of psychological and physical aggression, and a definition of partner abuse that could be used for clinical and legal purposes, additional research findings will be presented that further support the construct validity of various measures of psychological aggression since the aforementioned measures of psychological aggression have been used in a number of studies to be discussed later.

When Physical Aggression Occurs, it Is Often Preceded by Psychological/Verbal Aggression

In a longitudinal study of the etiology of partner violence, Murphy and O'Leary (1989) found that psychological aggression was a precursor of physical aggression in young couples. The young couples were engaged to be married within one month of the initial assessment. Couples were recruited from the community and were similar to the counties from which they were drawn in terms of age at first marriage and religious affiliation. The couples were almost exclusively White and had 14.5 years of education, 1.5 years more than the average for the local area. Two hundred and seventy-two couples participated at each assessment. Psychological aggression was measured by a combined score based on the CTS and the Spouse Specific Aggression Scale. These scores were transformed into Z scores and summed to form a composite index of psychological aggression. (The correlations between the two measures of psychological aggression at the initial assessment were .47 for men and .68 for women for the nonphysically aggressive subjects in this study.) Couples were selected for not having been physically aggressive to their partner in the past year or at any other time prior to the assessment of psychological aggression. The psychological aggression scores were used to predict the onset of the first acts of physical aggression (as reported by either the husband or the wife).

Across a 6-month period (from premarriage to 6 months after marriage), the lag correlations of psychological aggression and physical aggression (assessed dichotomously) were all significant. In predicting the husband's first instance of physical aggression, based on his self report, the correlation was .31; based on the wife's reports, the correlation was .19. In predicting wives' first instance of physical aggression, based on self-report, the correlation was .15. Based on partner report, the correlation was .32. With a lag of 12 months from 6 to 18 months into marriage, the correlations again were all significant and ranged from .29 to .34. The 18- to 30-month correlations were only significant for self-reports of psychological aggression and physical aggression.

As might be expected, cross-sectional associations were higher than the lag correlations. In predicting husbands' physical aggression, the correlations were .40, based on self-report and .33 based on partner report. In predicting wives' physical aggression, the correlations were .38 based on self-report and .40 based on partner report. Moreover, at 1 year, the correlations were again all significant and ranged from .33 to .41. At 30 months into marriage, three of the four correlations were significant.

In contrast to the consistent association across 6- and 12-month periods of psychological and physical aggression, general marital satisfaction was not predictive of later physical aggression. Only one of 23 longitudinal correlations was predictive of later physical aggression. The above results support the general model that psychologically coercive behaviors precede and predict the development of physically aggressive behavior in marriage (O'Leary, 1988). The importance of the negative interchanges and psychological aggression in the development of partner violence has been described clinically (e.g., Deschner, 1984), and this research supports the hypothesized progression from psychological to physical aggression in early marriage.

In a different analysis of the couples in the longitudinal research noted above, O'Leary, Malone, and Tyree (1994) showed that there were direct paths from psychological aggression to physical aggression. Psychological aggression, as assessed at 18 months by the Spouse Specific Aggression Scale (O'Leary & Curley, 1986), had a direct path to physical aggression for men at 30 months with a path coefficient of .36. For women, there was a similar direct path from psychological aggression at 18 months to physical aggression at 30 months with a path coefficient of .29. The results discussed here are based on predictions of physical aggression at 30 months, although this aggression may not have been the first reported act of physical aggression in the relationship. In addition, we were able to show that men and women who have aggressive and defensive personality characteristics and who are experiencing a lack of satisfaction with their partners tend to engage in psychological aggression against their partners. In turn, as noted above, the psychological aggression was a precursor of physical aggression. In terms of gender differences, for women, there was a significant path from marital discord to physical aggression that did not exist for men. As we stated in the publication of these results, "We suspect that this finding may reflect the greater importance of relationship factors for women than men. Women may be more frustrated by marital discord, and impulsive women may be more likely to re-engage their partners after discordant interactions—even through aggressive physical contact." In addition to what was initially stated, women's marital discord usually is lower than men's and they may be more responsive to slights and negative interactions that are not reflected directly in psychological aggression.

The Effects of Psychological Aggression are Often as Deleterious as Those of Physical Aggression

One of the first studies to address the comparative role of psychological and physical aggression was that of Folingstad, Rutledge, Berg, Hause, and Polek (1990). Two hundred thirty-four women were interviewed to assess the relationship of emotional abuse to physical abuse. The women all had some history of physical abuse. Approximately one quarter of the women (26%) had no physical abuse in their relationships within the past 2 years while the remainder were experiencing long-term, ongoing abuse. Most of the women reported being out of the relationship; 33 still remained in the relationship. Recruitment occurred via announcements in newspapers, radio, and television as well as flyers in prisons, the department of social services, and in a local shelter.

Six types of emotional abuse were assessed for their frequency and impact: (1) threats of abuse; (2) ridicule; (3) jealousy, (4) threats to change marriage status; (5) restriction; and (6) damage to property.

The abuse with the highest negative impact was ridicule, and it was one of the three most frequent types of abuse. Forty-six percent of the sample rated emotional ridicule as the worst type of abuse, 15% of the sample rated threats of abuse as the worst type of abuse, and 14% rated jealousy as the worst type of abuse.

To address the question of the relative impact of emotional and physical abuse, subjects rated whether emotional or physical abuse had a more negative impact on them. Seventy-two percent of the women rated emotional abuse as having a more negative impact on them than the physical abuse. Of interest, the women who reported emotional abuse as worse than physical abuse experienced the same degree of severity of typical physical abuse and the same frequency of abusive incidents during the first 6 months and subsequent months of abuse. Approximately half of the sample (54%) could predict the physical abuse they might receive from the emotional abuse they received. Threats of abuse and restriction of the woman were predictors of later physical violence. Using a regression analysis, it was determined that threat of abuse was a very strong predictor that physical abuse would follow.

Marshall (1992a) also addressed the issue of impact of psychologically and physically aggressive behaviors. Of special import for the discussion here, 707 college women rated 46 various aggressive behaviors on how serious, aggressive, abusive, violent, and threatening it would be "if a man did the act to a woman" on a 10-point scale. The women rated symbolically (psychologically) aggressive and physically aggressive acts with a woman. Moreover, they rated how much emotional or psychological harm each of the acts would have on a woman. For 11 of 12 items like those that appear on the CTS and are called minor violence, the emotional impact ratings for students were all numerically higher than the physical impact ratings. The same pattern held for a sample of community women. Eleven of 12 items had higher emotional impact ratings than physical impact ratings. Marshall's data can be addressed in another way, namely, to evaluate the emotional impact of symbolic and psychological violence and compare that to the emotional impact of actual behavioral acts of violence. Unfortunately, items assessing symbolic or psychological aggression did not correspond directly to the actual behavioral acts of aggression. More specifically, threats of certain behavior did not correspond to engaging in those specific behaviors. However, it is clear from the students' ratings of emotional impact that threats of moderate violence and acts of moderate violence had almost the identical impact rating, 7.1 and 7.0, respectively. Moreover, threats of serious violence and acts of serious violence also had almost the same emotional impact rating, namely, 8.5 and 9.0, respectively. Threats of minor violence and acts of minor violence had different emotional impact ratings with the behavioral acts of aggression having higher impact ratings than the threats of minor violence, 7.0 versus 4.6. It appears clear from these data that the emotional impact of psychological violence can often be as negative as the emotional impact of physical violence, though for some behaviors the emotional impact of engaging in the acts can have greater impact than the threats of such acts. The research by Marshall has one important limitation, namely, that actual violence was not being evaluated by the college students or the community women. The ratings were done in a hypothetical sense. More specifically, women were asked how they would feel if a male partner did each of the acts. Replication and extension of this work with battered women would be useful to arrive at estimates of comparative effects of psychological and physical aggression.

Aguilar and Nightingale (1994) assessed the association of physical, sexual, and emotional abuse with self-esteem in 48 battered women. Using cluster analyses, four clusters of negative experiences were associated with battering experiences, namely, physical abuse, controlling/emotional abuse, sexual/emotional abuse, and miscellaneous abuse. The physical abuse category was comprised of items like those on the CTS (Straus, 1979): e.g., pushed, hit with fist, hit with an object, pinched, slapped, and choked. In addition, one non-physical abuse item, called derogatory names, clustered with the physical abuse items. The controlling/emotional abuse items included the following: told whom you can speak to; told whom you can see; told you cannot work; told what you can do. The sexual emotional cluster included the following: sexually abused, treated like a servant, told you are stupid, told you are crazy, treated as a sex object.

There was a fourth cluster that included only two items: bit and told how money is to be spent. As was evident from the cluster analyzes, the items that are derived from the cluster analysis procedure are not the same items that one would make from a logical analysis of items. For example, a physical abuse cluster has a nonphysical abuse item "called derogatory names." The particular items that fall into a cluster depend upon the specific items that were used in the cluster analysis, and the specific items determine whether one can obtain a cluster that reflects single or logically consistent groupings. Though the clusters found in this research do not fit into neat logically consistent packages, they did have empirical associations with self-esteem that are of significance. More specifically, women with high scores on the controlling/emotionally abuse cluster had lower self-esteem scores. In contrast, there was no association of physical abuse and sexual abuse with self-esteem. Unexpectedly, the fourth cluster, which included two items, being bit and being told how money was to be spent was associated with high self-esteem scores. This latter finding does not fit any particular theoretical or clinical description of battered women and it seems inconsistent with other findings. Without more explanation of the reasons for the results in this sample and until there is an attempt to replicate this finding, it seems fruitless to spend time attempting to explain the seemingly anomalous result. On the other hand, in keeping with the results of several other studies herein, the authors found greater association of psychological abuse with low self-esteem of women than with physical abuse.

In related research with 56 young, newly married couples, investigators addressed the association of psychological and physical aggression with later marital satisfaction and stability. Psychological and physical aggression were assessed with the Conflict Tactics Scale (Lawrence & Bradbury, 1995). Marital deterioration was defined as marital discord (Locke-Wallace Marital Adjustment Test of < 80) or marital dissolution. Survival analysis was the method used to assess the relationship of psychological aggression to the maintenance of marital satisfaction (or to marital dissolution). Basically, in this case, the survival analysis was a plotting of the risk for marital failure (discord or instability) of each subgroup (nonaggressive, psychologically aggressive, and physically aggressive), given the percent of couples in that subgroup who failed up to that point. Surprisingly, 32% of the couples experienced marital dissolution within the first 4 years of marriage, and 57% of wives and 55% of men reported discord over the 4 years.

Let us first address the association of aggression of the husband and his wife's report of marital deterioration. Although 57% of the wives of nonaggressive husbands experienced deterioration in their marriages, a similar percentage of wives (63%) of psychologically aggressive husbands reported deterioration. Finally, 75% of the wives of physically aggressive husbands experienced deterioration. There were no differences across the three groups. When aggression as reported by the wives was the independent variable and husbands' marital deterioration the dependent variable, the levels of deterioration were as follows: 13% for the nonaggressive group; 53% for the psychologically aggressive group; 88% for the physically aggressive group. These differences were significant, and they suggest that women's psychological and physical aggression can have a definite negative effect on the marital satisfaction/stability of the husband.

The absolute numbers, and, in turn, the cell sizes in this study are small, and the results reported for husbands' marital deterioration were more predictable than was the case for wives. The results for marital deterioration of wives, given aggression of their husbands, were not as we would expect, but the absence of differences could have been due in large part to the high rates of marital deterioration of the women in the nonaggressive group, namely, 57%. That is, even wives of nonaggressive husbands experienced marital deterioration for reasons that are not clear, and this high rate of deterioration made it difficult to detect differences across the groups.

Using a different design, Christian-Herman, O'Leary, and Avery-Leaf (in press) assessed the role of severe negative events in marriage on depression in women by interviewing the women within 1 month after a severe negative marital event. Women were recruited who had no history of a depressive episode in order to minimize the confound of past depression increasing the risk of later episodes. The sample of 50 women with no prior history of depression was recruited from a group of 273 women who responded to a newspaper advertisement. The types of events reported by the larger sample were comparable to those reported by the 50 subjects; the three most common negative marital events were as follows: (1) threat or actual separation/divorce, (2) affair or belief that an affair is ongoing, and (3) acts of physical aggression. Ratings of negative events were made by experienced marital researchers/therapists with a mean of 10 years of experience. Only 3% of the respondents reported a specific event which they perceived as severely negative but that was not judged to be negative by the outside raters. Those subjects were excluded. Thirty-eight percent of the women met diagnostic criteria for Major Depressive Episode when they were administered the SCID approximately 2 to 4 weeks after the occurrence of the severe negative marital event. This rate can be compared to the incidence rate of 2% reported by Eaton, Kramer, Anthony, Dryman, Shapiro, and Locke (1989) for women age 18-44 in the NIMH Epidemiological Catchment Area study. Thus, the negative marital event appeared to be a cause of the depression in a very significant percentage of these women. When a comparison was made about the most frequent types of negative marital events and the depression rates in those groups, the rates were as follows: (1) threats or actual separation/divorce: 63%; (2) perception that an affair was ongoing: 36%; (3) physical aggression: 10%. Results from a Chi-square analysis indicated that there were higher rates of depression in the first two groups than in the physical aggression groups. These findings were a surprise to us, but led us to conclude that issues of loss were more likely to lead to depression than problems of physical aggression. Nonetheless, the rate of having a major depressive episode was approximately five times higher than the ECA incidence rates for depression, suggesting that physical aggression also increases the likelihood of having a major depressive episode in women who have never been depressed before. Overall, the results indicate that threats or actual separation/divorce or believing that an affair was ongoing placed women at higher risk for a major depressive episode than having been the victim of some act(s) of physical aggression by the partner.

A direct comparison of the effects of physical and psychological aggression was made by assessing impact ratings in a sample of couples in which both spouses reported physical aggression (Vivian & Langhinrichsen-Rohling, 1994). Aggression was defined as mutually agreed upon bidirectional aggression in a sample of 57 couples. This sample represented 39% of the total clinic sample of 145 couples who had sought marital therapy at the University Marital Therapy Clinic at Stony Brook. Physical aggression was reported to have occurred in 77% of the population of couples overall who came to the clinic. Impact ratings were made with a 1-7 range, with 1 being extremely negative and 7 being extremely positive. For wives, the impact of physical aggression was 1.94 while the impact of psychological aggression was 1.75. The second anchor point (2) on the scale was "quite negative," so that one can see that physical and psychological aggression both clearly have a negative impact. The impact of psychological abuse on women was greater than that for men, but upon further examination, it was seen that the difference was a function of one group of highly victimized women. Indeed, the mean ratings for impact of psychological aggression for men and women were identical except for a group of couples where the woman was highly victimized physically but the husband reported only mild to moderate physical victimization. The two groups in which the ratings were identical for men and women were in a group of couples in which both the men and women engaged in low levels of physical aggression and a smaller group in which the husband was highly physically victimized. When depressive symptomatology was assessed, the levels were found to be similar across groups and the depressive symptomatology scores were not different across men and women. The mean Beck Depression score for men was 12.8 while the mean for women was 15.4. Given the variability, the differences between men and women were not significantly different. Both men and women were approximately in the moderate range of depressive symptomatology (Beck, Ward, Mendelson, Mock, Erbangh, 1961; scores of 14 or greater). The impact ratings of psychological and physical aggression generally show that both can have a "quite negative" impact. Further, this research as well as that of others shows that the impact of psychological and physical aggression is not differential unless one is in a relationship that is characterized by being highly victimized.

Another way to assess the impact of psychological and physical aggression is to evaluate the impact of these variables on dropout from treatment (Brown, O'Leary, & Feldbau, 1997). In a treatment program designed to reduce both psychological and physical aggression, selection was made on the basis of husband and wife reports of husband-to-wife physical aggression. At least two incidents of physical aggression had to occur within the last year to be selected for a program comparing a gender-specific program with a couples program. In addition, the wives had to report in an individual assessment that they had not received injuries for which they sought medical attention and that they would not be fearful of participating with their husbands in treatment. There were positive changes reported by wives who completed the two different treatment programs, but there were no differential changes associated with the two treatments. More specifically, wives reported reductions in both psychological and physical aggression, increases in marital satisfaction, and decreases in anxiety and depression. However, 47% of the 70 couples dropped out of treatment. That is, they did not attend at least 10 of 14 treatment sessions (70% of the sessions). There was no difference in the dropout rates across the two treatments, and thus dropout results were assessed across the combined treatments. Demographic variables such as age, education, and income were not predictive of dropout. To our surprise, severity of physical aggression was not associated with dropout either. On the other hand, psychological aggression of the men and women was predictive of dropout.

Psychological aggression of the men as reported by the wives and as reflected on 14 items of the dominance/isolation scale of Tolman's Maltreatment of Women Scale was predictive of dropout. Psychological aggression of the women based on husband's reports on the six items of the psychological aggression measure from the Conflict Tactics Scale was predictive of dropout. Essentially, we interpreted these results as indicating that men's severe psychological aggression was predictive of dropout since the Tolman measure assesses dominance and control. While the men and women in the treatment program did not have significantly different scores on the dominance and control measure, the men had significantly higher scores on 4 of the 14 items, i.e., "my partner acted like I am his personal servant"; "my partner ordered me around"; "my partner didn't want me to go to school or other self-improvement activity," and "my partner restricted my use of the telephone." There were no items on which the women had higher scores than men.

Mild psychological aggression as reported by husbands about the wives distinguished treatment completers from dropouts. Items on the psychological aggression scale of the CTS include: spouse insulted or swore at you; spouse refused to give sex or affection; spouse sulked and/or refused to talk about an issue; spouse stomped out of the room or house; spouse did or said something to spite you; and spouse threatened to leave the marriage. It is noteworthy that the mean level of husbands' mild psychological aggression was significantly higher than the wives' mild psychological aggression, but husbands' mild psychological aggression did not discriminate between completers and dropouts. It appears that when women engage in the above behaviors, they have a greater impact than when men engage in the same behaviors. Since men engaged in the behaviors more frequently than women, when women do display such psychological aggression, it may spell greater problems for the marriage in relationships characterized by considerable physical abuse. One reason for the greater predictability of dropout from treatment by psychological aggression of women (relative to physical aggression) may be that their physical aggression does not have as great a physical or psychological impact.

In a different research setting, batterers and their wives were followed over a 2 year period to assess predictors of marital dissolution (Jacobson, Gottman, Gortner, Berns, & Shortt, 1996). At the 2 year follow-up, 62% of the couples ($N = 24$) were still married while 38% ($N = 17$) had separated or divorced. Physical abuse did not discriminate between those relationships that terminated and those that did not. On the other hand, emotional abuse did. As they stated, "Over time, emotional abuse is a more important factor than physical abuse in contributing to wife's marital satisfaction, and in driving them out of the marriage."

The effects of psychological aggression are often intertwined with the effects of physical aggression (O'Leary & Jouriles, 1994), but the relative effects of psychological and physical aggression can be assessed in several ways. As was done by Folingstad et al. (1990), women who experience both types of aggression can rate the impact of them. One can assess depression, anxiety, fear, and self-esteem in women and men in relationships characterized by psychological aggression and those relationships characterized by both psychological and physical aggression. The other alternative, namely, physical aggression without psychological aggression is essentially nonexistent. More specifically, Stets showed that in a nationally representative sample, the Family Violence Survey of 1995, less than one half of one percent of individuals who are physically aggressive are not verbally aggressive. The effects of psychological and physical aggression can be examined indirectly by evaluating the different etiological paths leading to psychological and physical aggression in populations with (a) psychological aggression and (b) psychological and physical aggression. This approach has been used by Stets (1990) who found different patterns of relationships for the two groups. Using probit analyses in the National Family Violence Survey of 1985, she found that there were certain variables that were associated with using physical aggression that were not associated with verbal aggression alone, namely, women with a low occupation and income and men who approve of physical aggression. Stets' research provided support for the view that verbal and physical aggression are the result of a two-stage process with some factors being associated with physical aggression that are not associated with verbal aggression alone.

In populations where both psychological and physical aggression exist, the effects of psychological and physical aggression can be evaluated using various methods, e.g., discriminant function analyses, regression, and path analytic models. Unfortunately, in studies of the effects of physical aggression, there are very few that provide data about the relative predictive power of psychological and physical aggression. However, as noted earlier (Brown, O'Leary, & Feldbau, 1997), in our sample of men and women seeking treatment for physical abuse, psychological aggression and physical aggression were used to predict dropout. Only psychological aggression predicted drop out. Clearly more studies assessing the relative contribution of psychological and physical aggression are needed. For example, in this miniseries, Arias and Pape (1999) demonstrated how psychological aggression had power in predicting a decision to leave a relationship that was over and above that of the physical aggression alone. In addition, in a sample of battered women either seeking shelter or nonshelter services, Sackett and Saunders (1999) found that fear was uniquely predicted by psychological abuse. Indeed, psychological abuse was a much stronger predictor of fear than physical abuse. Psychological abuse and physical abuse each contributed unique variance in depression and self-esteem. However, physical abuse accounted for more variance in depressive symptomatology than psychological abuse. In predicting self-esteem, both psychological and physical abuse made unique contributions, and they were of similar magnitude.

Definition of Psychological Abuse in Intimate Relationships

Adequate definitions of psychological abuse in relationships do not exist for legal and formal diagnostic purposes. The absence of such a definition, in part, reflects the greater emphasis on physical abuse of a partner by policy makers, mental health professionals, and by legal experts. The absence of such a definition also reflects the apparent ease of arriving at a definition of physical abuse of a partner because any act of physical aggression of a partner is often seen as partner abuse, particularly in divorce and custody matters. However, one must squarely address the very common prevalence of partner abuse in general populations of young married individuals that ranges from about 30%-35% of the men *and* women self-reporting such aggression (McLaughlin, Leonard, & Senchack, 1992; Mihalic, Elliot, & Menard, 1994; O'Leary et al., 1989). Moreover, physical aggression in the form of slapping, pushing, and shoving occurs in between 50% to 65% of the couples in marital clinic samples (cf. O'Leary, in press). Legal prosecution of everyone who hit a partner would be totally impractical as such prosecution, if totally effective, could involve arrest of one or both members of approximately half of all young married couples. Thus, it has become necessary to arrive at definitions of partner abuse for diagnostic purposes that involve more than a single instance of slapping or pushing (O'Leary & Jacobson, 1997).

While measures of psychological abuse exist that are reliable, the measures were not developed for legal purposes to help arrive at what would be an accepted definition of psychological abuse. Interestingly, however, neither were measures of physical abuse developed in order to arrive at what would be a DSM-IV type definition or a legal definition of abuse. Because of the prevalence of physical aggression by both men and women from adolescence to late adulthood (O'Leary & Cascardi, 1988), in DSM-IV, partner abuse has been defined as the presence of at least two acts of physical aggression within a year (or one severe act) and/or physical aggression that leads the partner to be fearful of the other or that results in injury requiring medical attention (O'Leary & Jacobson, 1997). Based on existing research, parallel definitions of psychological abuse lead to a definition as follows: acts of recurring criticism and/or verbal aggression toward a partner, and/or acts of isolation and domination of a partner. Generally, such actions cause the partner to be fearful of the other or lead the partner to have very low self-esteem, and it is recommended that researchers in this area routinely assess the impact of psychological abuse. Any definition of a problem or disorder can be altered as new evidence is gathered about a problem or disorder, as has been the case for numerous diagnostic classifications within the *Diagnostic and Statistical Manual* of the American Psychiatric Association. This will undoubtedly be the case for Physical Abuse of Partner and could be the case for Psychological Abuse of Partner.

SUMMARY

Psychological aggression has been measured reliably with at least eight different measures. The measures of psychological aggression can be differentiated from measures of physical aggression in factor analyses though there are consistently significant correlations between psychological and physical aggression. Psychological aggression generally precedes physical aggression. This adage is true both when one thinks about the development of relationships across time as well as when one thinks about the escalation of arguments in longstanding relationships. The evidence shows that psychological aggression predicts later physical aggression, and both are associated with deterioration in relationships. Data about the impact of psychological and physical aggression come from several quarters. Overall comparisons of physical and psychological aggression of women in physically abusive relationships indicated that the psychological abuse had a greater impact than the physical abuse. Direct impact ratings of psychological and physical aggression in both hypothetical and actual aggressive situations experienced by women in physically abusive relationships indicate that psychological aggression can have as negative an impact as physical aggression, unless a woman is in a highly victimized relationship. Associations of psychological aggression have been shown to be as great or greater with low self-esteem than with physical aggression. Further, psychological aggression predicted dropout from treatment and separation/divorce whereas physical aggression did not. Finally, major depressive episodes were more common where there were either threats of separation or actual separation/divorce or believing that an affair was ongoing than where physical aggression was seen by the wives as the severe negative marital event.

The data presented in this manuscript in no way detract from the need to address issues of physical abuse. Rather, the data from a number of quarters indicate that psychological abuse can have a very negative impact and often one that is greater than physical abuse. As the impact of psychological aggression in relationships is accepted as having a role often as important as physical aggression, there will be greater attention to it. It is easier to have people from different professions such as law and mental health agree about what is physically abusive than what is psychologically aggressive, because there appears to be zero tolerance for physically abusive behaviors across disciplines. On the other hand, agreement about what level of psychological aggression would meet some legal or mental health criterion of psychological abuse seems harder because psychological aggression is so common, even in happily married couples. The ability to provide a readily acceptable definition of physical abuse may be illusory as it becomes evident that physical as well as psychological aggression is so common, particularly in young couples without marital discord (O'Leary & Cascardi, 1998). With such a realization, it may become evident that some judgment about the level of physical and psychological aggression, along with some impact ratings on the fear of the partner, may be necessary to move the field forward and to give the necessary significance to psychological aggression in a relationship and its adverse impact on the mental health of partners. Such an approach has been used with the diagnostic definition of physical abuse of partner (DSM-IV; O'Leary & Jacobson, 1997), and a parallel approach is offered herein as a practical means of having a definition of psychological abuse of partner.

REFERENCES

Aguilar, R. J., & Nightingale, N. N. (1994). The impact of specific battering experiences on the self-esteem of abused women. *Journal of Family Violence, 9,* 35–45.

Arias, I., & Pape, K. T. (1999). Contribution of psychological abuse to psychological adjustment and relationship stability among battered women. Article for miniseries on Psychological Abuse. *Violence and Victims, 13.*

Beck, A., Ward, C., Mendelson, M., Mock, J., & Erbaugh, J. (1961). An inventory for measuring depression. *Archives of General Psychiatry, 4,* 561–571.

Brown, P. D., O'Leary, K. D., & Feldbau, S. R. (1997). Dropout in a treatment program for self-referring wife abusing men. *Journal of Family Violence, 12,* 365–387.

Berkowitz, L. (1973, July). The case for bottling up rage. *Psychology Today, 7,* 24–31.

Boyle, D., & Vivian, D. (1996). Generalized versus spouse-specific anger/hostility and men's violence against intimates. *Violence and Victims, 11,* 293–318.

Buss, A. H., & Durke, A. (1957). An inventory for assessing different kinds of hostility. *Journal of Consulting and Clinical Psychology, 21,* 343–349.

Campbell., D. W., Campbell, J., King, C., Parker, B., & Ryan, J. (1994). The reliability and factor structure of the index of spouse abuse with African American women. *Violence and Victims, 9,* 259–274.

Christian-Herman, J. L., O'Leary, K. D., & Avery-Leaf, S. (in press). The impact of severe negative marital events in marriage on depression. *Journal of Clinical Psychology.*

Deschner, J. P. (1984). *The hitting habit.* New York: The Free Press.

Eaton, W. W., Kramer, M., Anthony, J. C., Dryman, A., Shapiro, S., & Locke, B. Z. (1989). The incidence of specific DIS/DSM-II mental disorder. Data from the NIMH Epidemiological Catchment Area program. *Acta Psychiatrica Scandinavica, 79,* 163–178.

Folingstad, D. R., Rutledge, L. L., Berg, B. J., Hause, E. S., & Polek, D. S. (1990). The role of emotional abuse in physically abusive relationships. *Journal of Family Violence, 5,* 107–119.

Hamberger, L. K., & Hastings, J. E. (1986). Personality correlates of men who abuse their partners: A cross validation study. *Journal of Family Violence, 1,* 37–49.

Hamby, S. L. (1996). The dominance scale: Preliminary psychometric properties. *Violence and Victims, 11,* 199–212.

Holtzworth-Munroe, A., & Stuart, G. L. (1994). Topologies of male batterers: Three subtypes and the differences among them. *Psychological Bulletin, 116,* 476–497.

Hudson, W. W. (1990). *Partner abuse scale.* Tempe, AZ: Walmyr Publishing Company.

Hudson, W. W., & McIntosh, S. (1981). The index of spouse abuse. *Journal of Marriage and the Family, 43,* 873–888.

Jacobson, N. S., Gottman, J. M., Gortner, E., Berns, S., & Shortt, J. W. (1996). Psychological factors in the longitudinal course of battering: When do the couples split up? When does the abuse decrease? *Violence and Victims, 11,* 371–392.

Landau, P. (1976, May). A guide for the assertive book buyer. *Human Behavior, 70,* 64–71.

Lambert, L. K., & Fantuzzo, J. W. (1988). *Assessing spousal abuse: Beyond the Conflict Tactics Scales.* Unpublished master's thesis. California State University, Fullerton, CA.

Lawrence, E., & Bradbury, T. (1995). *Longitudinal course of physically aggressive and nonaggressive newlywed marriages.* Paper presented at the 29th annual meeting of the Association for Advancement of Behavior Therapy, Washington, DC.

McFarlane, J., Parker, B., Soeken, K., & Bullock, L. (1992). Assessing for abuse during pregnancy: Severity and frequency of injuries and associated entry into prenatal care. *Journal of the American Medical Association, 267*(23), 3176–3178.

McLaughlin, I. G., Leonard, K. E., & Senchak, M. (1992). Prevalence and distribution of premarital aggression among couples applying for a marriage license. *Journal of Family Violence, 7,* 309–319.

Marshall, L. L. (1992a). Development of the Severity of Violence Against Women Scales. *Journal of Family Violence, 7,* 103–121.

Marshall, L. L. (1992b). The Severity of Violence Against Men Scales. *Journal of Family Violence, 7,* 189–203.

Mihalic, S. W., Elliot, D. S., & Menard, S. (1994). Continuities in marital violence. *Journal of Family Violence, 9,* 195–225.

Murphy, C. M., & Cascardi, M. (1993). Psychological aggression and abuse in marriage. In R. L. Hampton, T. P. Gullotta, G. R. Adams, E. H. Potter, & R. P. Weissberg (Eds.), *Family violence: Prevention and treatment* (pp. 86–112). Sage: Newbury Park, CA.

Murphy, C, M., & O'Leary, K. D. (1989). Psychological aggression predicts physical aggression in early marriage. *Journal of Consulting and Clinical Psychology, 57,* 579–582.

O'Leary, K. D. (in press). Conjoint therapy for partners who engage in physically abusive behavior. *Journal of Aggression, Maltreatment, and Trauma.*

O'Leary, K. D. (1988). Physical aggression between spouses: A social learning perspective. In V. B. Van Hasselt, R. L. Morrison, A. S. Bellack, & M. Hersen (Eds.), *Handbook of family violence* (pp. 31–56). New York: Plenum.

O'Leary, K. D. (1993). Through a psychological lens: Personality traits, personality disorders, and levels of violence. In R. J. Gelles & D. R. Loseke (Eds.), *Current controversies on family violence* (pp. 7–29). Sage: Newbury Park, CA.

O'Leary, K. D., Barling, J., Arias, I. Rosenbaum, A., Malone, J., & Tyree, A. (1989). Prevalence and stability of physical aggression between spouses: A longitudinal analysis. *Journal of Consulting and Clinical Psychology, 57,* 263–268.

O'Leary, K. D., & Cascardi, M. (1998). Physical aggression in marriage: A developmental analysis. In T. N. Bradbury (Ed.), *The developmental course of marital dysfunction.* (pp. 343–374). Cambridge, MA: Cambridge University Press.

O'Leary, K. D., & Curley, A. D. (1986). Assertion and family violence: Correlates of spouse abuse. *Journal of Marital and Family Therapy, 12*(3), 281–289.

O'Leary, K. D., Curley, A. D., Rosenbaum, A., & Clarke, C. (1985). Assertion training for abused wives: A potentially hazardous treatment. *Journal of Marital and Family Therapy, 11*(3), 319–322.

O'Leary. K. D., & Jacobson, N. S. (1997). Partner relational problems with physical abuse. *DSM IV Sourcebook* No. 4 (pp. 701–721). Washington, DC: American Psychiatric Press, Inc.

O'Leary, K. D., & Jouriles, E. N. (1994). Psychological abuse between adult partners: Prevalence and impact on partners and children. In L. L'Abate (Ed.), *Handbook of developmental family psychology and psychopathology* (pp. 330–349).

O'Leary, K. D., Malone, J., & Tyree, A. (1994). Physical aggression in early marriage: Prerelationship and relationship effects. *Journal of Consulting and Clinical Psychology, 62,* 594–602.

Rathus, J. H., O'Leary, K. D., & Meyer, S. L. (1997). *Attachment, proximity control, and wife abuse.* Unpublished manuscript. University at Stony Brook, Stony Brook, NY.

Rhodes, N. R. (1985). *The assessment of psychological abuse: An alternative to the Conflict Tactics Scale.* Doctoral dissertation, Fuller Theological Seminary, 1985. Diss. Abstr. Int. 46: 2076B.

Rodenburg, F. A., & Fantuzzo, J. W. (1993). The measure of wife abuse: Steps toward the development of a comprehensive assessment technique. *Journal of Family Violence, 8*(3), 203–228.

Sackett, L. A., & Saunders, D. G. (1999). The impact of different forms of psychological abuse on battered women. Special Miniseries on Psychological Abuse. *Violence and Victims,*

Shepard, M. F., & Campbell, J. A. (1992). The abusive behavior inventory. *Journal of Interpersonal Violence, 7,* 291–305.

Stets, J. E. (1990). Verbal and physical aggression in marriage. *Journal of Marriage and the Family, 52,* 501–514.

Straus, M. A. (1979). Measuring intrafamily conflict and violence: The conflict tactics (CT) scales. *Journal of Marriage and the Family, 41,* 75–78.

Straus, M. A. (1994). Leveling, civility, and violence in the family. *Journal of Marriage and the Family, 35,* 13–29.

Straus, M. A., & Smith, C. (1990). Family patterns and child abuse. In M. A. Straus & R. J. Gelles (Eds.), *Physical violence in American families* (pp. 245–261). New Brunswick, NJ: Transaction Press.

Straus, M. A., Gelles, R. J., & Steinmetz, S. K. (1979). *Behind closed doors: Violence in the American family.* New York: Anchor/Doubleday.

Sullivan, C. M., Parisian, J. A., & Davidson, W. S. (1991, August). *Index of psychological abuse: Development of a measure.* Poster presentation at the annual conference of the American Psychological Association, San Francisco, CA.

Suitor, J. J., Pillemer, K., & Straus, M. A. (1990). In M. A. Straus & R. J. Gelles (Eds.), *Physical violence in American families* (pp. 305–317). New Brunswick, NJ: Transaction Press.

Straus, M. A., Hamby, S. L., Boney-McCoy, S., & Sugarman, D. (1995). The Revised Conflict Tactics Scales (CTS2). Durham, NH. Family Research Laboratory.

Tolman, R. M. (1989). The development of a measure of psychological maltreatment of women by their male partners. *Violence and Victims, 4,* 159–178.

Tolman, R. M. (1999). The validation of the psychological maltreatment of women inventory. *Violence and Victims,*

Vivian, D., & Langhinrichsen-Rohling, J. (1994). Are bi-directionally violent couples mutually victimized?. A gender sensitive comparison. *Violence and Victims, 9,* 107–124.

Walker, L. E. (1979). *The battered woman.* New York: Harper & Row.

Acknowledgments. This work was supported in part by NIMH grants MH57985 and MH47801.

Offprints. Requests for offprints should be directed to Daniel O'Leary, Psychology Department, State University of New York, Stony Brook, NY 11794–2500.

Violence and Victims, Volume 17, Number 1, 2002

Perceived Verbal Conflict Behaviors Associated With Physical Aggression and Sexual Coercion in Dating Relationships: A Gender-Sensitive Analysis

Jennifer Katz
University of Rochester School of Medicine

Andrew Carino
Angela Hilton
Washington State University

We studied perceived partner verbal behaviors associated with participants' use of dating aggression. Men's reports of their partners' demanding, controlling, and psychologically abusive behaviors during conflicts were expected to predict men's perpetration against partners. In contrast, women's reports of their partners' withdrawal were expected to predict women's perpetration. Data were collected from heterosexual undergraduates *(N = 223)* in exclusive dating relationships. Participants' reports of partner demands and partner psychological abuse were associated with participants' use of physical aggression and sexual coercion. Reports of partner withdrawal and partner controlling behaviors were associated with participants' sexual coercion only. Significant moderating effects of gender emerged. As expected, partner demands, controlling behaviors, and psychological abuse were associated with physical aggression and sexual coercion in men, but not women. Partner withdrawal was associated with sexual coercion in both women and men. We conclude that gender-sensitive approaches are necessary to understand and prevent verbal conflict patterns associated with physical aggression and sexual coercion in intimate relationships.

Keywords: abuse; dating violence; intimate partner violence; sexual abuse; gender; verbal conflict

Intimate aggression is a prevalent social problem that has gained much empirical attention over the recent past. One topic that has caused great controversy involves the equivalence, or lack thereof, of male-to-female versus female-to-male perpetration in heterosexual couples (e.g., Dobash, Dobash, Wilson, & Daly, 1992). Those who adopt a gender-sensitive view of aggression believe that the social context of gender and associated differences in dominance and social power is important in understanding risk for intimate aggression. It is important to stress that gender-sensitive does not mean gender-biased. Rather, gender-sensitive approaches are necessary to better understand and prevent both male- and female-perpetrated aggression within heterosexual couples.

Physical aggression in dating relationships typically involves acts of shoving, grabbing, and throwing objects. In contrast, sexual coercion involves attempts to force an unwilling partner into sexual activity through verbal tactics and/or physically aggressive means. Both men and women initiate physical aggression against intimate partners (Makepeace, 1986), and some research suggests that women in dating relationships more frequently initiate physical aggression than men (e.g., Capaldi & Crosby, 1997). There are more consistent gender differences in both the frequency and severity of sexual coercion (Smith, Pine, & Hawley, 1988; Struckman-Johnson & Struckman-Johnson, 1994). Women are more commonly victims of sexual coercion by partners, and women experience more extreme forms of coercion, such as intercourse, than men (Waldner-Haugrud & Magruder, 1995).

These data suggest that both women and men are at risk for experiencing some sort of aggression by dating partners. Although we strongly believe that neither male- nor female-perpetration is acceptable, we also believe that studying aggression from a gender-sensitive perspective will be fruitful in advancing basic knowledge about the context in which intimate aggression occurs. Because heterosexual couples are strongly influenced by gender-based scripts for interaction (e.g., Rose & Frieze, 1989), it seems important to consider possible gender-related differences in conflict behaviors associated with perpetration against intimate partners.

Gender and Conflict Behaviors

Social scientists in both the popular media (e.g., Tannen, 1990) and in scholarly journals recognize that women and men in close relationships often behave very differently from each other during conflict situations. Reasons for these behavioral differences include different socialization experiences (Tannen, 1990) and different levels of ascribed status and interpersonal power (Aries, 1997). Regardless, in our Western culture, women generally are socialized to maintain connectedness with others, whereas men are socialized to maintain high autonomy (Nadien & Denmark, 1999). Not surprisingly, during conflict situations with intimates, women tend to be more conflict-engaging whereas men tend to be more conflict-avoiding (e.g., Christensen & Shenk, 1991; Hall, 1984).

We hypothesized that different conflict behaviors enacted by dating partners may precipitate female- versus male-perpetrated aggression. Women and men have different socialization experiences that shape their expectations and goals for heterosocial interaction. Therefore, certain partner behaviors may be differentially associated with women's versus men's use of aggression during conflicts because specific partner behaviors may be seen as especially frustrating or threatening. To the extent that women attempt to maintain relationship intimacy, female-perpetrated aggression may be more likely to occur when male partners are seen as unwilling to be actively engaged in the relationship. In contrast, to the extent that men attempt to maintain personal autonomy, male-perpetrated aggression may be more likely to occur when female partners are seen as engaging in behaviors designed to unduly influence them or their behavior. That is, women's perceptions of male partner passivity/withdrawal during conflict situations may be associated with women's use of aggression, whereas men's perceptions of female partner demands/coercion may be related to men's use of aggression.

This conceptualization is consistent with observational research with physically aggressive couples. For instance, Capaldi and Crosby (1997) concluded that female aggression sometimes was used to obtain male partner attention during a problem-solving task; this is consistent with our hypothesis that female aggression may be used to engage male partners. Likewise, Coan, Gottman, Babcock, and Jacobson (1997) found that physically violent men often verbally rejected influence from their wives during behavioral interaction tasks. Men may use verbal tactics as well as aggression to reject female partners' influence and maintain their sense of autonomy. We wish to stress, however, that individuals do not cause partner aggression by engaging in specific conflict behaviors. Intimate aggression is caused by many factors, including the background of the aggressor and multiple aspects of the conflict situation (Riggs & O'Leary, 1986). Rather than studying causes of perpetration, our intent was to identify the types of conflict situations within which young men and women are at increased risk for using physical aggression and sexual coercion against dating partners.

Conflict Behaviors and Aggression

Aggressive couples engage in high levels of conflict (e.g., Riggs & O'Leary, 1986), and dating aggression is often conceptualized as the result of an escalation of negative affect during a conflict situation gone awry. For instance, Ryan (1995) found that dating men's own use of threats and verbal abuse were highly predictive of men's physical aggression, and White, Merrill, and Koss (1999) found that partner verbal abuse was the single best predictor of dating men's physical aggression. Verbal conflict behaviors associated with sexual coercion in ongoing romantic relationships have not been well studied. However, many verbal conflict behaviors have been linked to physical aggression in previous research on married and dating couples. Three types of verbal conflict behaviors associated with physical aggression include demand/withdraw patterns, controlling behaviors, and psychological abuse.

Demand/Withdraw Patterns. Christensen and Heavey (1990) have described an interaction pattern in which a demanding partner attempts to persuade a withdrawing partner to make a change. At the same time, the withdrawing partner attempts to avoid the demander's influence. Both partners then escalate their efforts; the more one partner demands, the more the other withdraws. Jacobson and Gottman (1998) have suggested that the demand/withdraw dynamic is related to power. The demanding partner wants something that the withdrawing partner does not want to provide; this renders the withdrawing partner more powerful since the withdrawing partner controls whether the demander's request will be met. The person who brings up a conflict topic, whether male or female, is usually the one in the demanding role (Klinetob & Smith, 1996). Regardless, consistent gender differences in demand/withdraw patterns in distressed marriages have been documented. Women more frequently seek change through demands, and men more frequently avoid change through withdrawal (Christensen, 1988; Christensen & Shenk, 1991).

To our knowledge, demand/withdraw patterns have not been studied in aggressive dating couples or as related to sexual coercion. However, there have been several studies of physically aggressive men and their spouses. Aggressive men engage in the demanding role more than non-aggressive men (Babcock, Waltz, Jacobson, & Gottman, 1993; Berns, Jacobson, & Gottman, 1999; Holtzworth-Monroe, Smutzler, & Stuart, 1998). Regardless of these base rates of demand behaviors among male perpetrators, however, we hypothesized that there would be gender differences in aggressive responses to demand versus withdraw behaviors. More specifically, dating men's use of aggression was expected to be associated with men's reports of "partner demands/I withdraw." In contrast, women's use of aggression was expected to be associated with women's reports of "I demand/partner withdraws."[1]

Controlling Behaviors. Stets and Pirog-Good (1987) suggested that the desire or need for control motivates the propensity to use violence (see also Stets, 1991). When one partner is motivated to exert control over another during a conflict situation and such attempts are unsuccessful, that partner may escalate to aggressive tactics. For instance, Riggs and Caufield (1997) found that physically violent men were significantly more likely than non-violent men to believe that violence would help them win an argument with their female dating partners. Men appear to be no more likely than women to be controlling in dating relationships (Stets & Pirog-Good, 1990), although we predicted that men would be more likely than women to aggress in response to perceived partner controlling behaviors. Research also suggests that controlling behaviors are associated with the use of sexual coercion within dating relationships (Burke, Stets, & Pirog-Good, 1989; Stets & Pirog-Good, 1989). In the present study, we expected that perceived partner controlling behaviors would be associated with men's perpetration against female partners.

Psychological Abuse. Another verbal conflict behavior associated with dating aggression is psychological abuse. Psychologically abusive behaviors are enacted in order to dominate over or emotionally injure another (Tolman, 1989). Kasian and Painter (1992) described several different types of psychological abuse within dating couples, including expressions of jealousy, verbal threats, diminishment of self-esteem, and isolation of the partner. Although social and emotional control are aspects of psychological abuse, and both controlling behaviors and psychological abuse are means of influence over another, psychological abuse involves a broader category of behaviors than controlling behaviors specifically.

Research with dating couples suggests physically abusive couples engage in elevated levels of verbal abuse (e.g., Capaldi & Crosby, 1997; White et al., 1999). Men consistently report sustaining more psychological abuse than women (Kasian & Painter, 1992; Pederson & Thomas, 1992). Psychological abuse also has been implicated in sexual coercion in dating relationships. Both men and women were found to use pressure and manipulation behaviors to gain increased sexual activity with committed dating partners, although only men used these psychologically abusive tactics with casual dating partners as well (Christopher, Owens, & Stecker, 1993). In the present study, perceived partner psychological abuse was expected to be associated with men's perpetration against female partners.

Hypotheses

Relative to non-aggressive couples, aggressive couples were expected to endorse more frequent destructive verbal conflict behaviors, including demand/withdraw patterns, partner controlling behaviors, and partner psychological abuse. Further, different verbal behaviors were expected to predict women's versus men's use of physical aggression and sexual coercion. Perceptions of partner withdrawal and disengagement during conflicts (as indexed by reports of I demand/partner withdraws) were expected to predict women's perpetration. In contrast, perceptions of partner influence and control (as indexed by reports of partner demands/I withdraw, partner control, and partner psychological abuse) were expected to predict men's perpetration. Physical aggression and sexual coercion were examined as two forms of intimate aggression. Relationship satisfaction (which may color perceptions of verbal conflict behaviors) and reports of partner aggression (given that aggression in dating couples tends to be mutual; Gray & Foshee, 1997) served as control variables in these analyses.

METHOD

Participants

Undergraduates at a large state university ($N = 223$; 115 men, 108 women) were recruited from a subject pool for a study of "Communication in dating relationships." All were involved in an exclusive heterosexual dating relationship lasting at least 2 months.

Participants ranged in age from 18 to 25 ($M = 19.48$, $SD = 1.39$). Most self-identified as Caucasian (84%; $n = 188$), others self-identified as Black (2%; $n = 5$), Asian (6%; $n = 13$), Hispanic (2%; $n = 5$), or "other" (5%; $n = 12$). The median annual parental income was $70,000. The average length of participants' dating relationships was 1 year ($SD = 2.89$ months, range 2-24 months). None was married, and 10 (4.5%) reported cohabiting.

Measures

The Conflict Patterns Questionnaire. The Conflict Patterns Questionnaire (CPQ; Christensen & Sullaway, 1984) was designed to assess perceptions about dyadic communication during disagreements. Two subscales from this measure were utilized for this study: I demand/partner withdraws and partner demands/I withdraw. The 3-item I demand/partner withdraws subscale focuses on the respondent pressing the other to discuss a problem and then criticizing, nagging, and making demands, while the partner avoids discussion, withdraws, or refuses to discuss the matter further. The 3-item partner demands/I withdraw scale is identical, although the respondent and partner are in opposite roles. Respondents use a Likert-type scale (1 = very unlikely, 9 = very likely) to rate each item. Estimates of internal consistency have ranged from .62-.86, with a mean of .71 (Berns et al., 1999). In this sample, internal consistency estimates (Cronbach's alphas) were .68 and .69 for the I demand/partner withdraws and partner demands/I withdraw subscales, respectively. Scores on the CPQ are related to observations of demand and withdraw behaviors (Berns et al., 1999). Excellent construct validity has been established (e.g., Christensen & Shenk, 1991).

Controlling Behaviors. Controlling Behaviors (Stets, 1995) were assessed by asking respondents how often they enact various coercive behaviors toward their partner. Examples of items include, "I regulate whom s/he sees" and "I set the rules in my relationship with him/her." Ten items pertain to the respondent's own controlling behaviors, termed the I control scale in this study. Ten additional items were used to assess the respondent's perceptions of his or her partner's controlling behavior (e.g., "My partner regulates whom I see," "My partner sets the rules in our relationship"). This scale was termed the Partner control scale. Items were rated on a 5-point Likert scale (0 = never, 4 = very often). Responses were summed, with higher scores reflecting greater frequency of controlling behaviors. Stets (1995) reported that the items on the original 10-item scale formed a single factor with an omega reliability of .87. Estimates of internal consistency (Cronbach's alpha) for both scales were calculated as .83 in the present study.

The Psychological Maltreatment Inventory. The Psychological Maltreatment Inventory (PMI) is based on the Psychological Maltreatment of Women Inventory developed by Tolman (1989) to assess the psychological abuse of women by their male partners. Kasian and Painter (1992) adapted this measure for use with both sexes in a dating population. The PMI has 60 items. Eleven items pertain to positive partner behavior. The remaining items assess the partner's use of different types of psychological abuse, including diminishment of self-esteem, jealousy, and verbal abuse. Responses to each item are made on a 6-point scale (1 = never, 6 = more than 20 times). A psychological abuse composite was created by summing responses to all 49 of the psychological abuse items. Possible scores range from 49 to 294, with higher scores reflecting more frequent psychological abuse enacted by partners. Adequate reliability, evidence for the internal factor structure, and construct validity are reported by the authors. Cronbach's alpha was .87 in this study.

Dating relationship satisfaction was indexed by the Quality of Marriage Index-Revised (QMI-R; Norton, 1983). The QMI is a self-report measure of relationship satisfaction. The six items which comprise the QMI have an intercorrelation of .76, and represent a unidimensional construct tapping the evaluative aspect of relationship satis-faction. Scores range from 1 to 7. Very low scores have been associated with a shorter estimated future of the relationship and a greater number of discu ssions about leaving the relationship. In this study, questions were re-worded to apply to dating, rather than marital, relationships. QMI scores are highly correlated with scores on other commonly used measures of relationship quality (Heyman, Sayers, & Bellack, 1994). Cronbach's alpha for this sample was .94.

The Revised Conflict Tactics Scale. The Revised Conflict Tactics Scale (CTS2; Straus, Hamby, Boney-McCoy, & Sugarman, 1996) is a 78-item scale which assesses specific behavioral tactics used by respondents and their partners during conflict situations. Questions pertain to the presence of aggression in ongoing dating relationships. The physi-cal aggression and sexual coercion perpetration subscales were used in the current study. Examples of milder and more severe physical aggression items are "I threw something at my partner that could hurt," and "I used a knife or gun on my partner," respectively. Examples of milder and more severe sexual coercion items are "I made my partner have sex without a condom," and "I used force (like hitting, holding down, or using a weapon) to make my part-ner have sex," respectively. Responses were scored on an 8-point scale, ranging from "This has never happened" (0) to "More than 20 times in the past year" (6). There is an addition-al response option indicating, "Not in the past year, but it did happen before" (7). The CTS2 was scored by adding the midpoints for the response categories chosen by the respondent. Midpoint scores range from 0 to 25. For category 7 ("Not in the past year, but it did happen before"), responses were scored as 1 (yes). In this sample, Cronbach's alphas were .74 and .68 for physical and sexual perpetration, respectively. The correlation between the physical and sexual perpetration scales was modest, r (119) = .29, $p < .01$.[2]

Procedure. In a small group format, participants completed a short assessment battery after providing informed consent. Participation was anonymous. After testing, participants were fully debriefed and counseling referrals were provided. An experimenter was avail-able to answer questions.

RESULTS

Use of aggression (CTS2) in dating relationships was fairly common. In the current sam-ple, 23% ($n = 49$) of the participants were involved in an ongoing dating relationship in which they had used physical aggression against their partners, although only 8% ($n = 18$) of the sample reported perpetrating severe aggression. The modal forms of moderate aggression were "I grabbed my partner" and "I pushed or shoved my partner," which were endorsed by 15% ($n = 33$) of the entire sample; the modal form of severe aggression was "I burned or scalded my partner on purpose" which was endorsed by 5% ($n = 10$) of the sample. About 33% of participants ($n = 74$) reported using sexual coercion against their dating partners. The modal form of sexual coercion was "I insisted on sex when my part-ner did not want to (but did not use physical force)," which was endorsed by 25% ($n = 56$) of participants. Victimization reports were comparable. About 29% ($n = 65$) of partici-pants reported sustaining physical aggression; the modal form was "My partner pushed or shoved me," which was endorsed by 15% ($n = 33$) of the sample. About 38% of partici-pants ($n = 86$) reported sustaining sexual coercion. The modal form was "My partner insisted on sex when I did not want to (but did not use physical force)," which was endorsed by 28% ($n = 62$) of the sample.

Most participants who reported using aggression also sustained aggression. Of those who reported that their relationship was physically aggressive, 75% ($n = 46$) reported both sustaining and perpetrating physical aggression, 20% ($n = 12$) reported sustaining only, and 5% ($n = 3$) reported perpetration only. No gender differences in classification within a one-sided versus mutually aggressive relationship emerged in a chi-square analysis, χ^2 (3, $n = 210$) = 5.43, *ns*. Of those who reported that their relationship was sexually coercive, 59% ($n = 59$) reported both sustaining and perpetrating sexual coercion, 27% ($n = 27$) reported sustaining only, and 15% ($n = 15$) reported perpetration only. Significant gender differences in classification within a one-sided versus mutually sexually coercive relationship emerged in a chi-square analysis, χ^2 (3, $n = 210$) = 9.89, $p < .02$. A greater proportion of men (33%) than women (19%) reported mutual sexual coercion, whereas a greater proportion of women (10%) than men (3%) reported one-sided sexual coercion.

We also compared men and women's mean levels of perpetration in two one-way analyses of variance (ANOVAs). Results suggested no differences in reports of physical perpetration, $F(1, 122) = 2.06$, *ns*. In contrast, men reported greater sexual perpetration ($M = 7.67$) than women, $M = 2.75$), $F(1, 122) = 7.99$, $p < .001$.

Conflict Behaviors in Aggressive Versus Non-Aggressive Dating Relationships

A 2×2 multivariate analysis of variance (MANOVA) was conducted to compare the conflict behaviors of male and female participants in aggressive versus non-aggressive relationships. A dating relationship was classified as aggressive if at least one episode of either physical or sexual perpetration was endorsed. Based on these criteria, reports from just under half of the sample indicated current involvement in an aggressive relationship ($n = 96$). Those participants who denied perpetrating either physical aggression or sexual coercion comprised the non-aggressive group ($n = 125$). Conflict behaviors included participant's reports of demand/withdraw patterns, partner control behaviors, and partner psychological abuse. Because of missing values, only 221 observations were included in this analysis.

Participants in aggressive versus non-aggressive relationships significantly differed in their reported conflict behaviors, Wilks's Lambda $F(4, 214) = 7.40$, $p < .001$. Univariate follow-up tests revealed significant between-subjects differences in reports of I demand/partner withdraws, $F(1, 217) = 11.88$, $p < .001$, partner demands/I withdraw, $F(1, 217) = 10.29$, $p < .002$, partner controlling behaviors, $F(1, 217) = 13.42$, $p < .001$, and partner psychological abuse, $F(1, 217) = 30.77$, $p < .001$. Aggressive participants endorsed greater use of I demand/partner withdraws (Magg = 10.60 versus Mnon = 8.46), partner demands/I withdraw (Magg = 10.09 versus Mnon = 7.95), partner controlling behaviors (Magg = 17.34 versus Mnon = 14.05), and partner psychological abuse (Magg = 83.15 versus Mnon = 63.36) than their non-aggressive counterparts.

MANOVA results also indicated significant gender differences in conflict tactics, Wilks's Lambda $F(4, 214) = 3.49$, $p < .01$. Univariate follow-up tests revealed significant differences in reports of partner psychological abuse, $F(1, 217) = 10.01$, $p < .01$. Men reported sustaining greater psychological abuse from partners, $M = 78.62$, than women, $M = 64.85$. There were no significant conflict behavior x gender interactions at the multivariate level, Wilks's Lambda $F(4, 214) = 1.13$, *ns*. These results indicated that dating aggression occurs within a unique context of verbal conflict tactics. Physically aggressive and/or sexually coercive young adults endorsed greater use of destructive verbal conflict behaviors in their partners than non-aggressive counterparts.[3]

Conflict Behaviors Associated With Perpetration

Zero-order correlations among participants' use of physical aggression, sexual coercion, perceived verbal conflict behaviors, and relationship satisfaction are reported in Table 1.[4] Participants' reports of partner demands/I withdraw and partner psychological abuse were positively associated with their use of both physical aggression and sexual coercion. However, reports of I demand/partner withdraws and partner controlling behaviors were associated with sexual coercion only.

Next, we calculated second-order correlations between perceived verbal conflict behaviors and perpetration, controlling for both participants' relationship satisfaction (which may color perceptions of verbal conflict behaviors) and reports of partner perpetration (given that dating aggression tends to be mutual). An identical pattern of results was obtained. Participants' use of physical aggression remained significantly related to perceived partner demands/I withdraw, $r(218) = .28, p < .001$, and partner psychological abuse, $r(218) = .32, p < .01$. Likewise, participants' use of sexual coercion remained significantly related to perceived partner demands/I withdraw, $r(218) = .22, p < .01$, I demand/partner withdraws, $r(218) = .17, p < .02$, partner control behaviors, $r(115) = .21, p < .01$, and partner psychological abuse, $r(218) = .41, p < .001$. These results suggested that the associations between perceived verbal conflict behaviors and the use of physical aggression, sexual coercion, or both, could not be accounted for by either general relationship satisfaction or partners' perpetration.

Gender Differences in Perceived Verbal Conflict Behaviors Associated With Perpetration

Next, we investigated whether the associations between perceived verbal conflict behaviors and participants' use of physical aggression and sexual coercion were moderated by gender. That is, reports of partner demands/I withdraw, partner controlling behaviors, and partner psychological abuse were expected to predict men's perpetration, but not women's. In contrast, reports of I demand/partner withdraws were expected to predict women's perpetration, but not men's. To examine these hypotheses, simultaneous regression equations were conducted with participants' use of physical aggression and sexual coercion as separate criterion variables. Given that perpetration scores were positively skewed, each criterion variable was transformed by squaring to normalize the distributions. Separate equations were calculated for each type of conflict behavior.

Participants' reports of partner perpetration (either physical aggression or sexual coercion) and relationship satisfaction were entered to control for the mutual nature of dating aggression and to control for general sentiment about the relationship, respectively. Participant gender and report of verbal conflict behaviors (i.e., I demand/partner withdraws, partner demands/I withdraw, partner control, or partner psychological abuse) also were entered as main effect predictors. In addition, the two-way interaction of gender × conflict behavior was entered. The presence of a significant gender times conflict behavior interaction would be consistent with our predictions about moderating effects of gender. Interaction terms were calculated as the product of the two component variables after each component variable was centered to reduce potential problems with multicolinearity (Cohen & Cohen, 1983).

Use of Physical Aggression. We first examined participants' perceptions about verbal conflict behaviors as predictors of participants' physical aggression. Given that only partner demands/I withdraw and partner psychological abuse were associated with physical

TABLE 1. Correlates of Perpetration Against Dating Partners ($N = 221$)

	1.	2.	3.	4.	5.	6.	7.
1. Use of Physical Aggression	—						
2. Use of Sexual Coercion	0.37***	—					
3. Partner Demand/I Withdraw	0.30***	0.27***	—				
4. I Demand/Partner Withdraw	0.12	0.28***	0.42***	—			
5. Partner Control	0.11	0.24***	0.42***	0.32***	—		
6. Partner Psychological Abuse	0.36***	0.42***	0.52***	0.40***	0.43***	—	
7. Relationship Satisfaction	-0.14*	-0.11	-0.39***	-0.26***	-0.19**	0-0.40***	—
Mean	4.92	5.29	8.88	9.40	15.55	72.03	33.20
SD	14.81	13.19	5.00	4.70	6.81	28.42	8.42

$*p < .05. **p < .01. ***p < .001.$

aggression (see Table 1), these two conflict behaviors were entered as predictors in separate regression equations. Results are reported in Table 2. As can be seen, the expected two-way interactions of gender × partner demands/I withdraw and gender × partner psychological abuse were significant within separate regression equations. In each equation, the two-way interaction accounted for a unique variance in participants' use of physical aggression (even after controlling for participants' relationship satisfaction and reports of partner physical aggression).

To explicate these significant interactions, we calculated the correlations between each of these verbal conflict behaviors and physical perpetration separately for men ($n = 114$) and women ($n = 107$). As predicted, participants' reports of partner demands/I withdraw were significantly related to the use of physical aggression among men, $r(113) = .37, p < .001$, but not women, $r(106) = .11$, ns. Likewise, reports of partner psychological abuse were related to the use of physical aggression among men, $r(113) = .39, p < .001$, but not women, $r(106) = .18$, ns.

Use of Sexual Coercion. We also examined perceived verbal conflict behaviors as predictors of sexual coercion. Given that all four of the conflict behaviors studied in this research were associated with sexual perpetration, each was entered as a predictor of sexual perpetration in separate regression equations. Results are reported in Table 3. As can be seen, there were significant two-way interactions between gender and each of the conflict behaviors in predicting sexual coercion. In each equation, the two-way interaction term accounted for unique variance in sexual coercion (even after controlling for participants' relationship satisfaction and reports of partner sexual coercion).

To explicate these significant two-way interactions, correlations between participants' reports of verbal conflict behaviors and participants' sexual perpetration were calculated separately for men and women. As predicted, reports of partner demands/I withdraw were related to sexual coercion among men, $r(113) = .29, p < .01$, but not women, $r(106) = .16$, ns. Unexpectedly, reports of I demand/partner withdraws were associated with perpetration among both men, $r(113) = .27, p < .01$, and women, $r(106) = .27, p < .01$. As predicted, however, sexual coercion was associated with men's reports of partner controlling behaviors, $r(113) = .23, p < .01$, and men's reports of partner psychological abuse, $r(113) = .53, p < .001$. In contrast, women's sexual coercion was not associated with either women's reports of partner controlling behaviors, $r(106) = .13$, ns, or partner psychological abuse, $r(106) = .09$, ns.

TABLE 2. Regression Equations Predicting Participants' Physical Aggression

| | Reports of Verbal Conflict Behaviors | | | |
	P Demand/ I Withdraw		P Psychological Abuse	
Control Variables	β	t value	β	t value
Partner Physical Aggression	.11	1.65	.07	0.97
Participant Relationship Satisfaction	.05	0.76	.04	0.50
Main Effect Predictors				
Participant Gender	-.14	-2.10*	-.11	-1.56
Verbal Conflict Behavior	.30	4.31***	.28	3.60***
Two-Way Interaction				
Gender × Verbal Behavior	-.20	-3.12**	-.20	-2.70**
$F(5, 215)$ for set		6.66**		6.06**
Adjusted R^2		.11		.10

Note. I refers to participants, whereas P refers to partners.
*$p < .05$. **$p < .01$. ***$p < .001$.

TABLE 3. Regression Equations Predicting Participants' Sexual Coercion

| | P Demand/I Withdraw | | Reports of Verbal Conflict Behaviors | | | | P Psychological Abuse | |
| | | | I Demand/P Withdraw | | P Control | | | |
	β	t value	β	t value	β	t value	β	t value
Control Variables								
Partner Sexual Coercion	.21	3.23**	.20	3.00**	.22	3.29**	.23	3.32**
Participant Satisfaction	.07	0.93	.01	0.19	-.02	-0.42	.11	1.77+
Main Effect Predictors								
Participant Gender	-.19	-2.87**	-.19	-2.88**	-.19	-2.82**	-.24	-3.71***
Verbal Conflict Behavior	.24	3.39***	.21	3.07**	.15	2.30*	.35	4.89***
Two-Way Interaction								
Gender × Verbal Behavior	-.17	-2.63**	-.17	-2.61**	-.17	-2.53*	-.42	-6.41***
$F(5, 215)$ for Set	7.13***		6.51***		5.99***		19.17***	
Adjusted R^2	.12		.11		.10		.29	

Note. I refers to the participants, whereas P refers to partners.
+$p < .08$. *$p < .05$. **$p < .01$. ***$p < .001$.

DISCUSSION

The purpose of the present study was to study perceived verbal conflict behaviors associated with the use of physical aggression and sexual coercion in dating relationships. Physically aggressive and/or sexually coercive participants endorsed greater use of destructive verbal conflict tactics than their counterparts. Further, significant correlations among participants' perceived verbal conflict behaviors and their perpetration against partners emerged. Participants' reports of partner demands/I withdraw and partner psychological abuse were associated with participants' use of physical aggression and sexual coercion. Participants' reports of I demand/partner withdraws and controlling behaviors were associated with use of sexual coercion only. These findings support the contention that physical aggression occurs within a unique context of destructive verbal tactics (e.g., Ryan, 1995; White et al., 1999), and provides evidence that sexual coercion does as well.

This gender-sensitive analysis further revealed differences in the correlates of male versus female perpetration. We predicted that men's reports of their partners' demanding, controlling, and psychological abuse during conflicts would be associated with men's perpetration. In contrast, we predicted that women's reports of their partners' withdrawal would be associated with women's perpetration. Results were most consistent with our hypotheses about men's perpetration. Specifically, reports of partner demands/I withdraw and of partner psychological abuse were associated with men's physical aggression and sexual coercion. Further, reports of partner controlling behaviors were associated with men's sexual coercion (but not physical aggression). These results supported the hypothesis that men may perpetrate against female partners when they view their partners as attempting to exert undue influence on them through demands and other destructive verbal tactics.

Women's use of aggression generally could not be predicted from their reports of their partners' verbal behaviors. Weak support for hypotheses specifically concerned with women's aggression as associated with partner withdrawal was found. More specifically, reports of I demand/partner withdraws were significantly associated with sexual coercion (but not physical aggression) among both women and men. Two possible explanations for this unexpected finding are offered. The most parsimonious explantion seems to be based on the nature of sexual coercion: demanding or pursuing behaviors coupled with the aggressor's refusal to accept partner withdrawal attempts. By definition, a sexually coercive individual demands increased sexual activity from a reluctant, withdrawing partner. This would explain the consistent relationship between I demand/partner withdraw scores and sexual coercion among both women and men. However, it also is possible that withdrawal from a partners' sexual demands during a conflict connotes emotional rejection or abandonment, whereas withdrawal from a partners' demands about other topics may not. In turn, perceived rejection or abandonment could be associated with aggression among both women and men. This notion remains speculative in the absence of additional information about actual conflict situations associated with sexual coercion, but suggests an interesting avenue for future research.

Additional studies employing alternative methods of assessing withdrawal might better support the hypothesized differences in precipitants of female- versus male-perpetration against dating partners. Perhaps women's use of aggression is more reliably predicted by their perceptions about their partners' willingness to be engaged in the conflict situation or the relationship generally rather than perceptions about specific withdrawal behaviors. Alternatively, perhaps women are more likely than men to engage in physical aggression due to self-defense (e.g., Katz, Yanez, & Kuffel, 2000; Makepeace, 1986), rather than in response to specific verbal behaviors. Further research also is needed to understand gender-related differences in correlates of varying levels of sexual coercion and aggression within intimate relationships.

Studying perceived partner verbal behaviors associated with the perpetration of dating aggression is an important step in understanding the larger context of conflict tactics that characterize aggressive dating couples. Observational studies of dating couples are one important direction for further research. For instance, Capaldi and Crosby (1997) observed couples and indexed incidents of physical aggression by dating partners during the observations. Similar studies could be conducted that examine both the enactment of aggression as well as the conflict behaviors that precipitate these aggressive acts. Additional verbal conflict behaviors should be studied as well. Attacking behaviors, negative mind-reading, criticism, threats, and other destructive verbal tactics could be associated with the escalation to aggression. Observational studies of violent married couples suggest that physically violent couples enact greater hostility (Burman, John, & Margolin, 1992; Margolin, Burman, & John, 1989), greater negative behaviors (Margolin, John, & Gleberman, 1988), and greater negative exchange (Cordova, Jacobson, Gottman, Rushe, & Cox, 1993) during marital conflicts. Physically violent husbands also display frequent defensiveness and withdrawal (Margolin et al., 1989). These and other destructive verbal conflict behaviors may characterize aggressive dating couples as well.

Of course, observational studies will provide only part of the picture. For instance, it is unlikely that researchers will be able to directly observe precipitants of sexual coercion. Sexual coercion within ongoing dating relationships has not been well studied in the past, although the present data suggest that such coercion is alarmingly prevalent. These data also indicated that somewhat different verbal behaviors were correlated with sexual coercion versus physical aggression and that sexual and physical perpetration scores were only modestly correlated. Overall, it appears that somewhat different conflict patterns may be associated with these two forms of relationship aggression. Therefore, future research may focus specifically on conflict patterns associated with sexual coercion in ongoing dating relationships. Although observational studies may be useful in determining conflict behaviors characteristic of sexually coercive couples, they are unlikely to allow researchers to observe direct precipitants of sexual coercion.

Another limitation of observational studies is that perceptions of partner behaviors do not always correspond with actual behaviors. Perceptions are likely key in understanding provocation to aggression. In the present study, we controlled for relationship satisfaction and reports of partner perpetration in order to control for aspects of the relationship that may influence perceptions of partner behaviors. In future studies, the development of more refined self-report measures about perceptions of partner behaviors would be helpful. For instance, research participants could be asked to provide retrospective accounts of conflict situations associated with previous episodes of physical or sexual aggression. Alternatively, participants might keep a journal documenting their perceptions of conflicts that escalate into physical aggression or sexual coercion. These and other qualitative research methods may allow researchers to develop more comprehensive hypotheses about conflict situations perceived to be associated with escalation to physical or sexual forms of aggression. These data could then be used to create more refined self-report measures of aggressive couples' verbal conflict tactics.

Another reason to study perceptions of partner behaviors is that aggressive versus non-aggressive individuals seem to make different interpretations of the same interpersonal behaviors enacted by others. Physically aggressive individuals often perceive that their romantic partners are behaving with hostile intent (e.g., Moore, Eisler, & Franchina, 2000), and sexually aggressive men tend to misperceive the meanings behind women's behaviors (Murphy, Coleman, & Haynes, 1986), often by disregarding what they actually say (Malamuth & Brown, 1994). Whether or not such perceptions occur before or after the enactment of aggression, such perceptions likely help aggressive individuals to justify or minimize their aggressive acts. Perceptions also are important to study because of consistent gender differences in interpretations of partner behaviors. For example, women tend to be more skilled than men in decoding others' nonverbal cues (Brody & Hall, 1993; Hall, 1984), perhaps as a result of their subordinate status as females (LaFrance & Henley, 1997). Therefore, gender-sensitive studies that include a focus on differing perceptions by men and women will be important in future research.

The present data should be interpreted in light of several limitations, including the use of a correlational design. We predicted and found support for the *a priori* hypotheses that specific verbal conflict behaviors are associated with perpetrating intimate aggression, and that different behaviors predict men's versus women's perpetration. It remains possible, however, that aggressive men and women tend to enact specific verbal conflict behaviors with their partners which are influenced by past episodes of aggression. For example, dating women who are abused by their male partners may subsequently engage in higher levels of demanding or psychologically abusive behaviors. Of course, it is likely that destructive verbal conflict patterns both precede and follow episodes of aggression. Future work employing longitudinal designs will help to separate out behavioral precipitants and sequelae of relationship aggression.

Relatedly, we focused primarily on individuals' perceptions of their partners' behaviors, although in many cases both partners' verbal behaviors are likely part of the negative escalation that precedes an aggressive episode. In future studies, data collection from both partners might provide a more comprehensive account of interaction patterns as well as provide a means for checking for reliability across partners. And finally, this study relied on reports from a homogenous white middle class sample of heterosexual college students. The present findings may not be generalized to married couples, same-sex couples, or couples from varying racial and socioeconomic status backgrounds. Further, these findings may not be generalized to couples characterized by severe violence and battering.

Before closing, one final point should be elaborated. It would be inaccurate to conclude from the present study that women cause their partners to be aggressive by engaging in demanding, controlling, or psychologically abusive behaviors. Certainly, aggression is only one response to destructive verbal partner behaviors. Further, aggressive men may be especially likely to perceive their partners as engaging in high levels of verbal coercion in order to justify their own aggressive behavior. Additional studies are needed to elucidate the complex interplay of verbal exchanges and perceptions about these exchanges related to intimate aggression.

In conclusion, the present data suggest that perceived verbal conflict behaviors are associated with the use of physical aggression and sexual coercion against dating partners. Aggressive individuals in ongoing dating relationships endorsed greater use of destructive verbal conflict patterns than their counterparts. Men's perceptions of their female partners' demanding and psychologically abusive behaviors were associated with men's use of physical aggression and sexual coercion against their partners. In contrast, women's perceptions of their male partners' behaviors were not reliably or uniquely associated with women's perpetration. Future research is needed to better delineate the complex cognitive and behavioral precipitants of intimate aggression. Continued research employing a gender-sensitive framework will be helpful in better understanding and preventing physical aggression and sexual coercion between intimate partners.

NOTES

1. Many abusive men are particularly sensitive to signs of rejection or abandonment by their female partners (e.g., Holtzworth-Munroe & Hutchinson, 1993; Murphy, Meyer, & O'Leary, 1994), which also may precipitate men's aggression. This hypothesis was not directly tested in the present study, as emotional rejection/abandonment was not directly assessed and cannot be inferred by measures of withdrawal from conflict. Behavioral withdrawal involves avoidance of or refusal to discuss a topic of disagreement introduced by one's partner. For example, manifestations of withdrawal behaviors assessed using the CPQ (Christensen & Sullaway, 1984) include avoiding partner-initiated discussions, refusing to discuss topics when partners nag and demand, and resisting action when partners provide pressure to change. In our view, passive withdrawal behaviors do not necessarily connote emotional rejection or abandonment (which may commonly manifest as active attempts to end the relationship or criticisms of the partner's character). Similarly, Gottman (1994) has observed that many spouses who avoid marital conflict situations remain emotionally engaged within stable marriages. Therefore, although behavioral withdrawal and emotional rejection/abandonment could be related in some cases, one cannot necessarily infer rejection from withdrawal behaviors, or vice versa.

2. The CTS scales have been criticized for a lack of attention to the context of intimate aggression (e.g., Kurz, 1990). However, since the purpose of the present research was to investigate this context, we felt that the strengths of the CTS2 (e.g., solid psychometric properties, assessment of multiple forms of aggression) outweighed this limitation.

3. Identical patterns of results emerged when comparing physically aggressive versus non-aggressive groups and the sexually coercive versus non-coercive groups separately.

4. One woman and one man did not provide complete data and, therefore, were excluded from further analyses.

REFERENCES

Aries, E. (1997). Women and men talking: Are they worlds apart? In M. R. Roth (Ed.), Women, men, and gender: *Ongoing debates* (pp. 91-103). New Haven, CT: Yale University Press.

Babcock, J. C., Waltz, J. Jacobson, N. S., & Gottman, J. M. (1993). Power and violence: The relation between communication patterns, power discrepancies, and domestic violence. *Journal of Consulting and Clinical Psychology, 61,* 40-50.

Berns, S. B., Jacobson, N. S., & Gottman, J. M. (1999). Demand-withdraw interaction in couples with a violent husband. *Journal of Consulting and Clinical Psychology, 67,* 666-674.

Brody, L. R., & Hall, J. A. (1993). Gender and emotion. In M. Lewis & J. M. Haviland, (Eds.) *Handbook of emotion* (pp. 447-460). New York: Guilford Press.

Burke, P. J., Stets, J. E., & Pirog-Good, M. A. (1989). Gender identity, self-esteem, and physical and sexual abuse in dating relationships. In M. A. Pirog-Good & J. E. Stets (Eds.), *Violence in dating relationships: Emerging social issues* (pp. 72-93). New York: Praeger Publishers.

Burman, B., John, R. S., & Margolin, G. (1992). Observed patterns of conflict in violent, nonviolent, and nondistressed couples. Behavioral Assessment, 14, 15-37.

Capaldi, D. M., & Crosby, L. (1997). Observed and reported psychological and physical aggression in young, at-risk couples. *Social Development, 6,* 184-206.

Christensen, A. (1988). Dysfunctional interaction patterns in couples. In P. Noller and M. A. Fitzpatrick (Eds.), *Perspectives on marital interaction* (pp. 31-52). Clevedon, England: Mutlilingual Matters.

Christensen, A., & Heavey, C. L. (1990). Gender and social structure in the demand/withdraw pattern of marital conflict. *Journal of Personality and Social Psychology, 59,* 73-81.

Christensen, A., & Shenk, J. L. (1991). Communication, conflict, and psychological distance in nondistressed, clinic, and divorcing couples. *Journal of Counseling and Clinical Psychology, 59,* 458-463.

Christensen, A., & Sullaway, M. (1984). *Communication Patterns Questionnaire.* Unpublished manuscript, University of California, Los Angeles.

Christopher, F. S., Owens, L. A., & Stecker, H. L. (1993). An examination of single men's and women's sexual aggressiveness in dating relationships. *Journal of Social and Personal Relationships, 10,* 511-527.

Coan, J., Gottman, J. M., Babcock, J., & Jacobson, N. (1997). Battering and the male rejection of influence from women. *Aggressive Behavior, 25,* 375-388.

Cohen, J., & Cohen, P. (1983). *Applied multiple regression/correlation analysis for the behavioral sciences* (2nd ed.). Hillsdale, NJ: Erlbaum.

Cordova, J. V., Jacobson, N. S., Gottman, J. M., Rushe, R., & Cox, G. (1993). Negative reciprocity and communication in couples with a violent husband. *Journal of Abnormal Psychology, 102,* 559-564.

Dobash, R. P., Dobash, R. E., Wilson, M. & Daly, M. (1992). The myth of sexual symmetry in marital violence. *Social Problems, 39,* 71-91.

Gottman, J. (1994). Why marriages succeed or fail. New York: Simon & Schuster.

Gray, H. M., & Foshee, V. (1997). Adolescent dating violence: Differences between one-sided and mutually violent profiles. *Journal of Interpersonal Violence, 12,* 126-141.

Hall, J. A. (1984). *Nonverbal sex differences: Communication accuracy and expressive style.* Baltimore: Johns Hopkins University Press.

Heyman, R. E., Sayers, S. L., & Bellack, A. S. (1994). Global marital satisfaction versus marital adjustment: An empirical comparison of three measures. *Journal of Family Psychology, 8,* 432-446.

Holtzworth-Munroe, A., & Hutchinson, G. (1993). Attributing negative intent to wife behavior: The attributions of maritally violent men. *Journal of Abnormal Psychology, 102,* 206-211.

Holtzworth-Monroe, A., Smutzler, N., & Stuart, G. L. (1998). Demand and withdraw communication among couples experiencing husband violence. *Journal of Consulting and Clinical Psychology, 66,* 731-743.

Jacobson, N. S., & Gottman, J. M. (1998). *When men batter women: New insights into ending abusive relationships.* New York: Simon & Schuster.

Kasian, M., & Painter, S. L. (1992). Frequency and severity of psychological abuse in a dating population. *Journal of Interpersonal Violence, 7,* 350-364.

Klinetob, N. A., & Smith, D. A. (1996). Demand/withdraw communications in marital interaction: A test of interpersonal contingency and gender role hypotheses. *Journal of Marriage and the Family, 58,* 945-957.

Kurz, D. (1995). Physical assaults by male partners: A major social problem (pp. 222-232). In M. R. Walsh (Ed.), *Women, men and gender: Ongoing debates.* New Haven, CT: Yale University Press.

LaFrance, M., & Henley, N. M. (1997). On oppressing hypotheses: Or, differences in nonverbal sensitivity revisited. In M. R. Roth (Ed.), *Women, men, and gender: Ongoing debates* (pp. 104-119). New Haven, CT: Yale University Press.

Makepeace, J. M. (1986). Gender differences in courtship violence victimization. *Family Relations, 35,* 383-388.

Malamuth, N., & Brown, L. K. (1994). Sexually aggressive men's perceptions of women's communications: Testing three explanations. *Journal of Personality and Social Psychology, 67,* 699-712.

Margolin, G., Burman, B., & John, R. S. (1989). Home observations of married couples reenacting naturalistic conflicts. *Behavioral Assessment, 11,* 101-118.

Margolin, G., John, R. S., & Gleberman, L. (1988). Affective responses to conflictual discussions in violent and nonviolent couples. *Journal of Consulting and Clinical Psychology, 56,* 24-33.

Moore, T. M., Eisler, R. M., & Franchina, J. J. (2000). Causal attributions and affective responses to provocative female partner behavior by abusive and nonabusive males. *Journal of Family Violence, 15,* 69-80.

Murphy, C. M., Meyer, S. L., & O'Leary, K. D. (1994). Dependency characteristics of partner assaultive men. *Journal of Abnormal Psychology, 103,* 729-734.

Murphy, W. D., Coleman, E. M., & Haynes, M. R. (1986). Factors related to coercive sexual behavior in a nonclinical sample of males. *Violence and Victims, 1,* 255-278.

Nadien, M. B., & Denmark, F. L. (1999). *Females and autonomy: A lifespan perspective.* Allyn and Bacon.

Norton, R. (1983). Measuring marital satisfaction: A critical look at the dependent variable. *Journal of Marriage and the Family, 45,* 141-151.

Pederson, P., & Thomas, C. D. (1992). Prevalence and correlates of dating violence in a Canadian university sample. *Canadian Journal of Behavioral Science, 24,* 490-501.

Riggs, D. S., & Caufield, M. B. (1997). Expected consequences of male violence against their female dating partners. *Journal of Interpersonal Violence, 12,* 229-240.

Riggs, D. S., & O'Leary, K. D. (1986). Aggression between heterosexual dating partners: An examination of a causal model of courtship aggression. *Journal of Interpersonal Violence, 11,* 519-540.

Rose, S., & Frieze, I. H. (1989). Young singles' scripts for a first date. *Gender and Society, 3,* 258-268.

Ryan, K. M. (1995). Do courtship-violent men have characteristics associated with a "battering personality?" *Journal of Family Violence, 10,* 99-120.

Smith, R. E., Pine, C. S., & Hawley, M. E. (1988). Social cognitions about male victims of female sexual assault. *Journal of Sex Research, 24,* 101-112.

Stets, J. (1991). Psychological aggression in dating relationships: The role of interpersonal control. *Journal of Family Violence, 6,* 97-114.

Stets, J. (1995). Modelling control in relationships. *Journal of Marriage and the Family, 57,* 489-501.

Stets, J., & Pirog-Good, M. A. (1989). Patterns of physical and sexual abuse for men and women in dating relationships: A descriptive analysis. *Journal of Family Violence, 4,* 63-76.

Stets, J. E., & Pirog-Good, M. A. (1990). Interpersonal control and courtship aggression. *Journal of Social and Personal Relationships, 7,* 371-394.

Stets, J., & Pirog-Good, M. A. (1987). Violence in dating relationships. *Social Psychology Quarterly, 50,* 237-246.

Straus, M. A., Hamby, S. L., Boney-McCoy, S., & Sugarman, D. B. (1996). The revised Conflict Tactics Scale (CTS2): Development and preliminary psychometric data. *Journal of Family Issues, 17,* 283-316.

Struckman-Johnson, C., & Struckman-Johnson, D. (1994). Men pressured and forced into sexual experience. *Archives of Sexual Behavior, 23,* 93-114.

Tannen, D. (1990). You just don't understand: Women and men in conversation. New York: William Morrow.

Tolman, R. M. (1989). The development of a measure of psychological maltreatment of women by their male partners. *Violence and Victims, 4,* 159-177.

Waldner-Haugrud, L. K., & Magruder, B. (1995). Male and female sexual victimization in dating relationships: Gender differences in coercion techniques and outcomes. *Violence and Victims, 10,* 203-215.

White, J. W., Merrill, L. L., & Koss, M. P. (1999). *Predictors of premilitary courtship violence in a Navy recruit sample* (U.S. Naval Health Research Center Report, pp. 1-22).

Offprints. Requests for offprints should be directed to Jennifer Katz, PhD, P. O. Box Psych, Wynne Center for Family Research, Department of Psychiatry, University of Rochester School of Medicine & Dentistry, 300 Crittenden Blvd., Rochester, NY 14642.

Violence and Victims, Volume 18, Number 2, April 2003

Stalking and Psychological Abuse: Common Factors and Relationship-Specific Characteristics

Melanie Livet Dye
Keith E. Davis
University of South Carolina
Columbia, SC

The purpose of this study was to refine and elaborate models of personality and relationship-specific characteristics in the perpetration of stalking and psychological abuse. Three hundred and forty-two college students who had been in intimate relationships completed a series of questionnaires about their most recent breakup and their former relationship. Our hypotheses were supported, with harsh parental discipline, anxious attachment, and need for control of one's partner forming a common cluster in the prediction of stalking and psychological abuse. For psychological abuse, relationship dissatisfaction added to the predictive factors; whereas for stalking, the level of anger-jealousy over the breakup was the major added factor. Degree of anger-jealousy was influenced by being the recipient of a breakup and the level of passion.

Keywords: stalking; psychological abuse; abuse; dating behavior

S talking and psychological abuse are becoming subjects of increasing interest as distinct and potentially devastating forms of relationship violence. Awareness of stalking as a noteworthy issue was raised by the death of actress Rebecca Schaeffer, who was shot by a fan after having been stalked for 2 years (National Institute of Justice, 1996). While the public's attention has been directed towards celebrities stalked by strangers, as many as 80% of stalking incidents take place within the context of an intimate relationship (Tjaden & Thoennes, 1998). Furthermore, it has been hypothesized that stalking is most likely to occur in interpersonal relationships that have recently ended (Coleman, 1997). A probability sample of colleges and women within schools revealed a 13% stalking rate over a 7-month period (Fisher, Cullen, & Turner, 2000).

Interpersonal violence researchers have recently begun to consider psychological abuse as an important phenomenon in its own right as well. Frequency rates range from 11% in a sample of college women (Pipes & LeBov-Keeler, 1997) to percentages in the 90s in samples of battered women (Follingstad, Rutledge, Berg, Hause, & Polek, 1990; Stets, 1990) and high school students (Jezl, Molidor, & Wright, 1996). Coker, Davis, Arias, Desai, Sanderson, Brandt, and Smith (under review) reported lifetime prevalence of psychological abuse to be 31.7% for men and 28.7% for women.

In addition to being quite prevalent, stalking and psychological abuse have a negative impact on the emotional well-being of the victims. These effects include stress, anxiety, depression, fear, repulsion, shock, self-blame, lowered self-esteem, and loss of trust in people (Aguilar & Nightingale, 1994; Mechanic, in press; Murphy & Cascardi, 1999). Psychological abuse is perceived by the victims as having more devastating effects than physical aggression (Dutton, 1998; Follingstad et al., 1990; Gelles & Straus, 1988; Marshall, 1992) and often predicts and/or accompanies physical abuse (Murphy & O'Leary, 1989; Tolman, 1999). For these reasons, further investigation of both psychological abuse that occurs during the relationship and stalking occurring after the dissolution of the relationship seems warranted.

We will establish a relationship between measures of stalking and psychological abuse, and will show that these both share a set of similar predictors, suggesting similar underlying mechanisms, but that specific features of the relationship context and background personality variables also operate distinctively in the prediction of each. We will develop each of these major considerations below, starting with the relationship between psychological abuse and stalking, followed by relationship context predictors, and then by personality and parental background factors.

CONCEPTUAL DEFINITIONS OF STALKING AND PSYCHOLOGICAL ABUSE

Stalking was defined to include the overt following of the individual, thereby presenting a threat to his/her safety, and more covert unwanted pursuit behaviors that can be perceived as simple annoyance or harassment by the victim. Some examples include writing and calling after being told not to, sending unwanted gifts, making specific threats to damage his/her property, and spying and following him/her (Tjaden & Thoennes, 1998). Stalking-like behaviors can be defined as "the repeated and unwanted pursuit and invasion of one's sense of physical or symbolic privacy by another person, either stranger or acquaintance, who desires and/or presumes an intimate relationship" (Cupach & Spitzberg, 1998, pp. 234-235). In this study, stalking was measured using a self-report inventory pre-tested and refined in two studies by Davis, Ace, and Andra (2000).

Psychological abuse was defined as coercive or aversive behaviors, not including physical force or threat of harm, which are "intended to produce emotional harm . . . and which are directed at the target's sense of self" (Murphy & Cascardi, 1999, p. 209). Tolman (1999) defines psychological abuse in terms of isolation of the victim/dominance of the perpetrator and emotional/verbal maltreatment of the victim. Because no standard perpetrator measure existed, we adapted the short form of the Psychological Maltreatment of Women Inventory (PMWI) for this purpose. Preliminary evidence (Davis et al., 2000; Davis & O'Hearn, 1989) indicated that it was a promising measure of abuse.

Following Kurt's (1995) hypothesis that stalking can be seen as a form of interpersonal coercion similar to physical and psychological abuse, we expect to find a core of common antecedents for psychological abuse during a relationship and stalking after a breakup. We also expect the context—being in a relationship versus not—to bring some distinctive predictors into play. In line with White, Kowalski, Lyndon, and Valentine's (2000) model, we propose to separate the class of potential predictors into relationship specific (dyadic and situational) and personality characteristics of the perpetrators.

RELATIONSHIP-SPECIFIC FACTORS

Angry-Jealous Emotional Reactions to a Breakup. The stalking literature has identified a core set of feelings, that is, anger, jealousy, and obsessiveness, that seem to typify many stalking relationships (Meloy, 1998; Mullen, Pathe, & Purcell, 2000). Studies of campus samples also find that feeling vengeful, deceived, jealous, and angry was moderately correlated with stalking-like behaviors (Davis et al., 2000; Langhinrichsen-Rohling, Palarea, Cohen, & Rohling 2000; Sinclair & Frieze, 2000). It was therefore hypothesized that an angry and jealous reaction to the breakup would significantly correlate with stalking as well as potentially mediate the relationship between stalking and other predictor variables in the model.

Breakup Initiation. The role of the stalking perpetrator during the breakup was explored by Davis and colleagues (2000). Being the recipient of a breakup was associated with an increased likelihood of engaging in stalking-like behaviors. Furthermore, breakup recipients were significantly more upset about the breakup than instigators or when the breakup was mutual. Since the breakup recipient usually experiences more emotional distress than the breakup initiator (Davis & O'Hearn, 1989), the correlation between breakup initiator status and stalking should be replicated. Furthermore, the link between breakup initiator status and stalking was expected to be mediated by breakup anger-jealousy in our model.

Quality of the Relationship. The quality of the relationship, as based on Sternberg's triadic theory of love involving intimacy, passion, and commitment (1986), prior to the breakup was also explored in the present study. Previous findings point to the potential importance of passionate love as a correlate and predictor of stalking behaviors (Langhinrichsen-Rohling et al., 2000; Sinclair & Frieze, 2000). While passion may correlate with stalking, we hypothesized that this relationship would be mediated by breakup initiation status and emotional reaction to the breakup. When a passionate relationship breaks up, being the recipient of the breakup makes it more likely that anger-jealousy will be elicited and that stalking will occur.

While passion is expected to play a crucial role in a model of stalking, relationship satisfaction, as defined by high levels of commitment and intimacy, is hypothesized to affect the likelihood of emotionally abusing one's partner. While research on whether marital satisfaction predicts later physical aggression yields mixed results (Murphy & O'Leary, 1989; O'Leary, Malone, & Tyree, 1994), lack of satisfaction with the relationship seems to be related to later psychological abuse for couples (O'Leary et al., 1994), with partners who are more dissatisfied with the relationship engaging in higher rates of psychological abuse.

PERSONALITY CHARACTERISTICS

Trait Anger. While the role of angry temperament has been examined in the context of domestic and dating violence (Dye & Eckhardt, 2000; for a review, see Eckhardt, Barbour, and Stuart, 1997; Follingstad, Bradley, & Helff, in press), trait anger has also been found to correlate positively with psychological abuse perpetration (Dutton & Starzomski, 1993). Based on these results, it was predicted that anger would predict psychological abuse both directly and indirectly through need for control. Furthermore, we hypothesized that anger would affect relationship satisfaction, that is, the degree of commitment and intimacy, which in turn would predict psychological abuse.

Initial theoretical model for stalking

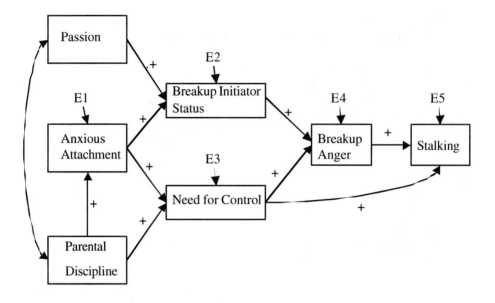

Initial theoretical model for psychological abuse

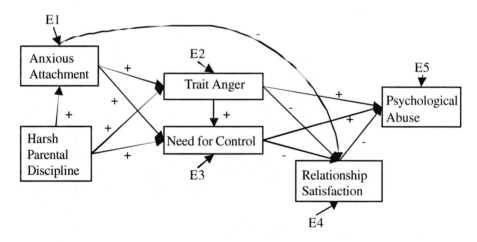

Figure 1. Proposed theoretical models.

Control of Partner. A control theory model of physical violence in dating relationships was first proposed by Stets and Pirog-Good (1987) and later elaborated by Follingstad and associates (Follingstad, Bradley, Laughlin, & Burke, 1999; Follingstad et al., 2002). In an attempt to regain control of his/her partner, the partner who is challenged will use physical force or psychological coercion to do so. Control of partner has also been investigated directly and indirectly in the stalking literature. While emotionally abusive and controlling behavior towards a spouse was more likely to have been endorsed by an ex-husband who stalked (Tjaden & Thoennes, 1998), a controlling pattern of behavior was found to relate to stalking perpetration in college student samples (Davis et al., 2000; Langhinrichsen-Rohling et al., 2000).

Need for control was hypothesized to directly impact psychological abuse as well as be mediated by relationship satisfaction. We expected that the need to control one's partner would influence levels of intimacy and commitment, which in turn would impact the likelihood of engaging in psychological abuse.

It was hypothesized that the present study would replicate Davis and associates' (2000) finding, with control being a significant predictor of stalking. Furthermore, we predicted that need for control would be mediated by the emotional reaction to the breakup, with participants who had a higher score on the need for control scale being more likely to react with anger and jealousy to the breakup and therefore more likely to enact stalking behaviors toward their ex-partner.

Attachment. Hazan and Shaver (1987) developed the first model of adult attachment in romantic relationships based on Ainsworth's studies of infant reactions to the separation and reunion with attachment figures. While Hazan and Shaver proposed three attachment styles, Bartholomew and Horowitz (1991) suggested a four-category model (secure, preoccupied, dismissing, and fearful) along two dimensions (self and others). After reviewing the attachment literature, Brennan, Clark, and Shaver's factor analysis (1998) provided further evidence of a four-category model with two dimensions, that they conceptualized as Anxiety (model of self) and Avoidance (model of others).

Several researchers have found the degree of anxious attachment to be related to physical and psychological abuse (Dutton, 1998; Follingstad et al., in press; Holtzworth-Munroe, Stuart, & Hutchinson, 1997) and to jealousy and surveillance (Guerrero, 1998). Follingstad and associates found that anxious attachment resulting from early experiences resulted in the development of an angry temperament, which in turn led to a controlling style and eventually physical aggression. In a study by Dutton, Saunders, Starzomski, and Bartholomew (1994), anxious attachment was correlated with both anger and psychological abuse, with these latter variables relating significantly to each other, in a sample of batterers. It was therefore hypothesized that the relationship between anxious attachment, need for control, and anger would be replicated in this study, with anxious attachment relating to psychological abuse through anger and need for control. Langhinrichsen-Rohling and colleagues (2000) provided evidence that victims of pursuit behaviors perceived their ex-partners as anxiously attached and Davis and associates (2000) found attachment anxiety to be mediated by anger-jealousy in the prediction of stalking. Anxious attachment was therefore expected to predict stalking indirectly through breakup status, need for control, and breakup anger.

Harsh Parental Discipline. While witnessing and experiencing parental violence has been repeatedly shown to be predictive of physical violence in later adult relationships, there is little data regarding the role of physical punishment in psychological abuse and stalking. Dutton and his associates (Dutton, 1995; Dutton, Starzomski, & Ryan, 1996) found that recollections of negative parental treatments by the abuse perpetrator were positively correlated with having an abusive personality and discriminated between low and high abusive personality perpetrators. Langhinrichsen-Rohling and Rohling (2000) discovered that recollections of parental divorce or separation were associated with more unwanted pursuit behaviors after a breakup, especially in male college students. Therefore, we hypothesized that the effect of parental punishment would be mediated by anxious attachment, need for control, and trait anger in the prediction of psychological abuse. In predicting stalking, harsh parental discipline would be mediated by anxious attachment and need for control.

To summarize, this study elaborates and tests two theoretical models of psychological abuse and stalking, which are presented in Figure 1.

METHOD

Participants

Participants were 87 male and 251 female undergraduates from the University of South Carolina in Columbia enrolled in a social psychology class. While 75% were Caucasian ($N = 253$), 23% were African American ($N = 78$), 2% were Asian American ($N = 7$), and 0.3% were Hispanic ($N = 1$). The mean age of participants was 21 ($SD = 3.31$). Only students who had been involved in a romantic relationship and had recently broken up were included in the present study. Participants had been with their ex-partner on average 2 years and 2 months and reported having broken up on average 19 months ago. While 59% of participants admitted to trying to get back together with their partner, 38% admitted to having broken up with that partner more than once.

Procedure

Participants were asked to complete a Relationship History Questionnaire anonymously that included all measures as well as relationship demographics information (current relationship status, dating history, duration of current relationship, age of first dating experience and first sexual intercourse, number of dating partners, and sexual orientation). Informed consent and debriefing procedures were followed.

Instruments

Stalking Behaviors. The 14-item Stalking scale was a revised version of the 16-item scale used by Davis and colleagues (2000). Items are rated on a 3-point Likert scale ranging from "did not do it" to "did it more than once." The scale yields a composite score and includes mild harassment items (e.g., "wrote, called, and e-mailed after s/he told me not to") and threat items (e.g., "made specific threats to hurt his/her other friends, if s/he did not stop seeing them"). Items that represented serious crimes (e.g., attempted to force sexual contact) and therefore potential confounds with other forms of violence (e.g., rape, kidnapping) were not included. These items had very low frequencies of endorsement in this sample. The 14-item scale was found to have adequate internal consistency, with an alpha level of .78.

Psychological Abuse Scale. The short version of the Psychological Maltreatment of Women Inventory is a 14-item scale designed to assess psychological abuse (Tolman, 1999). The items were reworded to assess perpetration of psychologically abusive behaviors by the respondents. Each item is scored on a 5-point Likert scale, ranging from "never" to "very frequently," with higher scores suggesting higher endorsement of these behaviors toward the partner. The dominance/isolation and emotional/verbal subscales were so highly correlated as perpetrator scales ($r = .51$, $p < .001$) that we combined them to form a single total score. In this study, the total scale had good internal consistency, with an alpha of .84.

Trait Anger Scale. The Trait Anger Scale was derived from the Affective Liability subscale (AFF) of the Propensity for Abusiveness Scale (PAS; Dutton, 1995). The anger subscale of the PAS was based on the Multidimensional Anger Inventory (Siegel, 1986). In this study, the Trait Anger Scale was composed of the three anger items of the AFF Scale.

The items are rated on a 5-point Likert scale, with 1 being "not at all true" and 5 being "completely true for me." In this study, the scale was found to have adequate internal consistency, with an alpha level of .72.

Control of Partner. The short version of the Need to Control Scale was used to assess the participants' need to control their partner (Follingstad et al., 1999). Items are rated on a 4-point Likert scale, ranging from "never or rarely" to "quite frequently." The higher the score, the higher the need to control is. The short version of the scale has excellent internal consistency reliability (with alpha levels above .90) and was shown to discriminate and predict severity levels as well as frequency levels of physical violence in dating couples (Follingstad et al., 1999; Follingstad et al., in press).

Attachment. The Experiences in Close Relationships (ECR) questionnaire is a 36-item self-report measure designed to assess adult attachment (Brennan et al., 1998). Each item is scored on a 7-point Likert scale, ranging from "disagree strongly" to "agree strongly," with higher scores indicating a more dysfunctional attachment style. In these analyses, only the Anxious Attachment Scale defined by fear of abandonment was used. The scale was shown to possess excellent internal consistency reliability, with an alpha level of .91 for Anxiety, good predictive validity for measures of interpersonal touch and sexual preferences, and excellent construct validity (Brennan et al., 1998).

Harsh Parental Discipline. The Harsh Parental Discipline Scale has for its origin "The Egna Minnen Betraffande Uppfostran" (EMBU; Perris, Jacobsson, Lindstrom, vonKnorring, & Perris, 1980), which was later shortened by Dutton (1995). The scale (10 items; e.g., "my parent punished me even for small offenses") assesses memories of maternal and paternal disciplinary behaviors. The scale items are rated on a 4-point Likert scale, with higher scores indicating a greater frequency of being harshly disciplined by one's parents. Because a large number of participants completed the scale only for one parent, the total score was calculated to represent disciplinary actions either by the father, or by the mother, or by both (an average of the two was computed). In this study, the scale was found to have an excellent internal consistency reliability, with an alpha of .91.

Breakup Anger-Jealousy. Five items were added to measure an angry and jealous reaction to the breakup: angry, upset, jealous, let down, and vengeful. The items were dichotomous as participants checked the ones applicable to their own situation. In this study, the scale alpha was .72.

Relationship Passion and Satisfaction. The Relationship Questionnaire is a 16-item measure assessing the quality of intimate relationships. The scale is based on the Factors for Intimate Relationships Scale created by Bretscher and Bergner (1991). Items are scored on a 9-point Likert scale, ranging from "absolutely uncharacteristic" to "absolutely characteristic." In this study, only the Passion subscale was used for the stalking model. The 5-item Passion subscale includes exclusiveness, sexual desire, preoccupation, enjoyment, and attractiveness. The alpha for the Passion scale was .78.

For the psychological abuse model, intimacy and commitment were combined to form a relationship satisfaction subscale. The 10-item satisfaction subscale includes trust, similarity between partners, authenticity of feelings, support, and acceptance. The scale has excellent internal consistency, with an alpha of .92.

Data Analysis

Descriptive and correlational analyses are presented. Path analysis was conducted to test the two theoretical models presented in Figure 1. The analyses, all conducted with the SAS software package, used the maximum likelihood method of parameter estimation and were performed on the correlation matrices. The two models were modified after review-ing the Goodness of Fit Indices (chi-Square, ratio chi-square to degrees of freedom, square root mean residual or SRMR, RMSEA Estimate, Bentler's Comparative Fit Index or CFI, Bentler and Bonnett's Non-Normed Index or NNI, and McDonald's Centrality Index or MCI), path coefficients, and the residual matrices. The chi-square should not be signifi-cant and the chi-Square ratio should be less than 3 to indicate good fit. The chi-square ratio is preferred as a more accurate estimation of model fit, since it is less dependent on sample size than the chi-square. While the CFI and NNI were considered excellent above .95 and MCI good above .90, the SRMR had to be below .08 and the RMSEA below .06 as indicators of a good fit between the model and data. Path coefficients were deemed sig-nificant if the standardized estimates of their t values were above 1.96 and the standard-ized path coefficients were nontrivial in magnitude (i.e., absolute values exceeded .05). Finally, Square Multiple Correlations for the endogenous variables were reviewed to determine the amount of variance accounted for by their antecedents. Modifications to the models were made only if they could be explained theoretically. Multivariate outliers were included in the analyses.[1] Furthermore, the distributions of variables included in the mod-els were checked for violation of normality.[2]

RESULTS

Stalking and Psychological Abuse Prevalence and Gender Differences

Results indicated that 35.67% of college students in this sample enacted a specific stalk-ing behavior at least twice in order to re-establish the relationship, and 21.05% of the stu-dents admitted to engaging in two forms of psychological abuse at least twice during their relationship.

TABLE 1. Means, Standard Deviations, Intercorrelations, and Coefficient Alphas Reliability Estimates for Stalking Models

Predictor	M	SD	Criterion Variable						
			1	2	3	4	5	6	7
1. Harsh parental discipline	1.29	0.38	[91]						
2. Breakup anger	6.32	1.48	09	[72]					
3. Passion	6.81	1.44	-00	22**	[78]				
4. Anxious attachment	3.50	1.22	12*	27**	10	[92]			
5. Breakup initiator status	1.12	0.15	-05	56**	20**	18**	[NA]		
6. Control	1.44	0.33	24**	19**	-03	36**	00	[88]	
7. Stalking	1.20	0.25	14*	32**	15**	26**	15**	33**	[79]

Note. Due to missing data, N varies from 279 to 342 per correlation; Harsh Parental Discipline = Recalled Negative Parental Treatment subscale of the Propensity for Abusiveness Scale; Control = Need for Control Scale; Breakup Initiator Status = partici-pant was the breakup recipient. Decimals omitted from correlations and reliability esti-mates. Alpha coefficient reliability estimates appear on the diagonal.
*p < .05. **p < .01.

TABLE 2. Means, Standard Deviations, Intercorrelations, and Coefficient Alphas Reliability Estimates for Psychological Abuse Models

			Criterion Variable						
Predictor	*M*	*SD*	1	2	3	4	5	6	7
1. Harsh parental discipline	1.29	0.38	[91]						
2. Trait anger	2.35	0.86	16**	[72]					
3. Relationship satisfaction	6.50	1.56	-08	-12*	[92]				
4. Anxious attachment	3.50	1.22	12*	40**	-13*	[92]			
5. Control	1.44	0.33	24**	36**	-20**	36**	[88]		
6. Psychological abuse	0.71	0.64	24**	27**	-23**	28**	66**	[84]	

Note. Due to missing data, *N* varies from 282 to 342 per correlation; Harsh Parental Discipline = Recalled Negative Parental Treatment subscale of the Propensity for Abusiveness Scale; Control = Need for Control Scale. Decimals omitted from correlations and reliability estimates. Alpha coefficient reliability estimates appear on the diagonal.
*$p < .05$. **$p < .01$.

Although, based on previous research using samples of college students, we did not expect gender differences on the stalking or psychological abuse measures, two independent *t*-tests were conducted on the stalking and psychological abuse scores. T-tests for the stalking measure ($t(121) = 0.72$, $p > .05$) and the psychological abuse scale ($t(140) = 0.01$, $p > .05$) were not significant, indicating that there were no gender differences. The correlations among predictors and criterion variables were also examined separately by gender. With two exceptions noted below, there were no significant differences between men and women in the correlations, therefore subsequent analyses used the combined sample.

Stalking and Psychological Abuse Correlations

Means, standard deviations, correlations, and coefficient alpha reliability estimates for the variables of interest for the stalking model are presented in Table 1 and for the variables included in the psychological abuse model in Table 2. Breakup status was dummy-coded prior to being entered in the analyses, with participants having been broken up with belonging to one group and participants who were the initiator of the breakup or whose breakup was mutual composing the other group.

Stalking was significantly correlated with passion ($r = .15$), need for control ($r = .33$), anxious attachment ($r = .26$), parental discipline ($r = .14$), breakup anger ($r = .32$), and being the recipient of the breakup ($r = .15$). There was a trend for the relationship between breakup anger and stalking to be stronger among men ($r = .47$) than among women ($r = .25$, $z = 1.96$, $p < .06$). Psychological abuse correlated positively with need for control ($r = .66$), anxious attachment ($r = .28$), parental discipline ($r = .24$), trait anger ($r = .27$) and negatively with relationship satisfaction ($r = -.23$). Stalking and psychological abuse were

Stalking model 1 (Original model)

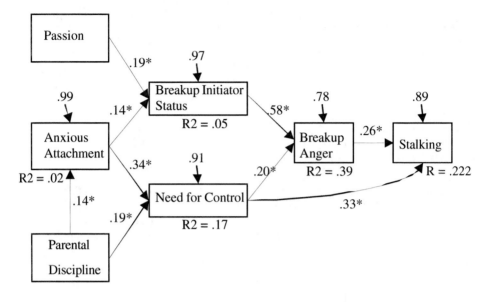

Stalking model 2 (Revised model)

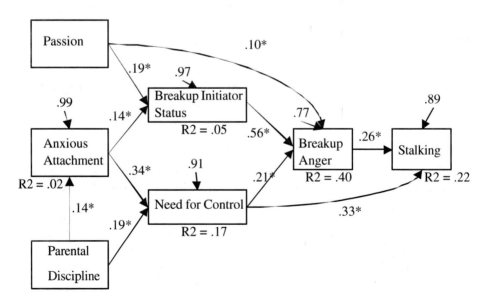

Figure 2. Stalking models with multiple square correlations and standardized path loadings.

positively correlated ($r = .35$), but in this case the relationship was stronger for men ($r = .54$) than for women ($r = .29$, $z = 2.44$, $p < .01$). All the correlations were in the expected direction.

Stalking and Psychological Abuse Path Analyses

Stalking Model (see figure 2). Estimation of the initial model revealed that, while the chi-square was significant, $\chi^2(11, N = 268) = 21.16$, $p < .05$, the chi-square ratio was 1.92. While the NNI was .93, the SRMR was .05, the RMSEA .06, the CFI was .96, and the MCI was .98, therefore indicating good model fit. The t values for all the paths were significant ($p < .05$) and all the residuals were below .10. Square multiple correlations for the endogenous variables indicated that 22% of the variance for stalking, 39% of the variance for breakup anger, 17% of the variance for need for control, 5% of the variance for breakup initiation status, and 2% of the variance for anxious attachment was explained by the preceding variables in the model. To test a secondary hypothesis that passion would affect breakup anger directly, a path was added from passion to breakup anger. Indeed, it is possible that the amount of passion in the relationship affected the amount of breakup anger/hurt directly, that is without being mediated by breakup status.

The revised model, presented in Figure 2, was then re-estimated. A review of the goodness of Fit Indices indicated that the revised model provided a good fit to the data: the chi-square was not significant $\chi^2(10, N = 268) = 17.23$, $p > .05$); the SRMR and RMSEA were both below .05; while the NNI was .94, the CFI was .97, and the MCI .99. The residuals were all below .10 and the R-squares were similar to those for the previous model, except for breakup anger ($r^2 = .40$). The t values for all the paths were significant ($p < .05$) and the standardized estimates of the paths were nontrivial in magnitude. The added path from passion to breakup anger was significant, therefore indicating that there is an indirect link between passion and stalking through breakup anger.

A chi-square difference between the initial model and the revised model was calculated to determine whether the addition of this path resulted in a significant improvement in the model's fit. Supporting our finding that this added path was significant, this difference was significant ($\chi^2(1, N = 268) = 3.93$, $p < .05$).

Psychological Abuse Model (see Figure 3). Based on the Fit Indices, the initial model of psychological abuse seemed to provide a good fit for the data. The chi-square was not significant ($\chi^2(3, N = 279) = 5.45$, $p > .05$) and the chi-square ratio was below 3. Furthermore, the SRMR and RMSEA were below .06 and the CFI, NNI, and MCI above .96. The residual correlations were also all below .10. However, three path coefficients did not reach significance ($t < 1.96$): anxious attachment to relationship quality, trait anger to relationship quality, and trait anger to psychological abuse. Based on these results, these three paths were removed in the subsequent model.

The revised model (see Figure 3) provided a superior fit to the data as indicated by the Goodness of Fit Indices: the Chi-Square was not significant ($\chi^2(6, N = 279) = 6.74$, p 05); the chi-square ratio was below 3; the RMR and RMSEA were below .03; and the CFI, NNI, and MCI were above .99. All the path coefficients were significant and the residuals were below .10. In this model, 47% of the variance for psychological abuse, 21% for need for control, 17% for trait anger, 4% for relationship quality, and 1% of anxious attachment was explained by preceding variables. The chi-square difference between these two models was not significant, $\chi^2(3, 279) = 1.29$, $p < .05$, indicating that, as expected, the deletion of these paths did not significantly alter the model.

Psychological model 1 (Original model)

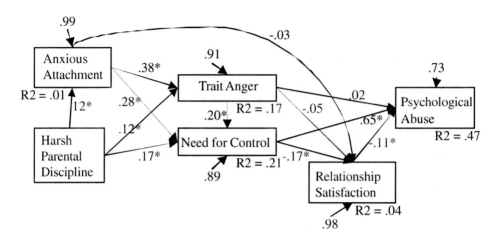

Psychological model 2 (Revised model)

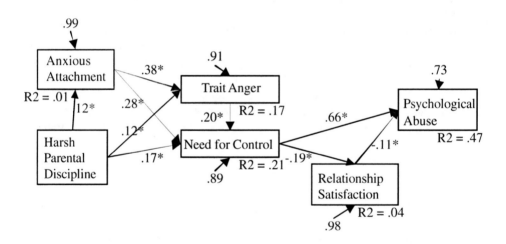

Figure 3. Psychological models with multiple square correlations and standardized path loadings.

DISCUSSION

We have established that stalking-like behaviors following a relationship breakup and the perpetration of psychological abuse during the relationship share a number of theoretically relevant antecedents. Among the shared antecedents are need for control, anxious attachment, and harsh parental discipline. Anger, jealousy, passion, relationship dissatisfaction, and breakup initiation status, however, enter into the prediction of these two outcomes in different ways depending upon the context. In an ongoing relationship, it appears that trait anger and relationship quality make an additional contribution to the prediction of psychological abuse; whereas in the context of relationship breakup, the contributors to the prediction of stalking are the context (whether one is the recipient vs. an initiator of the breakup), the level of passion prior to the breakup, and the degree of anger-jealousy associated with the breakup. The path models that we propose bring together a number of theoretically relevant variables and suggest further areas of research.

Harsh Parental Discipline, Anxious Attachment, and Need for Control: A Common Basis for Relationship Violence-Based Phenomena?

Consistent with previous literature (Davis et al., 2000; Langhinrichsen-Rohling et al., 2000; Stets, 1991; Tjaden & Thoennes, 1998), need for control of partners continues to be a central core component of both stalking and psychological abuse. Need for control not only predicted our two outcomes directly and indirectly through model-specific variables, but was also predicted by common variables in stalking and psychological abuse, that is, harsh parental discipline and anxious attachment. Individuals who reported a need to control their (ex-) partner tended to have been harshly punished by parental figures in childhood and to have developed an anxious attachment style, which subsequently increased the likelihood of stalking after a breakup or perpetration of psychological abuse when in a relationship.

The role of harsh parental discipline as an antecedent of both anxious attachment and need for control, and the role of anxious attachment as predictive of need for control are consistent with previous stalking and psychological abuse research (Davis et al., 2000; Dutton, 1995; Dutton et al., 1996; Langhinrichsen-Rohling et al., 2000; Langhinrichsen-Rohling & Rohling, 2000) and allow us to speculate about the underlying mechanisms of the development of a need to control one's partner. Our results indicate that harsh parental discipline may lead to the development of an anxious attachment style. Having received harsh and unfair parental punishment may lead the child to develop an insecure relationship with the caregiver. According to attachment theory (Bartholomew, Henderson, & Dutton, 2001), the child will then develop a negative sense of self (anxiety dimension), which will make him overly dependent on others for self-esteem and support (preoccupied) or fearful of intimacy because of fear of rejection (fearful). These internal working models will be re-activated in times of distress in an effort to re-establish their relationship with their partners, hence the relationship between anxious attachment and need for control.

The conclusions about harsh parental discipline's potential role need to be qualified in that when multivariate outliers were removed in the stalking analyses, harsh parental discipline was no longer contributing to the prediction of anxious attachment or need for control.

Relationship Characteristics Specific to Stalking and Psychological Abuse

Psychological Abuse. In the psychological abuse model, trait anger was significantly predicted by harsh parental discipline both directly and indirectly though anxious attachment. Furthermore, trait anger was predictive of psychological abuse through need for control. These findings are consistent with previous psychological maltreatment literature. Dutton and colleagues (1994), for instance, provided evidence that psychological abuse was related to both anger and anxious attachment.

Our results also further support Dutton and associates' theory of relationship violence development (Dutton, 1998) and dating violence findings (Follingstad et al., in press). Briefly, Dutton posits that difficulties in early attachment play a crucial role in later relationship violence. Follingstad and associates (in press) tested this theory in the context of dating violence and concluded that being anxiously attached predicted need for control indirectly through angry temperament. In our model, feelings of insecurity partly due to having been harshly punished as a child facilitate the development of an angry style as a way to handle the anxiety around real or imagined loss. The use of controlling tactics represents an effort to re-establish the relationship and is facilitated by the presence of anxious attachment both directly and indirectly through trait anger.

While trait anger appears to be an important antecedent of need to control in our psychological abuse model, relationship satisfaction was found to be predicted by need for control. Contrary to our expectations, however, anxious attachment and trait anger did not predict relationship quality directly. Anxious attachment and trait anger were negatively correlated with relationship satisfaction, but when introduced in the model, these direct paths were not significant. It therefore appears that the need to control one's partner, which stems from early attachment problems and the subsequent development of an angry style, not only affects psychological abuse directly, but is also mediated by the amount of commitment and intimacy in the relationship. The more controlling an individual is with his/her partner, the less committed and intimate the relationship becomes, that is, the less satisfied s/he is with the relationship, which increases the likelihood of psychological abuse perpetration. These findings are consistent with previous research on psychological abuse, which associated relationship dissatisfaction with psychological abuse perpetration (O'Leary et al., 1994). The controlling individual is therefore caught in a self-fulfilling prophecy cycle. He attempts to control his/her partner by fear of abandonment and, by doing so, affects the level of commitment and intimacy negatively and his/her satisfaction with the relationship, which then increases the likelihood that s/he will have to resort to emotionally abusive tactics in order to regain control over the relationship. Relationship satisfaction, and more specifically commitment and intimacy levels, should therefore be included in future models of psychological abuse.

Stalking. Passion, breakup initiator status, and anger-jealousy were included in our stalking model. Results indicate that passion does play a role in stalking not only in predicting breakup initiation status, but in also predicting breakup anger. The more passionate the relationship was, the less likely one was to initiate the breakup and therefore the more likely s/he was to be the recipient of the breakup, if there was a breakup. Furthermore, the more passionate the relationship, the more likely the participant was to experience feelings of anger and jealousy about the breakup, regardless of breakup initiator status.

Breakup initiation status was not only predicted by passion, but also by anxious attachment, and was predictive of breakup anger. In other words, fearing rejection and being dependent on one's partner for support and self-esteem decreased the likelihood of initiating the breakup and therefore increased the likelihood of being the recipient of the breakup, if there was a breakup. Breakup initiation status also predicted an angry and jealous reaction to the breakup, which was not surprising based on anxious attachment theory and since previous research revealed that the breakup recipient usually experiences more emotional distress than the initiator (Davis & O'Hearn, 1989).

The role of breakup anger appears to be a key in stalking relationships because an angry reaction to the breakup mediated the relationship between stalking and all the preceding variables, except need for control, which also has a direct link to stalking. The angrier the individual was about the breakup, the more likely s/he was to stalk his/her ex-partner when the preceding characteristics were also present.

While these results support our two conceptual models of stalking and psychological abuse, the study is not without limitations. First, while studying stalking in the college population is warranted, this sample came from a very restricted population of students in upper division psychology courses. The relationships found here will need to be replicated in broader samples to have their ecological validity established.

Second, the data are cross-sectional, not longitudinal, all rely on self-report methodology, and some of the measures are retrospective, for example, harsh parental discipline, and the levels of passion and satisfaction in the previous relationship. We cannot therefore exclude the possibility that current states of anger and jealousy may have colored respondents' memories of past relationships. Also, because of the common method variance, some of the relationships between variables may be inflated. The path models that we have tested and presented are thus plausible models of antecedents of stalking and psychological abuse, but not the only possible such models[3]. They have the virtue of being consistent with a growing body of literature on the antecedents of stalking and abuse (see Langhinrichsen-Rohling & Taylor, in press, for a similar model based on three studies by her research group) and of providing testable hypotheses for further research.

Another limitation is that the measures of both stalking-like behaviors and psychological abuse are relatively new. The measure of stalking has been pre-tested and refined in two studies by Davis, Ace, and Andra (2000). The item content is consistent with the highest frequency behaviors reported by victims (Tjaden & Thoennes, 1998; Cupach & Spitzberg, 2000) and the scale has shown modest, but statistically significant correlations with brief measures of psychological abuse and physical abuse. The measure of psychological abuse is built directly on Tolman's (1999) short form of his Psychological Maltreatment of Women Inventory. As expected, the perpetrator version of the PMWI was correlated with physical abuse measures-both frequency and severity (Davis, Ace, & Andra, 1999). Thus, while the key dependent variables are based on new measures, both have moderate internal consistency and evidence of construct validity.

In conclusion, we have established that two somewhat complex models of the antecedents of stalking and psychological abuse hold promise and support the premise that psychological abuse and stalking are forms of interpersonal coercion. The common constituents for these antecedents are need for control, forms of anger, anxious attachment, and the experience of harsh parental discipline. But in each case the form of the models must take account of relationship and context specific factors. For psychological abuse, relationship dissatisfaction and trait anger become important elements of the model; for stalking, anger-jealousy over the breakup, being the recipient of the breakup, and levels of passion in the relationship become important. These findings have a clear continuity with research on physical violence in relationships.

NOTES

1. All outliers were identified using multivariate statistical procedures (i.e., statistical comparison of Square Malanobis distance with appropriate Chi-Square). In the case of psychological abuse, 8 out of the 9 outliers fell at or above the 88th percentile on the abuse measure and represented one fourth of this group (i.e., scores at or above the 88th percentile). To exclude these scores would have been to eliminate the very participants we were trying to predict. Furthermore, there was no consistent correlational pattern of scores between anxious attachment, parental discipline, trait anger, need for control, relationship quality, and psychological abuse for these outliers, therefore indicating a plethora of alternative hypotheses for the model. We therefore decided to include these outliers in our models. In the

case of stalking, half of the 10 outliers fell below and half above the 90th percentile on the stalking measure. Again, correlational patterns of scores between passion, anxious attachment, parental shame, need for control, breakup status, breakup anger, and stalking were different for each participant, therefore leading no support to a specific alternative model hypothesis. The best fitting stalking model including the outliers (model 2) was then re-ran without the outliers. Results indicated slightly better Fit Indices, although the following paths were not significant in the stalking model: parental discipline to anxious attachment, parental discipline to need for control, and need for control to anger-jealousy.

2. Because the distributions of several manifest variables (i.e., passion, need for control, parental discipline, stalking, and psychological abuse) significantly departed from normality (i.e., the absolute value of skewness or kurtosis was greater than 1), these variables were transformed to moderate their skewness and/or kurtosis. The final models were then re-tested. Because violation of normality did not affect the results, they are not reported in the present article.

3. Other models that were theoretically defensible were also considered. Avoidant attachment was added as a variable that may potentially be influenced by harsh parental discipline and in turn impact need for control in both the stalking and psychological abuse models. These models did not fit the data as well and avoidant attachment was not found to be a significant variable. For these reasons, the results for these models are not presented in the present article.

REFERENCES

Aguilar, R. J., & Nightingale, N. N. (1994). The impact of specific battering experiences on the self-esteem of abused women. *Journal of Family Violence, 9,* 35-45.

Bartholomew, K., Henderson, A. J. Z., & Dutton, D. G. (2001). Insecure attachment and abusive intimate relationships. In C. Clulow (Ed.), *Adult attachment and couple work: Applying the "secure base" concept in research and practice* (pp. 43-61). London: Rutledge.

Bartholomew, K., & Horowitz, L. M. (1991). Attachment styles among young adults: A test of a four-category model. *Journal of Personality and Social Psychology, 61,* 226-244.

Brennan, K. A., Clark, C. L., & Shaver, P. R. (1998). Self-report measure of adult attachment: An integrative overview. In J. Simpson & W. Rholes (Eds.), *Attachment theory and close relationships* (pp. 46-76). New York: Guilford.

Bretscher, F., & Bergner, R. M. (1991). Relational qualities as factors in mate selection decisions. In M. K. Roberts & R. M. Bergner (Eds.), *Advances in descriptive psychology* (Vol. 6, pp. 107-123). Greenwich, CT: JAI Press.

Coleman, F. L. (1997). Stalking behaviors and the cycle of domestic violence. *Journal of Interpersonal Violence, 12,* 420-432.

Cupach, W. R., & Spitzberg, B. H. (1998). Obsessive relational intrusion and stalking. In B. H. Spitzberg & W. R. Cupach (Eds.), *The dark side of close relationships* (pp. 233-263). Hillsdale, NJ: Lawrence Erlbaum Associates.

Cupach, W. R., & Spitzberg, B. H. (2000). Obsessive relational intrusion. *Violence and Victims, 15,* 357-372.

Davis, K. E., Ace, A., & Andra, M. (1999). *Stalking measurement data.* Unpublished raw data.

Davis, K. E., Ace, A., & Andra, M. (2000). Stalking perpetrators and psychological maltreatment of partners: Anger-jealousy, attachment insecurity, need for control, and breakup context. *Violence and Victims, 15,* 407-425.

Davis, K. E., & O'Hearn, R. (1989, May). *Doing and being done to: Attachment style and the degree of post-breakup distress among formerly dating couples.* Paper presented at the Iowa Network on Personal Relationships, Iowa City, IA.

Dutton, D. G. (1995). A scale for measuring propensity for abusiveness. *Journal of Family Violence, 10,* 203-221.

Dutton, D. G. (1998). *The abusive personality: Violence and control in intimate relationships.* New York: The Guilford Press.

Dutton, D. G., & Starzomski, A. J. (1993). Borderline personality in perpetrators of psychological and physical abuse. *Violence and Victims, 8,* 327-337.

Dutton, D. G., Starzomski, A. J., & Ryan, L. (1996). Antecedents of abusive personality and abusive behaviors in wife assaulters. *Journal of Family Violence, 11,* 113-132.

Dutton, D. G., Saunders, K., Starzomski, A., & Bartholomew, K. (1994). Intimacy-anger and insecure attachment as precursors of abuse in intimate relationships. *Journal of Applied Social Psychology, 24,* 1367-1386.

Dye, M. L., & Eckhardt, C. I. (2000). Anger, irrational beliefs, and dysfunctional attitudes in violent dating relationships. *Violence and Victims, 15,* 337-350.

Eckhardt, C. I., Barbour, K. A., & Stuart, G. L. (1997). Anger and hostility in maritally violent men: Conceptual distinctions, measurement issues, and literature review. *Clinical Psychology Review, 17,* 333-358.

Fisher, B. S., Cullen, F. T., & Turner, M. G. (2000). *The sexual victimization of college women.* Washington, DC: U.S. Department of Justice.

Follingstad, D. R., Bradley, R. G., & Helff, C. M. (2002). A model for predicting dating violence in college students: Anxious attachment, angry temperament, and need for control. *Violence and Victims, 17,* 35-47.

Follingstad, D. R., Bradley, R. G., Laughlin, J. E., & Burke, L. (1999). Risk factors and correlates of dating violence: The relevance of examining frequency and severity levels in a college sample. *Violence and Victims, 14,* 1-17.

Follingstad, D. R., Rutledge, L. L., Berg, B. J., Hause, E. S., & Polek, D. S. (1990). The role of emotional abuse in physically abusive relationships. *Journal of Family Violence, 5,* 107-120.

Gelles, R. J., & Straus, M. A. (1988). *Intimate violence.* New York: Simon and Schuster.

Guerrero, L. K. (1998). Attachment-style differences in the experience and expression of romantic jealousy. *Personal Relationships, 5,* 273-291.

Hazan, C., & Shaver, P. R. (1987). Romantic love conceptualized as an attachment process. *Journal of Personality and Social Psychology, 52,* 511-524.

Holtzworth-Munroe, A., Stuart, G. L., & Hutchinson, G. (1997). Violent vs. nonviolent husbands: Differences in attachment patterns, dependency, and jealousy. *Journal of Family Psychology, 11,* 314-331.

Jezl, D. R., Molidor, C. E., & Wright, T. L. (1996). Physical, sexual, and psychological abuse in high school dating relationships: Prevalence, rates, and self-esteem issues. *Child and Adolescent Social Work Journal, 13,* 69-87.

Kurt, J. L. (1995). Stalking as a variant of domestic violence. *Bulletin of the Academy of Psychiatry and the Law, 23,* 219-223.

Langhinrichsen-Rohling, J., Palarea, R. E., Cohen, J., and Rohling, M. L. (2000). Breaking up in hard to do: Pursuit behaviors following the dissolution of romantic relationships. *Violence and Victims, 15,* 73-90.

Langhinrichsen-Rohling, J., & Rohling, M. (2000). Negative family-of-origin experiences: Are they associated with perpetrating unwanted pursuit behaviors? *Violence and Victims, 15,* 1-13.

Langhinrichsen-Rohling, J. & Taylor, J. (in press). After the break-up: Relationship factors associated with intimate relationship stalking. In M. Brewster (Ed.), *Stalking victims and offenders.* New York: Civic Research Institute, Inc.

Marshall, L. L. (1992). Development of the Severity against Women Scales. *Journal of Family Violence, 7,* 103-121.

Mechanic, M. B. (in press). Stalking victimization: Clinical implications for assessment and intervention. In K. E. Davis, I. H. Frieze, & R. Maiuro (Eds.), *Stalking: Perspectives on victims and perpetrators.* New York: Springer Publishing Co.

Meloy, J. R. (1998). The psychology of stalking. In J. R. Meloy (Ed), *The psychology of stalking: Clinical and forensic perspectives* (pp. 1-23). San Diego, CA: Academic Press.

Mullen, P. E., Pathé, M. & Purcell, R. (2000). *Stalkers and their victims.* New York: Cambridge University Press.

Murphy, C. M., & Cascardi, M. (1999). Psychological abuse in marriage and dating relationships. In R. L. Hampton (Ed.), *Family violence prevention and treatment* (2nd ed., pp. 198-226). Thousand Oaks, CA: Sage.

Murphy, C. M., & O'Leary, K. D. (1989). Psychological aggression in prediction of physical aggression in early marriage. *Journal of Consulting and Clinical Psychology, 57,* 579-582.

National Institute of Justice. (1996, April). *Domestic violence, stalking, and antistalking legislation: An annual report to Congress under the Violence against Women Act.* Washington, DC: U.S. Department of Justice.

O'Leary, K. D., Malone, J., & Tyree, A. (1994). Physical aggression in early marriage: Pre-relationship and relationship effects. *Journal of Consulting and Clinical Psychology, 62,* 594-602.

Perris, C., Jacobsson, L., Lindstrom, H., von Knorring, L., & Perris, H. (1980). Development of a new inventory for assessing memories of parental rearing behavior. *Acta Psychiatrica Scandinavica, 61,* 265-274.

Pipes, R. B., & LeBov-Keeler, K. (1997). Psychological abuse among college women in exclusive heterosexual dating relationships. *Sex Roles, 36,* 585-603.

Siegel, J. M. (1986). The multidimensional anger inventory. *Journal of Social Psychology, 51,* 191-200.

Sinclair, H. C., & Frieze, I. H. (2000). Initial courtship behavior and stalking: How should we draw the line? *Violence and Victims, 15,* 23-39.

Sternberg, R. J. (1986). A triangular theory of love. *Psychological Review, 93,* 119-135.

Stets, J. E. (1990). Verbal and physical aggression in marriage. *Journal of Marriage and Family, 52,* 501-514.

Stets, J. E. (1991). Psychological aggression in dating relationships: The role of interpersonal control. *Journal of Family Violence, 6,* 97-114.

Stets, J. E., & Pirog-Good, M. A. (1987). Violence in dating relationships. *Social Psychology Quarterly, 50,* 237-246.

Tjaden, P., & Thoennes, N. (1998). *Stalking in America: Findings from the national violence against women survey.* Denver, CO: Center for Policy Research.

Tolman, R. M. (1999). The validation of the Psychological Maltreatment of Women Inventory. *Violence and Victims, 14,* 25-37.

White, J., Kowalski, R., Lyndon, A., & Valentine, S. (2000). An integrative contextual developmental model of male stalking. *Violence and Victims, 15,* 373-388.

Offprints. Requests for offprints should directed to either Melanie Livet Dye, MA, Department of Psychology, University of South Carolina, Columbia, SC 29208 or to Keith E. Davis, PhD, Department of Psychology, University of South Carolina, Columbia, SC 29208. E-mail: daviske@sc.edu

Psychological Intimate Partner Violence During Pregnancy and Birth Outcomes: Threat of Violence Versus Other Verbal and Emotional Abuse

Jacqueline Gentry, BS
Beth A. Bailey, PhD
Department of Family Medicine, East Tennessee State University

Although physical abuse during pregnancy has been linked to poor birth outcomes, the role of psychological abuse is less well understood. Associations between birth outcomes and types of psychological abuse during pregnancy (being threatened, screamed at, or insulted) were examined in 489 women with no history of physical abuse. Being threatened was significantly associated with adverse birth outcomes, with women reporting any instance during pregnancy twice as likely to deliver a low birth weight baby. These results remained after controlling for background factors. Finally, most of the variance between threats and birth weight was accounted for by mediating health behaviors (specifically prenatal care utilization and pregnancy weight gain), suggesting pathways for the negative effects of being threatened by an intimate partner during pregnancy.

Keywords: intimate partner violence; psychological abuse; pregnancy; birth outcomes

In the United States, domestic abuse is a leading cause of injuries and death among women of childbearing age (D'Avolio et al., 2001). An estimated 42.4 million women have experienced rape, physical violence, and/or stalking by an intimate partner at some point in their lifetime (Black et al., 2011), and the U.S. Department of Justice National Violence Against Women survey estimates that 1.9 million women are victimized by intimate partner violence (IPV) annually (Tjaden & Thoennes, 2000). However, regional differences exist in the prevalence of IPV. One study found that women in small rural areas report the highest prevalence of IPV (22.5%), compared to 15.5% for urban women (Peek-Asa et al., 2011).

Pregnant women are not immune to IPV. Rates may be difficult to estimate, however, because of reluctance of women to disclose IPV, especially during pregnancy (Tjaden & Thoennes, 2000). A comprehensive review of the literature conducted in the mid-1990s concluded that the prevalence of IPV during pregnancy in the United States ranges from 1% to 20%, depending on the way IPV is assessed and on the population studied. Population-based studies, such as the U.S. Centers for Disease Control and Prevention (CDC) Pregnancy Risk Assessment Monitoring System, suggest that the prevalence of pregnancy IPV is 5.7% or less (CDC, 1997). Projects using behaviorally specific questions have put the rate of pregnancy IPV in the United States at 10%–15% (Coker, Sanderson, & Dong, 2004; Curry, 1998; Dunn & Oths, 2004; McFarlane, Parker, & Soeken, 1996; Norton, Peipert, Zierler, Lima, & Hume, 1995). When psychological abuse is included, rates of 36% to as high as 81% have been reported in various populations (Bailey & Daugherty, 2007; Shumway et al., 1999). Based on these statistics, researchers have estimated that every year in the United States, more than 300,000 pregnant women are victimized by an intimate partner (Bullock, Mears, Woodcock, & Record, 2001; Ventura, Martin, Curtin, & Mathews, 1999).

IPV during pregnancy can affect the health of both the newborn and the mother. A recent systematic review examined the impact of IPV on birth outcomes (Roy & Salihu, 2004). Mothers experiencing IPV were found to be significantly more likely to have adverse pregnancy outcomes including maternal, fetal, and neonatal mortality than nonabused mothers. In addition, fetal morbidity such as low birth weight, preterm delivery, and small size for gestational age are also more frequent among women experiencing IPV (Roy & Salihu, 2004). These effects on both infant birth weight and gestational age have been quantified in several studies. Deficits in birth weight of 150–250 g have been reported (Curry & Harvey, 1998; Dye, Tolliver, Lee, & Kenney, 1995), in addition to a nearly three-fold increased risk of delivering a low birth weight baby after experiencing physical IPV during pregnancy (Fernandez & Krueger, 1999). Pregnant women experiencing IPV are also at more than double the risk of delivering preterm compared with nonabused women (Fernandez & Krueger, 1999).

Although a considerable amount of research has analyzed the effects on birth outcomes of IPV in general, or physical violence specifically, the impact of psychological abuse is less well understood. Psychological IPV involves verbal and emotional abuse and threats and can be characterized by continuous feelings of susceptibility to danger, loss of power and control, and entrapment, as compared to the physical aspects of IPV that include pushing, hitting, and other assaultive behaviors (American Medical Association [AMA], 1992). Psychological IPV can affect chronic health conditions and can lead to many of the same health outcomes typically associated with physical IPV (Coker, Smith, Bethea, King, & McKeown, 2000). In fact, one study found that psychological IPV scores were even more strongly associated with many direct and indirect health outcomes than were physical IPV scores (Coker et al., 2002). However, physical aggression by men against their partners rarely occurs without psychological abuse, making it difficult to separate out the effects of each (O'Leary, 1999).

Both physical and psychological abuse during pregnancy have been linked to psychological outcomes such as high levels of stress and anxiety (Campbell, Poland, Waller, & Ager, 1992). Indeed, literature on battered women has suggested that psychological abuse greatly increases the risk for symptoms of posttraumatic stress disorder (PTSD; Street & Arias, 2001). Women who are victims of psychological abuse during pregnancy may be at elevated risk for depression compared to nonpregnant women experiencing psychological abuse (Martin, Beaumont, & Kupper, 2003), whereas those experiencing any type of abuse during pregnancy have been found to have more severe alcohol and family/social problems and higher rates of psychiatric problems and comorbidity compared to nonabused women (Tuten, Jones, Tran, & Svikis, 2004). Consequently, abuse may be a risk factor for negative pregnancy health experiences and behaviors including substance use and inadequate weight gain and prenatal care utilization, suggesting pathways by which IPV, and especially psychological IPV, may impact pregnancy outcomes (Murphy, Schei, Myhr, & Du Mont, 2001).

The goal of this study was to examine the association between psychological abuse during pregnancy and birth outcomes. The first question of interest was whether overall psychological abuse predicted birth weight and gestational age at delivery, controlling for potentially confounding background variables. The second question of interest was whether birth outcomes differed by type of psychological abuse. The final question examined was whether any links identified between psychological abuse and birth outcomes could be explained by differences in pregnancy health behaviors, including smoking, alcohol use, prenatal care utilization, and weight gain.

METHODS

Participants

Study subjects were participants in the first phase of a pregnancy smoking intervention program recruited from six prenatal provider offices in Northeast Tennessee. Of the 514 program participants whose pregnancy lasted at least 20 weeks (and thus had available birth outcome data), 4 reported no intimate partner during pregnancy and were necessarily eliminated from the sample. An additional 21 women reported either physical or sexual IPV during pregnancy, and they were also excluded from the sample so that the effects of psychological abuse independent of physical violence could be examined. This resulted in a final study sample of 489 women.

Procedure

Study procedures were approved by the affiliated university institutional review board. Following informed consent, participating women completed in-depth interviews during their second or third trimester of pregnancy (mean gestational age at time of interview was 18 weeks, range of 16–38 weeks), either before or after a scheduled prenatal visit. Interviews were conducted in private offices and were directed by a study research assistant. Most participants read the survey tools and marked their own responses on the forms. Where reading comprehension was a potential problem ($n = 18$), the research assistant read the questions aloud to the participant and facilitated form completion. Interviews, which included many assessments not relevant to this study, took up to an hour to complete. Participants received a $20 incentive for their time.

Assessments

Of interest in this study were several tools completed as part of the pregnancy interview. First, a detailed demographic and medical history tool was completed. In addition, pregnancy smoking and alcohol use were assessed via self-report, using well-validated standardized tools that included timeline follow-back assessment of alcohol use and detailed smoking history information.

The HITS (Hurt, Insulted, Threatened with harm, and Screamed) screening tool, a four-item questionnaire asking respondents how often their partner physically Hurt, Insulted, Threatened with harm, and Screamed at them (Sherin, Sinacore, Li, Zitter, & Shakil, 1998) was used to assess psychological abuse during pregnancy. A fifth item inquiring about sexual abuse was added to the HITS for this study. Answers were on a 5-point scale from *never occurred during pregnancy* to *frequently occurred during pregnancy*. Women who indicated a positive response on either the physical abuse or sexual abuse item were eliminated from the sample. The three remaining items assessed psychological abuse: Has an intimate partner *insulted* you fairly often; Has an intimate partner *screamed at* you fairly often; and Has an intimate partner *threatened* you. Previous work with this instrument produced an internal consistency of $\alpha = .80$ for the three psychological abuse items, and a correlation of $r = .81$ with the psychological abuse items on the gold standard Conflict Tactics Scale (Sherin et al., 1998). For purposes of the current report, the following abuse variables were constructed, consistent with previous use (Sherin et al., 1998). First, for each of the three dimensions of psychological abuse (insulted, screamed at, threatened), two variables were constructed. First, if a woman indicated she had experienced any level of that type of abuse during pregnancy, she was considered positive on an Any Abuse variable for that dimension. Second, if she indicated the type of abuse occurred sometimes, fairly often, or frequently, she was considered to have a High Frequency of Abuse for that dimension. Finally, two overall psychological abuse variables were constructed, including one Any Abuse variable that was considered positive if a woman reported that any of the three types of psychological abuse had occurred at any point during her pregnancy. The second overall variable, High Frequency of Abuse, was considered positive if a woman reported at least one category of abuse had occurred at least as often as "Sometimes" during pregnancy. Thus, eight psychological abuse variables, representing the three dimensions and overall abuse for Any Occurrence or High Frequency Occurrence, were used in this study.

Following delivery, prenatal medical charts and hospital delivery charts were reviewed for additional pregnancy variables and birth outcomes. Of interest in the current report were several variables. First, pregnancy weight gain was recorded in pounds. Second, prenatal care utilization was calculated using the Adequacy of Prenatal Care Utilization (Kotelchuck, 1994) Index, which is based on timing of entry into prenatal care and adherence to the schedule of recommended prenatal visits. Prenatal care utilization is classified as inadequate, intermediate, adequate, or adequate plus. Finally, baby's birth weight in grams and gestational age at delivery in weeks were recorded and analyzed dichotomously. Babies were classified as low birth weight if they weighed less than 2,500 g at delivery and were considered to be born preterm if they were delivered prior to 37 completed weeks' gestation.

Data Analysis

Before primary analyses were undertaken, all variables were checked for normality of distribution and analysis assumptions were verified. In addition, most participants (81%) completed a second pregnancy interview after 30 weeks' gestation, and this interview also included the HITS. These responses were checked for any women who experienced physical violence late in pregnancy and would additionally need to be eliminated from the sample. None of the women with available data reported physical violence as part of this second assessment, and thus the full sample of 489 women was retained.

Initially, *t* tests and chi-square analyses were used to compare women who experienced psychological abuse with women who did not on all background and pregnancy variables as well as on birth outcomes. Logistic regression analysis was used to examine the associations between abuse and birth outcomes while controlling for background differences. Potentially mediating factors (smoking, alcohol use, prenatal care utilization, and pregnancy weight gain) were also entered in these analyses to examine possible reasons for associations between psychological abuse and birth outcomes.

RESULTS

Of the 489 women in the study sample, 130 (26.6%) reported at least one instance of psychological abuse during pregnancy, whereas 58 (11.9%) reported a high frequency of at least one type of psychological abuse. Of the three dimensions of psychological abuse examined, being Screamed at occurred most frequently (22.7% any, 8.6% high frequency), followed by being Insulted (18.4% any, 8.2% high frequency) and being Threatened (4.9% any, 2.5% high frequency).

Differences between women who experienced any type of psychological abuse during pregnancy and those who did not are presented in Table 1. As can be seen, abuse status was not significantly associated with age, income, or number of children. However, women with fewer years of formal education were more likely than remaining women to have reported psychological abuse. Although women who experienced any abuse were slightly less likely to have adequate prenatal care utilization and to gain less weight, these differences were not statistically significant. However, compared with those who reported no psychological abuse, women who reported abuse were significantly more likely to report both pregnancy smoking and alcohol use.

Bivariate associations between psychological abuse during pregnancy, both overall and by type, and infant birth outcomes were next examined. The associations between psychological abuse dimensions and birth weight status are presented in Table 2. Overall psychological abuse, any occurrence or high-frequency occurrence, was not significantly related to low birth weight status. In addition, neither level of being Insulted nor Screamed at was linked to low birth weight. However, being Threatened by an intimate partner was significantly associated with low birth weight status. Compared with women who did not report being Threatened, those who reported any instance of this were twice as likely to

TABLE 1. Characteristics of Women by Pregnancy Psychological Abuse Status

	No Psychological Abuse (*n* = 359)	Any Psychological Abuse (*n* = 130)	*t*	*p*
Background Factors				
Age (years)	24.4	24.0	0.71	.480
Education (years)	12.8	12.3	2.52	.012
Income[a]	$10,000–$14,999	$10,000–$14,999	8.72	.096
Number of children	0.9	1.0	0.85	.398
Pregnancy Factors				
Smoked cigarettes (%)	56.8%	76.2%	15.13	<.001
Used alcohol (%)	6.1%	9.2%	15.13	<.001
Prenatal care[b] (% adeq/+)	73.3%	62.4%	5.35	.148
Weight gain (lb)	30.1	28.7	0.77	.443

Note. N = 489.
[a]Modal income category.
[b]Adequacy of Prenatal Care Utilization Index, percentage adequate or adequate plus.

TABLE 2.   Percentage of Women Who Delivered a Low Birth Weight Baby by Psychological Abuse Status

Type of Psychological Abuse[a]	Any Abuse		High Frequency of Abuse	
	No	Yes	No	Yes
Insulted	13.8%	17.8%	14.3%	17.5%
Screamed at	14.3%	14.4%	14.1%	16.7%
Threatened	13.8%	29.2%*	14.0%	33.3%*
All types	14.2%	15.4%	14.2%	17.2%

Note. $N = 489$. Cell values represent a percentage who delivered a low birth weight ($<2,500$ g) baby.
[a]Based on responses on the HITS intimate partner violence assessment administered during pregnancy.
*$p < .05$ for corresponding χ^2 test.

deliver a low birth weight baby ($\chi^2 = 4.36$, $p = .027$). In addition, those who reported a high frequency of being Threatened were nearly two and a half times more likely to deliver a low birth weight baby, with one-third of these women giving birth to a baby weighing less than 2,500 g ($\chi^2 = 3.51$, $p = .041$). None of the abuse variables significantly predicted preterm delivery ($p > .05$ for all analyses, data not shown).

To control for possible background differences and to examine potential explanatory factors, a logistic regression analysis was performed to predict low birth weight status from any occurrence of being Threatened by an intimate partner during pregnancy. These results are presented in Table 3. As can be seen, background factors did not significantly predict birth weight status. However, potentially mediating factors (smoking, alcohol use, prenatal care utilization, pregnancy weight gain) accounted for nearly 12% of the variance in birth weight in this sample, with prenatal care utilization and pregnancy weight gain the strongest predictors. After control for these mediating factors, the experience of being threatened by an intimate partner was no longer significantly associated with birth weight status.

DISCUSSION

Rates of pregnancy psychological IPV were high in the current sample of mostly rural, low-income women. This adds support to previous findings of increased incidence of IPV in rural populations and suggests this disparity may extend to psychological abuse as well (Peek-Asa et al., 2011). In this study, psychological abuse in general did not predict low birth weight or preterm delivery. However, the specific psychological abuse category of being Threatened was related to birth weight, with fear induced by threats a better predictor of birth weight than attacks on self-esteem by insults or being screamed at by a significant other. Threats appear to affect birth weight through indirect effects because we found that women who experience threats engage in negative health behaviors that are in turn associated with birth weight deficits.

That pregnancy outcomes could be negatively impacted by psychological IPV through negative health behaviors has been suggested by other work. For example, several reports

TABLE 3. Logistic Regression Results Predicting Low Birth Weight Status From Any Threatening Psychological Abuse During Pregnancy

Variables Entered	Overall R^2	χ^2	Step R^2 Change	p	Predictors B	p
Background	.014	3.74	.014	.443		
Age					0.047	.111
Education					−0.079	.312
Income					0.025	.639
Number of children					−0.027	.835
Potential mediators	.133	32.25	.119	<.001		
Pregnancy smoking					−0.519	.112
Pregnancy alcohol use					0.475	.419
Prenatal care utilization[a]					−1.620	<.001
Pregnancy weight gain					−0.030	.001
Threatening abuse	.141	2.28	.008	.131	−0.839	.113

Note. Results of logistic regression predicting birth weight. Background variables entered as a block on Step 1, potential mediating factors entered as a block on Step 2, and any threatening abuse entered on final step. $N = 489$.
[a]Adequacy of Prenatal Care Utilization Index.

have suggested a significant association between the experience of psychological IPV and heavy alcohol and recreational drug use (Coker et al., 2002; Feldner, Babson, & Zvolensky, 2007; Jun, Rich-Edwards, Boynton-Jarrett, & Wright, 2008), with this substance use in turn substantially increasing the risk for lower birth weight (Mariscal et al., 2006; Ventura, Hamilton, Mathews, & Chandra, 2003). Most recently, Ferri et al. (2007) suggested that the experience of threats by an intimate partner may be associated with decreased birth weight. In their large sample of urban women in Brazil, those who experienced threats were more than twice as likely to deliver a low birth weight baby as those who did not, consistent with findings in this study. This effect remained after control for potentially confounding background factors and was stronger than the nonsignificant effect between actual physical IPV and birth weight. Unfortunately, threats were the only type of psychological abuse examined in this study, and birth weight was the only outcome reported. However, the researchers did find that although some of the association between threats and birth weight was explained by mental health and health behaviors, not all of the relationship was explained by emotional health, smoking and alcohol use, and use of prenatal care (Ferri et al., 2007). In contrast, an investigation with a nationally representative sample of Canadian women found no significant association between threats of violence and either low birth weight or preterm birth (Urquia, O'Campo, Heaman, Janssen, & Thiessen, 2011). However, this study also found no link between actual physical abuse and birth outcomes, and lack of these expected findings could be largely a result of a very low incidence of pregnancy IPV (3.3%) in this sample.

The mechanism by which threats during pregnancy may impact birth outcomes, outside of the role of health behaviors, could not be determined from this study, but other research may provide some possible answers. Previous studies have shown that some women consider the psychological harm of physical aggression to be more severe than that caused by actual physical abuse (Marshall, 1992). Related to this, others have demonstrated a strong association between being threatened and PTSD (Ferri et al., 2007), with PTSD having been associated with significantly lower birth weight in multiple studies (Seng, Low, Sperlich, Ronis, & Liberzon, 2011). This may suggest that threats induce a biological stress response. Women who are victims of IPV have been found to have more severe symptoms of depression, anxiety, and incidence of PTSD, in addition to higher levels of evening cortisol and morning and evening dehydroepiandrosterone (DHEA; Pico-Alfonso, Garcia-Linares, Celda-Navarro, Herbert, & Martinez, 2004). Gitau, Cameron, Fisk, and Glover (1998) found that maternal cortisol concentration may have a major effect on fetal cortisol concentration, which is linked to abruption and hemorrhage as well as disturbances in uterine tone (Green et al., 2005). Maternal anxiety in pregnancy may also be related to increased uterine artery resistance index, which can cause lower birth weight (Teixeira, Fisk, & Glover, 1999).

This study was not without limitations. Information regarding pregnancy IPV, smoking, and alcohol use was collected via self-report. Women may not have been willing to disclose IPV or substance use, leading to underreporting and misclassification of those affected. Although all women who reported physical and/or sexual abuse were eliminated from the sample, some women who experienced physical abuse may not have been willing to disclose their experience, and thus effects that have here been attributed to psychological abuse could in fact be caused by undisclosed physical abuse. Finally, generalizability of this study may be limited to the geographical area and population from which the sample was taken, with the results applicable only to other low-income, rural areas in the Southeast.

The findings from this study have the potential to contribute substantially to our knowledge about the impact of psychological IPV on birth outcomes, and, in particular, how threats may relate to low birth weight. The way in which data were collected and analyzed allowed for an examination of the independent effect of different types of psychological IPV during pregnancy and control for potentially confounding factors. Information from this study may help in the development of interventions targeting this and similar populations. Future research is needed to further explore the pathways by which experiencing threats from an intimate partner during pregnancy may impact birth outcomes and to evaluate whether these findings generalize to other populations.

REFERENCES

American Medical Association. (1992). Diagnostic and treatment guidelines on domestic violence. *Archives of Family Medicine, 1*, 39–47.

Bailey, B. A., & Daugherty, R. A. (2007). Intimate partner violence during pregnancy: Incidence and associated health behaviors in a rural population. *Maternal Child Health Journal, 11*, 495–503.

Black, M. L., Basile, K. C., Breiding, M. J., Walters, S. G. S. L., Chen, M. T. M., & Stevens, M. R. (2011). *National Intimate Partner and Sexual Violence Survey (NISVS): 2010 Summary Report.* Atlanta, GA: National Center for Injury Prevention and Control, Centers for Disease Control and Prevention.

Bullock, L. F. C., Mears, J. L. C., Woodcock, C., & Record, R. (2001). Retrospective study of the association of stress and smoking during pregnancy in rural women. *Addictive Behaviors, 26*, 405–413.

Campbell, J. C., Poland, M. L., Waller, J. B., & Ager, J. (1992). Correlates of battering during pregnancy. *Research in Nursing & Health, 15*(3), 219–226.

Centers for Disease Control and Prevention. (1997). *PRAMS 1996 Surveillance Report.* Atlanta, GA: Division of Reproductive Health, National Center for Chronic Disease Prevention and Health Promotion, Centers for Disease Control and Prevention.

Coker, A. L., Davis, K. E., Arias, I., Desai, S., Sanderson, M., Brandt, H. M., & Smith, P. H. (2002). Physical and mental health effects of intimate partner violence for men and women. *American Journal of Preventive Medicine, 23*(4), 260–268.

Coker, A. L., Sanderson, M., & Dong, B. (2004). Partner violence during pregnancy and risk of adverse pregnancy outcomes. *Paediatric and Perinatal Epidemiology, 18*(4), 260–269.

Coker, A. L., Smith, P. H., Bethea, L., King, M. R., & McKeown, R. E. (2000). Physical health consequences of physical and psychological intimate partner violence. *Archives of Family Medicine, 9*(5), 451–457.

Curry, M. A. (1998). The interrelationships between abuse, substance use, and psychosocial stress during pregnancy. *Journal of Obstetric, Gynecologic, and Neonatal Nursing, 27*, 692–699.

Curry, M. A., & Harvey, S. M. (1998). Stress related to domestic violence during pregnancy and infant birth weight. In J. C. Campbell (Ed.), *Empowering survivors of abuse: Health care for battered women and their children* (pp. 98–108). Thousand Oaks, CA: Sage.

D'Avolio, D., Hawkins, J. W., Haggerty, L. A., Kelly, U., Barrett, R., Durno Toscano, S. E., . . . Bell, M. (2001). Screening for abuse: Barriers and opportunities. *Health Care for Women International, 22*(4), 349–362.

Dunn, L. L., & Oths, K. S. (2004). Prenatal predictors of intimate partner abuse. *Journal of Obstetric, Gynecologic, and Neonatal Nursing, 33*, 54–63.

Dye, T., Tolliver, N., Lee, R., & Kenney, C. (1995). Violence, pregnancy and birth outcome in Appalachia. *Paediatric and Perinatal Epidemiology, 9*, 35–47.

Feldner, M. T., Babson, K. A., & Zvolensky, M. J. (2007). Smoking, traumatic event exposure, and post-traumatic stress: A critical review of the empirical literature. *Clinical Psychology Review, 27*(1), 14–45.

Fernandez, F. M., & Krueger, P. M. (1999). Domestic violence: Effect on pregnancy outcome. *Journal of the American Osteopathic Association, 5*, 254–256.

Ferri, C. P., Mitsuhiro, S. S., Barros, M. C., Chalem, E., Guinsburg, R., Patel, V., . . . Laranjeira, R. (2007). The impact of maternal experience of violence and common mental disorders on neonatal outcomes: A survey of adolescent mothers in Sao Paulo, Brazil. *BMC Public Health, 7*(1), 209.

Gitau, R., Cameron, A., Fisk, N. M., & Glover, V. (1998). Fetal exposure to maternal cortisol. *The Lancet, 352*(9129), 707–708.

Green, N. S., Damus, K., Simpson, J. L., Iams, J., Reece, E. A., Hobel, C. J., . . . Schwarz, R. H. (2005). Research agenda for preterm birth: Recommendations from the March of Dimes. *American Journal of Obstetrics and Gynecology, 193*(3), 626–635.

Jun, H. J., Rich-Edwards, J. W., Boynton-Jarrett, R., & Wright, R. J. (2008). Intimate partner violence and cigarette smoking: Association between smoking risk and psychological abuse with and without co-occurrence of physical and sexual abuse. *American Journal of Public Health, 98*(3), 527–535.

Kotelchuck, M. (1994). The Adequacy of Prenatal Care Utilization Index: Its U.S. distribution and association with low birth weight. *American Journal of Public Health, 84*, 1486–1489.

Mariscal, M., Palma, S., Llorca, J., Pérez-Iglesias, R., Pardo-Crespo, R., & Delgado-Rodríguez, M. (2006). Pattern of alcohol consumption during pregnancy and risk for low birth weight. *Annals of Epidemiology, 16*(6), 432–438.

Marshall, L. L. (1992). Development of the severity of violence against women scales. *Journal of Family Violence, 7*(2), 103–121.

Martin, S. L., Beaumont, J. L., & Kupper, L. L. (2003). Substance use before and during pregnancy: Links to intimate partner violence. *The American Journal of Drug and Alcohol Abuse, 29*(3), 599–617.

McFarlane, J., Parker, B., & Soeken, K. (1996). Abuse during pregnancy: Associations with maternal health and infant birth weight. *Nursing Research, 45*, 37–42.

Murphy, C. C., Schei, B., Myhr, T., & Du Mont, J. (2001). Abuse: A risk factor for low birth weight? A systematic review and meta-analysis. *Canadian Medical Association Journal, 164*, 1567–1572.

Norton, L. B., Peipert, J. F., Zierler, S., Lima, B., & Hume, L. (1995). Battering in pregnancy: An assessment of two screening methods. *Obstetrics and Gynecology, 85*, 321–325.

O'Leary, K. D. (1999). Psychological abuse: A variable deserving critical attention in domestic violence. *Violence and Victims, 14*(1), 3–23.

Peek-Asa, C., Wallis, A., Harland, K., Beyer, K., Dickey, P., & Saftlas, A. (2011). Rural disparity in domestic violence prevalence and access to resources. *Journal of Women's Health, 20*(11), 1743–1749.

Pico-Alfonso, M. A., Garcia-Linares, M. I., Celda-Navarro, N., Herbert, J., & Martinez, M. (2004). Changes in cortisol and dehydroepiandrosterone in women victims of physical and psychological intimate partner violence. *Biological Psychiatry, 56*(4), 233–240.

Roy, A., & Salihu, H. M. (2004). Intimate partner violence and birth outcomes: A systematic review. *International Journal of Fertility and Women's Medicine, 49*(4), 159–164.

Seng, J. S., Low, L. K., Sperlich, M., Ronis, D. L., & Liberzon, I. (2011). Post-traumatic stress disorder, child abuse history, birthweight and gestational age: A prospective cohort study. *BJOG: An International Journal of Obstetrics & Gynaecology, 118*(11), 1329–1339.

Sherin, K. M., Sinacore, J. M., Li, X. Q., Zitter, R. E., & Shakil, A. (1998). HITS: A short domestic violence screening tool for use in a family practice setting. *Family Medicine, 30*, 508–512.

Shumway, J., O'Campo, P., Gielen, A., Witter, F. R., Khouzami, A. N., & Blakemore, K. J. (1999). Preterm labor, placental abruption, and premature rupture of membranes in relation to maternal violence or verbal abuse. *Journal of Maternal Fetal Medicine, 8*, 76–80.

Street, A. E., & Arias, I. (2001). Psychological abuse and posttraumatic stress disorder in battered women: Examining the roles of shame and guilt. *Violence and Victims, 16*(1), 65–78.

Teixeira, J., Fisk, N. M., & Glover, V. (1999). Association between maternal anxiety in pregnancy and increased uterine artery resistance index: Cohort based study. *British Medical Journal, 318*(7177), 153–157.

Tjaden, P., & Thoennes, N. (2000). *Full report of the prevalence, incidence, and consequences of violence against women: Findings from the National Violence Against Women Survey.* Washington, DC: United States Department of Justice.

Tuten, M., Jones, H. E., Tran, G., & Svikis, D. S. (2004). Partner violence impacts the psychosocial and psychiatric status of pregnant, drug-dependent women. *Addictive Behaviors, 29*(5), 1029–1034.

Urquia, M. L., O'Campo, P. J., Heaman, M. I., Janssen, P. A., & Thiessen, K. R. (2011). Experiences of violence before and during pregnancy and adverse pregnancy outcomes: An analysis of the Canadian Maternity Experiences Survey. *BMC Pregnancy and Childbirth, 11*(1), 42.

Ventura, S. J., Hamilton, B. E., Mathews, T. J., & Chandra, A. (2003). Trends and variations in smoking during pregnancy and low birth weight: Evidence from the birth certificate, 1990–2000. *Pediatrics, 111*(Suppl. 1), 1176–1180.

Ventura, S. J., Martin, J. A., Curtin, S. C., & Mathews, T. J. (1999). Births: final data for 1997. *National Vital Statistics Report, 47*(18), 1–96.

Acknowledgments. This study was supported by a grant from the Tennessee Department of Health to Dr. Beth Bailey.

Correspondence regarding this article should be directed to Beth A. Bailey, PhD, Department of Family Medicine, East Tennessee State University, P.O. Box 70621, Johnson City, TN 37614. E-mail: nordstro@etsu.edu

Violence and Victims, Volume 15, Number 2, 2000

Measuring Interference With Employment and Education Reported by Women With Abusive Partners: Preliminary Data

Stephanie Riger
Courtney Ahrens
Amy Blickenstaff
University of Illinois at Chicago

This study examines the reliability and convergent validity of the Work/School Abuse Scale (W/SAS), a measure of the ways that abusive men interfere with women's participation in education and employment. Results indicate good reliability as measured by coefficient alpha and significant correlations with both a revised version of the Conflict Tactics Scale and the Psychological Abuse Index. The W/SAS is a useful measure of the ways in which physical force and other means of interfering with women's lives isolate them from activities that might provide income, social contacts, and a sense of accomplishment. It may also be used to examine whether changes in welfare policies affect levels of physical force and nonviolent interference in women's employment and education, as suggested by the Family Violence Option to the 1996 revisions in federal welfare policies.

Violence by intimates may be a critical barrier to employment of a sizable proportion of welfare recipients (Allard, Albelda, Colten & Cosenza, 1997; Nadel, 1998; Raphael, 1996). Many state welfare policies now require women to attempt to find work after a certain time period if they are to continue to receive government aid. Yet job training providers report that some men sabotage women's employment efforts by acts such as leaving visible marks of a beating on a woman just before she has a job interview or threatening her coworkers at work (Raphael, 1996). In recognition of the possibility of increased violence when women on welfare attempt to attain employment or education, the Family Violence Option to the 1996 federal welfare reform legislation offers states the opportunity to provide counseling and other services to women with abusive partners and temporarily to waive work and other requirements for them. The assumption underlying the Family Violence Option is that men who abuse women in other ways will also interfere with their attempts to go to work and/or to school. Yet, testing this assumption is problematic because we lack an adequate measure of actions by intimates that affect women's employment or education. As many women are now reaching their 2-year limit on consecutive receipt of government aid, the need for such a measure is pressing.

Some conceptualizations of violence, such as the Power and Control Wheel (Pence & Paymar, 1993) and Tolman's (1989) Psychological Maltreatment of Women Inventory include economic abuse and isolation. However, current measures of violence may not contain sufficiently specific questions about abuse related to women's attempts to become financially independent and to advance their skills and knowledge. This study assesses the validity of the Work/School Abuse Scale that measures the reported extent of partners' interference with women's employment and education.

Research on male violence against women has been hampered by the difficulty of measuring violence. Little agreement exists on how to define violence, and researchers vary in the range of behaviors they study (Crowell & Burgess, 1996). Some include only behaviors intended to harm, while others include acts that are not intended to harm but that cause damage nonetheless. Some consider only physical acts while others also include verbal and psychological abuse. The more inclusive the definition of violence, the higher the level of violence reported (Smith, 1994).

Two commonly cited sources of national data on violence against women are the National Crime Victimization Survey (reported in Bachman & Saltzman, 1995) and the National Family Violence Survey (reported in Straus, Gelles, & Steinmetz, 1980; Straus & Gelles, 1990). The National Crime Victimization Survey (NCVS), conducted by the United States government, did not include specific questions about violence between intimates before 1992, when changes were made to increase the accuracy of reporting crimes committed by intimates or family members (Bachman & Saltzman, 1995). Behavior-specific wording replaced criminal justice terminology to make it easier for respondents to understand the meaning of questions, and items were added that included a wide spectrum of violent acts. Such methodological changes resulted in increases in reported rates of violent victimizations against women.

The Conflict Tactics Scale (CTS), developed for the National Family Violence Survey, includes measures of the use of reasoning and verbal/symbolic aggression as well as physical violence such as pushing, shoving, grabbing, kicking, biting, and so forth (Straus, 1979). Despite its frequent use, the CTS has been criticized for not specifying whether violent acts were in attack or self-defense, not taking into account the degree of injuries sustained, not sufficiently discriminating among different kinds of violence, and not recognizing the use of violence as a means of control of women (Dobash, Dobash, Wilson, & Daly, 1992; Koss et al., 1994; Kurz, 1993; cf. Straus, 1990, 1993).

In response to these criticisms, the CTS was revised to distinguish between minor and severe levels of physical force and to assess injuries incurred as a result of the abuse (Straus, Hamby, Bohey-McCoy, & Sugarman, 1996). Yet, despite these revisions, several researchers continue to criticize the CTS, claiming that conceptualizing intimate violence as the use of tactics to resolve conflicts obscures the dynamic of power and control that is inherent in domestic violence (Bograd, 1988; Schechter, 1988; Yllo, 1993). These researchers argue from a feminist perspective that multiple forms of coercive control are used by abusers (and reinforced by the patriarchal nature of society) to dominate women. The Power and Control Wheel (Pence & Paymar, 1993) illustrates this spectrum of control and includes acts such as intimidation, emotional abuse, isolation, economic abuse, coercion and threats, male privilege, manipulation through the children, and minimization, denial, and blame.

In addition to the measures described above, several other instruments have also been developed to assess a wide variety of violent acts that include both physical and non-physical maltreatment [e.g., the Index of Spouse Abuse (Hudson & McIntosh, 1981); the Wife Abuse Inventory (Lewis, 1987); the Severity of Violence Against Women Scales (Marshall, 1992); the Measure of Wife Abuse (Rodenberg, 1993); the Abusive Behavior

Inventory (Shepard & Campbell, 1992); the Psychological Abuse Index (Sullivan, Tan, Basta, Rumptz, & Davidson, 1992); and the Psychological Maltreatment of Women Inventory (Tolman, 1989)]. Both the Psychological Maltreatment of Women Inventory and the Power and Control Wheel include the concept of preventing women from going to work or keeping a job, but this form of abuse is not extensively assessed.

The lack of attention to this issue may stem, in part, from the use of shelter residents as the sample in many studies of violence. Many domestic violence shelter residents may not have been employed or have attended school recently. Consequently, this issue may not be relevant to all victims. Nonetheless, when abusers do interfere with their partner's work or school participation, the consequences for the victim may be profound, serving to further isolate the victim and limit the financial resources that could enable her to leave the battering relationship. Even though these experiences may be relevant only to a subset of domestic violence victims, it is important to understand and assess such tactics.

The purpose of this study was to develop a measure of abusive acts by intimates that prevent or hinder women's employment and/or education. Previous research indicates that multiple, behaviorally specific questions yield greater disclosure by respondents (Crowell & Burgess, 1996); therefore, we attempted to be inclusive and specific in generating items for this scale. Interference with women's work and education may come not only from actions involving the use of physical force but also from acts in which force is not used but that nonetheless affect women's participation. For example, turning off an alarm clock may cause a woman to be late to work, risking her job security. Consequently, we included both items that describe the use of force and items that describe nonforceful but interfering acts. Here we present the Work/School Abuse Scale (W/SAS) and its subscales and examine its relationship to other measures of violence. Since both work and school increase women's independence and financial self sufficiency, we have combined them in one measure. However, we present the items separately in the Appendix so that the work or school items may be used independently.

METHOD

Participants and Procedure

Participants in this study were recruited through a larger study of domestic violence victims residing in shelters in Chicago (Riger, Blickenstaff, Ahrens & Camacho, 1998). Although 46% of the women in the larger study ($N = 57$) reported that their abusers had forbidden them to work and 25% reported that their abusers had forbidden them to go to school, only 35 respondents had actually been employed or gone to school during their relationship with the abuser, whether or not they had been forbidden. Of these 35 women, 15 had been both employed and gone to school during their relationship with the abuser, 18 had been employed but had not gone to school, and 2 had been in school but had not been employed. These 35 women, who had either been employed or gone to school during their relationship with the abuser, constitute the sample for the present study.

The average woman in this sample was 31 years old and had two children under 14 years of age living with her. Eleven percent were married, 83% were African American, 51% had at least a high school diploma, and 68% were receiving welfare benefits at the time of the study.

We interviewed women at 4 shelters between February and April, 1997. However, logistical problems allowed us to interview only 1 woman from the 4th shelter. The Illinois

Department of Public Aid provided demographic information on all residents of the 3 remaining shelters during February, March, and April, 1997, the months during which we collected data. A comparison of the 35 women who went to school or work during their relationship with their abuser with the total population of each of these three shelters during the time of data collection indicated that our participants did not differ from the general population, with two exceptions. We were unable to interview in Spanish; therefore our sample had fewer Latinas than representative from the one shelter that had a large Spanish-speaking population. In this same shelter, our sample was significantly more likely to be receiving welfare than the general shelter population (see Table 1). Other than these two exceptions, our sample, albeit small, nonetheless represents the population of interest and therefore meets the assumption of classic test theory (Allen & Yin, 1979).

There are several possible reasons for the oversampling of welfare recipients. First, the shelter staff somehow may have systematically approached more women on welfare to be participants in this study than they approached nonwelfare recipients. Second, the financial incentive of $20 to be a participant in this study may have induced more women with few resources (e.g., women on welfare) to participate. Third, women on welfare may have stayed longer at the shelter than nonwelfare recipients, giving them more opportunity to be part of this study. Because shelter staff were unable to keep records of whom they approached, who consented, and who declined to be study participants, it is impossible to ascertain which of these possibilities accounts for the over sampling of welfare recipients in this shelter. However, because the purpose of this study was to develop a scale, not to assess a representative sample of shelter participants, the over sampling of welfare recipients is not a problem. Moreover, the long-term goal of the present study was to develop a measure that would be useful in studying the impact of welfare policies on women; therefore, over representation of women on welfare may be helpful in developing a scale appropriate for this population.

Measures

In addition to developing a measure of work/school interference, we also assessed levels of physical and psychological violence; the psychometric properties of these measures are reported below.

Work/School Abuse Scale. A pool of 15 items was developed from discussions with domestic violence and job training providers and from a review of the literature, including anecdotal descriptions of ways that abusive men interfere with women's work and school participation. We wrote items that describe behaviors that both prevent women from going to work or school and that interfere with participation once women were at work or school. Some of the items refer to the use of physical force while others do not.

Items describing work/school interference tactics were measured on a 6-point scale ranging from "never" to "more than 4 times a week." However, responses indicate that the items had low variability; that is, harassers either used a tactic frequently or did not use that tactic at all (rather than varying the frequency with which they used each tactic). Therefore, responses to the items were dichotomized. Each of the 15 items was first asked in the context of work and then in the context of school, and the parallel work/school items were combined. If an abuser had used a tactic to interfere with either a victim's work or school participation, the combined item received a "1"; if an abuser had not used the tactic to interfere with either work or school participation, the combined item received a "0." Participants in the study completed these items as well as those' asking whether or not they had ever been forbidden to go to work or school, had to miss work or school as a result of the abuse, or were fired or had quit as a result of the abuse.

TABLE 1. Demographic Comparisons of Women Who Worked/Went to School With the General Shelter Population

	Shelter 1			Shelter 2			Shelter 3		
Variable	% Sample ($n = 14$)	% Total ($n = 141$)	χ^2	% Sample ($n = 8$)	% Total ($n = 179$)	χ^2	% Sample ($n = 13$)	% Total ($n = 123$)	χ^2
Ethnicity									
African American	92.9	78.3	75.0	57.7	92.3	82.8			
Latina	0.0	15.2	0.0	24.6	0.0	4.9			
Caucasian	7.1	6.5	2.48	12.5	13.1	24.60***	7.7	9.0	1.22
Married	7.1	27.7	2.80	12.5	34.6	1.68	15.4	26.0	0.71
Spouse was abuser	46.2	40.0	0.19	60.0	39.0	0.89	25.0	28.2	0.05
Medicaid for self	42.9	50.4	0.29	50.0	33.5	0.92	46.2	58.5	0.74
Medicaid for child	64.3	46.8	1.56	75.0	29.6	7.31	61.5	53.7	0.29
Welfare receipt	64.3	47.5	1.43	75.0	24.6	9.94**	61.5	41.5	1.93

Table does not include the percentages of Asian, Native American, and "Other" participants, as these numbers were negligible.
*$p < .05$.**$p < .01$.***$p < .001$.

Physical Abuse. A modified version of the physical aggression section of the Conflict Tactics Scale (CTS) (Straus, 1979) as modified by Sullivan et al. (1992) was used to measure physical violence by the person who caused the respondent to enter the shelter. Items assessed the frequency of actions such as being pushed, slapped, choked, beat up, and threatened or assaulted with a knife or gun. Items were measured on a 6-point scale ranging from "never" to "more than 4 times a week." Sullivan et al. (1992) reported that the modified scale had an internal consistency of .90; in our sample the internal consistency was .89 as measured by Cronbach's alpha. Even though our sample is small, it nonetheless yields a reliability estimate that is consistent with a larger sample in previous research.

Psychological Abuse Index (PAI). The Index of Psychological Abuse (Sullivan et al., 1992) assessed the frequency of psychological abuse, such as control of money and activities, verbal abuse, and threats and criticism of the respondent, friends, family, and children. Items were rated on a 6-point scale of increasing frequencies ranging from "never" to "more than 4 times a week." Sullivan et al. (1992) reported that the scale had an internal consistency of .97, indicating that the items reliably measure women's experiences with psychological abuse. In our sample, the IPA had an internal consistency of .89 as measured by Cronbach's alpha. Again, although our sample is small, the reliability estimate obtained is reasonably close the one produced by a larger sample in previous research.

RESULTS

Reliability

Reliability of the Work/School Abuse Scale (W/SAS) was assessed by examining the coefficient alpha, a widely used measure of internal consistency. Analyses of the dichotomized items revealed that 3 of the 15 items had poor psychometric properties (i.e., low corrected item total correlations, low item means, and low standard deviations). These 3 items (which asked a woman whether her abuser had sent or left something at work or school to harass her, or whether the abuser had threatened her coworkers or school friends) were omitted. The resulting 12-item scale (see Appendix) has an internal consistency of .82 (see Table 2). Coefficient alpha tends to be lower if the scale items are dichotomously coded (Allen & Yin, 1979), and if there are a small number of items in a scale (Cortina, 1993). An alpha of .82 for a 12-item scale indicates good reliability.

The sample was too small to permit factor analysis of the 12 items. However, since the items were written to represent two types of interference, we examined the level of reliability of two subscales consisting of these two types of behaviors. The Restraint Tactics sub-scale contained 6 items that assessed the use of tactics that prevent the respondent from going to work or school (e.g., steal car keys or money). The Interference Tactics subscale contained 6 items that assessed the use of tactics aimed at making the respondent leave work or school (e.g., lie about children's health or safety to make you leave work/school). These subscales have internal consistencies of .73 and .77, respectively, which, for scales consisting of small numbers of items that are dichotomously coded, indicate good reliability. Table 2 presents the 12 items that constitute the W/SAS, their psychometric properties, and the percent of women who reported experiencing each tactic.

Validity

We examined the convergent validity of the W/SAS; that is, we assessed the extent to which the W/SAS correlates with measures of physical abuse (modified CTS) and

TABLE 2. Psychometric Properties and Frequencies for the Work/School Abuse Scale

Scale Item	Item M	Item SD	CITCa Scale	CITCa Subscale	Frequency (%)
Restraint Tactics					
1. Sabotage the car	.29	.46	.41	.52	29
2. Not show up for child care	.41	.48	.44	.36	41
3. Steal car keys or money	.46	.51	.45	.56	46
4. Refuse to give a ride to work/school	.51	.51	.18	.25	51
5. Physically restrain you from going to work/school	.37	.49	.64	.60	37
6. Threaten you to prevent your going to work/school	.46	.51	.57	.54	46
Interference Tactics					
1. Come to work or school to harass you	.40	.50	.36	.42	40
2. Bother coworkers/school friends	.20	.41	.59	.53	20
3. Lies to coworkers/school friends about you	.37	.49	.50	.56	37
4. Physically force you to leave work/school	.26	.44	.58	.66	26
5. Lie about children's health or safety to make you leave work/school	.41	.47	.42	.39	41
6. Threaten you to make you leave work/school	.34	.48	.61	.58	34
Dropped items					
1. Send something to work/school to harass you	.06	.24	.14	—	6
2. Left things at work/school to harass you	.11	.32	.15	—	11
3. Threaten coworkers or school friends	.09	.28	.27	—	9

Note. N = 35. Items were scored 0 = no interference; 1 = interference.
[a] CITC = Corrected Item-Total Correlation.

psychological abuse. The subscales of the W/SAS are also positively correlated with the modified CTS and the PAI. Specifically, the Restraint Tactics scale is significantly related to the modified CTS physical assault subscale ($r = .37$; $p < .05$), indicating that the more physical abuse a woman suffers, the more the abuser tries to restrain her from going to work and/or school. The Interference Tactics scale is significantly related to both the modified CTS ($r = .38$; $p < .05$) and the PAI ($r = .36$; $p < .05$). Thus, the more physical and psychological abuse a woman suffered, the more the abuser also interferes with her work and/or school participation. The fact that the correlations among the W/SAS and the other measures of abuse are significant but modest (ranging from .36 to .43) indicates that these constructs are related but not identical, demonstrating the need for a separate measure of work/school interference.

The Relationship Between Restraining and Interfering Tactics and Work or School Participation

In addition to completing items included in the W/SAS, women in our sample were asked if their abuser forbade them to work or go to school, if they missed work or school because of abuse, and if they were fired from work or dropped out of school because of the abuse. Of those 35 women who worked or went to school during their relationship with the abuser, 46% had been explicitly forbidden by their abusers to get a job. Of the 33 women who did work, 85% of them missed work because of the abuse and 52% were fired or had to quit because of the abuse. Women who were forbidden but who worked anyway did not report experiencing more Restraint or Interference tactics than those who worked but who were not forbidden (see Table 3). However, women who reported missing work as a result of their partners' abuse experienced significantly more interference with work activities than those who did not miss work because of abuse. Specifically, women who missed work because of abuse reported

TABLE 3.   Relationship Between Restraint, Interference, the Total W/SAS, and Work Participation

Variable	Restraint Subscale			Interference Subscale			Total W/SAS Scale		
	M	SD	t	M	SD	t	M	SD	t
Forbidden to go to work									
Yes ($n = 16$)	.48	.30		.44	.34		.46	.28	
No ($n = 18$)	.37	.33	0.99	.23	.28	2.03	.30	.26	1.76
Miss work because of abuse									
Yes ($n = 28$)	.45	.31		.39	.32		.42	.28	
No ($n = 5$)	.37	.40	0.50	.07	.15	2.22*	.22	.19	1.55
Fired from/quit work because of abuse									
Yes ($n = 17$)	.56	.30		.46	.36		.49	.27	
No ($n = 16$)	.30	.29	2.46*	.25	.25	1.65	.28	.24	2.44

Note. Responses to Work and School Interference Scale were dichotomized ($0 =$ no interference; $1 =$ interference). Ns vary due to missing data. $* p < .05. ** p < .01.$

TABLE 4. Relationship Between School Restraint, School Interference, the Total W/SAS, and School Participation,

Variable	Restraint Subscale			Interference Subscale			Total W/SAS Scale		
	M	*SD*	*t*	*M*	*SD*	*t*	*M*	*SD*	*t*
Forbidden to go to school									
Yes (*n* = 11)	.51	.35		.45	.40		.48	.35	
No (*n* = 24)	.37	.31	1.24	.26	.26	1.65	.32	.23	1.67
Miss school because of abuse									
Yes (*n* = 9)	.43	.33		.47	.34		45	.32	
No (*n* = 7)	.29	.37	0.85	.17	.24	2.01*	.23	.28	1.49
Dropped/kicked out of school because of abuse									
Yes (*n* = 6)	.62	.32		.57	.35		.59	.33	
No (*n* = 10)	.22	.26	2.76*	.20	.23	2.52*	.21	.20	2.94*

Note. Responses to Work and School Interference Scale were dichotomized (0 = no interference; 1 = interference). *N*s vary due missing data. * $p < .05$. ** $p < .01$.

significantly higher scores on the Interference scale than those women who did not miss work. Women who were fired or quit as a result of abuse reported significantly higher scores on the Restraint scale and the total W/SAS than those women who did not stop working.

School participation is also related to the W/SAS and its subscales. Of the 35 women who had gone to work or school during their relationship with the abuser, 31% were explicitly forbidden to attend school by the abuser. Of the 17 women who did go to school, 53% reported that they missed school and 35% reported having dropped out or having been kicked out of school because of abuse. Women who were forbidden but who went anyway, and women who missed school because of abuse did not report higher scores on the Restraint or Interference Tactics scales (see Table 4). However, women who reported leaving school because of abuse also reported experiencing significantly higher scores on both the Restraint and Interference Tactics scales and the total W/SAS.

DISCUSSION

These findings indicate that the W/SAS is a reliable and valid measure of interference with women's work and/or school participation. The scale has the advantage of asking explicitly about behaviors intended to interfere with women's daily activities that have not specifically been included in most other measures. The W/SAS may be used as a measure of the impact of welfare reform on women whose changed welfare status prompts them to attempt to work or go to school as well as to give a more complete picture of the ways that violence affects women's lives.

We did not have a sufficiently large sample to conduct factor analyses on the items. Therefore, the two subscales, Restraint and Interference, require confirmation in future studies. Until then, having the subscales might be useful for descriptive purposes or for conceptualizing the overall constructs. The two subscales of the W/SAS may be related differentially to work and school participation, although the small size of this sample makes these findings inconclusive. It appears that the use of tactics that interfere with women while they are at work is related to their missing work, while the use of tactics that make it difficult for them to get to work is related to being fired or quitting because of abuse. With respect to school, both types of tactics restrict women from getting to school, and those involving interference with women while they are at school are related to their leaving school.

Although the W/SAS appears to be useful, a cautionary note is in order. The small sample size limits the confidence that we can have in these findings. Due to the pressing need, given welfare reform, for a measure of abusive interference with women's work and school participation, however, we are putting forth this scale as a timely first step. Future studies will need to replicate these findings with a larger sample to confirm the reliability and validity of this scale and its subscales. Nevertheless, the validity of this study is supported by several aspects of the results: (a) the sample, although small, is representative of the population from which it is drawn; (b) the estimates of reliability for the existing measures of physical and psychological abuse are similar to those found in larger samples; and (c) the reliability estimates are good, especially for scales consisting of small numbers of items that are dichoto-mously coded. Finally, the modest (but significant) correlations between the W/SAS and the existing measures of physical and psychological abuse indicate that the W/SAS is measuring a related but different construct.

In addition to larger samples, future studies should include women from diverse settings. This sample was drawn exclusively from residents of inner-city domestic violence shelters and therefore probably represented women who were severely abused and who had few resources. It is possible that women who suffer abuse but who do not go to domestic violence shelters experience interference with work and education in ways that differ from this sample. Furthermore, the majority of women in this sample were African American. The factor structure underlying the W/SAS may differ for varying ethnic groups of women (see, e.g., Campbell et al., 1994), and forms of interference not included in this scale may be experienced by women of other ethnic or socioeconomic backgrounds.

The Family Violence Option to the federal welfare reform legislation assumes that men who are abusive to their female partners in other ways will also interfere with women's attempts to go to work and/or school. Support for this assumption comes from the significant correlations in this study between work and school interference and between both physical and psychological abuse. If women with abusive partners try to go to school or get a job, they may experience high levels of interference by their partners. Thus, victims of abuse who are welfare recipients may be caught in a double bind. They are being urged to move from welfare to work, but their attempts to do so may be thwarted by their abusive partners.

Researchers have previously identified the tendency of abusive partners to discourage women from maintaining relationships with friends and family and to isolate them from outside contacts (Browne, 1987). Male violence often occurs when women attempt to leave a relationship or in other ways to assert their independence (Dobash & Dobash, 1984; Ellis, 1992; Harlow, 1991; Mahoney, 1991). Getting a job or going to school may be seen by abusers as precursors to women's leaving. The self-esteem that attends accomplishment, the new social contacts that women make, and the income they receive from work or job training all may increase women's independence and self-assertion, consequently threatening men's authority and control. Hence, attempts to become employed or to further their education may subject women to increased violence by men who abuse their female partners. The W/SAS provides a means of identifying the scope and frequency of this violence, enabling us to further understand the role of violence in women's lives.

REFERENCES

Allen, M. J., & Yin, W. M. (1979). *Introduction to measurement.* Monterey, CA: Brooks/Cole.

Allard, M. A., Albelda, R., Colten, M.E., & Cosenza, C. (1997). *In harm's way? Domestic violence. AFDC receipt and welfare reform in Massachusetts.* Boston, MA: Center for Social Policy Research, University of Massachusetts Boston.

Bachman, R., & Saltzman L. E. (1995, August). *Violence against women: Estimates from the redesigned survey* (NCJ-154348). Washington, DC: Bureau of Justice Statistics, U.S. Department of Justice.

Bograd, M. (1988). Feminist perspectives on wife abuse: An introduction. In K. Yllo & M. Bograd (Eds.), *Feminist perspectives on wife abuse* (pp. 11–26). Newbury Park, CA: Sage.

Browne, A. (1987). *When battered women kill.* New York: Macmillan/Free Press.

Cortina, J. M. (1993). What is coefficient alpha? And examination of theory and applications. *Journal of Applied Psychology, 78,* 98–104.

Crowell, N. A., & Burgess, A. W. (1996). *Understanding violence against women.* Washington, DC: National Academy Press.

Dobash, R. E., & Dobash, R. P. (1984). The nature and antecedents of violent events. *British Journal of Criminology, 24,* 269–288.

Dobash, R. P., Dobash, R. E., Wilson, M., & Daly, M. (1992). The myth of sexual symmetry in marital violence. *Social Problems, 39,* 71–91.

Ellis, D. (1992). Woman abuse among separated and divorced women: The relevance of social support. In E. C. Viana (Ed.), *Intimate violence: Interdisciplinary perspectives* (pp. 177189). Washington, DC: Hemisphere.

Harlow, C. W. (1991). *Female victims of violent crime.* Rockville, MD: U.S. Department of Justice.

Hudson, W. W., & McIntosh, S. (1981). The assessment of spouse abuse: Two quantifiable dimensions. *Journal of Marriage and the Family, 43,* 873–888.

Koss, M. P., Goodman, L. A., Browne, A., Fitzgerald, L. E, Keita, G. P., & Russo, N. F. (1994). *Male violence against women at home, at work, and in the community.* Washington, DC: American Psychological Association.

Kurz, D. (1993). Physical assaults by husbands: A major social problem. In RJ. Gelles & D.R. Loseke (Eds.), *Current controversies on family violence* (pp. 88–103). Newbury Park, CA: Sage.

Lewis, B.Y. (1987). Psychosocial factors related to wife abuse. *Journal of Family Violence, 2,* 1–10.

Mahoney, M.R. (1991). Legal images of battered women: Redefining the issue of separation. *Michigan Law Review, I,* 43–49.

Marshall, L. L. (1992). Development of the severity of violence against women scales. *Journal of Family Violence, 7,* 103–121.

Nadel, M. V. (1998). Domestic violence: Prevalence and implications for employment among welfare recipients (HEHS-99-12). Washington, DC: U.S. General Accounting Office.

Pence, E., & Paymar, M. (1993). *Education groups for men who batter: The Duluth model.* New York: Springer Publishing.

Raphael, J. (1996). Domestic violence and welfare receipt: Toward a new feminist theory of welfare dependency. *Harvard Women's Law Journal, 19,* 201–227.

Rodenberg, F. A. (1993). The measure of wife abuse: Steps toward the development of a comprehensive assessment technique. *Journal of Family Violence, 8,* 202–228.

Schechter, S. (1988). Building bridges between activists, professionals, and researchers. In K. Yllo & M. Bograd (Eds.), *Feminist perspectives on wife abuse* (pp. 299–312). Newbury Park, CA: Sage.

Shepard, M. F., & Campbell, J. A. (1992). The abusive behavior inventory: A measure of psychological and physical abuse. *Journal of Interpersonal Violence, 7,* 291–305.

Smith, M. D. (1994). Enhancing the quality of survey data on violence against women: A feminist approach. *Gender and Society, 8,* 109–127.

Straus, M. A. (1979). Measuring intrafamily conflict and violence: The Conflict Tactics (CT) Scales. *Journal of Marriage and the Family,* 75–88.

Straus, M. A. (1990). The Conflict Tactics Scale and its critics: An evaluation and new data on validity and reliability. In M. A. Straus and R. J. Gelles (Eds.), *Physical violence in American families: Risk factors and adaptions to violence in 8.145 families* (pp. 49–73). New Brunswick, NJ: Transaction Publishers.

Straus, M. A. (1993). Physical assaults by wives: A major social problem. In R. J. Gelles & D. R. Loseke (Eds.), *Current controversies on family violence* (pp. 67–87). Newbury Park, CA: Sage.

Straus, M. A., & Gelles, R. J. (1990). How violent are American families? Estimates from the National Family Violence Resurvey and other studies. In M. A. Straus & R. J. Gelles (Eds.), *Physical violence in American families: Risk Factors and adaptations to violence in 8.145 families* (pp. 95–112). New Brunswick, NJ: Transaction Publishers.

Straus, M. A., Gelles, R. J., & Steinmetz, S. (1980). *Behind closed doors: Violence in the American Family.* Garden City, NY: Anchor Press.

Straus, M. A., Hamby, S. L., Boney-McCoy, S., & Sugerman, D. B. (1996). The revised Conflict Tactics Scale (CTS2): Development and preliminary psychometric data. *Journal of Family Issues, 17,* 283–316.

Sullivan, CM., Tan, C., Basta, J., Rumptz, M., & Davidson, W.S. (1992). An advocacy intervention program for women with abusive partners: Initial evaluation. *American Journal of Community Psychology, 20,* 309–332.

Tolman, R.M. (1989). The development of a measure of psychological maltreatment of women by their male partners. *Violence and Victims, 4,* 159–177.

Yllo, K. (1993). Through a feminist lens: Gender, power, and violence. In Gelles & Loseke (Eds.), *Current controversies on family violence* (pp. 47–60). Newbury Park: Sage.

Offprints. Requests for offprints should be directed to Stephanie Riger, Department of Psychology (M/C 285), University of Illinois at Chicago, 1062 Behavioral Sciences Building, 1007 West Harrison Street, Chicago, IL 60607-7137.

Work/School Abuse Scale Form

The following questions are about things that _____ (ABUSER'S NAME) may have done to bother you at work or to keep you from going to work. During your relationship with _____, did he ever ...

1. Come to your work to harass you? YES NO N/A
2. Bother your coworkers? YES NO N/A
3. Lie to your coworkers about you? YES NO N/A
4. Sabotage the car so you couldn't go to work? YES NO N/A
5. Not show up for child care so you couldn't go to work? YES NO N/A
6. Steal your keys or money so you couldn't go to work? YES NO N/A

Work/School Abuse Scale Form   (Continued)

7. Refuse to give you a ride to work?	YES	NO	N/A
8. Physically restrain you from going to work?	YES	NO	N/A
9. Threaten you to prevent your going to work?	YES	NO	N/A
10. Physically forced you to leave work?	YES	NO	N/A
11. Lied about your children's health or safety to make you leave work?	YES	NO	N/A
12. Threatened you to make you leave work?	YES	NO	N/A

The following questions are about things that (ABUSER'S NAME) may have done to bother you at school or to keep you from going to school. During your relationship with_____, did he ever...

1. Come to school to harass you?	YES	NO	N/A
2. Bother your school friends or teachers?	YES	NO	N/A
3. Lie to your friends/teachers about you?	YES	NO	N/A
4. Sabotage the car so you couldn't go to school?	YES	NO	N/A
5. Not show up for child care so you couldn't go to school?	YES	NO	N/A
6. Steal your keys or money so you couldn't go to school?	YES	NO	N/A
7. Refuse to give you a ride to school?	YES	NO	N/A
8. Physically restrain you from going to school?	YES	NO	N/A
9. Threaten you to prevent your going to school?	YES	NO	N/A
10. Physically forced you to leave school?	YES	NO	N/A
11. Lied about your children's health or safety to make you leave school?	YES	NO	N/A
12. Threatened you to make you leave school?	YES	NO	N/A

Violence and Victims, Volume 14, Number 1, 1999

Effects of Men's Subtle and Overt Psychological Abuse on Low-Income Women

Linda L. Marshall
University of North Texas

A social influence approach to the psychological abuse of women (Marshall, 1994; 1996) was expanded and tested. Distinctions are made between obvious acts (e.g., verbal aggression, controlling behaviors), overt acts which are easily recognized and described, and subtle acts which are least likely to be recognized as psychologically abusive. Men's violence and sexual aggression, and overt (dominating acts, indifference, monitoring, discrediting) and subtle (undermining, discounting, isolating) psychological abuse were examined as they related to women's psychological and emotional state and perceptions of their relationship. Results of regression equations with 834 low-income women in long-term heterosexual relationships are reported. In general, subtle psychological abuse had stronger and more consistent associations with women's state and relationship perceptions than did their partners' overt psychological abuse, violence, or sexual aggression. The importance of extending research beyond obvious acts was underscored by findings showing that subtle psychological abuse accounted for a small but significant proportion of the variance in outcome variables even after the effects of violence and sexual aggression (Step 1) and overt psychological abuse (Step 2) were controlled in eight of the nine regression equations. In contrast, when subtle and overt psychological abuse were entered first (in Steps 1 and 2, respectively), violence and sexual aggression (Step 3) made significant contributions in only two of the nine equations.

M y perspective on psychological abuse developed from theories and research on "normal" nonviolent samples from different (sub)disciplines (especially social psychology and communication). This view can best be described as a social influence perspective (Marshall, 1994). Briefly, psychological abuse results from normal intrapersonal and interpersonal processes occurring in everyday interactions. Interpersonal processes can make us feel very good or very bad. These influence processes are the same ones that enable therapists and others to help individuals improve themselves or overcome problems. The abuse is in the effect of an act.

This approach does not discount the effects of obviously abusive controlling or verbally aggressive acts. Indeed, important insights are gained from questionnaires, interaction records, and coding of acts during communication (Babcock, Waltz, Jacobson, & Gottman, 1993; Jacobson, Gottman, Gortner, Burns, & Shortt, 1996; Lloyd, 1996; Vivian & Malone, 1997). I simply propose that the prevailing perspective misses too much that is abusive because many acts can cause psychological and emotional harm. If measures are limited to dominance, obvious control or clear verbal aggression, knowledge will be biased. We will learn a great deal about various forms of aggression in relationships, for example,

---

verbal aggression as it accompanies violent or distressed relationships (Margolin, John, & Gleberman, 1988; Murphy & Cascardi, 1993; O'Leary, Malone, & Tyree, 1994), but little about harm that can be done to women through everyday interactions with men who may or may not have any intent to inflict harm or control their partner.

My social influence approach draws on vast bodies of research (e.g., on anger, attribution, compliance tactics, self-concept, nonverbal behavior, persuasion, expectancy effects, relationship development and dissolution, uncertainty, positive illusions, unintended thought), showing how others often have very strong effects on our attitudes, beliefs, and behaviors without intent, without their awareness, and without our own awareness. In this perspective, the intent of the psychologically abusive act is irrelevant. Thus, an act may be done out of love, to have fun or be playful, or to dominate. Regardless of the intent or the style used, an act may still harm the target and a combination or repetition of messages can cause serious damage. Similarly, the woman's recognition of the act and/or its effects are irrelevant. Social psychology is replete with examples of theories and experiments on many different topics, showing that people often have no awareness that their attitude, belief, behavior, or opinion was influenced by a behavioral induction, characteristics of the situation, or another person's behavior. Thus, there is no need to posit awareness in order to posit effect.

By removing the necessity of considering awareness and intent and by recognizing the potential for everyday interactions to be harmful, it is clear the context must not be restricted to conflict. Although the amount and intensity of conflict, especially in violent relationships, are important and harmful to the relationship and well-being of the individuals, conflictual situations constitute only one portion of communication in relationships. Moreover, statements made during conflicts may be more readily discounted or ignored afterwards as resulting from the heat of the moment. Granted, the statements could still cause hurt feelings which may be long lasting, but the cognitive processing of those statements may be less likely to result in self-questioning than if a hurtful statement was made in a calmer context.

Consider, for example, being told you are fat or ugly, an item on the revised Conflict Tactics Scale (ugly, an item on the revised Conflict Tactics Scale (CTS2; Straus, Hamby, Boney-McCoy, & Sugarman, 1996). If your partner yelled this during a conflict, it may hurt and you may think about it for a long time, but you could also attribute it to anger or your partner's personality. In contrast, your partner mentions you seem to be putting on weight (or your clothes seem tighter), or your hairstyle could be more attractive. He says he wants everyone to know how beautiful you are and how lucky he is to have you. In this situation, you may be hurt and think about it for a long time, but rather than attributing it to something about the situation or your partner's personality, you are likely to think there is something wrong with you that should be "fixed." If such statements recur, the belief will be strengthened to an extent not likely if such statements only occur as put-downs. Even if your partner told you he was wrong or did not mean to imply you were getting fat, you would still be likely to look at yourself differently. In contrast, you would be less likely to look at yourself differently had he yelled the comment or had said it only when he was in a bad mood.

This example highlights an important distinction that is difficult to describe. Psychological abuse may be obvious, overt, or subtle. Verbal aggression and controlling or dominating acts or statements are examples of obvious acts. Such acts are easily recognizable, readily coded and interpreted as harmful (Babcock et al., 1993; Jacobson et al., 1996; Lloyd, 1996; Vivian & Malone, 1997). An act of psychological abuse would be considered overt when an observer would be able to note the potential for harm and/or the woman would be able to describe the act or resulting feeling with relative ease. Some studies including obvious acts of verbal aggression or control also have measured behaviors which are less clear than obvious acts, but nonetheless overt. Acts may be considered subtle psychological abuse when it would be more difficult for an observer to see the potential for harm, the woman likely would have more difficulty describing the act and her resulting feelings, and/or the act could easily be done in loving and caring ways.

Obvious, overt, and subtle psychological abuse may all result in harm, but the type or locus of harm may differ. Obvious acts may result in anger at the partner and, over time, wear a woman down so she feels overwhelmed. This may be especially likely if the partner is also violent. Obvious acts are likely in distressed relationships and those on their way to the divorce court. Overt acts of psychological abuse may also result in anger and adversely affect a woman's perceptions of her relationship and her partner. Depending on the content of messages, overt acts may harm a woman's well-being in general or in specific areas. However, because subtle acts of psychological abuse are more intangible, they are likely to harm a woman's sense of self and her mental health and well-being more than her perceptions of the relationship and her partner.

Several years ago I conducted an exploratory study of 93 women who had been seriously psychologically abused (Ellington & Marshall, 1997; Marshall, 1994, 1996; Vitanza, Vogel, & Marshall, 1995). The extensive questionnaires and in-depth, semistructured interviews (pilot-tested with 14 women residing in battered women's shelters) were designed to learn more about 40 conceptually distinct categories of psychological abuse listed in Marshall (1994). Verbal aggression was not explored during interviews because it is relatively easy to observe and measure. Symbolic acts of aggression and threats of violence also were not explored during interviews because they are so closely associated with violence that they are usually assessed on the Conflict Tactics Scale (CTS) and the Severity of Violence Scales (Marshall, 1992a; 1992b). Women gave examples and described the effects of 20 to 40 types of psychological abuse during 4-hour interviews.

Transcripts of the interviews made it clear that even types of psychological abuse presumed to be obvious and clearly dominating (e.g., inducing physical debility, showing physical domination) were enacted in loving, joking, or playful ways as well as serious or threatening ways. Further, no male partner used only one style. Even the most violent men did not always inflict psychological abuse with an aggressive or dominating style. Men were often very gentle and loving when they enacted behaviors in the various categories of psychological abuse. Thus, the importance of assessing both subtle and overt psychological abuse was underscored.

As noted by O'Leary and Jouriles (1994), we must begin to disentangle the effects of psychological abuse and physical violence. In addition, sexual aggression is another harmful (Campbell, Miller, Cardwell, & Belknap, 1994; Kilpatrick, Best, Saunders, & Veronen, 1988) but understudied form of abuse in intimate relationships (Crowell & Burgess, 1996). This study expands Marshall (1996) examining the effects of subtle and overt psychological abuse, violence, and sexual aggression on women's emotional state and relationship perceptions. Violence, overt psychological abuse and/or sexual aggression by a male partner may affect women's self esteem (Arias, Lyons, & Street, 1997; Campbell et al., 1994; Cascardi & O'Leary, 1992; Follingstad, Rutledge, Berg, Hause, & Polek, 1990; Pipes & LeBov-Keeler, 1997; Sommers & Check, 1987; Stets, 1991), stress (Campbell, 1989; Cascardi & Vivian, 1995; Dutton, 1992; Marshall & Rose, 1990), health (Barnett & Hambeiger, 1992; Bergman & Brismar, 1991; Campbell, 1989; Cascardi, Langhrinsen, & Vivian, 1992; Riggs, Kilpatrick, & Resnick, 1992; Stuart & Campbell, 1989), emotional distress (Arias et al., 1997; Campbell, 1989; Campbell et al., 1994; Kilpatrick et al., 1988) and risk of suicide (Gondolf, Fisher, & McFerron, 1990; Kurz & Stark, 1989; Stuart &

Campbell, 1989). These effects harm women's emotional, cognitive, and physical state. These same types of abuse have been shown to affect perceptions women have about their relationship and their partner. For example, the quality of women's relationship (e.g., satisfaction, distress) is affected by violence and verbal aggression (Arias et al., 1997; Barnett & Hamberger, 1992; Frieze & McHugh, 1992; Kasian & Painter, 1992; O'Leary et al., 1994) as is women's fear (Kilpatrick et al., 1988; Jacobson, Gottman, Waltz, Rushe, Babcock, & Holtzworth-Munroe, 1994; Kelly & DeKeseredy, 1994; Saunders, 1996). In fact, even in nonviolent relationships, women fear their partner's verbal aggression (i.e., saying nasty things) as found by O'Leary and Jouriles (1994) in a re-analysis of an earlier study. If several obvious and subtle types of abuse are included in more studies, different types of effects may become evident.

Too little is known about subtle and overt forms of psychological abuse to make specific predictions but general trends were expected. Women are likely to recognize their partner's dominating, controlling, and aggressive behavior. Therefore, men's overt psychological abuse, violence, and sexual aggression were expected to affect the perceptions women had about their partner and relationship. Based on past research, these forms of aggression would also be likely to affect women's intrapersonal state. However, based on the social influence literature and the conceptualization described here, it was likely that subtle psychological abuse would have more of an effect on women's state and well-being than the other three forms of partner abuse. The exception was that perception of physical health would be more affected by violence and sexual aggression than by either type of psychological abuse because of the potential for physical harm from these acts.

This study is part of a longitudinal project examining the effects of psychological abuse, violence and sexual aggression on low-income women. Understanding these women is important for several reasons. Unless income is attenuated, ethnicity and socioeconomic status are likely to be confounded. In general, poverty is associated with poor physical and mental health. These effects may be exacerbated if women's vulnerability is increased by any type of partner abuse. In addition, women of lower socioeconomic status are more at risk than middle-class women for domestic violence (Mihalic & Elliott, 1997; Zawitz, 1994) and harm (Stuart & Campbell, 1989), homelessness (Brice-Baker, 1994; Shinn, Knickman, & Weitzman, 1991; Wood, Valdez, Hayashi, & Shen, 1990) and killing their partner (Roberts, 1996) as a result of domestic violence. Further, women who sustain partner violence use medical and other resources more than those in nonviolent relationships (Bergman & Brismar, 1991; Cascardi et al., 1992), especially if they are poor (McClosky, 1996). Low-income women must rely on public resources which may or may not be responsive to their needs which result from their partner's behavior (Kurz & Stark, 1989). The ultimate goal of the larger study is to identify points at which intervention could be of most benefit to women and to identify likely resources that could provide effective, ethnically appropriate intervention. Therefore, it was necessary to have a broad-based sample of ethnically diverse women who had and had not sustained violence from their partner at the beginning of the study.

METHOD

Sample

The data reported here are from the first of seven waves of interviews in a longitudinal study. Women were recruited through newspaper articles, personal encounters (e.g., on the street, in businesses, at health fairs or their homes), flyers (in businesses, libraries, churches), and by referral from participants over the course of 20 months. This study, Project HOW: Health Outcomes of Women, was described as focusing on factors that harm and help women's health. To schedule an interview, women had to be in a long-term (at least 1 year) heterosexual relationship, between the ages of 20 and 47 years, and live within 175% of poverty or be receiving public aid. The age range was chosen to correspond to census categories and to encompass ages at which relationship violence may increase and decrease. The purpose of limiting household income was to keep ethnicity from being confounded with class and to ensure that most women in the study would need to rely on public resources for help. Federal poverty tables were used to cross-tabulate income from work and number of people in the household unless women were receiving Aid to Families with Dependent Children (AFDC), food stamps, or a rent subsidy.[1] There was no requirement regarding the presence or absence of violence or any other type of abuse.

Of the 998 women who began the first interview, 164 were found not to qualify. During the interviews it was often discovered that their relationship was not ongoing with close contact (e.g., their partner was in prison, or they were married but separated). These interviews were not completed. The second primary reason for disqualification was income. Women were asked about their household income and the number of people supported by that income during screening, but many apparently determined the amount more exactly before their interview. Consequently, they reported more money during interviews than during screening. These women were dropped after their interview. All women were paid $15 in cash and received a tote bag and T-shirt with the project logo.

Of the 834 women in the study, 303 (36.3%) were African Americans, 271 (32.5%) were Euro-Americans, and 260 (31.2%) were Mexican Americans. The mean age of women was 32.81 years. Participants were seriously dating (24.1%), cohabiting (12.8%), in a self-defined common-law marriage (21.7%), or legally married (41.4%) to their partner. The duration of these relationships ranged from 1 to 33 years ($M = 7.70$ years).

Instruments

Women were interviewed in one of two storefront offices in the geographical area targeted for the study. The mean length of the structured interviews was 2.5 hours. Trained undergraduate females conducted the interviews. The results reported here are from measures of psychological abuse, physical and sexual aggression by women's partner, women's personal characteristics and emotional state at the time of the interview, and factors reflective of and related to their relationship. The state and relationship measures chosen for this study assessed constructs likely to affect women's overall sense of well-being. Pilot testing with a similar population resulted in revising, simplifying wording, and modifying ratings scales.

Violence and Sexual Aggression. The Severity of Violence Against Women Scale (SVAWS; Marshall, 1992a) was used to assess acts of violence and sexual aggression women sustained from their partner. Nineteen of the 46 items assess threats of violence which were not used in this study because of the high correlation ($r = .85$) with acts of violence. Twenty-one items assessed physical aggression, ranging from relatively minor acts (e.g., holding women down, pinning them in place, grabbing suddenly or forcefully), through acts classified as mild and moderate, to severe acts which could cause serious injury or death (e.g., use of a club-like object, beat up). Six items measured sexual aggression by the partner (e.g., physically forced to have sex, made to have anal sex against her will). Women reported the perceived number of times their partner had done each act during their entire relationship on 6-point rating scales (0 = never, 1 = once, 5 = a great many times). The internal consistency of the violence ($\alpha = .95$) and sexual aggression ($\alpha = .85$) scales were quite high.

Psychological Abuse. My earlier study showed that items to measure both overt and subtle psychological abuse must allow enactment to occur with a broad range of styles and message content areas (Marshall, 1994, 1996). Items were written so women would recognize the act whether it was done in a loving style (e.g., I love you so much that I hate to see you so upset by your family; it's too bad you see them so often), a dominating or controlling style, and/or a teasing or joking style. This was done with more success for some items (e.g., made you feel guilty) than others (e.g., yell at you). In addition, the content of items representing a partner's messages had to be less specific than items used in past research to allow relevance to a broad range of women.

Women were told "Both men and women do these kinds of things, but this time we want your partner's behavior. Some things may be nice and others may be unpleasant. Men may do these acts in a loving way, a joking way, or a serious way." Women rated the 184 items on 10-point frequency scales anchored by "never" and "almost daily." The elimination of items began when results from about two-thirds of the sample were available. It was important to have broadly relevant scales that were independent of whether or not women were battered, but it was also important to have items that were neither too common nor too uncommon. Consequently, items that were endorsed by more than about half the women were eliminated as were those endorsed by fewer than 15%. Used here are the initial versions of the Men's Psychological-Harm and Abuse in Relationships Measure-Overt scales and -Subtle scales (MP-HARM-O and MP-HARM-S; Marshall & Guarnaccia, 1998).

For present purposes, factor analysis with orthogonal rotation was conducted on the 35 items representing overt and the 33 items representing subtle psychological abuse. The number of factors to use for each scale (overt and subtle) was determined by examination of the eigen values, scree plots, and cross-loads. In addition to the empirical criteria (i.e., a gap in eigen value, flattening of the scree plot, and less than 2.5% of the variance accounted for by a factor), the factors were also examined for conceptual logic. (Results of the factor analyses are available from the author.) Representative items for the factors are listed in Table 1.

Factor analysis was first conducted on the 35 items indicative of overt psychological abuse. Although four items cross-loaded, the four factor solution resulted in interpretable, completely uncorrelated factors ($r = .00$). Factor 1, Dominate, consisted of 17 items representing overt attempts to dominate and control a woman. This factor accounted for 59.8% of the variance. Factor 2, Indifference, consisted of 5 items and accounted for 3.5% of the variance. Factor 3, Monitor, consisted of 6 items and accounted for 3% of the variance. Factor 4, Discredit, consisted of 7 items and accounted for 2.6% of the variance. The factor scores, which together accounted for 69% of the total variance, were used in analyses.

Factor analysis was then conducted on the 33 items representing subtle acts of psychological abuse. The three-factor solution was most clearly interpretable although two items cross-loaded. Factor 1, Undermine, consisted of 12 items and accounted for 61.4% of the variance. Factor 2, Discount, consisted of 11 items and accounted for 3.3% of the variance.

Factor 3, Isolate, consisted of 10 items and accounted for 3% of the variance. The factor scores, which together accounted for 67.7% of the total variance, were used in analyses.

TABLE 1.   Examples of Abbreviated Psychological Abuse Items

Overt Psychological Abuse

Dominate

    try to get you to say you were wrong even if you think you were right

    tell you something he did was your fault

    remind you of times he was right and you were wrong

    try to get you to apologize for something that wasn't your fault

    use an offensive or hurtful tone

    get angry or hurt if you talk about him or your relationship

    make you feel like nothing you say will have an effect

    make you feel like you can't keep up with changes in what he wants

Indifference

    act like you don't matter

    ignore you

    use money you need or keep money from you when you need it

    avoid you

Monitor

    check to see if you're doing what you said you would be doing

    check up on you

    act like he doesn't believe you

    try to keep you from seeing friends or family

Discredit

    tell others you have emotional problems or are crazy

    tell you friends or family don't care about you

    tell you what he likes about you then get upset about the same thing

    tell others things that make you look bad

Subtle Psychological Abuse

Undermine

    make you worry about your physical health and well-being

    make you worry about whether you could take care of yourself

    make you worry about your emotional health and well-being

    make you feel ashamed of yourself

    get you to question yourself, making you feel insecure and less confident

    make you feel guilty about something you have or haven't done

    say his hurtful actions were good for you or will make you a better person

(Continued)

TABLE 1.   Examples of Abbreviated Psychological Abuse Items (Continued)

Discount

act secretive or try to keep things from you

do things that make you feel small, less than what you were

discourage from interests he is not part of

do or say something that harms your self-respect or pride in yourself

act like you can do what you want then become upset if you do

act like there is something wrong with you mentally/emotionally

Isolate

discourage you from talking to his family, friends, or people he knows

make it difficult to go somewhere or talk to someone

point out he is the only one who really understands you

discourage you from having your own friends

keep you from having time for yourself

try to keep you from showing feelings

Women's State. The measures used to assess women's state covered a range of constructs related to well-being. Self-esteem was measured with Rosenberg's (1965) 10-item scale. This is the most widely used brief instrument available with adequate comparative data for ethnically diverse women. Women rated the accuracy of statements on 7-point scales anchored by "completely false," "I'm never like this" to "completely true," "exactly like me." Despite the modification in ratings, the scale was internally consistent ($\alpha = .83$).

Cohen, Kamarck, and Mermelstein's (1983) 14-item measure assessed how well women were handling stress. This is a general measure of perceived stress, with items reflecting difficulty in coping (e.g., felt nervous and stressed; been upset because of something that happened unexpectedly; felt difficulties were piling up so high that you could not overcome them). Responses were made on 7-point scales ranging from never (1) through about half the time (4) to always (7). Internal consistency was adequate ($\alpha = .76$).

Perception of physical health was measured with a slightly modified item developed by Hays, Sherbourne, and Mazel (1993). Women were asked to "Rate your overall quality of life in terms of your health. A zero is the worst possible and 10 is the best possible health quality of life." The item was in a section of the interview devoted to physical health (e.g., seeing a physician, health insurance, health conditions).

The Symptom Checklist 90 (Derogatis, Lipman, & Covi, 1973) assessed women's overall emotional distress. Both the SCL90 and SCL90-R are widely used with clinical and nonclinical samples. Women rated how much they had been bothered by each symptom during the past month on 5-point scales (not at all, a little bit, moderately, quite a bit, extremely). Internal consistency on the global distress scale was high ($\alpha = .98$).

Battered women may be at risk for suicide so a measure of severe depression or suicidal ideation was needed. Goldberg and Hillier's (1979) General Health Questionnaire is a multidimensional measure of emotional health. Five items reflecting severe depression and suicidal ideation were modified because the measure was developed for use with British samples. The items asked how often women felt that life is entirely hopeless; felt that life isn't worth living; thought of the possibility that you might do away with yourself; found yourself wishing you were dead and away from it all; found that the idea of taking your own life kept coming into your mind. Items were rated on 7-point scales ranging from never (1) through about half the time (4) to always (7). The scale was internally consistent ($\alpha = .92$).

Relationship-Related Measures. Two items measured women's fear of their partner's violence. Women were asked how many times they were afraid they might be seriously injured and afraid they might be killed using the same 6-point rating scale as used for the SVAWS (never to a great many times). Only 707 women were asked these questions. (Some early interviewers did not ask these questions unless women had been injured by their partner but the questions were supposed to be asked of every woman who had sustained any threat or act of violence.) This index had strong internal consistency ($\alpha = .88$).

Cloven and Roloff (1991) found that rumination about relationship conflicts was associated with the severity of the conflicts. (In turn, rumination has been associated with depression according to Nolen-Hoeksema, 1987.) A 5-item measure assessing women's rumination about problems in their relationship and with their partner was based on Cloven and Roloff's measure of mulling. The items assessed how much women thought about those problems; worried about those problems; how thoughts of those problems affected their daily activities; amount of effort they put into examining or evaluating those problems; and time they spent considering and thinking about those problems. The 7-point rating scale was anchored by "not at all" and "extremely much." This scale also showed strong internal consistency ($\alpha = .88$).

The measure of marital well-being used here (Acitelli, Douvan, & Veroff, 1989) has been used longitudinally with an ethnically diverse sample (Acitelli, Douvan, & Veroff, 1997; Crohan & Veroff, 1989; Hatchett, Veroff, & Douvan, 1995). The item addressing overall satisfaction was replaced with an item measuring stability. The six items (Taking things together, how happy is your relationship; When you think about your relationship, what each of you puts into it and gets out of it, how happy do you feel; How certain are you that you will be together one year from now; What about 5 years from now; How stable is your relationship; In the past 6 months, how often have you considered leaving him) were rated on 7-point scales ("not at all or never" to "completely or extremely often"). This brief scale was internally consistent ($\alpha = .92$).

RESULTS[2]

Many community samples contain few women who are battered to a degree comparable to those who enter shelters. To obtain a profile for this sample, the SVAWS violence subscales were used to classify women based on the most serious act of violence they had sustained from their partner. Table 2 shows a nearly equal proportion of women were with completely nonviolent partners as were with men who had inflicted severe, potentially life-threatening violence. Just under a third of the sample were at each extreme. The table also shows the mean frequency score (i.e., the sum of the 20 acts of violence) associated with each level of violence.

First, zero order correlations were calculated among the types of abuse, although multiple regression procedures are robust for multicollinearity. (Correlations nearing .80 may be acceptable in samples this large; Berry & Feldman, 1985.) Table 3 shows these correlations. Most correlations were less than .40. Only two correlations are moderately high;

TABLE 2. Distribution by Worst Act of Violence Sustained

	Percent in category	Range of scores	Mean score
No violent acts	31.5		
Acts of minor violence	16.2	1 to 14	2.27
Acts of mild violence	10.4	1 to 18	5.39
Acts of moderate violence	10.8	1 to 32	6.80
Acts of severe violence	31.1	1 to 99	21.05

TABLE 3. Correlations Among Predictor Variables

					Psychological Abuse			
Aggression					Overt		Subtle	
	1	2	3	4	5	6	7	8
1. violent acts								
2. sexual aggression	.55							
3. overt-Dominate	.29	.23						
4. overt-Indifference	.36	.26	..					
5. overt-Monitor	.26	.24	..	..				
6. overt-Discredit	.25	.29	..	..	..			
7. subtle-Undermine	.30	.30	.35	.27	..	.36		
8. subtle-Discount	.35	.25	.36	.56	.31	..	..	
9. subtle-Isolate	.35	.33	.25	..	.38	.46	..	..

The *n* for each correlation ranged between 822 and 834. Correlations are *p* < .000.

between overt Factor 2, Indifference, and subtle Factor 2, Discount, and between violence and sexual aggression. Then 9 multiple regressions were calculated allowing each type of abuse to enter in order of importance to explain the variance in women's state (self-esteem, stress, health quality, emotional distress, severe depression and suicidal ideation) and relationship (fear, rumination about problems, quality, duration) well-being. Abuse consisted of direct aggression (violence, sexual aggression), the overt (dominate, being indifferent, monitor, discredit) and subtle (undermine, discount, isolate) psychological abuse factors. Explanatory variables are reported in order of appearance.

The subtle psychological abuse factors emerged most often to explain the variance in women's state. Subtle Undermining (beta = −.357), Discounting (beta = −.126), and Isolation (beta = −.149) combined with overt Indifference (beta = −.098) to help explain women's self-esteem, $R = .46$, $p < .0001$. Subtle Undermining (beta = −.199), Discounting (beta = −.141), and Isolating (beta = −.128) helped explain health quality of life in this sample, $R = .27$, p < .0001. Similarly, subtle Undermining (beta = .388), Isolation (beta = .266), and Discounting (beta = .216) combined with overt Monitoring (beta = .073) emerged for global emotional distress, $R = .55$, p $< .0001$. Women's severe depression and suicidal ideation score was partially explained by subtle Undermining (beta $= .308$), Isolation (beta $= .170$) and Discounting (beta $= .117$) as well as sexual aggression (beta $= .077$) by their partner, $R = .41, p < .0001$. In contrast, overtly Dominating (beta $= .250$), Indifference (beta $= .225$), Discrediting (beta $= .105$), and Monitoring (beta $= .109$) acts as well as subtle Undermining (beta $= .078$) were significant predictors of women's stress, $R = .41, p < .0001$.

Although overt psychological abuse was expected to be more important for relationship variables, subtle acts again appeared to have more effect. Much of the variance in the index representing women's fear of severe injury or death at the hands of their partner was explained by men's violence (beta $= .528$) with significant contributions by overt Monitoring (beta $= .090$) and subtle Undermining (beta $= .117$), Isolation (beta $= .100$), and Discounting (beta $= .076$), $R = .67, p < .0001$. Women ruminated about problems as their partner subtly Undermined (beta $= .314$), Discounted (beta $= .290$), and Isolated (beta $= .214$) them, $R = .48, p < .0001$. Relationship quality was partially explained by subtle Discounting (beta $= -.428$), Isolation (beta $= -.236$), and Undermining (beta $= -.204$) as well as overt Indifference (beta $= -.085$) and violence (beta $= -.080$), $R = .63, p < .0001$. Finally, the duration of women's relationship was partially explained by overt Indifference (beta $= .131$), less subtle Isolation (beta $= -.168$), overtly Dominating acts (beta $= .102$) and sexual aggression (beta $= .095$), $R = .24$, p $< .0001$.

Additional Analyses

Although the various types of psychological abuse were expected to make significant contributions in the regression equations, violence and sexual aggression were expected to emerge much more often and be more important than was found. Further, subtle psychological abuse emerged much more consistently than overt psychological abuse which conflicts with the extant literature. Consequently, a series of hierarchical regression equations was calculated to confirm that subtle psychological abuse was, indeed, as important as it appeared.

In the first series of equations, men's violence and sexual aggression were entered at Step 1. The four types of overt psychological abuse were entered at Step 2 before the three types of subtle psychological abuse were entered at Step 3. This procedure stacks the deck against subtle psychological abuse. If subtle psychological abuse accounted for a significant amount of the variance even after controlling for men's direct aggression and overt psychological abuse, it would support the notion that acts which cannot be readily identified as harmful do indeed take their toll on women. In the second series of equations, the subtle psychological abuse factors were entered at Step 1, followed by overt psychological abuse at Step 2. Finally, men's direct aggression (violence and sexual aggression) was entered at Step 3.

In most community samples, violence scores would be less likely than more normally distributed variables (in this case overt and subtle psychological abuse) to make a significant contribution using these hierarchical procedures. This is because most of the violence in such samples is relatively minor with relatively low scores. Table 2 showed that was not an issue for this sample because over 30% had sustained severe, potentially life-threatening violence. The level of violence sustained by so many women in this study is likely similar to samples drawn from police reports, emergency rooms, and shelters. Moreover, all women were relatively poor when their data were collected. That, also, suggests that a reasonably large proportion is, in several ways, similar to samples of identified battered women.

The purpose of the hierarchical regressions was to confirm the results which indicated that subtle psychological abuse was generally more harmful than either overt psychological abuse or direct aggression. On the other hand, the procedures must be considered exploratory because this was the first study to examine all these different types of partner abuse together in such a systematic way. Consequently, the results are important to develop theory and hypotheses. As with Jacobson et al. (1996), alpha was not adjusted for the 18 regression equations.

To facilitate comparisons, the results from both series are presented side by side in Table 4. First, in eight of the nine equations the subtle psychological abuse factors made a small but significant contribution even when they were entered last, after the other types of abuse. Despite the appearance that violence and sexual aggression made major contributions to the state and relationship variables in the first series (on the left), these effects were sufficiently strong to make a significant contribution in only 2 (fear and relationship duration) of the 9 equations when they were entered last (on the right). The R at Step 1 was higher on the right side of the table when subtle abuse was entered, except in the equations for fear. Further, in all but one instance overt psychological abuse made a significant unique contribution when scores were entered after men's direct aggression, but nonsignificant in four of the nine equations when it followed subtle psychological abuse.

TABLE 4. Hierarchical Regression

Variables Entered	R	R^2chg	pchg	Variables Entered	R	R^2chg	pchg
Self-Esteem							
Step 1 Aggression	.25	.064	.0001	Step 1 Subtle	.45	.202	.0001
Step 2 Overt	.41	.105	.0001	Step 2 Overt	.46	.010	.05
Step 3 Subtle	.46	.047	.0001	Step 3 Aggression	.47	.004	ns
Stress							
Step 1 Aggression	.29	.083	.0001	Step 1 Subtle	.41	.169	.0001
Step 2 Overt	.41	.087	.0001	Step 2 Overt	.42	.007	ns
Step 3 Subtle	.42	.008	.05	Step 3 Aggression	.42	.003	ns
Health Quality of Life							
Step 1 Aggression	.19	.037	.0001	Step 1 Subtle	.27	.075	.0001
Step 2 Overt	.26	.030	.0001	Step 2 Overt	.28	.004	ns
Step 3 Subtle	.28	.013	.01	Step 3 Aggression	.28	.001	ns
Global Emotional Distress							
Step 1 Aggression	.36	.130	.0001	Step 1 Subtle	.54	.295	.0001
Step 2 Overt	.53	.151	.0001	Step 2 Overt	.55	.008	ns
Step 3 Subtle	.55	.023	.0001	Step 3 Aggression	.55	.002	ns

(Continued)

TABLE 4. Hierarchical Regression (Continued)

Severe Depression and Suicidal Ideation							
Step 1 Aggression	.30	.089	.0001	Step 1 Subtle	.41	.166	.0001
Step 2 Overt	.40	.071	.0001	Step 2 Overt	.42	.011	.03
Step 3 Subtle	.43	.022	.0001	Step 3 Aggression	.43	.005	ns
Fear of Severe Injury or Death							
Step 1 Aggression	.64	.414	.0001	Step 1 Subtle	.49	.243	.0001
Step 2 Overt	.66	.028	.0001	Step 2 Overt	.51	.013	.04
Step 3 Subtle	.67	.003	ns	Step 3 Aggression	.67	.189	.0001
Rumination About Relationship and Partner							
Step 1 Aggression	.30	.088	.0001	Step 1 Subtle	.48	.228	.0001
Step 2 Overt	.47	.136	.0001	Step 2 Overt	.48	.006	ns
Step 3 Subtle	.48	.009	.03	Step 3 Aggression	.48	.000	ns
Relationship Quality							
Step 1 Aggression	.42	.180	.0001	Step 1 Subtle	.62	.386	.0001
Step 2 Overt	.62	.207	.0001	Step 2 Overt	.63	.012	.003
Step 3 Subtle	.63	.016	.0001	Step 3 Aggression	.63	.004	ns
Relationship Duration							
Step 1 Aggression	.10	.011	.02	Step 1 Subtle	.17	.029	.0001
Step 2 Overt	.25	.050	.0001	Step 2 Overt	.24	.028	.0001
Step 3 Subtle	.26	.009	.05	Step 3 Aggression	.27	.013	.004

Aggression consists of violence and sexual aggression scores. Overt consists of the four factor scores (Dominate, Indifference, Monitor, Discredit) for overt psychological abuse. Subtle consists of the three factor scores (Undermine, Discount, Isolate) for subtle psychological abuse.

DISCUSSION

The results clearly show that an expanded view of psychological abuse is warranted. Surprisingly, the subtle forms of psychological abuse had an effect more frequently than overt psychological abuse, violence, or sexual aggression, regardless of whether intrapersonal or relationship measures were being examined.

As dictated by my approach to psychological abuse, there was little association between acts of physical or sexual aggression and psychological abuse. The correlations were generally low. The highest correlations between direct aggression and psychological abuse was only .36 (physical violence and overt indifference). The correlations suggest that suffering one form of abuse from a partner will not necessarily increase the likelihood of sustaining other forms of abuse. However, other researchers have found significant and sizable correlations between psychological and physical abuse (Straus et al., 1996).

Overall, the three types of subtle psychological abuse emerged more often to predict outcomes than did the four types of overt psychological abuse, violence, and sexual aggression. Even when the dependent variable was women's fear of injury or death as a result of their partner's violence, subtle and overt psychological abuse made independent contributions. The results of the two series of hierarchical multiple regression were even more impressive. Not only did subtle psychological abuse account for significant variance after controlling for men's violence, sexual aggression and overt psychological abuse, but it almost completely eliminated the effects of the other types of abuse when it was entered first on most measures.

It is not illogical that subtle psychological abuse would have broad effects. Enactment of the relevant items in Table 1 would likely cause a woman to feel uncertain about herself, unimportant and tentative during interactions with others. If uncertainty or discrepancies in a woman's sense of self were created or reinforced, the effects could be pervasive (Trope & Liberman, 1996). The woman may begin to view herself differently, for example, by mistrusting her perceptions. Processes (e.g., attributions, rumination, behavior change, expectancy effects) would be set in motion which are likely to result in confirming the problematic self-perceptions. Thus, many aspects of women's life could be affected by a partner who simply raised issues that created or reinforced a woman's personal vulnerabilities.

Of all the types of abuse, a man subtly undermining his partner emerged as a strong predictor most consistently. Apparently, having one's sense of self weakened results in the broadest effects. A sense of self is central to factors associated with personal well-being and is important for judgments about one's relationship. It is likely that most aspects of life could be affected if a woman did not believe in herself or trust her own perceptions. This type of psychological abuse always emerged in the logical direction.

Having been discounted or subtly isolated, the second and third subtle psychological abuse factors also emerged more often than overt psychological abuse or direct aggression for both women's state and relationship. When they were important, their contribution was in the logical direction. A partner enacting behaviors represented by the discount subscale could make a woman feel unimportant. If a woman felt insignificant, especially in her primary relationship, it could be very difficult for her to believe she was important in other parts of her own life or in the lives of others.

It should be noted that the subtle factor isolation is somewhat different than usually discussed in the partner violence literature. Most investigators have tended to conceptualize isolation as being done in very obvious ways. It has been thought of as a batterer keeping his partner away from others or making it difficult for her to communicate with others (e.g., restricting her use of a car or the telephone). Isolation in this study is more akin to alienation or psychological distance from others and even from oneself (e.g., somehow keep you from having time for yourself). Sustaining this type of subtle psychological abuse could result in a woman feeling as if she were alone or different from others even if she has a wide circle of friends. It could also keep her from enjoying the small, private pleasures most women enjoy (e.g., taking a long, hot bath).

The very nature of subtle psychological abuse would make it difficult to terminate and to treat, especially if acts appeared to be done out of love and concern for the woman rather than aggressively for purposes of control. It would be very difficult for both the woman and her therapist to recognize either that these acts were occurring or that these acts were causing emotional harm directly or through other intrapersonal or interpersonal processes. It may be that women who have endured subtle psychological abuse often seek therapy for symptoms caused by the abuse, but the likelihood that a partner's acts would be implicated as possible causal factors by the woman or her therapist is small. Further, from a social influence perspective, the woman would be unable to gain or maintain psychological and emotional well-being as long as her partner inflicted the subtle abuse.

Altogether, the types of overt psychological abuse also emerged more frequently than violence and sexual aggression. At first glance, it is difficult to imagine overt psychological abuse being done in a loving way, but both forms (i.e., subtle and overt) conceivably could be done in loving, joking, serious, and aggressive ways, except perhaps indifference. Thus, these acts may also be difficult to recognize but if alert to the possibility, the potential for harm inherent in the acts could be recognized by an observer or the woman herself. It is this characteristic of acts that make the label overt psychological abuse appropriate. In comparison to subtle acts, with overt acts it would be relatively easy to see the partner's behavior as one cause of associated symptoms.

Of the different types of overt abuse, monitoring and indifference emerged more often than dominating and discrediting. Overt types of psychological abuse were not more likely to be associated with relationship variables than with women's current physical and emotional state. Overall, overt psychological abuse may have the most effect indirectly by increasing women's perceived stress or decreasing their confidence in handling stressful events. Stress, then, may affect other aspects of women's well-being.

The most surprising finding for overt psychological abuse was the relatively little impact of the dominating factor, given its centrality in the partner violence literature. It only emerged twice. Both dominating and monitoring can be thought of as controlling behaviors, especially if done in serious or aggressive ways. Therefore, these factors are most similar to the way psychological abuse is usually addressed in the literature. There are several intriguing possibilities.

If dominating and monitoring actually have so little direct impact on women, programs and therapy for batterers and battered women may be focusing too much time and effort on something that is comparatively benign. It may be that most women are able to dismiss these types of acts as something about their partner that they have to put up with. In this case, men's behavior would be attributed to the men, not to women's own personality or behavior. For some women it may not be too bothersome, whereas it may eventually cause others to terminate the relationship. Thus, one reason why these controlling types of psychological abuse had so little effect could be that most women tend to leave men who dominate them or monitor their behavior.

On the other hand, with only four types of overt psychological abuse measured in this study, other overt and obvious acts of dominance or control are not precluded from having adverse effects on women. It must be remembered that the acts were not necessarily done in an aggressive, hostile, or possessive way. The partners of some women may enact the behaviors in a style or with specific messages that are congruent with traditional research and treatment, whereas others may enact the behaviors in very different ways. Alternatively, dominating or controlling acts may have serious effects only in the presence of a specific combination of factors in the relationship. Before concluding that controlling acts are not particularly harmful, research must combine the traditional approach to psychological abuse with the approach taken here.

There was a moderate correlation between overt indifference and subtle discounting. Examination of the items in Table 1 shows that both factors have elements of withdrawal or interpersonal distance. The overlap may reflect an underlying category of psychological abuse, perhaps withdrawal or rejection (Marshall, 1994). On the other hand, the relationship is not strong. It is possible that overt indifference occurs in most relationships that are in the process of dissolution as well as those that are psychologically abusive or distressed. In contrast, subtle discounting may be less likely to occur in dissolving relationships because there is also an element of commitment. For example, outside interests may be encouraged, rather than discouraged, in withdrawing, distancing, or divorcing couples.

The results are relative, not absolute. It is not that overt psychological abuse and direct aggression had little effect. Rather, in comparison to the effects of subtle psychological abuse, the effects of overt psychological abuse as well as violence and sexual aggression are relatively less likely and often weaker. Examination of the left side of Table 4 shows that overt psychological abuse significantly contributes to the explanation of the measures used in this study. Moreover, the unique contribution is often relatively large, even after the effects of direct aggression are controlled. Thus, even in the presence of direct aggression, overt psychological abuse is relatively harmful. In contrast, the right side of the table shows that overt psychological abuse makes relatively little contribution when the effects of subtle psychological abuse are controlled. Thus, in the presence of subtle psychological abuse, overt psychological abuse may do relatively little harm.

Neither violence nor sexual aggression contributed as much to the outcome measures as expected, but they were not unimportant. When either emerged with a significant contribution, its value usually decreased when any form of psychological abuse entered the equations. The primary (and logical) exception was on women's fear for their physical well-being. These results and the hierarchical procedures support anecdotal evidence from battered women who have said the psychological abuse was worse than the violence. The difference is that the most harmful psychological abuse was not of the dominating and controlling type that has been assumed. However, more research including the different forms of abuse is needed before conclusions can be drawn about these issues.

Because all women lived below or near the federal poverty level, the results may not generalize to women of higher economic status. Due to economic realities, more women in this study than in other studies may have too few alternatives to remaining with an abusive man. They, therefore, may be forced to make a stronger effort to effectively cope with abuse than would women with more economic resources. For example, it could be that violence and sexual aggression so rarely had an effect because these women were highly motivated to protect themselves from the harmful effects in order to remain with their partner for economic reasons. However, the likelihood that women's motivation to remain in their relationship could account for the relative lack of effect of obvious abuse (overt psychological abuse, violence, and sexual aggression) in comparison to subtle forms of abuse is not greater for two reasons. First, women who live in or close to poverty may be slightly better off financially in terms of eligibility for various types of public aid if they do not have a partner. (If so, this could change after all welfare reforms are fully implemented.) In addition, women willing to report domestic violence are exempt from some of the welfare reform limitations. Therefore, low-income women may be less motivated to stay with an abusive man than middle-class women whose economic status would decrease by loss of a partner's income. The second reason relates to the complexity of ties in the relationship which may be reflected in women's choice of terms for their relationship. Although 63% were married (common-law and legal), 24% of the sample were only dating their partner. Of the 288 women who were cohabiting, 37% did not consider themselves to be in a common-law marriage. There is no reason to believe women in this study would be more or less motivated to remain in a relationship than other samples with women whose relationships range from dating to married.

In sum, the results of this study underscore two major points. First, conceptualization of psychological abuse should be expanded beyond the predominante approach which associates emotional or psychological abuse too closely with obviously dominating and controlling acts such as physical violence. Second, it is possible, indeed important, to differentiate obvious, overt, and subtle acts of psychological abuse. All three forms are harmful and can be measured.

NOTES

[1]Reporting the range of income would be misleading because determination of poverty status was based on federal tables comparing income and number of people in the household who depend on that income. During screening, the cutoff for income from work was 175%, hoping to obtain a sample living below 200% of poverty. Poverty status based on work alone ranged from 0% of the federal poverty level to 338% (M = 91.22%, Med = 93%). This was over 200% because women were also eligible if they received aid designed to alleviate poverty. Later it was discovered that official designations of poverty must include the cash value of public aid (e.g., food stamps, child care). When aid was included, calculations could be made for 817 women who knew the cash value of their aid and both partners' income from work if they were cohabiting. The cash value of aid is often not known by recipients for several reasons (e.g., food stamps are electronically updated monthly, child care is valued differently depending on the program providing it, with a rent subsidy women know what they pay rather than the value of their home). Using this procedure, poverty status ranged from 0% to 399% (M = 106.97%, Med = 106%). All but two women were receiving at least one type of aid. (The woman who was least poor at 399% of poverty received both Medicaid and food stamps.) In addition, women who had insufficient data with which to calculate poverty status all received aid. Thus, all women were very poor or among the most disadvantaged of the "working poor" which would likely cause them to rely on free public and private services.

[2]Space prohibits examination of the pattern of results for each racial/ethnic group. Although there were only minor group differences on some independent and dependent variables used in this study, different variables emerged as important in regression equations calculated within each group. However, the general pattern was the same, with subtle psychological abuse having more impact than overt psychological abuse or direct aggression. These similarities and differences will be reported in a later article.

REFERENCES

Acitelli, L. K., Douvan, E., & Veroff, J. (1989). *Perceptions of self and spouse during marital conflict.* Presented at the International Conference on Personal Relationships. University of Iowa, Iowa City.

Acitelli, L. K., Douvan, E., & Veroff, J. (1997). The changing influence of interpersonal perceptions on marital well-being among black and white couples. *Journal of Social and Personal Relationships, 14,* 291–304.

Arias, I., Lyons, C. M., & Street, A. E. (1997). Individual and marital consequences of victimization: Moderating effects of relationship efficacy and spouse support. *Journal of Family Violence, 12,* 193–210.

Babcock, J. C., Waltz, J., Jacobson, N. S., & Gottman, J. M. (1993). Power and violence: The relation between communication patterns, power discrepancies, and domestic violence. *Journal of Consulting and Clinical Psychology, 61,* 40–50.

Barnett, O., & Hamberger, L. (1992). The assessment of maritally violent men on the California Psychological Inventory. *Violence and Victims, 7,* 15–28.

Bergman, B., & Brismar, B. (1991). A 5-year follow-up study of 117 battered women. *American Journal of Public Health, 81,* 1486–1489.

Berry, W. D., & Feldman, S. (1985). *Multiple regression in practice.* Newbury Park, CA: Sage.

Brice-Baker, J. R. (1994). Domestic violence in African-American and African-Caribbean families. *Journal of Distress and the Homeless, 3,* 23–38.

Campbell, J. C. (1989). Women's response to sexual abuse in intimate relationships. *Health Care for Women International, 10,* 335–346.

Campbell, J. C., Miller, P., Cardwell, M. M., & Belknap, R. A. (1994). Relationship status of battered women over time. *Journal of Family Violence, 9,* 99–111.

Cascardi, M., Langhrinsen, J.; & Vivian, D. (1992). Marital aggression: Impact, injury, and health correlates for husbands and wives. *Archives of Internal Medicine, 152,* 1178–84.

Cascardi, M., & O'Leary, K. D. (1992). Depressive symptomatology, self-esteem and self-blame in battered women. *Journal of Family Violence, 7,* 249–259.

Cascardi, M., & Vivian, D. (1995). Context for specific episodes of marital violence: Gender and severity of violence differences. *Journal of Family Violence, 10,* 265–293.

Cloven, D. H. & Roloff, M. E. (1991). *Sense-making activities and interpersonal conflict: Communicative cures for the mulling blues.* Western Journal of Speech Communication, 55, 134–158.

Cohen, S., Kamarck, T., & Mermelstein, R. (1983). A global measure of perceived stress. *Journal of Health and Social Behavior, 24,* 385–396.

Crohan, S. E., & Veroff, J. (1989). Dimensions of marital well-being among white and black newlyweds. *Journal of Marriage and the Family, 51,* 373–383.

Crowell, N. A., & Burgess, A. W. (1996). *Understanding violence against women.* Washington, DC: National Academy Press.

Derogatis, L. R., Lipman, R. S., & Covi, L. (1973). SCL-90: An outpatient psychiatric rating scale-preliminary report. *Psychopharmacology Bulletin, 9,* 13–28.

Dutton, M. A. (1992). Assessment and treatment of post-traumatic stress disorder among battered women. In D. W. Foy (Ed.), *Treating post-traumatic stress disorder: Cognitive behavioral strategies* (pp. 69–97). New York: Guilford Press.

Ellington, J. E., & Marshall, L. L. (1997). Gender role perceptions of women in abusive relationships. *Sex Roles, 36,* 349–369.

Follingstad, D. R., Rutledge, L. L., Berg, B. J., Hause, E. S., & Polek, D. S. (1990). The role of emotional abuse in physically abusive relationships. *Journal of Family Violence, 5,* 107–120.

Frieze, I. H., & McHugh, M. C. (1992). Power and influence strategies in violent and nonviolent marriages. *Psychology of Women Quarterly, 16,* 449–465.

Goldberg, D. P., & Hillier, V. F. (1979). A scaled version of the general health questionnaire. *Psychological Medicine, 9,* 139–145.

Gondolf, W. W., Fisher, E., & McFerron, J. R. (1990). The helpseeking behavior of battered women: An analysis of 6000 shelter interviews. In E. C. Viano (Ed.), *The victimology handbook: Research, treatment and public policy* (113–127). New York: Garland Publishing.

Hatchett, S., Veroff, J., & Douvan, E. (1995). Factors influencing marital stability among black and white couples. In B. Tucker & C. Mitchell-Kernan (Eds.), *The decline in marriages among African Americans: Causes, consequences and policy implications.* Newbury Park, CA: Sage.

Hays, R. D., Sherbourne, C. D., & Mazel, R. M. (1993). The RAND 36-item health survey 1.0. *Health Economics, 2,* 217–227.

Jacobson, N., Gottman, J., Gortner, E., Berns, S., & Shortt, J. (1996). Psychological factors in the longitudinal course of battering: When do the couples split up? When does the abuse decrease? *Violence and Victims, 11,* 371–392.

Jacobson, N., Gottman, J., Waltz, J., Rushe, R., Babcock, J., & Holtzworth-Munroe, A. (1994). Affect, verbal content and psychophysiology in the arguments of couples with a violent husband. *Journal of Clinical and Consulting Psychology, 62,* 982–988.

Kasian, M., & Painter, S. L. (1992). Frequency and severity of psychological abuse in a dating population. *Journal of Interpersonal Violence, 7,* 350–364.

Kelly, K. D., & DeKeseredy, W. S. (1994). Women's fear of crime and abuse in college and university dating relationships. *Violence and Victims, 9,* 17–30.

Kilpatrick, D. G., Best, C. L., Saunders, B. E., & Veronen, L. J. (1988). Rape in marriage and in dating relationships: How bad is it for mental health? *Annals of the New York Academy of Science, 528,* 335–344.

Kurz, D., & Stark, E. (1989). Not so benign neglect: The medical response to battering. In K. Yllo & M. Bograd (Eds.), *Feminist perspectives on wife abuse* (pp. 249–266). Newbury Park, CA: Sage.

Lloyd, S. A. (1996). Physical aggression, distress, and everyday marital interaction. In D. Cahn & S. Lloyd (Eds.), *Family violence from a communication perspective* (pp. 177–198). Newbury Park, CA: Sage.

Margolin, G., John, R. S., & Gleberman, L. (1988). Affective responses to conflictual discussions in violent and nonviolent couples. *Journal of Consulting and Clinical Psychology, 56,* 24–33.

Marshall, L. L. (1992a). Development of the Severity of Violence Against Women Scale. *Journal of Family Violence, 7,* 103–121.

Marshall, L. L. (1992b). The severity of Violence Against Men Scales. *Journal of Family Violence, 7,* 189–204.

Marshall, L. L. (1994). Physical and psychological abuse. In W. R. Cupach & B. H. Spitzberg (Eds.), *The dark side of interpersonal communication (pp. 281–311). Hillsdale, NJ:* Lawrence Erlbaum Associates.

Marshall, L. L. (1996). Psychological abuse of women: Six distinct clusters. *Journal of Family Violence, 11,* 369–399.

Marshall, L. L., & Guarnaccia, C. (1998). *Men's psychological-harm and abuse in relationships measure (MP-HARM): Overt and subtle psychological abuse.* Manuscript in preparation.

Marshall, L. L., & Rose, P. (1990). Gender, stress and violence in the adult relationships of a sample of college students. *Journal of Social and Personal Relationships, 4,* 299–316.

McCloskey, L. A. (1996). Socioeconomic and coercive power within the family. *Gender and Society, 10,* 449–463.

Mihalic, S., & Elliott, D. (1997). A social learning theory model of marital violence. *Journal of Family Violence, 12,* 21–47.

Murphy, C. M., & Cascardi, M. (1993). Psychological aggression and abuse in marriage. In R. L. Hamptom, T. P. Gullotta, S. R. Adams, E. H. Potter III, & R. P. Weissberg (Eds.), *Family violence: Prevention and treatment* (pp. 86–112). Newbury Park, CA: Sage.

Nolen-Hoeksema, S. (1987). Sex differences in unipolar depression: Evidence and theory. *Psychological Bulletin, 101,* 259–282.

O'Leary, K. D., & Jouriles, E. N. (1994). Psychological abuse between adult partners. In L. L'Abate (Ed.), *Handbook of developmental family psychology and psychopathology* (pp. 330–349). New York: John Wiley and Sons.

O'Leary, K. D., Malone, J., & Tyree, A. (1994). Physical aggression in early marriage: Prerelationship and relationship effects. *Journal of Consulting and Clinical Psychology, 62,* 594–602.

Pipes, R. B., & LeBov-Keeler, K. (1997). Psychological abuse among college women in exclusive heterosexual dating relationships. *Sex Roles, 36,* 585–603.

Riggs, D. S., Kilpatrick, D. G., & Resnick, H. C. (1992). Long-term psychological distress associated with marital rape and aggravated assault: A comparison to other crime victims. *Journal of Family Violence, 7,* 283–296.

Roberts, A. R. (1996). Battered women who kill: A comparative study of incarcerated participants with a community sample of battered women. *Journal of Family Violence, 11,* 291–304.

Rosenberg, M. (1965). *Society and the adolescent self-image.* Princeton, NJ: Princeton University Press.

Saunders, D. G. (1996). Feminist-cognitive-behavioral and process-psychodynamic treatment models for men who batter: Interaction of abuser traits and treatment models. *Violence and Victims, 11,* 393–414.

Shinn, M., Knickman, J. R., & Weitzman, B. C. (1991). Social relationships and vulnerability to becoming homeless. *American Psychologist, 46,* 1180–1188.

Sommers, E. K., & Check, J. V. P. (1987). An empirical investigation of the role of pornography in the verbal and physical abuse of women. *Violence and Victims, 2,* 189–209.

Stets, J. E. (1991) Psychological aggression in dating relationships: The role of interpersonal control. *Journal of Family Violence, 6,* 97–114.

Straus, M. A., Hamby, S. L., Boney-McCoy, S., & Sugarman, D. S. (1996). The revised Conflict Tactics Scale (CTS2): Development and preliminary psychometric data. *Journal of Family Violence, 17,* 283–316.

Stuart, E. P., & Campbell, J. C. (1989). Assessment of patterns of dangerousness with battered women. *Issues in Mental Health Nursing, 10,* 245–260.

Trope, Y., & Liberman, A. (1996). Social hypothesis testing: Cognitive and motivational mechanisms. In E. T. Higgins & A. W. Kruglanski (Eds.), *Social psychology handbook of basic principles* (pp. 239–270). NY: Guilford Press.

Vitanza, S., Vogel, L. C. M., & Marshall, L. L. (1995). Distress and symptoms of posttraumatic stress disorder in abused women. *Violence and Victims, 10,* 23–34.

Vivian, D., & Malone, J. (1997). Couples at risk for husband-to-wife violence: Screening potential of marital assessment inventories. *Violence and Victims, 12,* 1–19.

Wood, D., Valdez, B., Hayashi, T., & Shen, A. (1990). Homeless and housed families in Los Angeles. *American Journal of Public Health, 80,* 1049–1052.

Zawitz, M. W. (1994). *Violence between intimates.* Bureau of Justice Statistics, report #NCJ149259 available from BJS, P. O. Box 179, Annapolis Junction, MD 20701–0179.

Acknowledgments. Initial examination of subtle and overt psychological abuse was funded by grant #R29MH44217 from the National Institute of Mental Health and would not have been possible without the assistance of Dr. Stephanie Vitanza. This study was funded by grant #R49/CCR610508 from the National Center for Injury Prevention and Control of the Centers for Disease Control and Prevention. Special thanks are extended to Laura C. M. Vogel, Diane M. Sedillo, Barbara VanHorn, and Rebecca Weston. Portions of this study were presented at the Fifth International Family Violence Research Conference in Durham, NH. Thanks, also, go to Dan O'Leary and anonymous reviewers for their excellent suggestions on earlier versions of this manuscript.

Offprints. Requests for offprints should be directed to Linda L. Marshall, Department of Psychology, Denton, Texas 76203.

The Impact of Different Forms
of Psychological Abuse on
Battered Women

Leslie A. Sackett, PhD
Eastern Michigan University

Daniel G. Saunders, PhD
University of Michigan

Battered women receiving either shelter ($n = 30$) or nonshelter services (n = 30) from a domestic violence agency were interviewed regarding psychological abuse and its aftermath. Four types of abuse were derived from factor analysis: ridiculing of traits, criticizing behavior, ignoring, and jealous control. Sheltered women experienced ridicule and jealous/control more often than nonsheltered women. For the entire sample, ridiculing of traits was rated as the most severe form. Ignoring was the strongest predictor of low self-esteem. Both psychological abuse and physical abuse contributed independently to depression and low self-esteem. However, fear of being abused was uniquely predicted by psychological abuse. Implications for practice and research are discussed.

Practitioners and researchers are paying increasing attention to the psychological abuse of women (Follingstad, Rutledge, Berg, Hause, & Polek, 1990; Jones & Schechter, 1992; Loring, 1994; Tolman, 1989). A major reason for this focus is the realization that psychological abuse may be just as detrimental, or more detrimental, than physical abuse. In one study, 72% of the battered women reported that emotional abuse had a more severe impact than physical abuse (Follingstad et al., 1990). In another study, psychological abuse was more strongly associated with psychosocial problems than threats or physical abuse (Tolman & Bhosley, 1991). The focus of most previous work is on women who are both physically and psychologically abused. Almost all women who are physically abused also report verbal abuse (83%, Walker, 1984) or psychological abuse (99%, Follingstad et al., 1990). Another reason to focus on psychological abuse is the evidence that verbal aggression early in the relationship is a frequent precursor of physical aggression later (Murphy & O'Leary, 1989). Thus, identifying particular forms of psychological abuse may help prevent physical abuse later in the relationship.

Psychological abuse can also help to maintain abusive relationships. If severe enough, it may lead to self-doubt, confusion, and depression. Battered women may subsequently have a difficult time seeing their options and marshaling the resources needed to leave the relationship. At first, a battered woman may respond to criticism and put-downs by trying to change herself, convince her partner they need couple's counseling, or attribute his abuse to his drinking. Over time, many women realize that nothing they do seems to make a difference. Women may be especially affected by emotional abuse coming from a significant other because of the importance of mutuality to their psychological development (Miller, 1991). Qualitative research on battered women finds that battered women may experience a loss of identity directly related to coerced isolation, emotional abuse and "acts of diminishment" (Larkin & Popaleni, 1994; Mills, 1985; Smith, Tessaro, & Earp, 1995).

Along with the increased attention currently given to psychological abuse have come attempts to classify the various forms that it takes. Direct practice work with battered women and men who batter helped to create lists of a broad range of abusive behaviors (e.g., NiCarthy, 1982; Pence & Paymar, 1993; Sonkin, Martin, & Walker, 1985). Some practitioners drew parallels between battered women and prisoners of war, and thus the lists included techniques that are commonly used in brainwashing: degradation and threats with occasional indulgences, isolation, and invalidation of perceptions (Walker, 1984). Survey research that built on these observations and classifications has pointed to a number of different types. Tolman (1989) factor-analyzed 58 forms of psychological maltreatment and found two major dimensions: dominance-isolation and emotional-verbal. Aguilar and Nightingale (1994) divided abuse into "controlling/emotional" and "sexual/emotional," based on their cluster analysis. Using semistructured interviews, Follingstad and her colleagues (1990) created a list of five types: threats of abuse, ridicule; jealousy; threats to change marriage; restriction; and damage to property. Marshall (1996) uncovered six patterns of psychological abuse through a cluster analysis of a large sample. The patterns were as follows: (1) severe violence but without denigration or control of finances; (2) moderate violence and sexual abuse; (3) low on abuse but enforced isolation; (4) low levels of violence with overt criticism and several types of control; (5) several types of overtly dominating and controlling abuse and lower levels of sexual aggression; and (6) similar to cluster 5 but with different patterns of help-seeking.

Few attempts have been made to discover the forms of psychological abuse that have the most severe impacts. The women in the Follingstad et al. (1990) study reported that ridicule was the worst form. In the Aguilar and Nightingale study (1994), women who experienced "controlling/emotional" abuse had lower self-esteem scores. Dutton and Painter (1993) found that dominance/isolation was more strongly related to trauma and low self-esteem than emotional-verbal abuse 6 months after the abuse occurred.

The purpose of this study was to extend previous research on the different types of psychological abuse experienced by battered women and to examine whether some types of psychological abuse are rated as more severe than others. We predicted that, similar to the study by Follingstad and her associates (Follingstad et al., 1990), ridiculing of traits would be rated as more severe because it attacks a person's sense of self more directly than other types of abuse. For example, if a woman's behavior is criticized she may believe that she needs to change specific behaviors. Her hope for the relationship may continue and she is less likely to become depressed (Frieze, 1978). Ridiculing of her traits, however—an attack on her character—is more likely to shatter her sense of hope, security in the relationship, and even her sense of self. Depression, low self-esteem and further alienation and isolation from herself and others is likely to result. In our test of this hypothesis, we went beyond simple severity ratings to assess the impact of psychological abuse on distinct outcomes: depression, self-esteem, and fear.

We used more extensive measures of abuse and its impact than most other studies and therefore hoped to explore more fully questions about the impact of various forms of psychological abuse on battered women. Furthermore, we wanted to know if psychological abuse acts independently of physical abuse on depression, self-esteem, and fear, and if so, to what extent. Given the large overlap between physical and psychological abuse, it seems important to partial the effects of physical abuse from that of psychological abuse.

We also wanted to explore whether sheltered and nonsheltered women differ on levels of psychological abuse. Sheltered women generally suffer more severe physical abuse (e.g., Wilson, Vercella, Brems, Benning, & Renfro, 1992) and the pattern may be the same for psychological abuse. However, the two forms of abuse do not always correlate (e.g., Sabourin, 1991).

METHOD

Respondents

Respondents had sought help from a domestic violence agency in a midsized midwestern city. All of the women had been physically abused at least once. Thirty women were shelter residents and 30 were in nonresidential individual or group counseling for domestic violence. Average age was 34.7 years. (SD = 9.1). The majority of the women were White (62%); 30% were African American and 5% were Native American. One woman was Hispanic and one was Asian. Most of the women (63%) had some college and 25% were college graduates. Forty percent were employed full-time and 25% part-time. Most of the women (62%) had children (M = 1.2; SD = 1.2). Seventy percent of the women were currently living with their partners. The majority of partners were spouses (56%).

Procedure

Data collection took place over a 9 month period. Routine intake forms required by the state social service department provided some information for the study, such as demographics and abuse history. Other information was collected through an interview designed for the study. The women in the shelter were recruited by a staff member who gave the women information about the study a day or 2 after they entered the shelter. Following informed consent procedures, an interviewer was assigned to the woman. During the period that the 30 sheltered women were interviewed, 45 other women were sheltered. Many of these women were not interviewed because they left the shelter before an interview could be arranged.

The women who were not sheltered were recruited by their individual (n = 18) or group counselor (n = 12). When counselors wanted to refer a woman, information about the study was given to her and she completed informed consent procedures. The interviewers, trained by the first author, were staff members (n = 2) or volunteers (n = 5) of the domestic violence agency or undergraduates majoring in psychology (n = 3). The first author interviewed 21 of the women. The interviews lasted approximately 11/2 hours, but ranged from 1.25 hours to 3.5 hours. Fifteen of these women had never left their partners, 3 had stayed at a shelter at some time, and the remaining 12 stayed temporarily or permanently with friends, relatives, or on their own. Many of the women were referred to a special group for partners of men who were in treatment. Other women were referred by agencies, friends or themselves.

Measures

Depression. The Beck Depression Inventory (BDI) (Beck, 1967) was used to measure depression. The BDI contains 21 items that cover mood, guilt, loss of interest, and physical signs. It has good concurrent and construct validity (Beck, 1967). The internal reliability coefficient (alpha) in this study was .90.

Self-esteem. This construct was measured with a version of the Coopersmith Self-esteem Inventory (Coopersmith, 1967) designed for a general population. The scale contains 25 items with a response format of "like me" or "unlike me." The internal reliability coefficient (alpha) in this study was .90. It is demonstrated to have good convergent and discriminant validity (Johnson, Redfield, Miller, & Simpson, 1983).

Fear. A 6-item scale of battered women's fear was constructed for this study. Originally, 14 items were constructed and administered. The scale was reduced to 6-items through item analysis and by choosing items which clearly described emotional impact. The 6-item version had an internal reliability coefficient (alpha) of .86 which was higher than the 14-item version (see Appendix). The response format was: "never, less than once a month, once a month, 2-3 times a month, once a week, 2-3 times a week, and daily."

Profile of Psychological Abuse. This measure was developed for the study based on earlier work (Sackett, 1992). It initially contained 42 items drawn from clinical work, descriptions of the tactics of men who batter (Pence & Paymar, 1993), and the experiences of battered women as categorized by NiCarthy (1982). The items covered a wide variety of psychological abuse: humiliation, threats, invalidation of experiences, isolation, trivial demands, occasional indulgences, and emotional distance. The response format was the same as for the fear scale: "never, less than once a month, once a month, 2-3 times a month, once a week, 2-3 times a week, and daily." Seven items were removed because of ambiguous wording. The remaining 35 items were entered into a principal component factor analysis with varimax rotation. A scree test revealed that a 5-factor solution was optimal. All 5-factors were interpretable. One factor of 6 items was not retained because it did not reflect behaviors that were clearly abusive. As evidence for this, it did not correlate significantly with the womens' depression and low self-esteem.

Eight other items were deleted in order to improve the reliability of the subscales. The factor analysis was repeated with the 21-item version and the factor structure was consistent with the original analysis with 35 items with the exception of one item. The final 21 items are shown in the Appendix, along with the item-factor loadings and the internal alpha coefficients of the subscales. The factors were labeled as follows: Jealous Control (alpha = .85); Ignore (alpha = .80); Ridicule Traits (alpha = .79); and Criticize Behavior (alpha = .75).

Severity of Psychological Abuse. A single question asked about the severity level of abuse: "Overall, how would you rate the severity of the psychological abuse?" (not severe at all, mildly severe, very severe, extremely severe).

Demographics. Age, educational level (five levels), and income (nine levels) were taken from intake forms.

Violence. The intake form contained four questions on violence, with the first two requiring yes or no responses: Did the assailant use any of the following? (a gun? a knife, or other cutting instrument? hands/fist/feet? sexual assault? threats to kill?). Did the client ever receive any of the following injuries from the assailant? (cuts/burns/bruises; choking; internal injuries; strains/sprains/broken bones; head injuries). How often does any of the violence occur? (never, once a year or less, approximately 3-4 times a year, approximately once a month, approximately once a week, almost daily). Length of time the client has been exposed to abuse by the assailant? (no previous abuse, less than 1 year, 1 to 3 years, 3 to 5 years, more than 5 years).

Based on a factor analysis (principal component with varimax rotation) of the violence and injury items, the items "fist/feet/hands" and "cuts/burns/bruises" were labeled as "moderate violence" and all the rest as "severe violence." A variable called "Amount of Violence" was constructed by giving a double weight to the severe items, adding them to the less severe items and multiplying the total by the frequency of violence. An advantage of multiplying severity by frequency is that a more normal distribution is approached than when either variable is used alone. The item on the duration of violence in the relationship was kept intact.

Relationship Happiness. This construct was measured with items from a measure of relationship satisfaction developed by Veroff (1988). A factor analysis revealed one factor out of five that could clearly be labeled "relationship satisfaction." The highest loading items were: (1) "Would you say your relationship is: not too happy, just about average, a little happier than average, very happy?"; (2) "When you think about your relationship—what each of you puts into it, and gets out of it—how happy do you feel?"; (3) "When you think about your relationship—what each of you puts into it, and gets out of it—" how angry do you feel?"; (4) "How stable do you feel your relationship is?"; and (5) "All in all, how satisfied are you with your relationship." The response format was on a four point scale from "never" to "often." Factor scores were used in the analysis in order to use weighted items. The internal alpha coefficient of reliability was .78.

Analysis

We used a t-test to compare the sheltered and nonsheltered women on abuse and demographic variables. Hierarchical multiple regression analysis was used to test the relative impact of psychological and physical abuse on depression, self-esteem, and fear.

RESULTS

Compared with the women who had not been in the shelter, the sheltered women had less education and income and experienced more severe physical abuse (see Table 1). They also had higher scores on two of the psychological abuse scales: Ridicule Traits and Jealous Control (Table 1). Despite more physical and psychological abuse among the sheltered women, they did not have higher scores on depression and fear or lower scores on self-esteem. The average score for both groups of women on the Beck Depression Inventory was 18.1 ($SD = 12.5$), which is in the moderate range. There was considerable variation on this measure: 30% scored as nondepressed (0–9), 27% as mildly depressed (10–18), 27% as moderately depressed (19–29), and 17% as severely depressed (30 or over) (norms from Beck, Steer, & Garbin, 1988)

Table 2 shows the relationship among the independent and dependent variables for both groups of women combined. As predicted, psychological abuse severity was much more strongly related to ridiculing of traits than criticism of behavior. Psychological abuse severity also showed a significant but weak correlation with "jealous control." In addition, severity correlated positively with the amount of violence and fear and negatively with relationship satisfaction.

In the prediction of depression, the strongest bivariate correlation was with the amount of violence, followed by the global severity rating of psychological abuse. Ignoring and ridiculing of traits were also significantly related to depression. Unexpectedly, the duration of violence was negatively related to depression. The amount of violence also had the highest correlations with low self-esteem, followed by ignoring. Ridiculing of traits was also significantly related to lower self-esteem. Relationships with the fear of abuse were the strongest. Ridiculing of traits was the most strongly related to fear. Jealous/control, criticizing behavior, ignoring, and the amount of violence all had moderately high correlations with fearfulness.

Although Jealous/Control had relatively low correlations with depression and self-esteem, it had the highest correlation with physical abuse, compared with the other forms of psychological abuse (ave. $r = .32$).

TABLE 1.   Mean Comparisons of Sheltered and Nonsheltered Battered Women on Abuse and Demographic Variables (Standard Deviation in Parentheses)

	Sheltered $n = 30$	Nonsheltered $n = 30$	t
Psychological Abuse			
Ridicule Her Traits	24.6	20.4	2.08*
	(7.1)	(8.1)	
Jealous Control	40.7	31.7	2.95*
	(11.1)	(12.4)	
Criticize Behavior	9.8	9.8	.00
	(6.1)	(5.7)	
Ignore	22.5	23.3	−.34
	(9.2)	(8.5)	
Overall Frequency	5.5	5.6	−.49
	(0.8)	(0.8)	
Overall Severity	3.1	3.1	.00
	(0.8)	(0.8)	
Physical Abuse			
Severe Violence	4.9	3.2	2.79**
Duration	4.1	4.1	.12
Demographics			
Age	34.4	34.9	−.21
Education	3.2	4.1	−3.19**
Household Income	5.0	7.3	−3.73***

$*p < .05$; $**p < .01$; $***p < .001$.

The three dependent variables, depression, self-esteem, and fear, were correlated with each other in expected directions. Depression and low self-esteem were the most highly correlated.

The correlation matrices (six independent and three dependent variables) were compared between the two samples. Fifteen of the 18 correlations were similar. Sheltered women had much higher correlations between "ignore" and depression and self-esteem; and violence duration and depression.

Table 3 shows the results of the hierarchical multiple regression in the prediction of depression, self-esteem, and fear. Psychological abuse and violence variables were entered in separate blocks. Psychological abuse was entered first, followed by violence. The procedure was then reversed with violence entered first. In this way, the unique variance of psychological versus physical abuse could be determined.

Jealous/Control was not entered into the first two equations because it had the lowest correlation of the psychological abuse variables with depression and self-esteem and the sample was too small for using all of the variables. The psychological abuse variables

TABLE 2. Correlations Among the Dependent and Independent Variables

	1	2	3	4	5	6	7	8	9	10	11
1. Fear	—	-.25*	.29**	.56***	.47***	.66***	.52*	.31**	.01	.42***	-.34**
2. Self-Esteem		—	-.65***	-.17	-.31**	-.22*	-.17	-.08	.05	-.34**	.05
3. Depression			—	.18	.22*	.23*	.20	.31**	-.23*	.34***	-.40***
4. Jealous/ Control				—	.33**	.53***	.43***	.23*	-1.5	.49***	-.24*
5. Ignore					—	.47***	.55***	.17	-.03	.26*	-.16
6. Ridicule traits						—	.54***	.55***	.13	.36**	-.42***
7. Criticize behavior							—	.17	.35**	-.12	
8. Global severity of psychological abuse								—	-.04	.36**	-.61***
9. Duration of violence									—	.07	.16
10. Amount of violence										—	-.22*
11. Relationship satisfaction											—

*$p < .05$; ** $p < .01$; *** $p < .001$.

TABLE 3.   Hierarchical Multiple Regression

Independent Variable	Dependent Variable		
	Depression	Self-Esteem	Fear
Step 1: Psychological Abuse			
$R =$	.37	.32	.73
$R^2 =$	.13	.10	.53
Step 2: Violence			
$R =$	.48	.43	.73
$R^2 =$	.23	.19	.54
R square increase $=$	.10	.09	.01
F for increase $=$	7.40**	6.33**	1.24
Step 1: Violence			
$R =$	.43	.34	.42
$R^2 =$	.18	.12	.18
Step 2: Psychological Abuse			
$R =$	.48	.43	.73
$R^2 =$	.23	.19	.54
R square increase $=$	.05	.07	.36
F for increase $=$	3.70	4.93**	44.6***

$*p < .05; **p < .01; ***p < .001.$

accounted for 13% of the variance in depression. When the physical abuse variables were entered, the variance accounted for rose significantly by 10%. When the order was reversed, the violence variables accounted for 18% of the variance, showing a (not quite significant) 5% increase with the addition of the psychological abuse variables. Thus, psychological abuse and physical abuse made unique contributions in explaining depression, with a somewhat stronger contribution by physical abuse.

In the prediction of self-esteem, the variance accounted for when the psychological abuse variables were entered was 10%; with the addition of the violence variables, it rose significantly by 9%. When the violence variables were entered first, they accounted for 12% of the variance in predicting self-esteem; the addition of psychological abuse significantly increased the variance explained by 7%. Once again, psychological and physical abuse made independent contributions to the outcome variable.

In the prediction of fear, the global severity rating of psychological abuse was dropped from the equation. Although it was significantly related to fear ($r = .31$), the four types of psychological abuse were much more strongly related to it (ave. $r = .55$). The psychological abuse variables accounted for 53% of the variance. The entry of the physical abuse variables added only 1% to the variance. When the physical abuse variables were entered first, they accounted for 18% of the variance. The addition of the psychological abuse variables raised the percent variance by 36%, a very significant increase. Thus, psychological abuse was a much stronger predictor of fear than physical abuse.

DISCUSSION

The factor analysis of the Profile of Psychological Abuse revealed four major forms of abuse: Criticize Behavior, Ignore, Ridicule Traits, and Jealous/Control (Appendix). The Jealous/Control factor appears similar to the Dominance-Isolation factor of Tolman's (1989) Psychological Maltreatment of Women Inventory (PMWI), which also included items on jealousy and restriction of behavior. It also has items similar to the Controlling/Emotional Abuse items from the Aguilar and Nightingale study (1994). The Ignore factor has items similar to some of those on the Emotional-Verbal subscale of the PMWI (e.g., "sulked, refused to talk," "withheld affection"). The Criticize Behavior factor seemed closer to items on the Dominance-Isolation factor of the PMWI, whereas the Ridicule Traits factor seemed closer to items on the Emotional-Verbal factor of the PMWI. However, these similarities were not clear-cut.

An important feature of the Profile of Psychological Abuse is its ability to distinguish between criticism of behaviors and ridiculing of traits. It also has the advantage of using specific time referents (e.g., "once a month," "once a week," "2-3 times a week," etc.). The differing patterns of psychological abuse found in this and other studies probably reflect the behavior of different types of men who batter. Some men seem to restrict their partners' behavior out of jealousy, while others tend to blame their partners for the violence, treat them as inferiors, and use threats (Holtzworth-Munroe & Stuart, 1994). Battered women's experiences can also be clustered into different groups depending on the types of violence they experienced and their causal attributions for the violence (Follingstad, Laughlin, Polek, Rutledge, & Hause, 1991; Snyder & Fruchtman, 1981).

Battered women residing in a shelter reported more severe physical abuse. This finding is consistent with other studies (Saunders, 1994; Wilson et al., 1992), as are the findings that the sheltered women had less education and income. These women also experienced more ridicule of their personal characteristics and jealous control by their partners. Surprisingly, their depression, self-esteem, and fear did not differ from nonsheltered battered women. The shelter may have provided enough support in a short period of time for previous depression and fear to lift. Self-esteem is less likely to change in such a short period of time. However, one study found that the length of stay in a shelter was related to higher self-esteem and lower depression (Orava, McLeod, & Sharpe, 1996).

Another possibility is that the more severe abuse experienced by these women produced traumatic symptoms , such as "numbing" and dissociative responses, that kept other emotional responses from surfacing. The fight for survival and the recency of abuse might not have allowed them to feel depressed or fearful, at least for the time immediately after the abuse. Other research shows that sheltered women have more frequent symptoms of post-traumatic stress than other help-seeking battered women (Gleason, 1993; Saunders, 1994).

The average level of depression on the BDI for both samples was somewhat below that of another sample of battered women. In that sample 33% of the women were in the severe range (score over 30)(Orava, McLeod, & Sharpe, 1996).

As predicted, ridiculing of traits was related most strongly to the severity rating of psychological abuse. The other forms of psychological abuse, especially criticizing behavior and ignoring, are somewhat less likely to be taken personally. Jealous-controlling behavior, although most strongly related to the amount of physical abuse, might be viewed as a less severe form of psychological abuse for the same reason: it is not a direct attack on the self. Similarly, there was no relation between jealous/control and depression. Again, the women might be able to make external attributions, i.e., to readily see through the tactics and jealousy of their partners without blaming themselves. These findings are consistent with the distinction made between behavioral self-blame and characterological self-blame that Janoff-Bulman (1982) applied to rape survivors. Behavioral blame is a less severe form of blame and provides the victim with a sense of control that "there is something about myself that I can change to prevent an attack." These forms of attributions are less likely to have an impact on depression and self-esteem (Frieze, 1978). Jealous/control may also have been interpreted positively by many of these women, just has it does for many college women (Henton, Cate, Koval, Lloyd, & Christopher, 1983). At least early in the relationship, jealousy may be viewed as a sign of romantic love.

This study revealed that psychological and physical abuse had fairly independent effects on depression and self-esteem. However, psychological abuse had a much stronger impact than physical abuse on fear. Ridiculing traits, criticizing behavior, and jealous/control had the strongest relationship to fear. The intimidating behavior of the most controlling type of batterer may be partly responsible for the greater fear. The amount of physical abuse, but not its duration, was also significantly related to fear.

Depression was related to criticism, ignoring, ridicule, and violence as expected. The negative relation between depression and the duration of violence is more difficult to explain. It is possible that women experiencing the most severe violence had shorter relationships; those experiencing less severe violence might have been able to find ways to keep their hope alive and keep their depression lower. Alternately, as with the speculation we made about the severe trauma to sheltered women, the survival needs of those enduring longterm abuse may cause numbing and a suppression of feelings.

The amount of violence and ignoring were most strongly related to low self-esteem. The act of violence itself gives the message that the victim is unworthy and unlovable. In one study of the men's accounts, many of the men admitted that they were trying to convince their wives that they were worthless through a combination of verbal and physical abuse (Hyden, 1995). The finding on the use of ignoring shows that it needs to be taken seriously as a form of abuse, with the potential for long-term consequences. Being ignored may give one of the most negative messages possible about self-worth.

For practitioners, these results confirm the negative impact that psychological abuse has on battered women's emotional life and sense of self. Practitioners can help women to see why "character assassinations" are more devastating than specific criticisms, but also why specific criticisms might build unrealistic hopes. Ignoring needs to be discussed as an extreme form of abuse because it conveys the message: "you don't exist." Group work is particularly well suited to help battered women overcome psychological abuse because they can learn that their experiences are similar to those of other women, their experiences and emotions can be validated by others, and mutual support can occur. There is some evidence that such group work not only increases self-esteem and a sense of inner control but also may help to reduce psychological abuse (Tutty, Bidgood, & Rothery, 1993).

The conclusions of this study need to be viewed cautiously due to a number of limitations. The sample was relatively small and all of the women were seeking help. Not all of the women who were asked to participate were willing or able to do so. Nonparticipants tended to be those who left the shelter more quickly and were probably less traumatized. The results may also differ with nonhelp-seeking samples. The measure of physical aggression was derived from an intake form and had unknown reliability and validity. If it was less reliable than the psychological abuse variables, the relationship between physical abuse and the outcome variables would be attenuated. The measures of psychological abuse and fear were developed for this study. Although showing adequate scale reliability, tests of validity outside of the hypotheses of this study were not available. All of these limitations point the way for future research.

Despite these limitations, this study shows the utility of a new measure of psychological abuse. The findings suggest that the psychic injuries to battered women are typically caused as much by psychological abuse as physical abuse. Some forms of psychological abuse appear more damaging than others. With the replication of these results, counseling methods can be refined and tested for countering what are probably the most lingering effects of woman abuse—those which affect the survivor's very sense of self.

REFERENCES

Aguilar, R. J., & Nightingale, N. N. (1994). The impact of specific battering experiences on the self-esteem of abused women. *Journal of Family Violence, 9,* 35–46.

Beck, A. T. (1967). *Depression: Clinical, experimental and theoretical aspects.* New York: Harper & Row.

Beck, A. T., Steer, R. A., & Garbin, M. G. (1988). Psychometric properties of the Beck Depression Inventory. *Clinical Psychology Review, 8,* 77–100.

Coopersmith, S. (1967). *Self-esteem inventories.* Palo Alto, CA: Consulting Psychology Press.

Dutton, D. G., & Painter, S. (1993). Emotional attachment in abusive relationships. *Violence and Victims, 8,* 105-120.

Follingstad, D. R., Laughlin, J. E., Polek, D. S., Rutledge, L. L., & Hause, E. S. (1991). Identification of patterns of wife abuse. *Journal of Interpersonal Violence, 6,* 187–204.

Follingstad, D. R., Rutledge, L., Polek, D., & McNeill-Hawkins, K. (1988). Factors associated with patterns of dating violence toward college women. *Journal of Family Violence, 3,* 169–182.

Follingstad, D. R., Rutledge, L. L, Berg, B. J., Hause, E. S., & Polek, D. S. (1990). The role of emotional abuse in physically abusive relationships. *Journal of Family Violence, 5,* 107–120.

Frieze, I. H. (1978). *New approaches to social problems.* San Francisco: Jossey-Bass.

Gleason, W. J. (1993). Mental Disorders in battered women: An empirical study. *Violence & Victims, 8,* 53–68.

Henton, J., Cate, R., Koval, J., Lloyd, S., & Christopher, S. (1983). Romance and violence in dating relationships. *Journal of Family Issues, 4,* 467–482.

Holtzworth-Munroe, A., & Stuart, G. L. (1994). Typologies of male batterers: Three subtypes and the differences among them. *Psychological Bulletin, 116,* 476–497.

Hyden, M. (1995). Verbal aggression as prehistory of woman battering. *Journal of Family Violence, 10,* 55–73.

Janoff-Bulman, R. (1982). Esteem and control bases of blame: "Adaptive" strategies for victim versus observers. *Journal of Personality, 30,* 180–192.

Johnson, B. W., Redfield, D. L., Miller, R., & Simpson, R. E. (1983). The Coopersmith Self-Esteem Inventory: A construct validity study. *Educational and Psychological Measurement,* 907–913.

Jones, A., Schecter, S., (1992). *When love goes wrong.* New York: HarperCollins.

Larkin, J., & Popaleni, K. (1994). Heterosexual courtship violence and sexual harassment: The private and public control of young women. *Feminism & Psychology, 4,* 213–227.

Loring, M. T. (1994) *Emotional abuse.* New York: Lexington Books.

Jones, A., & Schechter, S., (1992). *When love goes wrong.* New York: HarperCollins.

Marshall, L. (1996). Psychological abuse of women: Six distinct clusters. *Journal of Family Violence, 11,* 379–410.

Miller, J. B. (1991). The development of women's sense of self. In J. V. Jordan et al., (Eds.), *Women's growth through connection.* New York: Guilford.

Mills, T. (1985). The assault on the self: Stages in coping with battering husbands. *Qualitative Sociology, 8,* 103–123.

Murphy, C., & O'Leary, K. D. (1989). Psychological aggression predicts physical aggression in early marriage. *Journal of Consulting and Clinical Psychology, 57,* 579–582.

NiCarthy, G. (1982). *Getting free: A handbook for women in abusive relationships.* Seattle: Seal Press.

Orava, T. A, McLeod, P. J., & Sharpe, D. (1996). Perceptions of control, depressive symptomatology, and self-esteem of women in transition from abusive relationships. *Journal of Family Violence, 11,* 167–186.

Pence, E., & Paymar, M. (1993). *Education groups for men who batter.* New York: Springer Publishing.

Sabourin, T. C. (1991). Perceptions of verbal aggression in interpersonal violence. In D. D.Knudsen & J. L. Miller (Eds.), *Abused and battered.* New York: Aldine de Gruyter.

Sackett, L. A. (1992). Assessing psychological abuse among battered women. Unpublished dissertation, University of Michigan, School of Social Work and Department of Psychology, Ann Arbor, MI.

Saunders, D. G. (1994). Posttraumatic stress symptom profiles of battered women: A comparison of survivors in two settings. *Violence and Victims, 9,* 125–138.

Sonkin, D. J., Martin, D., & Walker, L. E. A. (1985). *The male batterer: A treatment approach.* New York: Springer Publishing.

Smith, P. H., Tessaro, I., & Earp, J. A. L. (1995). Women's experiences with battering: A conceptualization from qualitative research. *Women's Health Issues, 5,* 173–182.

Snyder, D. K., & Fruchtman, L. A. (1981). Differential patterns of wife abuse: A data-based typology. *Journal of Consulting and Clinical Psychology, 49,* 878–885.

Tolman, R. M. (1989). The development of a measure of psychological maltreatment of women by their male partners. *Violence and Victims, 4,* 159–178.

Tolman, R. M., & Bhosley, G. (1991). The outcome of participation in a shelter-sponsored program for men who batter. In D. Knudsen & J. Miller (Eds.), *Abused and Battered: Social and Legal Responses.* New York: Aldine de Gruyter.

Tutty, L. M., Bidgood, B. A., & Rothery, M. A. (1993). Support groups for battered women: Research on their efficacy. *Journal of Family Violence, 8,* 325–344.

Veroff, J. (1988). First years of marriage: Wave III: Spouse questionnaire. Survey Research Center, Institute for Social Research. University of Michigan, Ann Arbor, MI.

Walker, L. E. (1984). The battered woman syndrom.

Wilson, K., Vercella, R., Brems, C., Benning, D., & Renfro, N. (1992). Levels of learned helplessness in abused women. *Women & Therapy, 13,* 53–67.

Acknowledgment. Leslie A. Sackett is currently at Columbia College, Columbia, SC.

Offprints. Requests for offprints should be directed to Daniel G. Saunders, University of Michigan, School of Social Work, 1080 University Avenue, Ann Arbor, MI 48109.

APPENDIX

Profile of Psychological Abuse

As much as possible, I would like you to disregard the physical abuse that has occurred in your current relationship. The question I am asking should be answered according to the psychological or emotional abuse that has occurred in your relationship. I know some of these questions may be hard to answer, but please try to be as accurate as possible. Response format under each item:

1	2	3	4	5	6	7
never	less than once	once a month	2–3 times a month	once a week	2–3 times a week	daily

Jealous Control
Internal Alpha Reliability = .85

Factor
Loading   How often does your partner:
.74   Become angry or upset if you want to be with someone else and not with him?
.70   Intercept your mail, telephone calls, or drill you about who called you, who wrote you a letter, or what you were talking about?
.70   Make you account for every minute you spend away from the house?
.65   Become jealous about your friends, family or pets?
.62   Ask for detailed reports of your hourly activities?
.61   Check up on you throughout the day? (calls you every 15 minutes, comes home early from work, has others tell him your whereabouts, etc.)
.57   Threaten to hurt a prized possession, pets, friends, or relatives if you don't comply with his wishes?
.48   Keep you up late yelling at you, either accusing you of having affairs or accusing you of other things?

Ignore
Internal Alpha Reliability = .80

.77   Make the TV, a magazine, the newspaper, or other people seem more important than you are?
.74   Ignore your need for assistance when you're sick, tired, or over-worked?
.71   Complain or ridicule you if you are upset or ask for emotional support?
.70   Ignore your suggestion to have sex or not do what excites or satisfies you?
.61   Ignore you when you begin a conversation?

Ridicule Traits
Internal Alpha Reliability = .79

.80   Ridicule the traits you admire or value most in yourself?
.66   Tell you that you are a horrible lover, worthless, or no good?
.54   Suggest you're crazy or stupid?
.50   Call you names with sexual connotations such as "slut" or "whore" or "cunt"?
.46   Make fun of your triumphs, discourage your plans, or minimize your successes?

Criticize Behavior
Internal Alpha Reliability = .75

.73   After you've cooked or cleaned, tell you it's not right and ask you to do it over again until he decides it's done right?
.61   Inspect your work and make overly critical comments?
.50   Request that everything be done in a precise way or it will be unacceptable to him?

Fear of Abuse
Internal Alpha Reliability = .84

Make you feel guilty or ashamed for something he demanded that you do?
Make you feel you as if you are "walking on egg shells" when you are around him?
How often:
Do you worry that what you do will make your partner angry?
Do you do things your partner wants you to do because you feel afraid?
Do you fear that your partner will hit you if you don't comply with his wishes?
Do you try to second-guess how your partner will act?

Violence and Victims, Volume 4, Number 3, 1989

The Development of a Measure
of Psychological Maltreatment of
Women by Their Male Partners

Richard M. Tolman*

This study describes the initial development of a scale of measurement of psychological maltreatment of women by their male partners. The initial version of the scale was administered to 407 men and 207 women at intake into a domestic violence program. All 58 items of the scale were endorsed by a large enough number of subjects to warrant inclusion in the final instrument. Factor analysis revealed a similar factor structure for the men and women, with dominance-isolation and emotional-verbal abuse factors emerging from the analysis. Intracouple reliability for each item of the scale was examined for the subset of men and women who were cohabiting couples ($n = 28$). Unsurprisingly, the agreement of men's and women's reports was low, though the scores on the domination-isolation subscale were significantly correlated.

A widely shared clinical observation is that men who physically and sexually abuse their partners also engage in a wide range of other abusive behaviors (Walker, 1979; Ganley, 1981; Nickle & Purdy, 1981). These behaviors have been alternatively characterized as nonphysical abuse (Hudson & McIntosh, 1981), emotional abuse (NiCarthy, 1986), indirect abuse (Gondolf, 1987), psychological abuse (Patrick-Hoffman, 1982), and mental or psychological torture (Russell, 1982).

Several conceptual frameworks for classifying the forms that nonphysical abuse takes have been proposed. For example, Sonkin, Martin, and Walker (1985) list six forms of psychological violence, including explicit threats of violence, implicit threats of violence, extreme controlling behavior, pathological jealousy, mental degradation, and isolating behavior. Russell (1982) and NiCarthy (1986) draw attention to the similarity of the behavior of batterers and the behaviors listed on Biderman's Chart of Coercion, which was included in an Amnesty International publication (1973) detailing techniques used in brainwashing prisoners of war. These categories include isolation, monopolization of perception, induced debility, threats, occasional indulgences, demonstrating "omnipotence," degradation, and enforcement of trivial demands. Other authors have developed more elaborate typologies of psychologically abusive behavior. For example, Patrick-Hoffman (1982), who did extensive qualitative interviews with women who reported being emotionally abused, identified 21 types of emotional abuse.

The systematic study of these abusive behaviors is important for several reasons. Presumably, nonphysically abusive behaviors are themselves damaging to the targets of those behaviors. Furthermore, when these behaviors occur in the context of a relationship in

---

* University of Illinois, Chicago.

---

which physical violence has occurred, the effects of other forms of abuse may be intensified (Edleson & Brygger, 1986; Ganley, 1981; Walker, 1979). Another clinical observation is that many men are able to stop their physically abusive behavior while under the scrutiny of a counseling program. Their use of other abusive behaviors, however, may continue or increase as a way of maintaining their control over their partners. Therefore, it is important to understand the interlocking nature of various abusive behaviors in relationships, the function and consequences of those behaviors, and the methods for effectively eliminating those behaviors.

The purpose of the present study was to begin the development of a measure that can be used to assess the nonphysically abusive behaviors exhibited by men who batter. The need for such a measure for use in evaluating interventions for men who batter has been noted in the literature (see, e.g., Gondolf, 1987; Edleson, 1988). To be maximally useful in such evaluations, a measure needs the following properties. First, the measure must be written in a form that can be administered to both the men themselves and their partners. Research strongly suggests that men minimize the extent of their own abusive behavior (Edleson & Brygger, 1986; O'Leary & Arias, 1988; Szinovacz, 1983), making reports from both the men and their partners necessary. It is as yet undetermined, however, whether men minimize nonphysically abusive behaviors to the same extent as the physical behaviors, though evidence from Edleson and Brygger (1986) indicates that reports of psychological threats may be less reliable than those of physical abuse. Second, the measure must include items that represent the relevant abusive behaviors. Finally, the measure should be easily administered to be useful for practitioners as well as researchers.

The measures commonly used in violence research to date meet some but not all of these criteria. For example, the widely used Conflict Tactics Scale (CTS) (Straus, 1979) is an 18-item self-report scale assessing the occurrence and frequency of behaviors used during interpersonal conflict. The CTS items include nonaggressive problem-solving behaviors, psychological aggression, physical threats, and direct physical aggression. The psychological aggression items are limited, however, drawing only on withdrawal (e.g., stomped out of the room or house) and verbal aggression (e.g., insulted or swore at the other one). The CTS is also designed to be a measure of all forms of intrafamily violence. Its generality, although valuable for an exploration of different types of family violence in the same study (Straus, 1981), limits its usefulness when one is attempting to study abuse of women in context (Dobash & Dobash, 1981).

The Index of Spouse Abuse (ISA) (Hudson & McIntosh, 1981) is a 30-item self-report measure with two subscales, one measuring physical (ISA-P) and the other measuring nonphysical abuse (ISA-NP) of a woman by her spouse or partner. The ISA accurately discriminates between abuse victims and women known not to be victims. The ISA also has good evidence for construct validity, and each subscale has high internal consistency. Compared with the psychological aggression items of the CTS, the ISA-NP contains many more items that attempt to measure nonphysical dimensions of abuse. For use in evaluation of programs for men who batter, however, the ISA-NP has several limitations. The ISA is written for women's reports only. The ISA has been criticized for including only a limited sample of nonphysically abusive behaviors (Gondolf, 1987). An examination of the items indicates some commonly reported abusive behaviors are not included (e.g., monitoring her time, isolation from family, withholding of affection).

The current study sought to improve on these currently available measures, while retaining the advantage of gathering data comparable to that of previous investigations. Therefore, a measure that would be compatible with the use of the CTS or the ISA-P was designed.

METHOD

Development of the Measure

Items for the Psychological Maltreatment of Women Inventory (PMWI) were derived from several sources. Items from two existing scales (CTS and ISA) were examined. Sixteen items were modified from the 18-item nonphysical abuse scale of the ISA. Five items were modified from the CTS (see Table 1).

TABLE 1.   Women's Scale Items

 1. My partner put down my physical appearance.
 2. My partner insulted me or shamed me in front of others.
 3. My partner treated me like I was stupid.
 4. My partner was insensitive to my feelings.
 5. My partner told me I couldn't manage or take care of myself without him.
 6. My partner put down my care of the children.
 7. My partner criticized the way I took care of the house.
 8. My partner said something to spite me.
 9. My partner brought up something from the past to hurt me.
10. My partner called me names.
11. My partner swore at me.
12. My partner yelled and screamed at me.
13. My partner treated me like an inferior.
14. My partner sulked or refused to talk about a problem.
15. My partner stomped out of the house or yard during a disagreement.
16. My partner gave me the silent treatment, or acted as if I wasn't there.
17. My partner withheld affection from me.
18. My partner did not let me talk about my feelings.
19. My partner was insensitive to my sexual needs and desires.
20. My partner demanded obedience to his whims.
21. My partner became upset if dinner, housework, or laundry was not done when he thought it should be.
22. My partner acted like I was his personal servant.
23. My partner did not do a fair share of household tasks.
24. My partner did not do a fair share of child care.
25. My partner ordered me around.

(Continued)

TABLE 1.   Women's Scale Items (Continued)

26. My partner monitored my time and made me account for where I was.

27. My partner was stingy in giving me money to run our home.

28. My partner acted irresponsibly with our financial resources.

29. My partner did not contribute enough to supporting our family.

30. My partner used our money or made important financial decisions without talking to me about it.

31. My partner kept me from getting medical care that I needed.

32. My partner was jealous or suspicious of my friends.

33. My partner was jealous of other men.

34. My partner did not want me to go to school or other self-improvement activities.

35. My partner did not want me to socialize with my female friends.

36. My partner accused me of having an affair with another man.

37. My partner demanded that I stay home and take care of the children.

38. My partner tried to keep me from seeing or talking to my family.

39. My partner interfered in my relationships with other family members.

40. My partner tried to keep me from doing things to help myself.

41. My partner restricted my use of the car.

42. My partner restricted my use of the telephone.

43. My partner did not allow me to go out of the house when I wanted to go.

44. My partner refused to let me work outside of the home.

45. My partner told me my feelings were irrational or crazy.

46. My partner blamed me for his problems.

47. My partner tried to turn our family, friends, and children against me.

48. My partner blamed me for causing his violent behavior.

49. My partner tried to make me feel like I was crazy.

50. My partner's moods changed radically, from calm to angry, or vice versa.

51. My partner blamed me when he was upset about something, even when it had nothing to do with me.

52. My partner tried to convince my friends, family, or children that I was crazy.

53. My partner threatened to hurt himself if I left him.

54. My partner threatened to hurt himself if I didn't do what he wanted me to do.

55. My partner threatened to have an affair with someone else.

56. My partner threatened to leave the relationship.

57. My partner threatened to take the children away from me.

58. My partner threatened to have me committed to a mental institution.

Note. Items modified from ISA: 2, 5, 12, 20–22, 25, 27, 32, 35, and 37. Items modified from CTS: 8, 11, 14 and 15.

TABLE 2.   Conceptual Framework for Item Development

1. Attacking her personhood, demeaning, belittling, undermining self-worth
2. Defining her reality, getting her to question her own perceptions, judgments
3. Controlling her contact with outside world, support systems
4. Demanding subservience, complying with rigid sex role expectations within the family
5. Withholding positive reinforcers within the relationship
6. Threatening nonphysical punishment for noncompliance with requests, status, and emotional regulation

Some items were suggested by the work of Patrick-Hoffman (1982), who identified 21 categories of emotional abuse. Other items were developed from behaviors reported in other descriptive clinical literature and the clinical observations of the author. Finally, some additional items were generated according to a conceptual scheme that divided abuse into several categories and subcategories (see Table 2). Excluded from the scale items were some behaviors sometimes described as psychological maltreatment, if those behaviors had a direct physical component (e.g., interrupted sleep or eating, forced sex), or were threats or implied threats of physical harm (e.g., threatened to hit, broke objects). These items were excluded to facilitate use of this measure with other existing measures of physical aggression, such as the CTS.

Fifty-eight items were selected for study. Versions for women and men were developed, using nearly identical phrasing for all items, but with pronouns and direction of abuse altered. The scale format chosen was similar to that of the ISA. Ratings of relative pervasiveness of occurrence were chosen (e.g., never, rarely, sometimes, frequently, very frequently) rather than estimates of frequency (e.g., how many times), because some items imply complex ongoing sequences of behavior (e.g., kept you from seeing your family) rather than a discrete one-time behavior. Respondents were asked to rate how often the behaviors occurred in the past 6 months. A fixed time frame presumably makes the scale more useful for evaluating change in treatment programs.

Initial pilot testing with a small group of men who batter revealed that the measure was readily understood and that the checklist was easily completed in 10 to 15 min. In addition, copies of the scale were distributed to women and men working with battered women and men who batter. Feedback from those workers suggested that the scale had high face validity and good content validity. Limited evidence for the content validity of the scale was indicated by the observation that few workers were able to suggest additional items not included on the current scale.

Subjects

The PMWI was administered to men who batter and battered women at intake into a domestic violence program. Although a small percentage of the men and women in the sample were partners, for the most part the men and women in the study were not related. The average age of male subjects was 31.9 years. Most of the men were white (76%), with blacks (15%), Hispanics (5%), and Native Americans (3%) represented in smaller number. The median income in the group was between $10,000 to $15,000. Only 52.4% of the men were employed full-time, with 30.6% totally unemployed. The mean educational level of the men was 12.76 years of schooling. The men in the sample had been in a relationship with their partners for an average of 6.48 years.

The average age of women in the sample was 32.6 years. Eighty-nine percent of the women were white, with Native Americans (5%), blacks (4%), and Hispanics (1%) constituting the remainder of the sample. Thirty-four percent of the women were employed full-time outside the home, and 22% had part-time employment. The average level of education of the women was 13.3 years. Women had been in their relationships an average of 6.9 years.

RESULTS

Item Means and Endorsement

Table 3 lists percentage of endorsement of items (e.g., did it ever happen in past 6 months) and mean item ratings (1 = never; 5 = very frequently) for men and women. No item had a percentage endorsement of less than 25% of the battered women. Percentage endorsement ranged from 0.29 (kept from medical care) to 0.98 (insensitive to feelings). Mean item ratings for the women ranged from 1.45 (threatened to hurt himself if partner did not do what he wanted) to 4.10 (insensitive to feelings).

TABLE 3.   Item Means and Percentage of Endorsement

	WOMEN			MEN		
	Mean	SD	%	Mean	SD	%
1. Put down physical appearance	2.67	1.23	.81	1.74	0.95	.48
2. Insulted in front of others	2.89	1.25	.85	1.89	0.92	.58
3. Treated her like she was stupid	3.37	1.21	.90	2.07	0.99	.66
4. Acted insensitive to feelings	4.10	1.01	.98	2.67	1.14	.83
5. Told could not manage	2.83	1.44	.75	1.61	0.90	.37
6. Put down care of children	2.86	1.36	.78	1.94	1.12	.50
7. Criticized way took care of house	2.95	1.35	.82	2.37	1.31	.64
8. Said something to spite	3.56	1.11	.94	2.47	1.09	.79
9. Brought up past to hurt	3.63	1.17	.91	2.39	1.09	.74
10. Called names	3.55	1.19	.86	2.74	1.15	.86
11. Swore at partner	3.69	1.20	.95	2.91	1.13	.90
12. Yelled and screamed	3.78	1.19	.90	2.91	1.08	.91
13. Treated like an inferior	3.55	1.23	.92	2.06	1.10	.62
14. Sulked, refused to talk	3.75	1.18	.90	2.47	1.24	.72

(Continued)

TABLE 3.   Item Means and Percentage of Endorsement (Continued)

	WOMEN			MEN		
	Mean	SD	%	Mean	SD	%
15. Stomped out of house	2.90	1.31	.82	2.25	1.13	.69
16. Gave silent treatment	3.07	1.28	.87	2.15	1.02	.68
17. Withheld affection	3.24	1.22	.91	2.02	1.05	.61
18. Did not let talk about feelings	3.53	1.11	.95	1.89	1.08	.50
19. Acted insensitive sexually	3.11	1.35	.86	1.76	1.02	.48
20. Insisted on catering to whims	3.35	1.23	.90	1.93	1.11	.53
21. Upset when chores not done	2.78	1.34	.79	2.07	1.21	.55
22. Acted like partner was servant	3.07	1.35	.84	1.59	0.95	.38
23. Did not do fair share of housework	3.46	1.39	.87	2.04	1.14	.59
24. Did not do fair share of child care	3.16	1.54	.93	1.75	1.02	.45
25. Ordered around	3.20	1.25	.89	1.95	1.06	.58
26. Monitored time	3.37	1.44	.85	2.10	1.19	.59
27. Acted stingy with money	3.02	1.60	.92	1.66	1.04	.38
28. Acted irresponsibly with money	3.29	1.44	.83	2.11	1.12	.60
29. Did not contribute enough support	2.92	1.54	.70	1.78	1.13	.41
30. Used money without consultation	2.91	1.48	.74	1.64	0.95	.43
31. Kept partner from medical care	1.57	1.03	.29	1.05	0.30	.04
32. Acted jealous or suspicious of friends	3.59	1.35	.90	2.26	1.29	.62
33. Acted jealous of other men	3.41	1.44	.87	2.37	1.38	.62
34. Did not allow going to school	2.53	1.52	.62	1.29	0.69	.19
35. Did not allow socializing with friends	3.00	1.41	.79	1.62	0.98	.37
36. Accused of having affair	2.70	1.57	.66	1.77	1.05	.45
37. Demanded she stay home with kids	2.47	1.52	.54	1.56	0.96	.30
38. Kept from seeing family	2.32	1.34	.60	1.29	0.71	.20
39. Interfered with family relationships	2.54	1.34	.68	1.29	0.67	.22
40. Kept partner from self-help	2.59	1.33	.69	1.23	0.61	.15

(Continued)

TABLE 3.   Item Means and Percentage of Endorsement (Continued)

	WOMEN			MEN		
	Mean	SD	%	Mean	SD	%
41. Restricted car use	2.25	1.41	.54	1.33	0.80	.21
42. Restricted telephone use	2.13	1.24	.56	1.21	0.59	.17
43. Did not allow to leave house	2.29	1.24	.62	1.35	0.73	.26
44. Did not allow to work	1.85	1.32	.35	1.21	0.65	.11
45. Told feelings irrational or crazy	3.52	1.26	.90	2.14	1.11	.61
46. Blamed for problems	3.78	1.29	.92	2.19	1.13	.64
47. Turned family against partner	2.48	1.43	.64	1.29	0.70	.18
48. Blamed for causing violence	3.88	1.31	.90	2.33	1.25	.64
49. Tried to make feel crazy	3.56	1.31	.89	1.36	0.77	.22
50. Changed moods radically	3.89	1.11	.90	2.62	1.19	.21
51. Blamed partner when upset	3.47	1.24	.92	1.87	1.06	.51
52. Tried to convince partner she was crazy	2.27	1.40	.55	1.24	0.66	.16
53. Threatened to hurt self if partner left	1.85	1.28	.38	1.35	0.81	.23
54. Threatened to hurt self if partner did not do what was wanted	1.45	.93	.33	1.14	0.47	.21
55. Threatened to have an affair with someone	2.05	1.26	.51	1.39	0.77	.25
56. Threatened to leave relationship	2.78	1.37	.75	1.99	1.07	.27
57. Threatened to take children away	2.09	1.37	.44	1.34	0.72	.24
58. Threatened to commit to an institution	1.48	1.02	.33	1.09	0.41	.05

The men, on the whole, had lower percentage of endorsement and mean item ratings than the women. Percentage endorsement ranged from 0.04 (kept partner from medical care) to 0.91 (yelled and screamed). The lowest item mean was 1.05 (kept partner from medical care); the highest 2.91 (swore at partner; yelled and screamed).

Factor Analysis

An exploratory factor analysis was undertaken to determine the factor structure of the checklist. The checklist was derived with some informed hunches about the dimensions of nonphysical abuse, but at this early stage of theoretical development an empirical approach to factor structure is appropriate for heuristic purposes as well as for data reduction for other analyses (Nunnally, 1978).

Separate factor analyses were done for the men's and women's reports. A principal components extraction indicated 13 factors with Eigen values greater than 1.000 for the women's data, and 14 factors for the men's data. Analysis of the factors using the Scree test revealed that two true factors in both analyses were likely to exist. The Varimax rotation method was used for both analyses, limiting the final solution to two factors.

The results of the factor solution for the women are presented in Table 4. Both factors seem readily interpretable. The first factor represents a dominance-isolation factor, which includes items dealing with isolation from resources, demands for subservience, and rigid observance of traditional sex roles. Two items do not appear to readily fit this factor. One item was Item 1: "My partner put down my physical appearance." At first glance, this item seems to belong to the emotional-verbal abuse dimension. This item, however, might be related to isolation and dominance in the sense that by demeaning his partner's physical appearance, a man may diminish her belief in her attractiveness to others outside the relationship, thereby assuring his exclusive access to her. The second item was Item 7: "My partner criticized the way I took care of the house," which has a verbal abuse element but also contains an implicit assumption that a man believes it is his partner's responsibility to care for the home and therefore fits the dominance factor. Both items have relatively low loadings on Factor 1, and Item 7 also loads highly on Factor 2 (0.38).

The items loading on the second factor represent an emotional-verbal factor that includes verbal attacks, behavior that demeans the women, and withholding of emotional resources. Item 20, "My partner demanded that I cater to his whims," which appears to fit with Factor 1, also loads highly on Factor 1 (0.47). Again, the item has a verbal (demanding) as well as a dominance element, which may explain the mixed factor loading.

TABLE 4. Factor Structure for Women at Intake

	LOADING		
	1	2	h^2
Items loading $>$ .4 on Factor 1			
26. Monitored time	.75	.06	.40
40. Kept her from helping self	.75	.29	.65
43. Did not allow to leave house	.74	.14	.40
38. Kept from seeing family	.70	.16	.52
39. Interfered with family relationships	.70	.17	.52
35. Did not allow socializing with friends	.69	.14	.40
34. Did not allow going to school	.68	.18	.65
42. Restricted telephone use	.67	.18	.48
32. Acted jealous or suspicious of friends	.67	.13	.46

(Continued)

TABLE 4.   Factor Structure for Women at Intake (Continued)

	LOADING		
	1	2	h^2
22. Acted like she was personal servant	.65	.35	.54
33. Acted jealous of other men	.63	.10	.41
44. Did not allow to work	.63	.11	.40
41. Restricted car use	.61	.18	.40
25. Ordered around	.59	.45	.55
36. Accused of having affair	.59	.13	.36
47. Turned family against her	.56	.39	.47
5. Told could not manage	.53	.30	.36
27. Acted stingy with money	.52	.33	.37
52. Tried to convince her she was crazy	.52	.38	.41
21. Became upset if household chores not done	.50	.29	.33
55. Threatened to have an affair	.48	.21	.27
30. Used money without consultation	.48	.46	.38
1. Put down physical appearance	.45	.28	.28
31. Kept her from medical care	.45	.15	.22
28. Acted irresponsibly with money	.44	.32	.30
7. Criticized way took care of house	.41	.38	.31

Eigen value: 18.96; variance explained: 32.7%

Items loading > .4 on Factor 2

46. Blamed her for problems	.24	.71	.56
51. Blamed her when upset	.36	.71	.63
48. Blamed for causing violence	.27	.69	.69
8. Said something to spite	.19	.67	.49
18. Did not let talk about feelings	.18	.65	.48
50. Changed moods radically	.29	.64	.50
13. Treated like an inferior	.36	.63	.53
45. Told feelings crazy or irrational	.34	.63	.52
17. Withheld affection	−.03	.62	.39
49. Tried to make feel crazy	.40	.61	.53
12. Yelled and screamed	.35	.60	.49
4. Acted insensitive to feelings	.21	.59	.39
14. Sulked, refused to talk	−.05	.55	.31

(Continued)

TABLE 4. Factor Structure for Women at Intake (Continued)

| | LOADING | | |
	1	2	h^2
20. Insisted on catering to whims	.47	.55	.53
19. Acted insensitive sexually	.21	.59	.34
11. Swore at her	.33	.54	.40
16. Gave silent treatment	−.05	.51	.27
15. Stomped out of house	−.03	.48	.24
3. Treated her like she was stupid	.41	.48	.38
10. Called names	.37	.47	.36
9. Brought up past to hurt	.41	.46	.38
2. Insulted in front of others	.42	.46	.39
56. Threatened to leave relationship	.11	.43	.20
Eigen value: 3.784; variance explained: 6.5%			

Items loading < .4 on both factors

	1	2	h^2
54. Threatened to hurt self if partner did not do what was wanted	.38	.05	.15
57. Threatened to take children away	.38	.27	.14
24. Did not do fair share of child care	.35	.25	.18
6. Put down care of children	.33	.25	.41
58. Threatened to commit to an institution	.32	.15	.13
23. Did not do fair share of housework	.19	.30	.13

Note. $N = 207$.

The factor analysis of the men's data resulted in a similar factor structure, with most items loading similarly on the two factors (see Table 5).

A multiple-group method of confirmatory analysis (Nunnally, 1978) was used to confirm the similarity in the factor structure. The factor structure for the women's analysis was hypothesized to be similar to the men's. To derive loadings for the men's data on the hypothesized factors, the item/item-total correlations for each item on each hypothesized factor was computed. As can be seen in Table 6, all items except for Item 31 ("I kept my partner from getting medical care that she needed") had high correlations with the hypothesized factor. Only Item 52 ("I tried to convince my partner that she was crazy") had a higher item/item-total correlation with a different factor than was hypothesized. Therefore, the data support the hypothesis that the factor structure for the men is similar to that for the women.

Although the data from the multiple-group method analysis support the hypothesis of factor similarity, it should be noted that many items did have high correlations with both factors, and the two subscale total scores are highly correlated for both the men ($r = .7320$) and the women ($r = .7376$).[1]

TABLE 5. Factor Structure for Men at Intake

	LOADING		
	1	2	h^2
Items loading > .4 on Factor 1			
12. Yelled and screamed	.72	.14	.54
4. Acted insensitive to feelings	.71	.14	.53
18. Did not let talk about feelings	.68	.21	.46
8. Said something to spite	.66	.24	.49
13. Treated my partner like an inferior	.66	.32	.53
14. Sulked, refused to talk	.66	.01	.31
50. Changed moods radically	.65	.22	.50
51. Blamed partner when upset	.65	.32	.63
10. Called names	.64	.20	.36
11. Swore at partner	.63	.15	.40
25. Ordered partner around	.60	.44	.55
17. Withheld affection	.58	.15	.37
20. Demanded obedience to whims	.57	.39	.53
28. Acted irresponsibly with finances	.56	.25	.30
3. Treated partner like she was stupid	.56	.33	.38
23. Did not do fair share of household tasks	.55	.15	.13
45. Told partner feelings were crazy	.55	.26	.52
9. Brought up something from past to hurt	.55	.37	.38
22. Acted like partner was personal servant	.54	.46	.54
19. Acted insensitive to partner's sexual needs	.54	.25	.34
16. Gave partner silent treatment	.53	.03	.27
56. Threatened to leave relationship	.53	.13	.20
15. Stomped out during disagreement	.52	.02	.24
46. Blamed partner for problems	.52	.32	.56
30. Used money without consultation	.45	.29	.39
2. Insulted or shamed in front of others	.43	.29	.39
48. Blamed her for causing violent behavior	.42	.23	.54
24. Did not do fair share of child care	.41	.36	.19
Eigen value = 16.97; variance explained = 29.3			
Items loading > .4 on Factor 2			
37. Demanded she stay home and take care of kids	.21	.66	.43
34. Did not allow school or self-help	.11	.62	.50

(Continued)

TABLE 5. Factor Structure for Men at Intake (Continued)

	LOADING		
	1	2	h^2
40. Kept her from doing things for herself	.21	.62	.65
26. Monitored partner's time and whereabouts	.34	.62	.57
38. Kept her from seeing her family	.10	.62	.52
35. Did not allow socializing with friends	.19	.60	.49
32. Acted jealous or suspicious of friends	.30	.55	.46
39. Interfered with other family relationships	.11	.54	.52
42. Restricted use of telephone	.14	.53	.48
36. Accused her of having affair	.19	.52	.36
33. Acted jealous of other men	.22	.52	.41
43. Did not let out of the house	.19	.51	.57
44. Refused to allow her to work outside home	.05	.48	.40
45. Restricted use of car	.23	.48	.40
57. Threatened to take children away	.11	.48	.22
54. Threatened to hurt self if she did not do what he wanted	.20	.47	.14
27. Acted stingy with money	.26	.44	.38
55. Threatened to have affair	.36	.44	.27
21. Upset when chores not done	.43	.44	.33
1. Put down partner's physical appearance	.28	.41	.28
Eigen value = 3.1; variance explained = 6.6			
Items loading < .4 on both factors			
49. Tried to make partner feel crazy	.39	.39	.53
29. Did not contribute enough to supporting family	.36	.32	.20
7. Criticized way partner took care of house	.33	.33	.31
47. Tried to turn family against my partner	.32	.29	.47
52. Tried to convince others partner was crazy	.29	.39	.41
5. Told partner she could not manage on own	.32	.39	.36
6. Put down partner's care of the children	.16	.39	.17
53. Threatened to hurt self if partner left	.16	.38	.16
58. Threatened to have partner committed	.01	.33	.13
31. Kept partner from medical care	—	.25	.22

Note. N = 407.

TABLE 6. Multiple-Group Method Comparison of Men's and Women's Factor Structure

	ITEM-SUBSCALE CORRELATION: MEN	
	D-I	E-Y
Dominance-isolation subscale		
1. Put down physical appearance	.46	.40
5. Told could not manage	.51	.40
7. Criticized way took care of house	.48	.41
21. Became upset if household chores not done	.63	.53
22. Acted like she was personal servant	.68	.64
25. Ordered around	.70	.67
26. Monitored time	.74	.51
27. Acted stingy with money	.70	.67
28. Acted irresponsibly with money	.56	.55
30. Used money without consultation	.53	.47
31. Kept her from medical care	.18	.07
32. Acted jealous or suspicious of friends	.67	.48
33. Acted jealous of other men	.60	.40
34. Did not allow going to school	.56	.34
35. Did not allow socializing with friends	.60	.40
36. Accused of having affair	.61	.36
38. Kept from seeing family	.52	.33
39. Interfered with family relationships	.48	.31
40. Kept her from helping self	.64	.42
41. Restricted car use	.55	.39
42. Restricted telephone use	.46	.33
43. Did not allow to leave house	.47	.36
44. Did not allow to work	.39	.23
47. Turned family against her	.47	.41
52. Tried to convince her she was crazy	.57	.64
55. Threatened to have affair	.56	.50
Average item-subscale correlation	.56	.41
Emotional-verbal subscale		
2. Insulted in front of others	.41	.51
3. Treated her like she was stupid	.55	.64

(Continued)

TABLE 6. Multiple-Group Method Comparison of Men's and Women's Factor Structure (Continued)

	ITEM-SUBSCALE CORRELATION: MEN	
	D-I	E-Y
4. Acted insensitive to feelings	.49	.72
8. Said something to spite	.52	.70
9. Brought up past to hurt	.56	.66
10. Called names	.47	.67
11. Swore at her	.44	.66
12. Yelled and screamed	.46	.72
13. Treated like an inferior	.61	.72
14. Sulked, refused to talk	.37	.62
15. Stomped out of house	.30	.49
16. Gave silent treatment	.33	.51
17. Withheld affection	.46	.59
18. Did not let talk about feelings	.52	.71
19. Acted insensitive sexually	.49	.60
20. Insisted on catering to whims	.60	.67
45. Told feelings crazy or irrational	.57	.64
46. Blamed her for problems	.50	.65
48. Blamed for causing violence	.42	.55
49. Tried to make feel crazy	.48	.55
50. Changed moods radically	.52	.72
51. Blamed her when upset	.59	.72
56. Threatened to leave relationship	.41	.56
Average item-subscale correlation	.48	.63

Note. D-I = dominance-isolation; E-V = emotional-verbal.

The mean scores for the domination subscale were 43.3 (SD = 15.8) for the men, and 70.7 (SD = 13.5) for the women. The men's mean score on the emotional-verbal subscale was 51.7 (SD = 15.7), and the women's emotional-verbal mean score was 79.4 (SD = 17.9).

Intracouple Reliability

Nonparametric analysis was used in analyzing intracouple reliability. Twenty-eight couples were identified from the large sample. Spearman's Rho was used to determine the degree of association between men's and women's reports on each item. The results of that analysis are presented in Table 7. The results show that a low degree of agreement exists between the men

TABLE 7.   Correlation of Male and Female Reports

	Rho	*P*
1. Put down physical appearance	.4423	.009
2. Insulted in front of others	.2460	.104
3. Treated like stupid	.1569	.213
4. Acted insensitive to feelings	.1552	.215
5. Told could not manage	.1909	.165
6. Put down care of children	.4036	.035
7. Criticized way took care of house	.5250	.002
8. Said something to spite	.1016	.314
9. Brought up past to hurt	.1570	.222
10. Called names	.3065	.060
11. Swore at partner	.3614	.029
12. Yelled and screamed	.0903	.324
13. Treated like an inferior	.2254	.134
14. Sulked, refused to talk	.2075	.145
15. Stomped out of house	.0586	.384
16. Gave silent treatment	−.0483	.404
17. Withheld affection	−.0585	.386
18. Did not let talk about feelings	.2639	.087
19. Acted insensitive sexually	.1601	.208
20. Insisted on catering to whims	.2475	.107
21. Became upset when household chores not done	.0269	.446
22. Acted like partner was personal servant	.0319	.436
23. Did not do fair share of housework	.0601	.383
24. Did not do fair share of child care	.2013	.191
25. Ordered around	.1041	.303
26. Monitored time	.0794	.347
27. Acted stingy with money	.1791	.186
28. Acted irresponsibly with money	.3565	.034
29. Did not contribute enough support	.3888	.025
30. Used money without consultation	.2421	.112
31. Kept partner from medical care	[a]	
32. Acted jealous or suspicious of friends	.3086	.055
33. Acted jealous of other men	.1303	.254

(Continued)

TABLE 7. Correlation of Male and Female Reports (Continued)

	Rho	*P*
34. Did not allow going to school	.3134	.056
35. Did not allow socializing with friends	.2780	.076
36. Accused of having affair	.4808	.005
37. Demanded partner stay home with children	.1831	.213
38. Kept from seeing family	.1241	.269
39. Interfered with family relationships	.3396	.039
40. Kept partner from doing things to help self	.4640	.006
41. Restricted car use	−.0076	.485
42. Restricted telephone use	.0452	.410
43. Did not allow to leave house	.3766	.024
44. Did not allow to work	.3155	.054
45. Told feelings irrational or crazy	.1434	.233
46. Blamed for problems	−.1304	.258
47. Turned family against partner	.4085	.017
48. Blamed for causing violence	.1389	.245
49. Tried to make feel crazy	.2300	.120
50. Changed moods radically	−.0778	.347
51. Blamed partner when upset	.0541	.392
52. Tried to convince she was crazy	.4846	.005
53. Threatened to hurt self if partner left	.3114	.053
54. Threatened to hurt self if did not do what was wanted	−.0996	.307
55. Threatened to have an affair with someone	.3211	.048
56. Threatened to leave relationship	.3100	.054
57. Threatened to take children away	.3740	.052
58. Threatened to commit to an institution	.6565	.000

[a]No men endorsed this item.
Note. N = 28.

and women on the items. Only a few items showed significant association. Generally these were items that appear to have high social acceptability (e.g., yelled and screamed) or low endorsement by both men and women (e.g., threatened to commit to a mental institution).

Wilcoxon tests were done for each item-pair to determine the degree of disagreement for each item. The results of those analyses are presented in Table 8. Again, it is evident that little agreement exists between the men's and women's reports. Gender differences on these items are statistically significant in all but a few cases. Nonsignificant items had apparent higher social acceptability or lower rates of endorsement.

TABLE 8. Wilcoxon Comparisons of Male and Female Report of Nonphysical Abuse

	NUMBER HIGHER				
	Women	Men	Ties	z	P
1. Put down physical appearance	15	5	8	-1.9973	
2. Insulted in front of others	11	6	11	-1.9172	ns
3. Treated her like she was stupid	19	5	4	-2.6714	
4. Acted insensitive to feelings	17	5	6	-2.7271	
5. Told could not manage	15	4	9	-2.7163	
6. Put down care of children	11	4	13	-2.3854	
7. Criticized way took care of house	12	4	12	-2.1459	
8. Said something to spite	19	5	4	-2.1857	
9. Brought up past to hurt	20	3	5	-3.0567	
10. Called names	15	5	8	-1.0366	ns
11. Swore at partner	17	5	6	-1.6557	ns
12. Yelled and screamed	12	5	11	$-.9941$	ns
13. Treated like an inferior	16	5	7	-1.7553	ns
14. Sulked, refused to talk	17	5	6	-2.4187	
15. Stomped out of house	12	8	8	$-.9520$	ns
16. Gave silent treatment	16	7	5	-1.9618	
17. Withheld affection	17	5	6	-1.9804	
18. Did not let talk about feelings	22	3	3	-4.0945	
19. Acted insensitive sexually	19	2	7	-3.6322	
20. Insisted on catering to whims	19	4	5	-3.4673	
21. Upset if chores not done	10	8	10	-1.6331	ns
22. Acted like partner was servant	18	5	5	-3.0145	
23. Did not do fair share of housework	17	7	4	-2.6857	
24. Did not do fair share of child care	11	7	10	-1.5678	ns
25. Ordered around	18	6	4	-2.9429	
26. Monitored time	19	6	3	-2.9732	
27. Acted stingy with money	15	4	9	-2.3340	
28. Acted irresponsibly with money	11	8	9	-1.5694	ns
29. Did not contribute enough support	18	2	8	-3.5466	
30. Used money without consultation	14	5	9	-2.1932	
31. Kept partner from medical care	5	1	22	-1.6773	ns
32. Acted jealous or suspicious of friends	19	3	6	-3.2303	

(Continued)

TABLE 8. Wilcoxon Comparisons of Male and Female Report of Nonphysical Abuse (Continued)

	NUMBER HIGHER				
	Women	Men	Ties	*z*	*P*
33. Acted jealous of other men	20	3	5	−3.3761	
34. Did not allow going to school	13	1	14	−3.1074	
35. Did not allow socializing with friends	21	1	6	−3.9283	
36. Accused of having affair	14	1	13	−3.2090	
37. Demanded she stay home with kids	7	4	17	−1.4670	ns
38. Kept from seeing family	12	2	14	−2.6680	
39. Interfered with family relationships	13	1	14	−3.013	
40. Kept her from self-help	14	0	14	−3.2958	
41. Restricted car use	9	2	16	−2.2357	
42. Restricted telephone use	11	2	15	−2.7605	
43. Did not allow to leave house	13	1	14	−3.0760	
44. Did not allow to work	9	1	18	−2.5992	
45. Told feelings irrational or crazy	22	5	1	−2.6187	
46. Blamed for problems	23	3	2	−3.5430	
47. Turned family against partner	14	1	13	−3.2090	
48. Blamed for causing violence	19	4	5	−3.0871	
49. Tried to make feel crazy	23	1	4	−4.1857	
50. Changed moods radically	20	5	3	−3.3365	
51. Blamed partner when upset	21	2	5	−3.8627	
52. Tried to convince partner crazy	14	1	13	−3.1806	
53. Threatened to hurt self if partner left	9	1	18	−2.5482	
54. Threatened to hurt self if partner did not do what was wanted	6	1	21	−1.8593	ns
55. Threatened to have an affair	11	1	16	−2.7848	
56. Threatened to leave relationship	13	2	13	−2.6694	
57. Threatened to take children away	7	0	21	−2.3664	
58. Threatened to commit to institution	5	1	22	−1.8869	ns

Note. ns = not significant.

In addition, intracouple reliability on each of the subscales was examined. The domination-isolation scale scores for the men and women were significantly correlated ($r = .4849$, $p = .007$). The verbal-emotional scale scores, however, were not significantly correlated (r = .3025, p = .265). The mean scores for the couples were comparable to those of the total sample: men's domination-isolation, x = 38.4, SD = 9.33; women's domination-isolation, x = 62.2, SD = 24.5; men's emotional-verbal, x = 53.9, SD = 15.61; women's emotional-verbal, x = 80.0, SD = 22.6.

Subscale Reliability

The internal consistency coefficients for the women's subscales were high (domination-isolation, α = 0.9451; emotional-verbal, α = 0.9292). The internal reliability for each men's subscale was also high (domination-isolation, α = 0.9087; emotional-verbal, α = 0.9335).

DISCUSSION

The high percentage endorsement by women of all the items indicates that the PMWI does include items that tap many abusive behaviors experienced by battered women. Although it was initially believed that the measure might be shortened to remove items endorsed by less than 10% of the battered women, no item failed to meet this criteria for inclusion.

The PMWI seems to have relevant subscales that may prove useful in both outcome studies and theoretical investigations. It has been argued that control and dominance behavior may be ignored in many programs for men who batter (Gondolf & Russell, 1986). A scale that measures a reduction in dominance behaviors, as well as other non-physically abusive behaviors, would therefore be useful in evaluation of outcome in those programs. This scale would provide a way of determining the breadth of change in men receiving intervention. One possible application is in determining differential impact of different types of intervention. For example, programs focusing exclusively on techniques to limit physical and verbal aggression might fail to create change on domination-isolation behaviors if these behaviors are not directly attended to during intervention.

Intracouple reliability for individual items is low. Men report much lower levels of nonphysical abuse than do their partners. Those items with the least apparent social desirability are less likely to be reported by men than by their partners. Although social desirability has been demonstrated to be related to reports of physical aggression (Arias & Beach, 1987), it remains to be demonstrated empirically with psychological maltreatment. Greater intracouple agreement is found on items that have lower endorsement by the men and the women, and on those items that contain an implicit criticism of the women. Despite low item agreement, the scores for the domination-isolation subscale reach moderate levels of intracouple agreement. The verbal-emotional scale, however, has a low intracouple reliability. The discrepancy may be explainable by the relatively higher number of low endorsement items in the dominance-isolation scale. The men and women are more likely to agree and accurately report the nonoccurrence of a socially undesirable act. The reliable reporting of occurrences of socially undesirable acts is most crucial to the utility of this measure.

Although it cannot be determined from this data alone, the question may be raised as to whether the men's reports are low or the women's high. The clinical literature overwhelmingly suggests that men are likely to underreport their abusive behavior. As men participate in treatment, however, they frequently begin to reduce their denial and minimization of their abusive behavior. Further examination of the intracouple reliability may yield different results if the scale is administered later in the treatment process. For example, Edleson and Brygger (1986) found greater intracouple reliability of reports of physical abuse when a modified conflict tactics scale was administered at a 6-month follow-up, as compared to at intake. Future investigations using the PMWI might compare retrospective reports of psychological maltreatment before the start of intervention with the level of psychological maltreatment reported at intake. Increased retrospective reporting on the part of the men, combined with consistent reporting of the men's partners would provide some evidence that men's reports are indeed underestimated at intake. It should be noted that the women's reports may also increase, as their intake reports may also be subject to minimization (Hudson & Mcintosh, 1981). It has been suggested that such minimization may serve as a coping mechanism for battered women (Klingbeil & Boyd, 1984).

It would seem that the measure, as currently formulated, would not yield sufficiently reliable reports from men at intake if used as an evaluation tool in programs for men who batter. It remains to be seen, however, if batterers' scores, though low, may still discriminate them from nonabusive men. Given the high internal consistency and high endorsement of items, summative subscale scores for the women can be reliably used as a measure of the psychological maltreatment women are experiencing in their relationships.

Many crucial unanswered questions remain as to the validity of the PMWI. No evidence exists at this point as to the validity of the measure beyond the content validity established through the informal clinician review of items and the evaluation of the endorsement rates. It is critical that future research establish the known-groups validity of the scale. It remains to be determined whether the scales discriminate between the behavior of abusive men and the behavior of men in distressed relationships that would not be characterized as abusive. In fact, one might argue that many of the items reflect behaviors that may occur in nondistressed relationships. For example, some of the behaviors in the emotional-verbal subscale (e.g., scream, say something to spite, withhold affection) probably occur in most relationships from time to time. It remains to be empirically established which behaviors, and what levels of those behaviors, distinguish psychological batterers from men in distressed and nondistressed relationships, and whether this measure can adequately make those discriminations.

One hypothesis for future investigation is that the items reflected on the dominance-isolation subscale will more effectively discriminate between battering and distressed relationships. Although conflict in nonabusive relationships may be characterized at times by verbal aggression and withdrawal of affection on the part of either partner, isolation from friends, family, and outside resources, and demands for subservience may be more characteristic of men who batter.

If the measure is to be useful in clinical evaluations, it must be demonstrated that it is sensitive to change. Therefore, an investigation using the PMWI as a pretest-posttest measure, along with additional criterion measures, could demonstrate its validity and sensitivity to change.

With regard to construct validity, with the current measure sharing some items from the ISA and the CTS, correlations with those measures would not provide a high level of evidence of validity. Further study is needed to determine whether the expanded set of items improves on the validity of the other measures. Future research can address this issue, by comparing the ISA and CTS items that are imbedded in the current scale, or by a direct comparison of the current scale with the complete sets of nonphysical abuse items of the ISA and CTS. Regarding the other measures, however, it is interesting to note that CTS scale items all load on the emotional-verbal factor. Those clinicians or researchers using only the CTS to evaluate physical and psychological aggression will miss an important dimension of nonphysical abuse. The ISA items, conversely, load on both factors, indicating that the use of that measure with women is tapping a broader domain of psychological maltreatment.

A final word of caution should be expressed about the tentativeness of the results reported here. Because the issue of measurement of the psychological maltreatment of women by their male partners is a critical matter that has not yet received much attention in the field, this article has reported work in progress. It is not intended, however, that the PMWI be adopted for use by practitioners before completion of further exploration of its reliability and validity and the establishment of clinical norms and formal scoring procedures.

NOTE

[1]The high correlation of the two subscales raises an important methodological issue. Many scales that appear to be unidimensional may indeed be multidimensional, with highly correlated subscales. Because of an inadequate sample of items for each subscale, a scale appears to be unidimensional, when it is actually multidimensional. When the number of items for each dimension is increased, the multidimensionality of the scale is clarified.

REFERENCES

Arias, I., & Beach, S. R. H. (1987). Validity of self-reports of marital violence. *Journal of Family Violence, 2,* 139–150.

Dobash, R. E., & Dobash, R. P. (1981). Social science and social action: The case of wife-beating. *Journal of Family Issues, 2*(4), 439–470.

Edleson, J. (1988, March). *Judging success in intervention: The case of men who batter.* Paper presented at the American Enterprise Institute for Public Policy Conference on Family Violence Research, Washington, DC.

Edleson, J., & Brygger, M. (1986). Gender differences in reporting of battering incidents. *Family Relations, 35,* 377–382.

Ganley, A. (1982). *Court-mandated counseling for men who batter: A three day workshop for mental health professionals.* Washington, DC: Center for Women Policy Studies.

Gondolf, E. (1985). Anger and oppression in men who batter: Empiricist and feminist perspectives and their implications for research. *Victimology, 10,* 311–324.

Gondolf, E. (1987). Evaluating programs for men who batter: Problems and perspectives. *Journal of Family Violence, 2,* 95–108.

Gondolf, E., & Russell, D. (1986). The case against anger control treatment for batterers. *Response, 10,* 31–34.

Hudson, W., & Mcintosh, S. (1981). The assessment of spouse abuse: Two quantifiable dimensions. *Journal of Marriage and the Family, 43,* 873–885.

Klingbeil, K., & Boyd, V. (1984). Emergency room intervention: Detection, assessment and treatment. In A. Roberts (Ed.), *Battered women and their families.* New York: Springer Publishing Co.

NiCarthy, G. (1986). *Getting free: A handbook for women in abusive relationships.* Seattle, WA: Seal Press.

Nunnally, J. (1978). *Psychometric theory.* New York: McGraw-Hill.

O'Leary, K. D., & Arias, I. (1988). Assessing agreement of reports of spouse abuse. In G. T. Hotaling, D. Finkelhor, J. T. Kirkpatrick, & M. A. Straus (Eds.). *Family abuse and its consequences: New directions in research* (pp. 218–227), Newbury Park, CA: Sage.

Patrick-Hoffman, P. (1982). *Psychological abuse of women by spouses and live-in lovers.* Unpublished doctoral dissertation, The Union for Experimenting Colleges and Universities.

Purdy, S., & Nickle, N. (1981). Practice principles for working with groups of men who batter, *Social Work with Groups, 4*(3–4), 111–122.

Russell, D. E. (1982). *Rape in marriage.* New York: Collier Books.

Sonkin, D. J., Martin, D., & Walker, L. E. A. (1985). *The male batterer: A treatment approach.* New York: Springer Publishing Co.

Straus, M. (1979). Measuring intrafamilial conflict and violence: The conflict tactics (CT) scale. *Journal of Marriage and the Family, 45,* 75–88.

Straus, M. (1981, July 21–25). *A reevaluation of the conflict tactics scale violence measures and some new measures.* Paper presented at the National Family Violence Research Conference, Durham, NH.

Szinovacz, M. (1983). Using couple data as a methodological tool: The case of marital violence. *Journal of Marriage and the Family, 45,* 633–644.

Walker, L. (1979). *The battered woman.* New York: Harper & Row.

Acknowledgments. The author gratefully acknowledges the staff and clients of the Domestic Abuse Project, Minneapolis, Minnesota, for their cooperation with this research, and Walter Hudson, for his methodological assistance and support. This research was supported by NIMH Grant IT32-MH17152.

Reprints. Requests for reprints should be directed to Richard M. Tolman, University of Illinois at Chicago, Jane Addams College of Social Work, Box 4348, Chicago, IL 60680.

Violence and Victims, Volume 19, Number 4, August 2004

Psychologists' Judgments of Psychologically Aggressive Actions When Perpetrated by a Husband Versus a Wife

Diane R. Follingstad

Dana D. DeHart

Eric P. Green

University of South Carolina
Columbia

Research literature suggests that clinical judgments of men's versus women's behavior and symptoms typically rate the men as more pathological and dangerous. To determine whether this view would extend to assessments of psychologically aggressive actions, two separate versions of a survey listing potentially psychologically abusive behaviors perpetrated by either a wife toward her husband or the identical actions perpetrated by a husband toward his wife were sent to a nationwide sampling of practicing psychologists. Results indicated that psychologists, irrespective of demographics, rated the husband's behavior as more likely to be psychologically abusive and more severe in nature than the wife's use of the same actions. Psychologists did not differentially rely on any of the three contextual factors (i.e., frequency/duration, intent of the perpetrator, and perception of the recipient) to influence their determination that a behavior was "psychological abuse" dependent upon whether the initiator of the psychological actions was the husband or the wife. Future research could assess more directly the rationale for the psychologists' differing views of male versus female behavior. In addition, more normative information is needed to inform mental health professionals as to the prevalence and severity of psychologically aggressive actions in the general population.

Keywords: psychological aggression; psychological abuse; professional judgments

T he study of physical abuse, and more recently of psychological abuse, in intimate relationships has focused almost exclusively on women as the victims and men as the perpetrators (e.g., Migliaccio, 2001; Simonelli & Ingram, 1998). The earliest books to be published were about battered women (e.g., Martin, 1976; Walker, 1979) and the bulk of the research literature has focused on the incidence and prevalence of physical abuse, impacts of abuse, and correlates of perpetration. While some sociological surveys (e.g., Straus, 1977-1978) or emergency room commitment rates (e.g., Coontz, Lidz, & Mulvey, 1994) have indicated similar rates of physical violence for men and women, and some authors have raised concerns regarding the plight of battered men as well (e.g., Steinmetz, 1977-1978), other authors (e.g., Dobash, Dobash, Wilson, & Daly, 1992) do not believe these data accurately reflect the reality of physical abuse in the "real world."

While it is still uncertain whether actual rates of the use of physical force are comparable by males and females, it is typically granted that the impact of violence by men toward women produces greater harm as evidenced by women's emergency room visits, their need for medical care, and women's deaths at the hands of their partners (e.g., Germain, 1984). Harned (2001) reported that being the recipient of physical violence in a *dating* relationship is more severe for women than men, although Coker and colleagues (2000) found that poor mental and physical health was associated with severe physical dating violence for both male and female recipients. Stets and Straus (1990) presented evidence to suggest that physical violence in marital relationships is more traumatic physically and psychologically for women. There is mounting evidence, however, that the use of physical force by females is quite prevalent, especially in milder forms in dating relationships, where rates of females using force typically matches or exceeds that of the males (e.g., Harned, 2001; Katz, Kuffel, & Coblentz, 2002). The prevailing assumption, however, both with professionals and lay persons, seems to be that men are more likely to engage in using physical force and that the impact of such by a man is greater than that exhibited by a woman.

While the perpetration of *physical* abuse, especially without weapons, seems inherently more dangerous when engaged in by a man toward his partner, there is only one study (Harned, 2001) to date which suggests that the perpetration of *psychological* abuse is inherently more harmful when engaged in by men as opposed to women. Most anecdotal information which makes a case for the negative effects of psychological aggression perpetrated by men typically derives from the battered women literature. If battering men engage in psychologically aggressive actions, the physical threat usually implied in their daily behavior would certainly render any psychological aggression as more salient. But, because psychological aggression occurs in most relationships without the threat of accompanying physical force, we currently have very limited information as to whether psychological aggression is differentially applied or more harmful when men versus women engage in it. (Note: To clarify nomenclature, "psychological aggression" is used in this article to denote the full range of aggressive actions of an emotional/verbal/mental nature while "psychological abuse" is used similarly to most of the research literature wherein the implication of the term is that egregious actions likely to result in psychological harm have taken place. Thus, psychological aggression as a concept encompasses psychological abuse, but also includes behaviors at the mild or moderate levels of the continuum. The literature in this area has yet to resolve the best way to handle the terminology.)

The bulk of literature on psychological abuse focuses on women as the victims of psychological abuse which has the force of implying that this is the more common and serious scenario. There are some notable exceptions in the research on psychological abuse by those investigators who asked male and female participants about their own behavior as well as that of their dating partners (e.g., White & Koss, 1991) or focused specifically on men who reported being the recipient of psychologically aggressive behavior (e.g., Simonelli & Ingram, 1998). Some very recent research by Hines and Malley-Morrison (2001) reported similar effects of "psychological abuse" on male recipients as have been reported by female recipients in the literature. Furthermore, Hines and Malley-Morrison (2001), Molidor (1995), and Simonelli and Ingram (1998) all indicated that men reported being recipients of actions designated as psychological abuse on questionnaires at similar rates to females. However, the assumption for most professionals that men are the most likely perpetrators of psychological abuse may follow if one assumes that men are the more likely perpetrators of physical abuse. If mental health professionals believe that men are more culpable and harmful in this form of maltreatment, it is likely that they would view the perpetration of particular behaviors differently when exhibited by a man versus a woman in a marital relationship. It was expected that the same psychological action engaged in by a husband toward his wife would more likely be viewed as psychological abuse than when a wife engaged in the behavior toward her husband.

Psychological aggression has become an area of investigation in its own right in the last 15 years as researchers have begun to attempt to measure it, look at its relationship with physical abuse, and determine the impact of psychological aggression upon recipients. While the area of psychological abuse is fraught with definitional and conceptual problems (see Follingstad, 2003), researchers have forged ahead to conduct studies, often defining psychological abuse as a function of the measure they used or devised. Unfortunately, there has been little effort to provide normative information regarding how professionals or the general public view particular behaviors which make up the items on psychological abuse measures. As a beginning step toward understanding professionals' views of psychological abuse, Follingstad and DeHart (2000) investigated the degree to which psychologists viewed specific psychological behaviors as constituting psychological abuse. Using categories of psychological abuse and items from the literature, a sample of psychologists were solicited to rate 102 items regarding a husband's behavior toward his wife, and, from these data, five clusters of psychological actions were identified which varied in terms of being rated as "always," "maybe," or "never" psychological abuse as well as in terms of severity (see Measures section for more specific information about the clusters). From that study, what was still unknown was whether the psychologists would have rated the behaviors similarly if the survey had indicated that these were behaviors of a wife toward her husband.

Whether these assumptions—that gender influences who is more likely to engage in physical abuse and that behaviors by one gender can more readily be interpreted as abuse—extend over into professional judgments of *psychological* actions engaged in by men versus women in intimate relationships has yet to be investigated. There are numerous studies which suggest that gender, in general, affects professional judgments (e.g., Dohrenwend & Dohrenwend, 1976; Gove & Tudor, 1973; Harris, 1977). Clinical assessments regarding dangerousness and commitment have indicated that gender is considered relevant for professionals' decision-making (e.g., Holstein, 1987; Warren, 1982). And, if sex differences in clinical judgments of behavior (broadly defined) are any indication, we would then hypothesize that mental health professionals would likely view a man's psychological actions as more malignant than the same actions by a woman. In general, mental health professionals (i.e., psychologists, social workers, psychiatrists) do not view male and female behaviors as equally disordered. For instance, Lowery and Higgins (1979) reported that experienced clinicians rated male clients as more disturbed than female clients with the same case description. Their study surveyed 120 professional therapists who rated the severity of cases of depression, schizophrenia, and alcoholism. Sex of the patient was varied in the vignettes, and by virtue of being male, those patients were viewed as more seriously pathological and in need of more restrictive treatments. Similarly, Wrobel (1993) found an effect of client gender on clinicians' assessments, such that men and women clients with descriptions of cognitive and affective symptoms of depression were respectively diagnosed as having more serious problems of organicity versus depression. Teri's (1982) study adds to the body of literature in which males are rated differentially than females regarding mental health variables by professionals. Case descriptions of clients with relationship problems varied as to whether the person behaved in line with expected gender stereotypes or not. On ratings of prognosis and future functioning, women clients were believed to have a more positive prognosis and a higher level of expected functioning than males were expected to exhibit. While two studies did not support poorer ratings for male clients by mental health professionals, their methodology may explain the disparate results. Zygmond and Denton (1988) used an extremely narrow sexual problem for the clients, thus potentially limiting the amount of variability which could be generated with a more ambiguous diagnosis, and Poole and Tapley (1988) required clinicians to rate general behaviors rather than make diagnostic or prognostic evaluations from their clinical vignettes.

The specific behavior of physical aggression has been "stereotypically more closely associated with males than females" (Coontz, Lidz, & Mulvey, 1994, p. 370), with gender stereotypes reserving the aggressive, dominant perception for men and the submissive, nurturant perception for women. Because of the historical view of male and female differences regarding aggression along with the literature suggesting that professionals rate males as more pathological and impaired, the major hypothesis for this study is that professionals' judgments of psychological aggression will also view these actions by males as more problematic than these actions by women. That is, similar actions will be viewed as more abusive and more severe when engaged in by a man toward his wife than when exhibited by a woman toward her husband.

The prior study by Follingstad and DeHart (2000) which established psychologists' ratings of behaviors by a husband toward his wife was used for comparison purposes with a comparable sample of psychologists who rated the same behaviors by a wife toward her husband. The same methodology was adapted but the language was reversed for this study to indicate that a wife was the initiator of these actions. The participants rating the wife's behaviors were expected to similarly rate psychologically aggressive behaviors along a continuum such that items rated as more seriously abusive in the prior study would also be rated as more severe when a wife engaged in the behavior. However, the participants were expected to rate behaviors by the wife as less likely to be psychological abuse and as less severe in nature than the same behaviors by the husband. This hypothesis was expected to hold true: (a) for all of the items combined; (b) for the clusters of items previously devised using the psychologists' ratings on the husband's data (i.e., threats to physical health, control over personal freedoms, general destabilization, domination and control, and ineptitude/poor relationship behavior); and (c) for many of the individual items. Female psychologists, compared to male psychologists, were expected to rate the wife's behaviors as even less likely to be psychological abuse than the husband's behaviors. Because demographic variables of the psychologists were not related to their ratings in the prior study, it was expected that no other demographic variables would influence the psychologists' ratings of the wife's behaviors. In the prior study, psychologists rated the contextual variable of the frequency/duration of the behavior as more important when deciding whether a particular behavior was psychological abuse than the intent of the husband or the wife's perception. When psychologists rated the wife's behavior in this study, it was expected that the husband's perception of harm would be a more important variable for determining whether to label a behavior as psychological abuse than the woman's intentions. Psychologists may need to be convinced that the woman was able to inflict harm on her spouse before rating a behavior as psychological abuse.

METHOD

Participants

For each of the two studies, surveys were mailed to 1,000 psychologists sampled in a random fashion from the American Psychological Association's membership rosters. Because the goal was to obtain responses from practicing psychologists, professionals from Divisions 29, 42, and 43 were sampled (i.e., Psychotherapy, Psychologists in Independent Practice, and Family Psychology). The psychologists received a packet containing a cover letter, instructions, the survey and a postage-paid return envelope. The purpose of the study was described to the participants as the desire to establish normative information regarding whether specific behaviors were viewed as constituting psychological abuse. The second study informed the participants that this survey only investigated psychological abuse from a female partner toward her husband because a previous study of a husband's behavior toward his wife had already been conducted. Informed consent was implied by the voluntary return of the survey.

The surveys for the second study were mailed approximately 9 months to 1 year following the initial data collection. Of the 1,000 surveys mailed for the second sample, 103 surveys were returned due to death or relocation of recipients, while completed surveys numbered 263. The response rate of 26% was substantially lower than that obtained in the previous study of husband-to-wife behaviors (45%) using identical methodological procedures. The lower response rate was in itself informative, as were several incomplete surveys returned with comments. These few participants were reluctant to consider whether behaviors enacted by a woman were abusive because they perceived that women lacked the requisite power to effectively enact psychologically abusive behaviors and they could not comprehend that females could coerce male partners into submission using only psychological tactics.

Demographics of the First Sample. The psychologist sample (see Follingstad & DeHart, 2000) consisted of 449 clinicians randomly selected from relevant divisions of the APA. Fifty-six percent of the psychologists were male (*N* = 251) and 44% were female (*N* = 198). The median age of the psychologists was 52 with a range from 26 to 88. Racial breakdown indicated that 97% were Caucasian with less than 1% each of African Americans, Hispanics, and Native Americans. Most participants were married (78%), 5% identified as cohabiting, 8% as divorced, 2% as separated, 2% as widowed, and 5% as single. The majority of participants (75%) identified private practice as their primary employment setting, 8% worked primarily in academic settings, 5% in a hospital setting, 5% in clinics, 1% in federal or state agencies, and 6% worked in other settings. Number of years of practice following the doctorate ranged from 1 to 55 years, with the median length of psychological practice being 18 years. Most (316) participants performed up to one third of their applied work with couples, 90 participants performed 34% to 67% of applied work with couples, and nine performed over two thirds of their applied work with couples. About two thirds knew at least one woman close to them who had been a victim of psychological abuse in an intimate relationship, and about one third of participants identified themselves as having been victims of such abuse.

Demographics of the Second Sample. The demographics which follow pertain to the version in which the wife initiated the behaviors. There were 147 male (56%) and 116 female (44%) psychologists in the sample. Participants ranged in age from 32 to 80, with the median age being 52. Ninety-six percent of the participants were White, 2% were

Native American, and less than 1% each were African Americans or Hispanic. Most participants were married (78%), 5% identified as cohabiting, 9% as divorced, 2% as separated, 3% as widowed, and 5% as single. The majority of participants (72%) identified private practice as their primary employment setting, 10% worked primarily in academic settings, 8% in a hospital setting, 8% in clinics, 5% in federal or state agencies, and 5% worked in other settings. Number of years of practice following a doctorate degree ranged from 2 to 50 years, with the median length of psychological practice being 19 years. Most (189) participants performed up to one third of their applied work with couples, 50 participants performed 34% to 67% of applied work with couples and three performed over two thirds of applied work with couples. Thirty-eight percent of participants resided in the north, 22% in the southeast, 9% in the southwest, 16% in the midwest, and 16% in the West. About two thirds reported knowing at least one person close to them who had been a victim of psychological abuse in an intimate relationship, with the median number of victims known being two. Just under one half of the participants (47%) identified themselves as having been victims of such abuse, and slightly over one half of those who had been personally victimized were female.

Measures

Psychological Abuse Survey. In the prior study, 102 psychologically aggressive items were identified from the research literature and clinical cases focusing on psychological abuse. The authors adopted some descriptions of psychologically aggressive behaviors directly from the literature and modified others for the survey, in order to provide participants with a wide range of relatively non-overlapping items. For the first study, all of the behaviors were exhibited by a husband toward his wife (HTOW) whereas the second study was characterized by the wife engaging in the behaviors toward her husband (WTOH). The 102 selected items were grouped thematically as fitting the following categories of psychological abuse identified in the literature and are listed in Table 1: (a) treatment as inferior, humiliation, degradation; (b) isolation, restriction or monopolization of mobility, information or social activity; (c) emotional or sexual withdrawal or blackmail; (d) verbal attacks/criticism; (e) economic deprivation; (f) threats of physical harm or threats to physical health; (g) destabilizing the woman's perception of reality; (h) use of male privilege and/or rigid gender role; (i) control of personal behavior; (j) jealousy/suspicion; (k) intimidation or harassment; and (l) failure to live up to role expectations. To enhance the likelihood that psychologists would take the time to complete the survey, two forms of the survey were devised with each form consisting of 51 behaviors and comprising roughly one half of the items for the identified categories of psychological abuse. The same forms were used for the second study, but the roles were changed such that the wife was the perpetrator and the husband was the recipient of the behaviors. Two of the items, which were considered unable to be reversed, were eliminated (i.e., "wanted to use spouse as prostitute" and "was stingy in giving spouse money to run the household").

The prior study (Follingstad & DeHart, 2000) with the psychologists rating the husband's perpetration of the behaviors identified five clusters which appeared to be mostly influenced by how likely the item was viewed as "psychological abuse" and the severity ratings. The cluster analysis used squared Euclidean distance measures and the Ward clustering method to ensure that item groups were combined in a manner that minimized within-group variance. The first two clusters (each with four items) were rated as equally severe in nature as evidenced by the high percentage of psychologists rating the behavior as "always" abusive and the high mean severity ratings. The first cluster involved serious threats to the woman's physical well-being while the second cluster involved serious

TABLE 1. Item Clusters and Percentages of Items for the Two Surveys

Items	Husband to Wife			Wife to Husband		
	Yes	Maybe	No	Yes	Maybe	No
Cluster A: Threats to physical health and destabilization-prisoner						
Threatened to hurt spouse	99	1	0	93	8	0[b]
Threatened to hurt spouse's family/ children/friends	99	0	1	93	7	0[b]
Threatened to disfigure spouse permanently	98	2	0	97	3	0
Prevented spouse from getting medical care	95	5	0	93	6	1
Forced spouse to eat from a bowl on the floor	100	0	0	91	8	2[ab]
Would not let spouse leave the house	94	6	0	79	8	3[a]
Would not let spouse sleep	89	11	0	72	26	2[a]
Cluster B: General destabilization (intimidation, isolation/restriction/monopolizing, degradation, destabilizing perceptions)						
Harassed spouse at work	95	4	1	81	18	1[a]
Demanded spouse's unconditional obedience	94	6	0	82	10	8[ab]
Forced spouse to beg for something essential	94	5	1	82	13	6
Called spouse derogatory names (e.g., whore)	93	7	0	76	24	0[a]
Tried to make spouse believe s/he was crazy	92	8	0	90	9	2
Tried to turn family/friends against spouse	88	10	2	81	16	2
Would not let spouse go anywhere without him/her	88	10	2	66	27	7[ab]
Threatened to hurt a pet	86	10	4	89	10	2
Controlled info by limiting phone and car use	85	13	2	76	20	5
Treated spouse as inferior	85	14	1	54	35	10
Threatened to take children away from spouse	83	16	1	77	23	0
Would not let spouse socialize with family/friends	83	15	2	58	36	7[a]
Damaged spouse's personal belongings	80	19	1	72	24	4
Denied spouse access to money	80	18	2	69	26	5
Threatened to have spouse committed to institution	79	20	1	64	35	2
Tried to convince others spouse was crazy	78	18	4	61	37	2[a]
Physically abused a pet	77	20	3	76	16	8
Threatened to deny spouse economic support	72	24	4	38	46	16[a]
Threatened to hurt himself or herself	52	41	7	61	32	7
Cluster C: Dominating/Controlling (jealousy/ suspicion, control of personal behavior, isolation/ restriction/monopolization, emotional withholding/blackmail, verbal abuse, treatment as inferior)						
Threatened to humiliate spouse in public	83	15	2	74	22	4
Insulted spouse in front of others	81	18	1	76	23	1
Made spouse account for whereabouts at all times	80	19	1	50	38	12[a]
Would not allow spouse to speak/look at other members of the same sex	80	18	2	59	33	8[a]
Decided what spouse could eat	78	18	4	37	43	20[ab]
Chose spouse's friends	77	20	3	42	42	16[a]
Decided activities in which spouse could engage	77	20	3	45	46	9[a]
Threw tantrums, breaking objects in the house	76	23	1	59	36	5[a]
Blamed spouse for things totally unrelated to him/her	74	23	3	58	35	7[a]
Made spouse ask every time s/he needed money	73	22	5	50	29	11[a]
Kept spouse from self-improvement activities	71	25	4	49	40	11[ab]
Listened to spouse's phone conversations secretly	70	24	6	60	34	6
Forced spouse to discuss past sexual relationships	68	31	1	33	49	18[a]
Intruded in spouse's work with immediate demands	68	28	4	58	34	8[a]

TABLE 1. continuued

Items	Husband to Wife			Wife to Husband		
	Yes	Maybe	No	Yes	Maybe	No
Decided whether spouse could smoke or drink	66	27	7	35	45	20[a]
Monitored spouse to always know where s/he was	66	31	3	35	53	12[a]
Followed spouse when s/he was away from home	65	32	3	38	52	10[a]
Refused to let spouse work outside the home	65	29	6	62	28	10
Insisted spouse answer any question s/he asked	5	29	6	24	55	21[a]
Treated spouse as inferior	65	28	7	54	35	10
Threatened to reveal secrets spouse had confided	64	31	5	64	29	7
Made decisions about spouse's appearance	63	32	5	13	56	31[ab]
Blamed spouse for his or her own problems	63	32	5	52	34	14[a]
Played cruel jokes on spouse	61	38	1	82	16	2
Checked spouse's belongings to confirm suspicions	61	33	6	31	53	16[a]
Criticized spouse's sexual performance/desirability	61	32	7	51	41	8
Left for long periods with no explanation	60	31	9	61	35	5
Used needed money for own addictions/ hobbies	52	32	11	59	27	14
Acted rude to guests to discourage visitors	56	35	9	49	39	12
Stayed angry until spouse cooperated	55	38	7	43	41	16[a]
Refused to pay fair share to maintain family	54	34	12	15	48	37[a]
Swore at spouse	52	44	4	37	51	12[a]
Denied spouse any private time	52	43	5	24	63	13
Threatened to have an affair	52	35	13	52	34	13[a]
Expressed jealousy of any members of the same sex in contact with spouse	51	42	7	32	48	20[a]
Would not let spouse talk about his/her feelings	51	36	13	53	33	14
Yelled and screamed at spouse	49	49	2	33	61	6[a]
Wanted spouse to be involved only in his/her interests	46	35	19	37	40	23
Assumed a frightening look, stance or mood	40	55	5	16	59	25[ab]
Was insensitive to spouse's sexual needs	40	47	13	27	61	12
Was reluctant to share spouse with the children	39	43	18	40	46	15
Was jealous and suspicious of spouse's friends	38	52	10	27	49	23
Criticized spouse's personal characteristics or ideas	37	56	7	32	58	11
Criticized spouse's strong points	37	50	13	25	55	20
Accused spouse of an affair/being promiscuous	35	59	6	17	65	17
Checked to see if spouse went where s/he indicated	34	56	10	10	65	24[a]
Verified that spouse was still home after s/he left	34	52	14	14	61	24
Denied spouse his/her own companionship	34	52	14	32	55	13
Withheld supportive behavior	34	49	17	28	54	18
Threatened to leave the relationship	32	55	13	31	58	11
Made major decisions without spouse	30	60	10	17	64	19[a]
Withheld affection/tenderness	30	58	12	23	62	15
Criticized spouse's weak points	30	58	12	23	62	15
Expressed disgust or hatred for other members of the opposite sex	25	48	27	12	51	38
Displayed radical mood changes	21	54	25	16	62	22
Used poor judgment when caring for children	12	52	36	25	49	26[a]
Cluster D: Ineptitude (rigid gender roles, role failure)						
Insisted on holding all money when out together	42	40	18	36	42	22
Expected dinner/housework done on his/her schedule	40	47	13	14	51	35[a]

TABLE 1. continued

	Husband to Wife			Wife to Husband		
Criticized spouse's physical appearance	37	60	3	37	60	2
Told spouse s/he could not manage alone	34	56	10	17	68	14[a]
Burdened spouse with errands to occupy his/her time	30	52	18	16	57	28[a]
Refused to talk about things important to spouse	30	51	19	24	55	21
Criticized the way spouse handled house/children	9	66	5	25	66	10
Would not let spouse drive when out together	29	49	22	13	60	28[a]
Did not do fair share of tasks and childcare	23	47	30	15	52	34
Refused to go to functions important to spouse	22	52	26	20	63	17
Refused to talk about problems (sulked, etc.)	20	53	27	22	50	29
Moved spouse far away from his/her support system	17	69	14	23	59	18
Refused to see spouse's family	17	59	24	18	59	24
Mismanaged the family's money	17	54	29	6	61	33
Was reluctant to have children	14	36	50	7	47	47
Did not live up to commitments	13	60	27	14	64	22
Showed more interest in own than spouse's activities	13	50	37	4	58	38
Showed a loss of sexual interest	9	55	36	8	58	35

[a]indicates $p < .05$ for both subsamples for the Abuse variable.
[b]$p < .05$ for both subsamples for the Severity variable.

degradation, isolation, and control of the woman. The third cluster consisted of 19 behaviors which would be destabilizing to the recipient, and included items representing psychological abuse categories of intimidation, degradation, isolation, restriction, monopolization, and destabilizing perceptions. The fourth cluster involved 56 items of lesser domination and control, while the fifth cluster's 18 items depicted the mildest ones with the potential to be abusive, but which could alternatively be interpreted as ineptitude on the part of the husband, such as role failure and boorish behavior, rather than behaviors intending to cause harm.

Because only one half of the items were located on each form of the survey, the overall reliability was calculated using each half. For the HTOW version, Cronbach alphas were .96 and .96, and for the WTOH version, the alphas were .95 and .96. The reliability estimates for the clusters were conducted similarly, using the items in a cluster from the first form, followed by using the items from the second form. Thus, for each cluster, there are two Cronbach alphas. In addition, these reliability estimates were calculated separately for the HTOW data and the WTOH data. The Cronbach alphas are as follows for the HTOW data: Cluster A—.90 and .89; Cluster B—.85 and .71; Cluster C—.94 and .94; and Cluster D—.85 and .91. For the WTOH data, the alphas are as follows: Cluster A—.63 and .74; Cluster B—.84 and .80; Cluster C—.94 and .94; and Cluster D—.82 and .88. Thus, the internal consistency for the clusters which were originally formed are quite high, and this remains true for the data from the WTOH sample for which the same clusters were used.

Analyses from the HTOW study indicated that the clusters appear to be reasonably distinct from each other in terms of their items being labeled as "psychological abuse" and the severity level assigned to them (Follingstad & DeHart, 2000). Cluster D is significantly different from all other clusters, as is Cluster C. Clusters B and A, while different from C and D, are not statistically different from each other. However, the items in Cluster

A represented those for which there was the highest agreement among the professionals that the behaviors were psychologically abusive, while Cluster B represented somewhat more of a range within items considered to be fairly severe.

For purposes of comparison, the clusters of items which were identified in the original study were also formed for the data involving the wife as the perpetrator of psychological abuse with one exception (see Table 1). Because the original study had generated two small clusters of similarly severe psychological abuse items and which were only distinguishable by the fact that they loaded on the two different forms, these two clusters (except for the elimination of the prostitution item) were combined into Cluster A (with 7 items) for this study. Thus, the third cluster from the prior study now became Cluster B (with 19 items), the fourth cluster became Cluster C (with 56 items), and the fifth cluster became Cluster D (with 18 items). (Note: A separate cluster analysis performed on the data from the WTOH study yielded quite similar clusters, suggesting that grouping the items into clusters from the HTOW study for comparison was a reasonable strategy.)

Participants read each item describing a psychologically aggressive behavior and decided whether they believed the behavior (a) is *never* abusive no matter what the circumstances ("no"); (b) *might be* considered abusive in some contexts or under some conditions ("maybe"); or (c) is *always* abusive, no matter what the circumstances ("yes"). The scoring for this variable is designated as "no" = 1, "maybe" = 2, and "yes" = 3. If the participant designated a behavior as "always" abuse, the participant then rates the severity of the abuse on a 5-point Likert scale (1 = not severe to 5 = very severe). If participants chose the "maybe" category, they then use 5-point Likert scales (ranging from 1 = not at all to 5 = very much so) to rate the extent to which (a) the frequency/duration of the behavior, (b) the wife's intention to create psychological distress, and (c) the husband's perception of harm to himself, would influence whether they would classify the behavior as abusive. Because mean scores on frequency/duration, intent, perception, as well as the severity rating were calculated using ratings by a subsample of participants (i.e., those who chose "maybe" or "yes" responses), a possibility of limited reliability remains for these ratings.

Demographics for the psychologists completing the husband-to-wife form (HTOW) ($N = 449$) and those completing the wife-to-husband form (WTOH) ($N = 263$) were equivalent with no significant differences emerging between the two groups. For each of the items of the two forms of the survey, the percentage of respondents who identified the behavior as definitely not abusive, as possibly abusive, and as definitely abusive was calculated (see Table 1).

To determine whether there were differences between the two forms of the survey which each consisted of one-half of the items, that is, Forms A and B, means for the five potential ratings were calculated for each form in each study. A MANOVA using all five ratings of Form A as the dependent variables with the two forms of the survey constituting the independent variable indicated that there was no overall significant difference ($F(1,710) = .01$, $p = .92$). The same finding occurred for Form B when a MANOVA, utilizing all five ratings for that form, compared that form across both studies, ($F(1,710) = .07$, $p = .79$). Thus, the two forms appear to be basically comparable.

RESULTS

Initially, all five ratings by psychologists (i.e., whether the behavior is psychological abuse [ABUSE], the degree to which frequency/duration [FREQ/DUR], intention of the perpetrator [INTENT], and perception of the recipient (PERCEPT) influenced a participant's determination that a behavior is psychological abuse, and the severity of the action [SEVERITY]) were included in a MANOVA to determine whether, overall, psychologists made different ratings dependent upon whether the husband or wife was committing the action. The overall MANOVA was significant [F (1,206) = 6.00, $p < .02$]. How frequently psychological actions were labeled "abusive" was significant in subsequent univariate tests [t (206) = 3.85, $p < .0001$], with the means indicating that actions by a husband were more likely to be considered psychologically abusive than those by a wife. Subsequent ratings of the severity of those actions by those who decided the actions were definitely "abusive" indicated significantly higher ratings of severity if the actions were perpetrated by a husband as compared with a wife [t (206) = 3.81, $p < .0001$]. While there was a trend, [t (187) = -1.86, $p < .064$], for participants who used the "maybe" category to more seriously consider the intent of a wife's actions compared to considering the intent of a husband's actions when deciding whether to label particular actions as psychological abuse, the three contextual factors were not utilized differentially to make determinations of psychological abuse if the initiator of the action was a husband or a wife.

While the overall data supported the hypothesis of differential rating of husbands' versus wives' behavior, exploratory analyses looking at subsets of the 100 items and the individual items themselves were conducted to better understand where the differences were apparent. Because of the large number of analyses that were to be conducted to assess differences at the item level, a random set of one-half of the participants for each of the surveys was generated on which to conduct the analyses. To provide cross-validation, the other half of the participants were subsequently subjected to the same analyses. In order to protect against significance occurring by chance, only those findings which resulted in p values at the .05 level for *both* samples were considered significant (Anderson, 2001).

The four major clusters (A, B, C, and D) were used for comparing the psychologists' ratings between the two studies. Clusters A, B, and C were all highly significantly different from each other in both samples (see Table 2) in that psychologists always rated the husband's actions toward his wife as more likely to be psychological abuse than a woman's perpetration of the same behaviors toward her husband. While Cluster D was significantly different for one of the samples, and demonstrated a trend in the other, the criterion of being significant at the .05 level for both samples was not met. The items in Cluster D represent the mildest actions and those which are potentially more controversial as to whether they represent "psychological abuse." Demographic variables such as participant sex, ethnicity, or marital status either did not influence the psychologists' ratings of the clusters of items across both samples or produced inconsistent findings with one exception. For Cluster B, which consists of items representing moderately severe controlling, isolating, monitoring, and destabilizing actions, female psychologists rated the items as more likely to be psychological abuse ($M = 2.82$) than the male psychologists ($M = 2.75$), no matter who perpetrated the actions. However, the mean differences were only .7 apart on a 3-point scale, suggesting that, clinically, this difference would not likely have much impact upon male and female psychologists' real-life determinations of psychological abuse. In addition, the three other clusters did not show any sex differences.

To further delineate the psychologists' view of husband to wife versus wife to husband psychological aggression, analyses were conducted on the severity ratings of behaviors which were elicited when participants labeled a particular behavior as definitely "psychological abuse." Overall, both cross-validation samples of the participants rated the severity of the total items differentially for the husband to wife versus wife to husband versions (see Table 2), with the husband's actions rated as more severe. Regarding the individual clusters, only Clusters A and B were rated as significantly different in terms of severity with the husband's behavior rated as more severe than that of the wife, even though all of the behaviors which participants rated in terms of severity were first designated as

TABLE 2. Means for Subsamples of the HTOW and WTOH Versions of the Survey With F Values and Significance Levels

Dependent Variables	Subsample 1					Subsample 2				
	HTOW M	WTOH M	df	F	p	HTOW M	WTOH M	df	F	p
Abuse										
Overall	2.49	2.29	1,354	28.72	.0001	2.48	2.29	1,352	24.76	.0001
Cluster A	2.96	2.86	1,354	20.56	.0001	2.96	2.85	1,353	23.58	.0001
Cluster B	2.82	2.71	1,354	11.63	.0007	2.83	2.68	1,353	15.92	.0001
Cluster C	2.51	2.25	1,354	37.03	.0001	2.48	2.27	1,353	25.24	.0001
Cluster D	2.05	1.90	1,354	8.44	.004	2.03	1.95	1,353	2.62	.107
Severity										
Overall	3.60	3.34	1,353	12.38	.0005	3.58	3.32	1,352	12.34	.0005
Cluster A	4.66	4.29	1,346	35.44	.0001	4.64	4.24	1,353	38.65	.0001
Cluster B	3.84	3.57	1,346	38.65	.0001	3.81	3.45	1,353	15.02	.0001
Cluster C	3.15	3.02	1,346	1.79	.182	3.08	2.89	1,353	3.71	.055
Cluster D	2.63	2.63	1,346	0.00	.997	2.55	2.60	1,353	0.18	.674
Frequency/ Duration										
Overall	3.64	3.64	1,349	0.00	.977	3.69	3.62	1,340	0.36	.550
Intent Overall	3.64	3.67	1,349	0.09	.770	3.72	3.72	1,340	0.00	.997
Perception										
Overall	3.45	3.48	1,342	0.03	.860	3.61	3.50	1,343	0.98	.320

HTOW: Behaviors perpetrated by the husband toward the wife.
WTOH: Behaviors perpetrated by the wife toward the husband.

"psychologically abusive" (See Table 2). The only demographic variable which demonstrated significant results on severity ratings across both subsamples was the sex of the participant. For Clusters A and B, female psychologists generally rated the psychologically aggressive behaviors as more severe in nature, irrespective of who engaged in them $[F (1,353) = 5.50, p < .022$ and $F (1,354) = 4.70, p < .031$ for Cluster A; $F (1,353) = 4.21, p < .041$ and $F (1,354) = 9.44, p < .002$ for Cluster B].

Analyses at the individual item level revealed that 43 of the 100 items were rated significantly differently by both subsamples of the psychologists dependent upon who was the perpetrator for the ABUSE variable. Many of these items indicated very large differences with p values greater than .0001. In addition, 17 other items were significant at the .05 level for one of the two cross-validation samples. All but one of the significant items were rated as more likely to be psychological abuse when engaged in by a man than by a woman, the exception being the item indicating that the person used poor judgment in relation to the children. (Note that items which were rated significantly different between the two surveys are indicated by [a] on Table 1.) There were fewer individual items which were rated differently on the two surveys in terms of severity. Only nine items were rated by both of the randomly generated subsamples as more severe psychological abuse when exhibited by a man than when exhibited by a woman toward their spouse. Thus, while many more items are likely to be perceived as psychological abuse when perpetrated by a man, professionals who label the behaviors as "psychologically abusive" do not differ that often in terms of the degree of severity they assign to the action. (The nine items which were rated differently in terms of severity are indicated by [b] on Table 1.)

Psychologists did not rate the three contextual variables differently as to the degree to which the factors would influence a determination of psychological abuse if the psychologists originally thought the behavior "might be" abusive (see Table 2). Neither the frequency/duration of the behavior (FREQ/DUR), the intention of the perpetrator (INTENT), nor the perception of the recipient (PERCEPT) were rated differently by the psychologists as likely to influence their decision whether a behavior was psychological abuse if they were making the determination regarding a husband's behavior versus a wife's behavior. The lack of overall findings for these three variables was consistent with the lack of significance when utilizing item clusters and individual items as the object of analysis. None of the demographic variables influenced the ratings of the overall contextual variables.

When the data from both studies were combined, psychologists rated the frequency and/or duration variable as more likely to influence them to designate a behavior, about which they were previously uncertain, as psychological abuse than either knowing the intention of a person to harm their spouse [t (207) = 3.72, $p < .0001$] or knowing the perception of the person on the receiving end of the behavior [t (207) = 7.21, $p < .0001$]. Also, knowing the intent of the perpetrator when engaging in a psychological action was rated as more likely to influence psychologists' judgments of psychological abuse than knowing the perception of the recipient [t (207) = 3.36, $p < .001$]. For the HTOW data alone, the first two comparisons remained significant [t (101) = 3.37, $p < .001$ and t [101] = 4.87, $p < .0001$, respectively] but the psychologists did not consider knowing the intentions of the husband versus knowing the perception of the wife as likely to differentially affect their judgments [t (101) = 1.01, $p < .32$]. In contrast, using only the WTOH data, there was a trend for psychologists to consider the frequency/duration of a behavior as more important for judging it to be psychological abuse than the perpetrator's intention [t (105) = 1.19, $p < .059$]. The frequency/duration was rated as significantly more likely to affect judgments of psychological abuse than knowing the perception of the recipient of the action [t (105) = 5.30, $p < .0001$] and knowing the woman's intention was considered more important for labeling a behavior as psychological abuse than knowing the husband's perception [t (105) = 4.15, $p < .0001$].

DISCUSSION

As hypothesized, psychologists deciding whether particular actions were definitely, maybe, or never psychological abuse were more likely to consider actions of a husband toward his wife to be abusive than when a wife engaged in the identical behaviors toward her husband. Thus, the stereotypical association between physical aggression and males (Coontz, Lidz, & Mulvey, 1994) appears to extend to an association of psychological abuse and males. Analyses to determine where this difference was most salient indicated that three of the four clusters of psychological actions were highly discrepant (while the fourth narrowly missed significance in both samples) and that almost one half of the individual items were perceived differently as to their "abusiveness" dependent upon the gender of the perpetrator. Even some of the more severe items (i.e., "wouldn't let spouse socialize with family/friends," "threatened to deny spouse economic support," "wouldn't let the spouse go anywhere without him/her") resulted in fairly large percentages of psychologists more likely to classify the behavior as *possibly* abusive (rather than definitely abusive) when a wife engaged in the behavior than when a husband acted the same way. While the psychologists were not asked to give rationales for their decisions, some themes for the items which were considered less offensive for a wife to engage in were as follows: (a) Men may not be able to be trusted, so it is less of a problem and probably not abusive for a wife to monitor her husband (e.g., "Made spouse account for whereabouts at all times;" "Would not allow spouse to speak/look at other members of the opposite sex;" "Checked spouse's belongings to confirm suspicions;" "Followed spouse when he/she was away from home"); (b) Women don't have the same responsibility/equality regarding support of the household (e.g., "Refused to pay fair share to maintain family;" "Threatened to deny spouse economic support;" "Made spouse ask every time he/she needed money;" "Made major decisions without spouse"); (c) It is possible that women engage in certain behaviors as a way of taking care of the man or because he cannot take care of himself, therefore she is not actually controlling him (e.g., "Decided what spouse could eat;" "Chose spouse's friends;" "Decided activities in which spouse could engage;" "Made decisions about spouse's appearance"); and (d) Women do not have as much power as men, therefore certain actions would not have much impact (e.g., "Demanded spouse's unconditional obedience;" "Tried to convince others spouse was crazy;" "Kept spouse from self-improvement activities;" "Assumed a frightening look, stance or mood"). The mildest behaviors found in the fourth cluster were not rated much differently as to whether a husband or wife did the behavior, probably because the behaviors already were perceived by the psychologists as least likely to constitute psychological abuse irrespective of the gender of the person engaging in the behavior.

The findings suggested that, *overall*, if a psychologist decided that behavior was psychologically abusive, that the perception of the behavior was still different if it was engaged in by the husband as opposed to the wife. Thus, if psychologists thought an action by a wife toward her husband was actually "abusive," they did not think it was as bad, problematic, or pathological than if the husband engaged in that behavior. This disparity was most evident in the two most serious clusters of items wherein the husband's actions were viewed as more severe in nature. Thus, it appears that equality of severity ratings is evident when milder and moderate items are being considered, but less so when items of a more severe nature are being rated. This discrepancy in severity ratings is again likely to be the result of the themes listed above regarding the discrepancy in rating the behavior as abusive—the wife would not have the same responsibilities to maintain, she would be unlikely to carry out her threats, her actions would have less impact on the man than vice versa, and women might need to engage in some of these actions to keep the man's behavior in check. Regarding individual items, only nine items out of 102 were viewed differently when perpetrated by a husband versus a wife, suggesting that differences in severity ratings consist of a trend for the psychologists to rate more severe items differently without the difference being starkly evident on individual items. However, three of the most severe items were among those with the different severity ratings, and while it appears that the psychologists clearly felt they had to label these items as psychologically abusive based on their content, they rated a wife's actions as less *severe* than a husband's actions for the following items: "Threatened to hurt spouse;" "Threatened to hurt spouse's family, children or friends;" and "Forced spouse to eat from a bowl on the floor." One likely reason could be that the psychologists were taking the viewpoint that a man's threats would be more frightening and that the woman might not be able to physically carry out the threats. That view, however, would raise the issue as to whether the potential *impact* of an action should influence the rating of its severity or whether some extreme behaviors should be viewed as offensive/psychologically abusive irrespective of the possible impact.

Frequency/duration of a behavior was almost always viewed by psychologists as a more important contextual factor to consider when deciding whether to call a behavior psychological abuse than either of the other contextual factors—the perpetrator's intention to harm or the recipient's perception of harm. As stated in the prior study, psychologists may desire a more objective indicator for determining when a behavior has moved beyond being problematic to becoming "psychological abuse," and knowledge of frequency and/or duration of a behavior would allow for a more behavioral assessment than the murky appraisal of a person's genuine intentions or of a partner's reaction to an event while partialling out potential biases, motivations, or distortions which might be present. However, when comparing psychologists' ratings regarding the importance of the perpetrators' intentions versus the recipients' perceptions, the psychologists rated the wife's perspective as more important for determining that psychological abuse had occurred whether she was the perpetrator of the action or the recipient of it. While current sensitization about wife battering would seem an explanation for psychologists' preference for the perspective of a woman who is a potential recipient of psychological abuse over the potential perpetrator's perspective, it is less easy to understand why psychologists would reverse their preference when a woman is the potential perpetrator. Because more of the psychologists were rating the woman's actions as "not" or "maybe" psychological abuse to begin with, it is possible that they were already judging her intentions as unlikely to be malignant, but considered it wise to check their perspective against other data that might be available. In addition, if the psychologists typically viewed the woman's actions as less severe, they may have subsequently considered the man's viewpoint as not particularly important for making the larger determination of labeling the behavior as psychological abuse or not. That is, if a wife's intentions are viewed as benign, then even if the man perceived the behavior otherwise, the assumption would be that he is likely mistaken and therefore his viewpoint would not need to be weighed as heavily. When a husband engages in the listed behaviors, the findings suggest that the man's actions, at the outset, were more often judged as abusive and severe; therefore, it is likely that the psychologists believed, by virtue of his actions, that they know the man's intentions, and therefore were more willing to take into consideration the wife's perceptions as to whether she felt psychologically harmed.

Because the prior study with only ratings of the husband's actions found demographic variables to have no real influence on the ratings, the fact that demographic variables overall and specifically regarding the ratings of the wife's actions did not have much influence on the ratings of abuse or severity was somewhat expected. Due to the small number of non-Caucasian psychologists in the sample, appropriate analyses could not be conducted for ethnicity. Of course, education as a factor had no variability, rendering it unuseable for analysis. However, the psychologists who participated were reasonably balanced for sex and marital status, and two variables were added to determine whether someone close to the person or the person himself/herself having been in a psychologically abusive relationship would influence ratings. On only one cluster did female psychologists rate the items as more abusive and on only two clusters did female psychologists rate the severity of items they had already designated as psychologically abusive as more severe than male psychologists. However, these mean differences were so small as to be unlikely to impact clinical decision-making. Interestingly, there were no significant interactions of the demographics with the different surveys, such that when female psychologists did rate behaviors as more likely to be abusive or as more severe, they made these determinations regardless of the sex of the perpetrator of them.

Because this study attempted to provide a wide range of psychologically aggressive behaviors for psychologists to rate, it is of note that so many of the items were rated by a substantial number of psychologists as "always abusive" based solely on a very brief description. For example, "blaming spouse for own problems" was endorsed as always psychological abuse by 63% of the psychologists for the husband's behavior and by 52% for the wife's behavior. "Swearing at a spouse" was judged to be abusive by 52% of the psychologists when the husband swore and by 37% of the psychologists when the wife swore. While there has certainly been much sensitization regarding intimate aggression and victimization in recent years, it is hard to understand how so many psychologists could unequivocally determine that most of these items are always abuse with no knowledge from the brief scenario as to the context or the impact of the behavior. While almost every item might be considered psychological aggression, there are numerous contextual factors which might prevent a professional from moving many of these behaviors into the range of abuse. Consider the following questions with regard to "swearing at a spouse." What if the person swore in a joking manner? What if it were a mild swear word? What if it were the first time the person had ever sworn at the spouse? What if the spouse had just engaged in reprehensible behavior toward the partner, who then swore in retaliation? What if the recipient of the swearing was a person who swore all the time himself/herself, such that swearing had no impact on them? What if the swearing was used for impact to get the partner to pay attention because he/she would not listen to important information otherwise? Additional contextual factors could be raised as well and the differential impact of swearing across relationships ranges vastly. Thus, the labeling of psychological actions as "psychological abuse" may require much more development of the concept and factors influencing it before psychologists can isolate most psychological actions as "abusive" within a relationship (see Follingstad, 2003). For example, the current use of checklists which briefly describe a behavior the researcher considers "psychological abuse" may need to be modified in order to more accurately assess whether an egregious action actually occurred.

There are several limitations of this study. First of all, while the items on the survey include many items found on current measures of psychological abuse and represent a range of psychological dimensions, they do not constitute a systematic way of assessing psychologically abusive actions. Some dimensions may be overrepresented and some may require more description before judgments can be even cursorily made. Second, because the study utilizing the survey in which the wife engaged in behaviors toward her husband had a poorer return rate, questions can be raised regarding why this survey was less likely to be returned by psychologists than the version using the husband as the perpetrator. However, some of the spontaneous comments of those returning the survey not completed did suggest that a number of professionals had difficulty perceiving that women could be effectively psychologically abusive, further adding to the view that men are more likely to be the psychologically aggressive individuals in relationships. Third, while this research design investigated psychologists' impressions as to how salient several contextual factors would be for their decision making regarding psychological abuse, further research will be required to empirically demonstrate whether their perceptions are borne out in judgments made regarding cases in which these factors vary. Fourth, this study could not include at this time the issue of the impact of behaviors, other than through indirectly asking whether the recipient's perception of harm would be important for making these decisions. Thus, participants had to basically assume that behaviors which seemed more severe would have more serious impacts while behaviors perceived as milder would be viewed as having low impact. While one would expect that there would be a reasonable correlation between these in the real world, there could certainly be behaviors which would be objectively rated as severe, but have low impact, and vice versa.

The findings of this study suggest that clinical judgments regarding the assessment of psychological abuse parallel prior literature wherein professionals judged men's interpersonal actions as more likely to be dangerous, pathological, and as having menacing implications than the same behaviors exhibited by women. What is uncertain is whether these judgments were based upon predictions these clinicians made based upon actual experiences with clients, whether these judgments are representative of what actually exists (i.e., men are more dangerous and menacing in terms of psychological interactions), or whether these judgments are based upon heuristics which may lead to errors in decision making. It is possible that the tendency of persons toward producing consistent, therefore stable, perceptions even when they might make logical errors in so doing (Amabile & Hastorf, 1976) may influence the judgment to perceive a woman's actions as less problematic than a man's actions. Because women have been historically viewed as less aggressive and more affiliative, professionals might utilize this view and even apply it in a general way to descriptions of aggressive behavior by women by assuming it either must not be particularly abusive, or if it is abusive, it must not be particularly severe. If this is the case, clinicians may need to examine their assumptions to see whether they have different standards for identical behavior exhibited by men and women in intimate relationships. Another study might investigate this type of decision making of professionals to understand the rationales, assumptions, stereotypes, etc., which might be influencing the differences found in this study. What exactly do psychologists consider or weigh when inferring that egregious psychological behavior has occurred?

Another area of investigation triggered by this study could be an assessment of whether the various categories/dimensions of psychological aggression are differentially influenced by particular contextual factors. This research could move away from sterile descriptive sentences of psychological actions to situations in which couples' more complex interactions are the setting for the psychological actions. The field of psychological abuse is in dire need of a more sophisticated understanding of psychological actions which takes into account normative information both of prevalence and attitudes, objective (if possible) standards, and the influence of short-term and long-term contexts on the interpretation of behaviors in intimate relationships.

At worst, the findings of this study suggest that there is an inherent (and potentially biased) view that men's psychological behavior is more likely to constitute "psychological abuse" and is likely to be more severe than women's identical behavior when we have little normative information regarding this phenomenon. Rather, the mental health field's exposure to the phenomenon of psychological abuse has typically been the anecdotal information regarding psychological components of physically abusive relationships. And, there may be an underlying assumption fueling this view of men's actions that could be an erroneous parallel to the physical abuse phenomenon—that the impact of a man's psychological actions are, by virtue of being exhibited by a man, likely to have a more deleterious impact than a woman's psychological actions against her partner. At best, this study's findings raise intriguing questions which could stimulate interesting research as to why judgments about psychologically aggressive behavior are made differently simply on the basis of gender.

REFERENCES

Amabile, T., & Hastorf, A. H. (1976). Person perception. In B. Seidenberg & A. Snadowsky (Eds.), *Social psychology: An introduction*. New York: The Free Press.

Anderson, N. H. (2001). *Empirical direction in design and analysis*. Mahwah, NJ: Lawrence Erlbaum Associates.

Coker, A. L., McKeown, R. E., Sanderson, M., Davis, K. E., Valois, R. F., & Huebner, E. S. (2000). Severe dating violence and quality of life among South Carolina high school students. *American Journal of Preventive Medicine, 19*(4), 220-227.

Coontz, P. D., Lidz, C. W., & Mulvey, E. P. (1994). Gender and the assessment of dangerousness in the psychiatric emergency room. *International Journal of Law and Psychiatry, 17*(4), 369-376.

Dobash, R. P., Dobash, R. E., Wilson, M., & Daly, M. (1992). The myth of sexual symmetry in marital violence. *Social Problems, 39*(1), 71-90.

Dohrenwend, B. P., & Dohrenwend, B. S. (1976). Sex differences in psychiatric disorders. *American Journal of Sociology, 81*, 1147-1154.

Follingstad, D. R. (2003). *Rethinking current approaches to understanding and investigating psychological abuse: A call for controversy.* Unpublished manuscript, University of South Carolina.

Follingstad, D. R., & DeHart, D. D. (2000). Defining psychological abuse of husbands toward wives: Contexts, behaviors, and typologies. *Journal of Interpersonal Violence, 15*(9), 891-920.

Germain, C. P. (1984). Sheltering abused women: A nursing perspective. *Journal of Psychosocial Nursing, 22*(9), 25-31.

Gove, W., & Tudor, J. (1973). Adult sex roles and mental illness. *American Journal of Sociology, 78*, 50-73.

Harned, M. S. (2001). Abused women or abused men? An examination of the context and outcomes of dating violence. *Violence and Victims, 16*(3), 269-285.

Harris, A. R. (1977). Sex and theories of deviance: Toward a functional theory of deviant typescripts. *American Sociological Review, 42*, 8-16.

Hines, D. A., & Malley-Morrison, K. (2001). *Effects of emotional abuse against men in intimate relationships.* Unpublished manuscript.

Holstein, J. A. (1987). Producing gender effects on involuntary mental hospitalization. *Social Problems, 34*, 141-155.

Katz, J., Kuffel, S. W., & Coblentz, A. (2002). Are there gender differences in sustaining dating violence?: An examination of frequency, severity, and relationship satisfaction. *Journal of Family Violence, 17*(3), 247-271.

Lowery, C. R., & Higgins, R. L. (1979). Analogue investigation of the relationship between clients' sex and treatment recommendations. *Journal of Consulting and Clinical Psychology, 47*(4), 792-794.

Martin, D. (1976). *Battered wives.* New York: Simon & Schuster.

Migliaccio, T. A. (2001). Marginalizing the battered male. *Journal of Men's Studies, 9*(2), 205-226.

Molidor, C. E. (1995). Gender differences of psychological abuse in high school dating relationships. *Child and Adolescent Social Work Journal, 12*(2), 119-134.

Poole, D. A., & Tapley, A. E. (1988). Sex roles, social roles and clinical judgments of mental health. *Sex Roles, 19*(5/6), 265-272.

Simonelli, C. J., & Ingram, K. M. (1998). Psychological distress among men experiencing physical and emotional abuse in heterosexual dating relationships. *Journal of Interpersonal Violence, 13*(6), 667-681.

Steinmetz, S. K. (1977-1978). The battered husband syndrome. *Victimology: An International Journal, 2*(3-4), 499-509.

Stets, J. E., & Straus, M. A. (1990). Gender differences in reporting marital violence and its medical and psychological consequences. In M. A. Straus & R. J. Gelles (Eds.), *Physical violence in American families.* New Brunswick, NJ: Transaction.

Straus, M. A. (1977-1978). Wife-beating: How common and why? *Victimology: An International Journal, 2*(3-4), 443-458.

Teri, L. (1982). Effects of sex and sex-role style on clinical judgment. *Sex Roles, 8*(6), 639-649.

Walker, L. E. (1979). *The battered women.* New York: Harper & Row.

Warren, C. A. (1982). *The court of last resort.* Chicago: University of Chicago Press.

White, J. W., & Koss, M. P. (1991). Courtship violence: Incidence in a national sample of higher education students. *Violence and Victims, 6*(4), 247-256.

Wrobel, N. H. (1993). Effect of patient age and gender on clinical decisions. *Professional Psychology: Research and Practice, 24*(2), 206-212.

Zygmond, M. J., & Denton, W. (1988). Gender bias in marital therapy: A multidimensional scaling analysis. *The American Journal of Family Therapy, 16*(3), 262-272.

Offprints. Requests for offprints should be directed to Diane R. Follingstad, PhD, Department of Psychology, University of South Carolina, Columbia, SC 29208. E-mail: Follingstad@sc.edu

Violence and Victims, Volume 16, Number 3, 2001

Abused Women or Abused Men?
An Examination of the Context and
Outcomes of Dating Violence

Melanie S. Harned

University of Illinois at Urbana-Champaign

The present study examines the controversial issue of whether women and men are equally abused in dating relationships. Undergraduate and graduate students ($n = 874$) completed a survey about their experiences and perpetration of psychological, sexual, and physical aggression within dating relationships. To enable a more contextualized understanding of these phenomena, motives for and outcomes of dating violence were also assessed. Women and men reported comparable amounts of overall aggression from dating partners, but differed in the types of violence experienced. Women were more likely to experience sexual victimization, whereas men were more often the victims of psychological aggression; rates of physical violence were similar across genders. Contrary to hypotheses, women were not more likely to use physical violence in self-defense than men. However, although both genders experienced similar amounts of aggressive acts from dating partners, the impact of such violence is more severe for women than men.

Since the early 1980s, research has made it increasingly clear that violence in intimate relationships is not limited to married couples. Although prevalence rates vary considerably depending on how intimate violence is defined and measured, approximately one-third of those who date use or experience physical aggression within the context of their dating relationships (Sugarman & Hotaling, 1989). One of the most heated debates that has risen out of this research pertains to gender differences in rates of dating violence perpetration and victimization. Specifically, significant controversy exists about whether women and men are equally abused by and abusive toward their dating partners.

Research has indicated that women are more likely to report perpetrating (e.g., Follingstad, Wright, Lloyd, & Sebastian, 1991; Foshee, 1996; Pedersen & Thomas, 1992; Stets & Henderson, 1991) and men are more likely to report experiencing (e.g., Pedersen & Thomas, 1992; Stets & Henderson, 1991) physical violence in dating relationships. However, studies have also found that men and women do not differ on rates of physical aggression used or experienced (e.g., Makepeace, 1986; White & Koss, 1991) and that women are the primary victims of physical aggression in dating relationships (e.g., Follingstad et al., 1991; Stets & Pirog-Good, 1987). On the whole, however, the research findings have generally been considered to indicate that women are at least equally as likely to use physical aggression toward dating partners as men and, thus, that women and men are equally abusive.

Feminists and woman abuse researchers have contested this conclusion on several grounds. The vast majority of research on this issue has utilized variations of the Conflict Tactics Scales (CTS; Straus, 1979) or similar instruments that simply tally up the types of physical aggression used or experienced, but fail to consider the context in which violence occurs or the consequences it has for those who experience it. Critics have suggested that although women and men may commit similar amounts of violent acts, women suffer more damage and are more likely to engage in physical aggression for purposes of self-defense (e.g., Currie, 1998; DeKeseredy & Schwartz, 1998). The failure to consider these issues can foster a decontextualized and, thus, distorted understanding of violence within intimate relationships. Although many have argued these points on purely ideological grounds, some relevant empirical evidence does exist.

Research examining gender differences in motives for using physical aggression has yielded mixed results. Some data demonstrate that women are more likely than men to use physical aggression for self-defensive purposes among high school students (Foshee, 1996), college students (Makepeace, 1986), a shelter-based sample of battered women (Saunders, 1986), and physically violent couples in marital treatment (Cascardi & Vivian, 1995). Other research has addressed this issue by examining who initiates violence in intimate relationships. For example, DeKeseredy and Schwartz (1998) report that the majority of women in their college sample who used physical aggression toward dating partners never initiated violence. Similarly, Molidor and Tolman (1998) surveyed high school students and found that 70% of females and 27% of males reported that their dating partner had initiated the violence.

Conflicting findings have indicated that women initiate physical violence as often or more often than men and that men are more likely to report using physical aggression in retaliation for being hit first. For example, using data from the National Family Violence Resurvey, Stets and Straus (1990) found that women reported initiating violence toward their spouses about as often as men. DeMaris (1992) surveyed college students and found that both men and women reported that, when one partner could be identified as the usual initiator of violence, it was most often the woman. In addition, Follingstad and colleagues (1991) found that college men were more likely than women to report using physical violence in retaliation for being hit first. In summary, research on gender differences in motives for using physical aggression has yielded inconsistent results, perhaps reflecting the variation in samples and measurement techniques used.

Research examining the consequences of violence in intimate relationships has generally supported contentions that women report more severe outcomes. Studies have found that women experiencing physical aggression from dating partners report more emotional difficulties and physical injury than similarly victimized men (Follingstad et al., 1991; Foshee, 1996; Makepeace, 1986). For example, Molidor and Tolman (1998) asked high school students about the worst incident of physical violence experienced from a dating partner. Boys reported little or no effects from the violence in over 90% of the incidents and only 5% reported physical injury. Conversely, 48% of girls said that it hurt a lot and 34% reported physical injury; only 9% of girls indicated that the violence had no effect on them. Comparable results have been obtained in studies of married couples; women experiencing physical aggression are more likely than men to require medical attention, incur injury, and report depression (Morse, 1995; Stets & Straus, 1990). Such research findings are also supported by clinical observations of male batterers indicating that the impact of female aggression on men is irritation and annoyance rather than fear or injury (Hamberger, Lohr, Bonge, & Tolin, 1997).

The present study addresses the central issues in this debate while overcoming some of the limitations of previous research in this area. First, conclusions that women and men are equally abusive toward dating partners have been drawn almost exclusively from data on physical aggression. The present study conceptualizes dating violence more broadly to include incidents of psychological, sexual, and physical aggression and, therefore, may yield quite different results. Previous research has consistently found that women are more likely to experience and men are more likely to perpetrate sexual aggression in the context of dating relationships (e.g., Foshee, 1996; Makepeace, 1986). Results pertaining to rates of psychological aggression have been mixed, perhaps reflecting the different ways this construct has been defined. For example, research has found that dating men and women typically do not differ on rates of verbal aggression experienced or perpetrated (Stets & Henderson, 1991; White & Koss, 1991). However, studies utilizing broader definitions of psychological aggression have yielded inconsistent results (Foshee, 1996; Kasian & Painter, 1992; Stets, 1991). Further research is clearly needed to provide a more complete understanding of the amounts and types of violence experienced by women and men in dating relationships.

A second goal of the present study is to examine further the motives of men and women who perpetrate physical violence in dating relationships. As reviewed above, previous research in this area has largely been inconclusive. Given the central role that motivational hypotheses play in feminists' rebuttals of the argument that women and men are equally physically violent, it is important to gather additional evidence relevant to this issue. As with previous research, it is therefore hypothesized that women will be more likely to perpetrate physical violence for self-defensive purposes than men. Finally, the present study examines a variety of outcomes (i.e., physical, psychological, and school related) in association with dating violence. It is hypothesized that women who experience violence from dating partners will report worse outcomes than similarly victimized men.

METHOD

Procedure

All data were collected via an electronic survey that was located on the Internet. The survey was initially pilot tested on a sample of 34 undergraduates and appropriate revisions were made. The final study employed a stratified random sampling procedure in which the categories used for stratification included:

1. *Gender,*
2. *Race* (African American, Asian American, East Asian, Hispanic, Caucasian and Other),
3. *Class* (Freshman, Sophomore, Junior, Senior, Graduate/Professional).

Graduate/professional students were randomly selected from the entire graduate student body at the university, whereas undergraduates were randomly sampled from among those students whose last names fell in the first half of the alphabet. Although the undergraduate sampling procedure was nontraditional, there is no reason to believe that students in the first half of the alphabet would differ in any systematic way from those in the latter half. Three thousand students were selected for the initial sample.

A letter was sent to all members of the sample inviting them to participate in the study and follow-up postcards were mailed approximately five weeks later. Ultimately 1,150 students completed the survey, yielding an overall response rate of 38%. To ensure that only responses from members of the sample were included, each student was required to use a preassigned log-in identification number when completing the survey online. Only responses for which the log-in could be matched to a member of the sample were included

Table 1.   Demographics of the Entire Student Body, the Full Sample, and the Dating Sample

	Entire Student Body %	Full Sample (*n* = 1,139) %	Dating Sample (*n* = 874) %
Gender			
Female	49	600 (53)	489 (56)
Male	51	539 (47)	385 (44)
Race/Ethnicity			
African-American	8	72 (6)	53 (6)
Asian-American	10	110 (10)	75 (9)
Caucasian	67	816 (72)	660 (76)
East Asian	3	61 (5)	25 (3)
Hispanic	5	42 (4)	30 (3)
Other	7	38 (3)	31 (3)
Class			
Freshman	20	294 (26)	222 (26)
Sophomore	16	186 (16)	151 (17)
Junior	18	204 (18)	160 (18)
Senior	21	182 (16)	162 (19)
Graduate/Professional	25	272 (24)	178 (20)

in the dataset. Of the 1,150 students who completed the survey, 1,139 (99%) provided usable data and were included in the database. As can be seen in Table 1, the full sample was representative of the university student body as a whole.

Sample Characteristics

Only those respondents who reported having dated while enrolled at the university were included in the present analyses. Dating was defined as having engaged in any type of dating behavior ranging from one-time dates to long-term relationships and included both same- and opposite-sex dating partners. Of the 1,139 students in the full sample, 874 (77%) had dated whereas 265 (23%) had not. Daters ranged in age from 17 to 52 (*M* = 21.3, *SD* = 3.74) and 31 (4%) identified as homosexual, whereas 19 (2%) identified as bisexual; additional demographic data can be found in Table 1.

Measures

Participants completed materials described as a questionnaire about student life at the university. With the exception of the physical injury scale (located immediately following the physical assault measure), all measures assessing outcomes were placed prior to the measures assessing stressors to minimize potential demand effects. The measures used in the present study are described below; see Table 2 for correlations and reliability indices.

Table 2. Scale Correlations and Reliabilities Among Women and Men

	1	2	3	4	5	6	7	8	9	10	11	12	13	14	15
1. Positive Affect	.82/.81	-.73*	-.49*	-.58*	-.23*	-.37*	-.12*	-.09	-.18	-.03	-.02	-.05	-.02	.03	-.01
2. Depression	-.74*	.91/.90	.61*	.74*	.29*	.42*	.13*	-.06	.26	.08	.10	.07	.03	-.03	.03
3. Anxiety	-.64*	.71*	.87/.85	.61*	.28*	.24*	.04	-.06	.17	.12*	.13*	.02	.01	.04	.07*
4. Posttraumatic Stress	-.56*	.68*	.54*	.92/.90	.36*	.40*	.23*	-.03	.42*	.14*	.17*	.19*	.14*	.06	.08
5. BSQ	-.30*	.37*	.29*	.33*	.97/.96	.15*	.09	.07	-.12	.04	.06	.08	.03	.00	-.02
6. School Withdrawal	-.32*	.44*	.29*	.39*	.17*	.59/.62	.23*	-.14	.41*	.01	.06	.12*	.03	-.04	-.02
7. Academic Withdrawal	-.16*	.26*	.13*	.37*	.23*	.26*	.68/.74	.03	.25	.29*	.37*	.21*	.22*	.12*	.03
8. Physical Injury	-.10	.10	.11	.20*	.26*	.00	.04	.71/.54	.21	.16	.19	.21	.03	.58*	.42*
9. Motives for Violence	-.20	.15	.02	.29*	.17*	-.06	.08	.25	.78/.75	.63*	.62*	.21	.22	.32*	.14
10. ABI (V)	-.29*	.29*	.29*	.37*	.21*	.06	.24*	.40*	.26*	.87/.84	.83*	.27*	.29*	.37*	.18*
11. ABI (P)	-.26*	.28*	.28*	.35*	.22*	.08	.22*	.07	.50*	.65*	.81/.79	.23*	.36*	.29*	.15*
12. SES (V)	-.19*	.17*	.14*	.24*	.23*	.02	.24*	.13	.19	.39*	.29*	.71/.72	.40*	.39*	.15*
13. SES (P)	-.07	.07	.10*	.07	.08	.03	.15*	.11	.04	.18*	.29*	.29*	.53/.66	.21*	.11*
14. CTS (V)	-.11*	.14*	.12*	.16*	.19*	.00	.10*	.73*	.42*	.50*	.38*	.28*	.14*	.84/.84	.71*
15. CTS (P)	-.08	.12*	.12*	.13*	.15*	-.03	.08	.39*	.46*	.30*	.46*	.11*	.13*	.70*	.83/.83

Note. Correlations for women are shown below the diagonal; correlations for men are shown above the diagonal. Coefficient alphas are in italics and appear in the diagonal; alphas for men precede the slash and alphas for women follow the slash. BSQ = Body Shape Questionnaire; ABI = Abusive Behavior Inventory—Psychological Abuse sub-scale; SES = Sexual Experiences Survey; CTS = Conflict Tactics Scale—Physical Abuse subscale; (V) = Victimization; (P) = Perpetration.

*p < .05.

Psychological Outcomes. A 21-item version of the Mental Health Index (MHI; Veit & Ware, 1983; Ware, 1984) assessed symptoms of anxiety, depression, and positive affect during the past month. Reliability indices for the MHI are excellent for the general population ($\alpha = .96$; Ware, 1984). Symptoms of posttraumatic stress disorder (PTSD) occurring during the past month were assessed via the PTSD Checklist—Civilian Form (PCL-C; Weathers, Litz, Herman, Huska, & Keane, 1993). The PCL-C consists of 17 items corresponding to the DSM-IV criteria for PTSD and assesses symptoms that apply generically to any traumatic event. The PCL has been found to have excellent reliability ($\alpha = .97$), high test-retest reliability, and high convergent validity among combat veterans (Weathers et al., 1993). Finally, body shape concern was measured using a 10-item revised version of the Body Shape Questionnaire (BSQ-R-10; Mazzeo, 1999). This scale assesses preoccupation with body image and has been found to be highly reliable ($\alpha = .96$) and valid in samples of female undergraduates (Mazzeo, 1999).

School-Related Outcomes. Hanisch and Hulin's (1991) scales assessing work and job withdrawal were revised in the present study for the academic context. Congruent to their definition of work withdrawal, *academic withdrawal* was defined as a student's attempts to remove him/herself from their immediate academic situation while still maintaining enrollment in the university. A 6-item scale assessed behaviors such as completing course assignments late and arriving late to class. Parallel to Hanisch and Hulin's (1991) construct of job withdrawal, *school withdrawal* was defined as a student's intentions of leaving the university. A 3-item scale was used and included items such as thoughts of quitting school and likelihood of quitting. Previous research has found good reliability indices for the original work withdrawal ($\alpha = .78$) and job withdrawal ($\alpha = .73$) scales in a sample of working women (Schneider, Swan, & Fitzgerald, 1997).

Psychological Abuse. A 12-item version of the Abusive Behavior Inventory—Psychological Abuse subscale (ABI; Shepard & Campbell, 1992) was used to assess experiences and perpetration of psychological abuse within dating relationships occurring at the university. This scale was reliable among a sample of abusive and non-abusive men and women (alphas ranged from .79 to .92) and demonstrated good validity among abuser and non-abuser groups (Shepard & Campbell, 1992). This measure yielded scores on four subscales suggested by the test developers:

1. *Emotional abuse* (i.e., insults, humiliation, degradation),
2. *Isolation* (i.e., restriction of social contact),
3. *Intimidation/Threats* (i.e., attempts to frighten, threats of harm to self or others), and
4. *Economic abuse* (i.e., restriction of financial resources).

In the present study five items from the original scale were deleted: four that assessed behaviors more relevant to married couples (e.g., told you that you were a bad parent) and one that assessed reckless driving. Each item was asked twice with slightly different wording to assess participants' own experiences of psychological abuse as well as their perpetration of such behaviors toward their dating partners. All items were scored using a 5-point scale ranging from 0 (Never) to 4 (Very Frequently).

Sexual Abuse/Assault. The 10-item Sexual Experiences Survey (SES; Koss & Oros, 1982) was used to assess participants' experiences of sexual victimization and aggression within dating relationships since they had been students at the university. Reliability indices of .74 for women (victimization) and .89 for men (perpetration) have been reported for the SES and the measure has been found to demonstrate excellent one-week test-retest reliability (Koss & Gidycz, 1985). Categories of sexually abusive/assaultive experiences congruent with legal definitions and recommended by the test developers were used including:

1. *Rape* (i.e., unwanted completed vaginal/penile, oral, or anal intercourse or penetration by other objects that was perpetrated using threats of bodily harm, actual force, or when the victim was impaired by drugs/alcohol),
2. *Attempted rape* (i.e., unwanted attempted sexual intercourse that was perpetrated using threats of bodily harm, actual force, or when the victim was impaired by drugs/alcohol),
3. *Sexual coercion* (i.e., unwanted completed sexual intercourse subsequent to the use of overwhelming verbal pressure or misuse of authority), and
4. *Sexual contact* (i.e., unwanted sexual behavior including fondling, kissing, or petting but not intercourse that occurred subsequent to overwhelming verbal pressure, misuse of authority, threats of bodily harm, or actual force).

Each item was asked twice with slightly different wording to measure participants' experiences of both sexual victimization and aggression. All items were scored using a 5-point scale from 0 (Never) to 4 (Very Frequently).

Physical Assault. The 12-item Revised Conflict Tactics Scales – Physical Assault sub-scale (CTS2; Straus, Hamby, Boney-McCoy, & Sugarman, 1996) was used to assess participants' physical victimization and aggression within dating relationships since they had been students at the university. This scale has been found to be reliable (α = .86) and to demonstrate preliminary evidence of construct validity in a sample of male and female undergraduates (Straus et al., 1996). Using the definitions proposed by the test developers, two subscales were created:

1. *Minor violence* (i.e., pushing, shoving, grabbing, slapping, twisting hair or arms, or throwing something) and
2. *Severe violence* (i.e., kicking, beating up, burning or scalding, slamming against a wall, choking, punching or hitting with something that could hurt, or using a knife or gun).

Each item was asked twice to assess participants' experiences and perpetration of physical violence with dating partners. All items were scored using a 7-point scale from 0 (Never) to 6 (More than 20 times).

Physical Injury. A 5-item version of the CTS2-Injury subscale (Straus et al., 1996) assessed injuries resulting from physical violence experienced from a dating partner while at the university. Straus and colleagues (1996) found this scale to be highly reliable (α = .95) and to demonstrate preliminary evidence of construct validity in a college student sample. Items assess such things as having a sprain, bruise, or cut or seeing a doctor because of a fight with a dating partner. All items were scored using a 7-point scale from 0 (Never) to 6 (More than 20 times).

Motives for Using Physical Violence. A 12-item version of the Motivations and Effects Questionnaire (MEQ; Follingstad et al., 1991) assessed motives for using physical violence. Although no psychometric data are available for this instrument, it has been used in a previous study involving male and female college students (Follingstad et al., 1991). Items include such things as using physical violence to show anger, due to jealousy, for self-defense, and to control the other person. All items were scored using a 6-point scale from 1 (Never) to 6 (Always). Psychometric data and results of exploratory principal components analyses are presented below.

Data Preparation

Missing data were imputed on the outcome measures that were at least 10 items in length and provided continuous measures of symptom severity. For scales containing 10–19 items (i.e., BSQ-R-10, PCL-C) imputation was used for those participants who had only one item missing. For scales consisting of 20 or more items (i.e., MHI), imputation was used for those participants with up to two missing items. The formula used for imputation was: Item mean + (Person mean − Mean of item means for answered items). Omitted responses were not imputed for scales shorter than 10 items in length or for scales assessing dating abuse or motives for violence.

RESULTS

The Incidence and Frequency of Dating Violence Victimization and Perpetration

The first step in data analysis was to determine the incidence of each of the three types of dating violence measured. In all cases, respondents were considered to have experienced or used a type of violence if they endorsed at least one item on the relevant measure. In addition, the frequency of violent behaviors were calculated by summing the relevant poly-tomous scale items. Incidence and frequency rates are presented in Table 3 separately for women and men.

Gender Differences in Dating Violence Victimization and Perpetration

Planned gender comparisons were conducted for each type of dating violence victimization and perpetration using the frequencies (i.e., not incidence rates) and are presented in Table 3. In addition, comparisons were conducted among respondents who reported only same-sex, only opposite-sex, and both same- and opposite-sex dating partners. Effect sizes (d) were calculated using Cohen's (1977) formula, which describes sizes of effects in standard deviation units. Conventional cutoff scores for small, moderate, and large effects are .2, .5, and .8, respectively (Cohen, 1977).

   Psychological Abuse. Independent t-tests indicated that men reported more overall psychological victimization ($d= 0.21$), isolation ($d = 0.15$), intimidation/threats ($d = 0.26$), and economic abuse ($d = 0.35$) from dating partners than did women. Given that men typically have more power and, thus, greater resources than women in our society, the high rate of economic abuse among men was especially counterintuitive. Additional analyses revealed that gender differences were only evident for the item "Has a dating partner prevented you from having money for your own use?" ($t (866) = 5.57, p < .001$). It is unclear by what mechanism a dating partner would be able to prevent another from having money for his/her own use, except perhaps within the context of a cohabiting relationship. However, only 6% of women and 6% of men who endorsed this item indicated that they were currently living with a dating partner. Thus, it is possible that this item may have been misinterpreted; for example, the item may have been endorsed by men who feel that they have to spend too much money entertaining women dating partners, a different issue than abuse. Only one significant gender difference in the frequency of psychological aggression was found; men reported perpetrating more emotional abuse than women ($d = 0.16$). ANOVAs did not reveal any significant differences in the frequencies of psychological victimization

Table 3. Incidence, Frequency, and Gender Comparisons of Dating Violence Victimization and Perpetration

| | Experienced | | | | | | | Perpetrated | | | | | | |
| | Women | | | Men | | | | Women | | | Men | | | |
	%	M	SD	%	M	SD	t	%	M	SD	%	M	SD	t
Psychological Abuse Total	82	5.06	5.65	87	6.26	5.51	3.13**[c]	85	4.80	4.35	84	5.13	4.35	1.08[d]
Emotional abuse	71	2.22	2.42	77	2.46	2.29	1.46[b]	78	2.10	1.87	77	2.42	2.17	2.38*[b]
Isolation	57	1.83	2.52	72	2.20	2.25	2.27*[b]	64	1.70	1.99	61	1.56	1.79	1.11[c]
Intimidation/threats	51	0.90	1.26	68	1.23	1.25	3.88***[c]	58	0.89	0.98	63	0.95	0.97	0.93[c]
Economic abuse	7	0.12	0.47	20	0.36	0.89	5.21***[c]	8	0.11	0.42	12	0.17	0.53	1.77[c]
Sexual Abuse/Assault Total	39	1.15	2.07	30	0.83	1.89	2.36*[e]	8	0.15	0.59	26	0.57	1.37	6.11***[e]
Sexual contact	32	0.53	0.92	25	0.42	0.90	1.77[e]	7	0.09	0.33	23	0.34	0.71	7.07***[e]
Attempted rape	17	0.27	0.70	9	0.14	0.50	2.93**[f]	2	0.02	0.15	7	0.08	0.33	3.51***[e]
Sexual coercion	13	0.17	0.50	8	0.12	0.43	1.73[e]	2	0.02	0.18	8	0.10	0.38	3.98***[e]
Rape	12	0.18	0.55	8	0.15	0.57	0.82[e]	1	0.01	0.13	3	0.04	0.24	2.16*[f]
Physical Assault Total	22	1.16	3.54	21	1.41	4.10	0.95[d]	19	0.77	2.61	1	0.52	2.62	1.42[g]
Minor violence	22	0.95	2.63	20	1.05	2.93	0.52[d]	18	0.62	1.94	11	0.42	1.85	1.50[g]
Severe violence	8	0.21	1.10	11	0.36	1.34	1.80[d]	6	0.16	0.82	3	0.10	0.88	1.02[g]

[a]$df = 871$. [b]$df = 870$. [c]$df = 869$. [d]$df = 868$. [e]$df = 867$. [f]$df = 866$. [g]$df = 865$.
*$p < .05$. **$p < .01$. ***$p < .001$.

or aggression among respondents who indicated only same-sex, only opposite-sex, and both same- and opposite-sex dating partners.

Sexual Abuse/Assault. Women reported experiencing more overall sexual victimization ($d = 0.16$) and attempted rape ($d = 0.21$) from dating partners than did men. The lack of a gender difference for rape was particularly unexpected. However, 100% of raped women reported only male dating partners, whereas 9% of raped men reported dating either only men (6%) or both men and women (3%). This suggests that a moderate proportion of men's rapes may have been perpetrated by other males. Furthermore, ANOVAs indicated significant differences among men who reported only same-sex, only opposite-sex, and both same- and opposite-sex dating partners in frequencies of overall sexual victimization, $F(2, 377) = 3.02, p < .05$, and attempted rape, $F(2, 377) = 3.74, p < .03$. Post-hoc Tukey tests revealed that men who reported only same-sex dating partners experienced significantly more overall sexual victimization ($d = 0.59$) and attempted rape ($d = 0.68$) than men who reported only opposite-sex dating partners. No significant differences in frequency of sexual victimization were found among women who reported only same-sex, only opposite-sex, and both same- and opposite-sex dating partners.

Finally, men reported perpetrating more sexual abuse and assault of all types: overall sexual aggression ($d = 0.42$), unwanted sexual contact ($d = 0.49$), attempted rape ($d = 0.24$), sexual coercion ($d = 0.27$), and rape ($d = 0.15$). No significant differences in the frequency of sexual aggression were found among respondents who indicated only same-sex, only opposite-sex, and both same- and opposite-sex dating partners.

Physical Assault. No differences in frequencies of physical victimization or aggression were found between women and men or among respondents who indicated only same-sex, only opposite-sex, and both same- and opposite-sex dating partners.

Motives for Using Physical Aggression

Of the 92 women and 42 men who reported perpetrating physical violence, 83 (90%) of the women and 39 (93%) of the men completed the scale assessing their motives for using physical violence. An exploratory principal components analysis with varimax rotation indicated two interpretable subscales that were reliable for both women and men. Four items formed an *Anger/Jealousy* component (α's $= .78$ for women and .72 for men) that included using physical violence to show anger, to punish, due to jealousy, and to retaliate for emotional hurt. The second component was termed *Self-Defense* (α's $= .68$ for women and .86 for men) and included two items assessing the use of physical violence to protect oneself and in retaliation for being hit first. Six additional items did not load on interpretable and reliable components for both women and men and thus were analyzed as single items using Bonferroni corrected alpha levels. Incidence rates and results of independent samples *t*-tests are presented in Table 4. Women were more likely to use physical aggression toward dating partners due to anger/jealousy ($d = 0.39$); no other significant gender differences in motives were found.

Outcomes of Dating Violence Victimization

Hierarchical regression analyses were conducted to determine:

1. whether each of the three types of dating violence victimization significantly predicted negative outcomes (Step 1) and,
2. whether women and men were differentially affected by similar experiences of dating violence (Step 2 Gender X Victimization interactions).

Table 4. Incidence, Frequency, and Gender Comparisons of Motives for Using Physical Aggression

	Women			Men			
	%	M	SD	%	M	SD	t
Subscales							
Anger/Jealousy	88	7.76	3.98	64	6.28	3.47	1.99*[a]
Self-Defense	42	3.34	2.15	56	3.74	2.37	0.94[a]
Single Items							
Inability to express self verbally	50	2.00	1.29	41	1.64	1.04	1.52[b]
To feel more powerful	15	1.30	0.88	5	1.05	0.22	1.76[b]
To get control over the person	27	1.49	0.98	44	1.72	1.00	1.20[b]
To prove love	4	1.06	0.32	15	1.33	0.95	2.34[a]
Because it was sexually arousing	7	1.10	0.37	18	1.28	0.69	1.92[b]
To get attention	23	1.48	1.05	31	1.54	0.94	0.29[a]

Note. An alpha level of $p < 05$ was used for the subscales, whereas a Bonferroni corrected alpha level of $p < .009$ (.05/6) was used for the single items. [a]$df = 120$. [b]$df = 119$.
*$p < .05$.

Psychological Outcomes. As can be seen in Table 5, psychological and sexual victimization were significantly associated with worse psychological outcomes of all types. Physical victimization, however, only significantly predicted higher levels of anxiety, posttraumatic stress, and body shape concern. In addition, gender interacted with psychological abuse in predicting all psychological outcomes, with physical assault in predicting all but one psychological outcome, and with sexual victimization in predicting body shape concern.

The above interactions indicate that women and men experience comparable amounts of depression, anxiety, and posttraumatic stress at low levels of physical and psychological victimization, but that women report more severe outcomes as the frequency of violence increases. In addition, women report more positive affect than men at low levels of psychological and physical victimization; however, because men's positive affect remains unchanged and women's decreases considerably as victimization becomes more frequent, positive affect is comparable across genders at high levels of violence. Finally, interactions indicate that women's body shape concern is higher than men's at all levels of victimization, but that it increases as victimization becomes more frequent, whereas men's remains relatively stable.

School-Related Outcomes. Regression analyses indicated that all three types of dating violence victimization significantly predicted higher levels of academic withdrawal: psychological abuse ($\beta = .27, p < .001, R^2 = .07$), sexual abuse/assault ($\beta = .22, p < .001, R^2 = .05$), and physical assault ($\beta = .11, p < .002, R^2 = .01$). Victimization experiences did not significantly predict school withdrawal and no significant gender by victimization interactions were found for either school-related outcome.

Table 5. Hierarchical Regressions: Predicting Psychological Outcomes From Victimization, Gender, and Gender by Victimization Interactions

	Positive Affect		Depression		Anxiety		Posttraumatic Stress		Body Shape Concern	
	β	ΔR^2	β	ΔR^2	β	ΔR^2	β	ΔR^2	β	ΔR^2
Psychological Abuse										
Step1		.03***		.04***		.04***		.07***		.01**
PSYA	−.18***		.19***		.20***		.27***		.09**	
Step 2		.02***		.03***		.02***		.02***		.16***
PSYA	−.03		.09		.12*		.14**		.03	
Gender	.06		.12***		.09**		.07*		.39***	
PSYA X Gender	−.19***		.15**		.12*		.18***		.13**	
Sexual Abuse/Assault										
Step 1		.02***		.02***		.01**		.05***		.04***
SA	−.13***		.14***		.10**		.23***		.19***	
Step 2		.01*		.01**		.01*		.00		.14***
SA	−.06		.08		.02		.19***		.07	
Gender	.07*		.10**		.08*		.03		.37***	
SA X Gender	−.10		.07		.09		.05		.12*	
Physical Assault										
Step 1		.00		.00		.01*		.01**		.01*
PA	−.05		.05		.08*		.11**		.09*	
Step 2		.01*		.02***		.01*		.01*		.16***
PA	.02		−.03		.04		.05		.00	
Gender	.06		.11**		.08*		.05		.39***	
PA X Gender	−.10*		.12**		.06		.09*		.14**	

Note. Gender was coded such that 1 = Female and 0 = Male. PSYA = Psychological abuse; SA = Sexual abuse/assault; PA = Physical assault.

Physical Injury. Experiences of physical aggression from a dating partner significantly predicted higher levels of physical injury ($\beta = .64, p < .001, R^2 = .41$). In addition, both physical victimization ($\beta = .44, p < .001$) and an interaction between gender and physical victimization ($\beta = .34, p < .001$) significantly predicted physical injury, whereas gender did not ($R^2 = .49$). This interaction indicates that men report slightly more injuries at low levels of physical violence, whereas women experience more injuries as physical violence becomes more frequent.

DISCUSSION

The present results indicate that violent experiences are, unfortunately, quite common in college students' dating relationships. Psychological abuse appears to be so highly prevalent as to be considered normative, with 82% of women and 87% of men reporting some experience of this type. Sexual victimization was reported by 39% of women and 30% of men, whereas 22% of women and 21% of men reported experiencing physical aggression from dating partners. With the exception of the high rate of sexual victimization among men, comparable rates of these types of violence have been generated in some previous research (e.g., DeKeseredy & Schwartz, 1998; Follingstad et al., 1991 ; White & Koss, 1991). The high incidence of sexual victimization found among men is potentially due, in part, to the fact that same-sex dating relationships were assessed; 10% of the men experiencing sexual victimization reported dating other men.

Both women and men reported perpetrating less sexual abuse/assault than was experienced by men and women daters, respectively. In addition, women reported experiencing considerably more physical violence than men reported perpetrating. These discrepancies may be due to methodological reasons; the respondents were not couples reporting on the same incidents, but individuals reporting on incidents that may or may not have occurred with other members of the sample. In addition, 6% of the sample indicated homosexual or bisexual orientations and thus may have been reporting on violence occurring in same-sex relationships. However, given that such discrepancies have often been found in previous research (e.g., DeKeseredy & Schwartz, 1998; Makepeace, 1986), other explanations are possible.

Several authors have proposed that men tend to underreport their perpetration of abuse. Whereas women's use of minor violence (e.g., slapping) toward male dating partners is often considered acceptable if not encouraged in certain situations (Stets & Straus, 1990), such behaviors are generally less tolerated in men. Thus, men may underreport their perpetration of physical aggression toward dating partners because it is socially undesirable (DeKeseredy & Schwartz, 1998). Moreover, Currie (1998) posits that men may recall more instances of violent behavior by women because it contradicts feminine sex role stereotypes of passivity. Women, on the other hand, may downplay or normalize men's violence because it conforms to stereotypes of men as aggressive. In contrast, some research has found that socially desirable response sets are related to less willingness to report one's own perpetration of marital violence for both men and women (Arias & Beach, 1987). Although it is impossible to determine from the present data why such discrepancies were found, future research should attempt to address this issue in more detail.

The present results indicate that women and men experience comparable amounts of overall aggression in dating relationships, but that they differ in the types of aggression experienced. Specifically, men were more likely to experience psychological and women were more likely to experience sexual victimization; however, of these differences only rates of overall sexual aggression and perpetration of unwanted sexual contact yielded moderate effect sizes. Rates of physical violence were comparable across genders.

Although findings such as these have often been used to support arguments that women and men are equally abused, critics have noted that such statistics fail to consider the context in which abuse occurs. Many have suggested that women are more likely to use physical violence for purposes of self-defense than men and, thus, to consider women and men to be equally violent would essentially be blaming women for their own abuse (Stets & Straus, 1990). The present study, however, found that women and men were equally likely to use physical violence for self-defensive purposes. Moreover, women reported using physical violence due to anger/jealousy more often than men. Thus, the present data failed to confirm hypotheses. However, although it is often implied or assumed that recognition of women's physical aggression as neither defensive nor retaliatory is inconsistent with feminist goals, it is important to note that women's use of aggression in dating relationships in no way undermines the seriousness of their own victimization (White & Kowalski, 1994). Furthermore, recognizing the reality of women's use of physical violence may help to dispel the myth of the nonaggressive woman, which some feminists argue has been used to sustain male power over women (White & Kowalski, 1994).

In general, the present findings are consistent with previous research in demonstrating that sexual and physical victimization are associated with negative psychological and physical outcomes (e.g., Goodman, Koss, & Russo, 1993). However, this is the first study to link school-related outcomes to experiences of dating violence. In addition, despite some contentions that psychological victimization constitutes "soft-core abuse" (Fox, 1993), the present results indicate that this type of aggression has considerable negative psychological and school-related consequences. In fact, psychological abuse was found to significantly predict more types of psychological distress than physical violence, which is typically considered to be more "severe" in nature. These findings are particularly significant given the apparently normative nature of experiences of psychological abuse in college students' dating relationships.

Of particular relevance to the current topic, however, were findings that gender moderated the relationship between victimization experiences and many outcomes. Overall, these interactions indicate that women's outcomes worsen considerably as victimization becomes more frequent, whereas men's outcomes either remain stable or decline only slightly. These findings therefore support hypotheses that victimized women will report more damage than men, although this was found to be true primarily for psychological and physical outcomes at high levels of psychological and physical aggression. Although such findings are often explained by arguing that men are larger and stronger than women and, thus, can inflict more physical damage (e.g., DeMaris, 1992; Foshee, 1996; Stets & Straus, 1990), it is unclear whether such arguments can explain why women suffer worse psychological outcomes. It is also possible that male aggression is generally more damaging than female aggression due to the systematic, structural differences in power between women and men that place women in subordinate positions to men in most areas of life, including within the context of intimate relationships (Malik & Lindahl, 1998). Future research should attempt to disentangle the possible reasons that women suffer greater harm than men, both physical and psychological, when experiencing aggression from a dating partner.

Although firmly based on a large and representative sample, the present findings nevertheless possess some limitations. The overall response rate obtained for the survey (38%), although typical for this type of research, may generate unknown biases; for example, those with higher rates of perpetration may not have felt comfortable participating. In addition, the use of self-report and the lack of anonymity may have inhibited disclosure of dating abuse experiences. Furthermore, the use of a college student sample may limit the general-izability of the findings. It is also noted that the present data are cross-sectional in nature and, thus, that definitive statements about a potentially causal relationship between victimization and negative outcomes cannot be made. Finally, the present study did not assess all of the types of motivations for using physical violence (e.g., professed ignorance, coercive communication, alcohol related) that have been identified in previous research (Hamberger et al., 1997) and only motives for using physical aggression were examined. Future research would benefit from using a more exhaustive measure of motives for dating violence that also assesses reasons for engaging in psychological and sexual aggression.

CONCLUSION

The present study is consistent with previous research in demonstrating that women and men experience comparable amounts of violent acts from dating partners. However, these findings are clearly inconsistent with medical, legal, and social service accounts indicating that women are more often abused within intimate relationships than men (Morse, 1995). This discrepancy is perhaps largely due to researchers' failure to consider the consequences of aggressive acts, which appear to be quite different for women and men. In particular, women experiencing violence from dating partners report much more psychological and physical damage than similarly victimized men.

This raises the question of whether abuse, and perhaps victimization in particular, should be defined in terms of acts or consequences. Studies utilizing traditional act-defined approaches generally find that women and men are equally abusive, whereas a definition that requires evidence of damage would indicate that women are more often abused by their dating partners than men. Stets and Straus (1990) have suggested that definitions based on acts are congruent with moral principles of non-violence and may be more relevant to primary prevention efforts, whereas measuring abuse in terms of outcomes may be preferable when providing estimates of acute care needs. As this distinction implies, what is at stake in this debate is the provision of services and resources for women abused in intimate relationships, which has been challenged on the basis of research that defines abuse in terms of acts. For example, in New Hampshire such research has been used to direct resources away from shelters for battered women in order to open shelters for battered men, which were subsequently closed "because of the complete absence of clientele" (Currie, 1998; p. 109).

More generally, feminist definitions of abuse emphasize one person's power and control over another rather than the actual violent acts that are perpetrated (Muehlenhard & Kimes, 1999). Accordingly, feminists have been less concerned with determining whether women or men are more aggressive, and have focused instead on examining the context and outcomes of such violent acts. As White and Kowalski (1994) write, "the important questions concern the cultural, social, and psychological circumstances surrounding incidents of aggression by women and men" (p. 504). In accord with this viewpoint, the present results indicate that to accurately determine whether women and men are equally abused within dating relationships, one must go beyond simple summations of aggressive acts to consider the impact they have on those who experience them. When this is done it becomes evident that women are more often abused by their dating partners than men not because they experience violent acts more frequently, but because they suffer more damage.

REFERENCES

Arias, I., & Beach, S. R. H. (1987). Validity of self-reports of marital violence. *Journal of Family Violence, 2,* 139–149.

Cascardi, M., & Vivian, D. (1995). Context for specific episodes of marital violence: Gender and severity of violence differences. *Journal of Family Violence, 10,* 265–293.

Cohen, J. (1977). *Statistical power analysis for the behavioral sciences* (Rev. ed.). New York: Academic Press.

Currie, D. H. (1998). Violent men or violent women?: Whose definition counts? In R. K. Bergen (Ed.), *Issues in intimate violence* (pp. 97–111). Thousand Oaks, CA: Sage Publications.

DeKeseredy, W. S., & Schwartz, M. D. (1998). *Woman abuse on campus: Results from the Canadian National Survey.* Thousand Oaks, CA: Sage Publications.

DeMaris, A. (1992). Male versus female initiation of aggression: The case of courtship violence. In E. C. Viano (Ed.), *Intimate violence: Interdisciplinary perspectives* (pp. 111–120). Washington, DC: Hemisphere Publishing Co.

Follingstad, D. R., Wright, S., Lioyd, S., & Sebastian, J. A. (1991). Sex differences in motivations and effects in dating violence. *Family Relations, 40,* 51–57.

Foshee, V. (1996). Gender differences in adolescent dating abuse prevalence, types and injuries. *Health Education Research, 11,* 275–286.

Fox, B. J. (1993). On violent men and female victims: A comment on DeKeseredy and Kelly. *Canadian Journal of Sociology, 18,* 321–324.

Goodman, L. A., Koss, M. P., & Russo, N. F. (1993). Violence against women: Physical and mental health effects. Part I: Research findings. *Applied & Preventive Psychology, 2,* 79–89.

Hamberger, L. K., Lohr, J. M., Bonge, D., & Tolin, D. F. (1997). An empirical classification of motivations for domestic violence. *Violence Against Women, 3,* 401–423.

Hanisch, K. A., & Hulin, C. L. (1991). General attitudes and organizational withdrawal: An evaluation of a causal model. *Journal of Vocational Behavior, 39,* 110–128.

Kasian, M., & Painter, S. L. (1992). Frequency and severity of psychological abuse in a dating population. *Journal of Interpersonal Violence, 7,* 350–364.

Koss, M. P, & Gidycz, C. A. (1985). Sexual Experiences Survey: Reliability and validity. *Journal of Consulting and Clinical Psychology, 53,* 422–423.

Koss, M. P., & Oros, C. J. (1982). Sexual Experiences Survey: A research instrument investigating sexual aggression and victimization. *Journal of Consulting and Clinical Psychology, 50,* 455–457.

Makepeace, J. M. (1986). Gender differences in courtship violence victimization. *Family Relations, 35,* 383–388.

Malik, N. M., & Lindahl, K. M. (1998). Aggression and dominance: The roles of power and culture in domestic violence. *Clinical Psychology: Science and Practice, 5,* 409–423.

Mazzeo, S. E. (1999). Modification of an existing measure of body image preoccupation and its relationship to disordered eating in female college students. *Journal of Counseling Psychology, 46,* 42–50.

Molidor, C., & Tolman, R. M. (1998). Gender and contextual factors in adolescent dating violence. *Violence Against Women, 4,* 180–194.

Morse, B. J. (1995). Beyond the Conflict Tactics Scale: Assessing gender differences in partner violence. *Violence and Victims, 10,* 251–272.

Muehlenhard, C. L., & Kimes, L. A. (1999). The social construction of violence: The case of sexual and domestic violence. *Personality and Social Psychology Review, 3,* 234–245.

Pedersen, P., & Thomas, C. D. (1992). Prevalence and correlates of dating violence in a Canadian university sample. *Canadian Journal of Behavioural Science, 24,* 490–501.

Saunders, D. (1986). When battered women use violence: Husband-abuse or self-defense? *Violence and Victims, 1,* 47–60.

Schneider, K. T., Swan, S., & Fitzgerald, L. F. (1997). Job-related and psychological effects of sexual harassment in the workplace: Empirical evidence from two organizations. *Journal of Applied Psychology, 82,* 401–415.

Shepard, M. F., & Campbell, J. A. (1992). The Abusive Behavior Inventory: A measure of psychological and physical abuse. *Journal of Interpersonal Violence, 7,* 291–305.

Stets, J. E. (1991). Psychological aggression in dating relationships: The role of interpersonal control. *Journal of Family Violence, 6,* 97–114.

Stets, J. E., & Henderson, D. A. (1991). Contextual factors surrounding conflict resolution while dating: Results from a national study. *Family Relations, 40,* 29–36.

Stets, J. E., & Pirog-Good, M. A. (1987). Violence in dating relationships. *Social Psychology Quarterly, 50,* 237–246.

Stets, J. E., & Straus, M. A. (1990). Gender differences in reporting marital violence and its medical and psychological consequences. In M. A. Straus & R. J. Gelles (Eds.), *Physical violence in American families: Risk factors and adaptations to violence in 8,145 families* (pp. 151–165). New Brunswick, NJ: Transaction Publishers.

Straus, M. (1979). Measuring intrafamily conflict and violence: The Conflict Tactics (CT) Scales. *Journal of Marriage and the Family, 41,* 75–88.

Straus, M. A., Hamby, S. L., Boney-McCoy, S., & Sugarman, D. B. (1996). The revised Conflict Tactics Scales (CTS2): Development and preliminary psychometric data. *Journal of Family Issues, 17,* 283–316.

Sugarman, D. B., & Hotaling, G. T (1989). Dating violence: Prevalence, context, and risk markers. In M. A. Pirog-Good & J. E. Stets (Eds.), *Violence in dating relationships: Emerging social issues* (pp. 3–32). New York, NY: Praeger Publishers.

Veit, C. T., & Ware, J. E. Jr. (1983). The structure of psychological distress and well-being in general populations. *Journal of Consulting and Clinical Psychology, 51(5),* 730–742.

Ware, J. E. (1984). The General Health Rating Index. In N. K. Wenger, M. E. Mattson, C. D. Furberg, & J. Elinson (Eds.), *Assessment of quality of life in clinical trials of cardiovascular disease* (pp. 184–188). New York: LeJacq Publishing Co.

Weathers, F. W., Litz, B. T., Herman, D. S., Huska, J. A., & Keane, T. M. (1993, October). *The PTSD Checklist: Reliability, validity, and diagnostic utility.* Paper presented at the annual meeting of the International Society for Traumatic Stress Studies, San Antonio, TX.

White, J. W., & Koss, M. P. (1991). Courtship violence: Incidence in a national sample of higher education students. *Violence and Victims, 6,* 247–256.

White, J. W., & Kowalski, R. M. (1994). Deconstructing the myth of the nonaggressive woman: A feminist analysis. *Psychology of Women Quarterly, 18,* 487–508.

Acknowledgments. Portions of this article were presented at the 25th Annual Conference of the Association for Women in Psychology, Salt Lake City, UT, March, 2000. Funding for this research was provided by the Office of Women's Programs and the Department of Women's Studies at the University of Illinois at Urbana-Champaign. The author would like to thank Patricia Morey and Marilyn Best for making this research possible, as well as Louise Fitzgerald and Fritz Drasgow for providing feedback and statistical advice.

Offprints. Requests for offprints should be directed to Melanie S. Harned, MA, 603 East Daniel Street, Department of Psychology, University of Illinois at Urbana-Champaign, Champaign, IL 61820.

Violence and Victims, Volume 14, Number 1, 1999

Psychological Abuse: Implications for Adjustment and Commitment to Leave Violent Partners

Ileana Arias
Karen T. Pape
The University of Georgia

The contribution of psychological abuse, beyond that of physical abuse, to battered women's psychological adjustment and their intentions to terminate their abusive relationships was examined. Sixty-eight battered women residing in shelters for battered women provided information on their: (1) physical and psychological abuse; (2) psychological symptomatology; (3) strategies for coping with and perceptions of control over partner violence; and (4) intentions to return to their abusive partners. Multiple regression analyses indicated that frequency and severity of physical abuse was not a significant predictor of posttraumatic stress disorder (PTSD) symptomatology nor of women's intentions to terminate their abusive relationships. However, psychological abuse was a significant predictor of both PTSD symptomatology and intentions to permanently leave abusive partners even after controlling for the effects of physical abuse. PTSD symptomatology moderated the relationship between psychological abuse and intentions to terminate the abusive relationships: resolve to leave the abusive partner as a function of level of psychological abuse was significant only among women characterized by low levels of PTSD symptomatology. Greater use of emotion-focused coping strategies, absolutely and relative to problem-focused coping, had direct effects on PTSD symptomatology. However, neither coping nor perceptions of control moderated the effects of psychological abuse on psychological adjustment. The results of the investigation suggested that psychological abuse and ensuing PTSD symptomatology are important variables to assess among physically battered women.

P sychological abuse, frequently defined as, "verbal and nonverbal acts which symbolically hurt the other, or the use of threats to hurt the other..." (Straus, 1979, p. 77), has been shown to covary significantly with physical abuse among married couples (Follingstad, Rutledge, Berg, Hause, & Polek, 1990), dating high-school students (Molidor, 1995), and pregnant teenage and adult women (Parker, McFarlane, Soeken, Torres, & Campbell, 1993). Contrary to expectations, women have been shown to object, fear, and resent psychological abuse and its effects more than those of physical abuse (Follingstad et al., 1990; Herbert, Silver, & Ellard, 1991; O'Leary & Curley, 1986; Walker, 1984). It is surprising, therefore, that researchers have focused little attention on the occurrence and impact of psychological abuse on women's physical and mental health. Lack of empirical interest may in part be a function of the need to respond to the severe consequences of physical battering and the expectation that psychological abuse will have fewer, less severe, and more transient consequences than physical abuse. Additionally, as Vitanza, Vogel, and Marshall (1995) suggested, difficulties in operationalizing and measuring psychological abuse may have impeded progress. Notwithstanding, there has been some empirical attention devoted recently to the impact of psychological abuse on women's physical and mental health.

Aguilar and Nightingale (1994) employed a sample of 48 battered and 48 nonbattered women to examine the impact of physical abuse on women's self-esteem. While battered women were characterized by significantly lower levels of self-esteem relative to nonbattered women, psychological abuse was the only significant predictor of low self-esteem within the battered subsample. In a sample of 234 women with a history of battering, Follingstad and her colleagues (1990) found that only three of the participants had never experienced any form of psychological abuse. Seventy-two percent of the women in this sample reported that they experienced psychological abuse more negatively than physical abuse. Women who experienced psychological abuse more negatively, relative to those who experienced physical abuse more negatively, reported more fear of the partner, shame, loss of self-esteem, depression, and anxiety. Interestingly, there were no differences between women who experienced psychological abuse more negatively and those who experienced physical abuse more negatively on severity or frequency of the physical abuse they endured.

More recently, Marshall (1996) examined the physical and psychological correlates of psychological abuse among a sample of 578 women who volunteered their participation for a study of women in "bad or stressful long term relationships with a man" (p. 383). Only 13% of Marshall's sample had never been physically assaulted by the partner while 3% had never experienced an incident of psychological abuse. Higher frequencies of psychological abuse were related to higher frequencies of serious or chronic illness and visits to a physician; more frequent use of psychotherapeutic services and psychotropic medication; lower levels of relationship satisfaction and more frequent attempts to leave the partner; and lower levels of perceived power and control.

In a community sample consisting of 232 married women, Arias, Street, and Brody (1996) found that psychological abuse was a significant predictor of depressive symptomatology and problem drinking. The effects of psychological abuse on problem drinking continued to be significant even after controlling for depression. In the aforementioned sample, Arias and Street (1996) found that the negative effects of women's psychological abuse extended to their children: psychological abuse was a significant predictor of emotionally neglectful and maltreating parenting which, in turn, predicted both boys' and girls' depression and low self-esteem.

The studies reviewed suggest that psychological abuse has a negative impact on women's physical and psychological health. However, these studies did not control for the effects of physical abuse when examining those of psychological abuse. Because both forms of abuse frequently co-occur, it is difficult to obtain sizable samples of women who are only psychologically abused or only physically abused in order to examine unique effects. Statistical control is an available alternative. There appears to be only one study that attempted to statistically control for the effects of physical abuse in determining the psychological impact of psychological abuse. Kahn, Welch, and Zillmer (1993) administered the MMPI-2 to 31 battered women residing in a shelter and instructed them to indicate whether or not they had been subjected to each of nine psychologically abusive partner behaviors such as criticisms, threats, isolation, and intimidation, and nine physically abusive behaviors such as pushing, punching, hairpulling, and use of weapons. While 68% of participants scored high on the *PS* and *PK* supplementary scales (posttraumatic stress disorder scales), experience of psychological abuse only emerged as a unique predictor of the average clinical T-score when both types of abuse were included as predictors in the regression equations.

The results of investigations completed to date suggest that it is important to examine the impact of psychological abuse on women's psychological adjustment. Psychological abuse has been associated with negative psychological sequelae and ineffective coping (Arias et al., 1996). However, it is important to control for the potential confounding effects of physical abuse. In the current investigation, we were interested in the extent to which psychological abuse was related to women's psychological adjustment above and beyond the effects of their physical abuse. To the extent that terminating abusive relationships is desirable, it is also important to specify variables that facilitate or hamper battered women's attempts to leave their abusers. Because women have been shown to be more likely to leave their abusive partners as a function of abuse severity and increases in abuse frequency and severity (Herbert, Silver, & Ellard, 1991; Marshall, 1996; Strube, 1988), we were interested in the impact of psychological abuse on women's intentions to terminate their abusive relationships, again, controlling for the potential confounding effects of physical abuse. Further, we were interested in examining conditions under which severity of psychological abuse would and would not motivate women to intend to terminate their relationships. Existing literature suggests that the presence of PTSD symptomatology may be such a factor.

Walker (1984) suggested that the psychological symptoms frequently experienced by battered women overlap greatly with symptoms comprising diagnostic criteria for posttraumatic stress disorder (PTSD; APA, 1994). Assessment of PTSD among battered women indicates that, indeed, PTSD is prevalent among battered women with prevalence estimates ranging from a low of 33% (Astin, Lawrence, & Foy, 1993; Cascardi, O'Leary, Lawrence, & Schlee, 1995) to a high of 84% (Kemp, Rawlings, & Green, 1991). Variability in prevalence estimates appears to be a function of differences across studies in the method of diagnostic assessment, the population sampled, and the length of time since the traumatic event, i.e., the violent episode(s). Higher rates are more likely to result from self-report assessments among shelter women conducted immediately, e.g., 1–2 days, after a violent event. The high prevalence of PTSD among battered women merits attention since the disorder may interfere with a woman's functioning after she leaves her abusive partner and attempts to live on her own. Additionally, PTSD symptomatology may be stressful enough to interfere with women's attempts to escape abusive relationships.

PTSD has been shown to be more likely to develop among victims who engage in dissociative strategies, such as distraction, to cope during the trauma and after (Ronfeldt, Bernat, Arias, & Calhoun, 1996). Perceptions of control over stressful events and the use of problem-focused coping strategies, such as developing a plan of action, relative to the use of emotion-focused coping, such as fantasizing about good outcomes, have been shown to be more effective in reducing distress (Lazarus & Folkman, 1984). Specific to battering, Herbert, Silver, and Ellard (1991) found that battered women who remained with their abusers were more likely to employ emotion-focused strategies to cope with their abuse than women who terminated their abusive relationships. Thus, it seems reasonable to expect that women who engage in ineffective, emotion-focused coping and feel powerless or helpless may be more likely to develop PTSD symptomatology in response to abuse.

This investigation then was designed to test the following hypotheses:

1. physical and psychological abuse will be positively related;
2. psychological abuse will be a significant predictor of battered women's psychological, i.e., PTSD, symptomatology and their intentions to leave the abusive partner even after controlling for the effects of physical abuse;
3. the relationship between psychological abuse and intentions to leave the abusive relationship will be moderated by PTSD symptomatology such that the relationship will be stronger among women who do not suffer from high levels of PTSD symptomatology than among those who do; and
4. perceptions of control over the violence and type of coping strategies used in response to physical abuse will moderate the relationship between psychological abuse and PTSD symptomatology such that the relationship will be stronger for women who do not perceive themselves to be in control over their partners' violence and for women who engage in emotion-focused coping.

METHOD

Participants

Sixty-eight women currently residing in battered women's shelters in Atlanta, Georgia, and surrounding counties participated in this project. All of the women were either married for at least 1 year (61%) or had cohabited with their current partners for at least 1 year (39%). Women on average were 36 years old and had 12.60 years of education. Forty-eight percent were White American, 43% African American, 3% Latino American, and 6% Native American. Fifteen percent of the women identified themselves as Protestant, 13% Catholic, and 72% indicated "other" religious affiliations.[1] Fifty-six percent of the women were employed outside the home earning an average personal annual income of $22,000, and all had children living at home.

All assessments were conducted within 2 weeks of each woman's arrival at the shelters. Each woman completed the assessment independently, in private, and anonymously. Women were paid $10.00 each for their participation.

Measures

Conflict Tactics Scale-Form R (CTS-R). The CTS-R (Straus, 1990) is a 19-item self-report measure designed to assess the ways in which family members and intimately related partners resolve conflict. It is composed of three subscales: (1) reasoning, (2) verbal aggression, and (3) violence. Behaviors ranging from "discussed the issue calmly" to "did or said something to spite the other one" to "used a knife or gun" are assessed, employing seven response categories indicating the frequency of behavior: 1 = never, 2 = once, 3 = twice, 4 = 3–5 times, 5 = 6–10 times, 6 = 11–20 times, and 7 = more than 20 times. Participants indicated the frequency at which their partners had engaged in each of the 19 behaviors of the CTS-R during the preceding year. Scores for each of the subscales were calculated by weighting each item (i.e., multiplying the response category code [1 through 7] by the number of the item [1 through 19]), and summing the weighted items comprising each of the subscales. Total physical abuse scores could range between 135 (no violence during the preceding year) and 945 (all forms of violence occurring more than 20 times each during the preceding year). The CTS-R has been shown to be a reliable and valid measure (Straus, 1990).

Psychological Maltreatment of Women Inventory (PMWI; Tolman, 1989). The PMWI is a 58-item self-report questionnaire used to evaluate the psychological maltreatment of women. The items reflect an individual's attempt to isolate, dominate, humiliate, and threaten his/her partner and comprise two separate but related subscales: dominance/ isolation (e.g., "My partner monitored my time and made me account for where I was;" "My partner tried to keep me from seeing or talking to my family") and emotional/verbal abuse (e.g., "My partner tried to make me feel like I was crazy;" "My partner insulted or shamed me in front of others"). Participants were asked to indicate the frequency at which their partners engaged in each psychologically abusive behavior during the preceding year on a scale ranging from 1 (never) to 5 (very frequently). Total PMWI scores range from 58 (no psychological abuse) to 290 (all forms of psychological abuse occurring frequently). Victims' reports of psychological abuse on the PMWI have been found to be characterized by high internal consistency (Dutton & Hemphill, 1992; Tolman, 1989) and free of socially desirable responding effects (Dutton & Hemphill, 1992).

Ways of Coping Checklist-Revised (WCCL-R). The WCCL-R (Folkman & Lazarus, 1985; Forsythe & Compas, 1987) is a 66-item self-report measure that assesses a range of coping strategies, including both problem-focused (e.g., "I made a plan of action and followed it;" "I changed something so things would turn out all right") and emotion-focused strategies ("I had fantasies or wishes about how things might turn out;" "I rediscovered [focused on] what is important in life"), employed to manage the internal and external demands of stressful encounters. Factor analyses conducted on a sample of college undergraduates (Folkman & Lazarus, 1985) have resulted in eight scales: one problem-focused scale, six emotion-focused scales, and one mixed scale containing both problem- and emotion-focused items. The problem-focused scale consisting of 11 items and a composite emotion-focused scale consisting of the 24 items of the six emotion-focused scales have been shown to be reliable and were employed in this investigation.

Participants were asked to indicate the extent to which they employed each strategy to cope with their partners' most recent violent episode on a 4-point Likert scale ranging from 1 (does not apply and/or is not used) to 4 (used a great deal). Scores were calculated separately for the problem- and emotion-focused coping scales by summing the ratings for the items pertaining to each scale (Forsythe & Compas, 1987). Thus, scores for problem-focused coping could range from 11 to 44, while scores for emotion-focused coping could range from 24 to 96. As problem- and emotion-focused coping are believed to be interdependent (Folkman & Lazarus, 1980, 1985), combinations of problem- and emotion-focused coping reflect differences in coping patterns, and the ratio of problem-focused to emotion-focused coping has been found to be more sensitive to interaction between cognitive appraisals and coping (Forsythe & Compas, 1987). Accordingly, the ratio of problem- to emotion-focused coping was employed. Resulting ratios could range from 44/24 or 1.83, reflecting exclusive use of problem-focused coping, to 11/96 or .11, reflecting an exclusive use of emotion-focused coping. Equal use of both types of coping strategies would be reflected by a ratio of approximately .47.

Symptom Checklist-90-Revised (SCL-90-R). The SCL-90-R (Derogatis, 1977) is a 90-item checklist assessing psychological symptomatology. Specifically, respondents are asked to indicate how much personal discomfort each symptom on the scale has caused. The SCL-90-R is a widely used instrument consisting of nine symptom dimensions: somatization, obsessive-compulsive, interpersonal sensitivity, depression, anxiety, hostility, phobic anxiety, paranoid ideation, and psychoticism. Participants were instructed to indicate how much distress each item on the SCL-90-R had caused during the preceding year on a 5-point scale ranging from 0 (not at all) to 4 (extremely). Saunders, Arata, and Kilpatrick (1990) developed a 28-item scale within the SCL-90-R that successfully discriminated between crime-related posttraumatic stress disorder (PTSD) positive and negative women. Items comprising the PTSD subscale include SCL-90-R items such as "suddenly scared for no reason," "thoughts and images of a frightening nature," "feelings of hopelessness about the future," and "your mind going blank." PTSD subscale scores are calculated by adding a participant's responses across the 28 items and dividing the total by 28, resulting in a mean item score. The mean item score for the subscale can range from 0 to 4, and a cutoff score of .89 correctly classified 89.3% of the respondents in the Saunders et al. study. In conjunction with a history of victimization, this cutoff score indicates the high probability that the individual will meet criteria for PTSD. Since it is recommended that diagnosis of PTSD be made on the basis of structured diagnostic interviews, we employed this SCL-90-R sub-scale as a continuous measure of PTSD symptomatology and not the presence or absence of the disorder *per se.*

Procedure

Participants were informed that they would be participating in a study examining the ways that women appraise relationship conflict and the various ways that couples resolve conflictual issues. All participants completed an informed consent form. Each participant was asked to complete a packet of questionnaires that included demographic information, the CTS-R, the PMWI, and the SCL-90-R. Participants then were asked to briefly describe in writing the most recent violent event in which they were the recipient of their partners' physical aggression. They were instructed to rate the extent to which they believed they had control over the violence they described on a scale from 1 (no control) to 7 (complete control) and then to indicate the likelihood that they would end the relationship on a 7-point scale, ranging from 1 ("I will never end this relationship") to 7 ("I am 100% sure that I will end this relationship").

RESULTS

Table 1 presents the means and standard deviations for the variables examined in this investigation. The women in our sample on average were characterized by fairly high levels of physical abuse and very high levels of psychological abuse. Eighty-four percent of the women reported being survivors of severe violence such as being beaten, choked, and threatened or actually assaulted with weapons. The average psychological victimization score was 202 out of a possible score of 290, suggesting that participants in this investigation survived frequent exposure to abusive behaviors assessed by the PMWI. Likewise, participants were characterized by fairly high levels of PTSD symptomatology. Indeed, 60 participants (88%) had scores of .89 or greater, the cutoff for suspected PTSD clinical criteria. Participants on average employed a moderate number of coping strategies in response to partner violence and were equally likely to rely upon emotion- and problem-focused coping. Women saw themselves as having little control over their partners' violence and expressed strong intentions to leave their abusive partners permanently.

TABLE 1. Means, Standard, Deviations and Range of Obtained Scores

Variable	Mean	Standard Deviation	Range
Physical abuse (CTS-R)	474.04	209.69	135–945
Psychological abuse (PMWI)			
Total	201.99	50.83	80–285
Dominance/isolation	86.39	25.95	31–130
Emotional/verbal	91.39	19.01	33–115
PTSD symptomatology (SCL-90-R)	1.86	.75	.11–3.25
Coping (WCCL-R)			
Emotion focused	59.63	14.31	32–96
Problem focused	28.72	6.77	15–44
Ratio	.50	.12	.25–.92
Perceptions of control	1.98	1.73	1–7
Intention to end relationship	6.23	1.38	2–7

As expected, there was a significant relationship between physical and psychological abuse[2] among our sample of battered women (r [66] = .52, $p < .001$). Surprisingly, multiple regression analysis results indicated that physical abuse did not account for significant variance in either PTSD symptomatology ($R^2 = .02$, F [1, 64] = 1.54, ns) or women's intentions to end their abusive relationships ($R^2 = .06$, F [1, 63] = 3.78, $p = .06$). On the other hand, psychological abuse was a significant predictor of both PTSD symptomatology ($R^2 = .11$, F [1, 64] = 8.09, $p < .01$) and intentions to end the relationship ($R^2 = .24$, F [1, 63] = 19.40, $p < .001$), indicating that greater levels of psychological abuse were associated with greater levels of PTSD symptomatology and a greater resolve to leave the abusive partner. When we controlled for the effects of physical abuse by including it as a predictor in the regression equations, psychological abuse continued to account for significant variance in both PTSD symptomatology (full model $R^2 = .11$; partial $R^2 = .09$; $\beta = .35$, t [63] = 2.52, $p < .05$) and intention to end the abusive relationship (full model $R^2 = .24$; partial $R^2 = .18$; $\beta = .50$, t [62] = 3.81, $p < .001$).

In order to test for the potential moderating effects of PTSD symptomatology on the association between abuse and intentions to terminate the relationship, multiple regressions were conducted separately for physical abuse and for psychological abuse. In each regression, the main effects of abuse and PTSD symptomatology and their interaction (i.e., their product) were entered as predictors of intentions. A significant model with a significant interaction term indicates a significant moderating effect (Baron & Kenny, 1986). PTSD symptomatology proved to be a significant moderator of the effects of both physical (full model $R^2 = .15$; partial $R^2 = .09$; $\beta = -1.19$, t [61] = -2.57, $p = .01$) and psychological abuse (full model $R^2 = .30$; partial $R^2 = .05$; $\beta = -1.24$, t [61] = -2.16, $p < .05$). In order to examine the moderating effect of PTSD, we computed a median split to create low (< median) and high ($\geq$ median) PTSD symptomatology groups and calculated correlations between abuse and intentions to end the abusive relationship for each of these groups separately. While the relationship between physical abuse and intentions to terminate was significant for women in the low PTSD symptomatology group (r [34] = .54, p = .001), there was no significant relationship for women in the high PTSD symptomatology group (r [32] = −.07, *ns*). Likewise, psychological abuse and intentions to terminate were highly related among women in the low PTSD symptomatology group (r [33] = .71, p < .001), but there was no significant association for women in the high PTSD symptomatology group (r [32] = .18, *ns*). Thus, it appeared the presence of high levels of PTSD symptomatology interfered with the intention to leave the abusive partner in response to both physical and psychological abuse.

Because of the significant association between physical and psychological abuse, we conducted a second set of regressions examining the moderating effects of PTSD symptomatology while controlling for the remaining form of abuse. As was the case when we examined main effects, the interaction between PTSD symptomatology and physical abuse was no longer significant after controlling for the effects of psychological abuse. However, the interaction between psychological abuse and PTSD symptomatology continued to be significant even after controlling for physical abuse (full model R^2 = .31 ; partial R^2 = .06; β = −1.33, t [60] = −2.25, p <.05).

We conducted similar sets of regression analyses to examine potential risk factors for the presence of high levels of PTSD symptomatology in the context of high levels of psychological abuse. The three coping variables (i.e., emotion-focused, problem-focused, and the ratio) and perceptions of control were examined as moderators of the relationship between psychological abuse and PTSD symptomatology in separate regression analyses. Emotion-focused coping and the ratio of emotion- to problem-focused coping strategies were significant predictors of PTSD symptomatology (emotion-focused: R^2 = .13, F [1, 64] = 9.23, p < .01; ratio: R^2 = .07, F [1, 64] = 5.04, p < .05): greater use of emotion-focused coping and greater use of emotion-focused relative to problem-focused coping were associated with greater levels of PTSD symptomatology. While the ratio of emotion- to problem-focused coping strategies was no longer a significant predictor of PTSD symptomatology after controlling for the effects of psychological abuse, emotion-focused coping continued to account for unique variance significantly (t [62] = 2.61, p = .01). However, none of the three coping variables nor perceptions of control moderated the effects of psychological abuse on PTSD symptomatology.

DISCUSSION

The results of the current investigation underscore the importance of assessing and addressing psychological abuse among battered women. Psychological abuse of women was a strong and significant predictor of PTSD symptomatology and intentions to terminate the abusive relationship, accounting for 11% and 24% of the total variance, respectively. More important, the effects of psychological abuse were significant even after controlling for the effects of physical abuse. Surprisingly, physical abuse failed to account significantly for variance in either PTSD symptomatology or intentions to terminate the relationship. All participants in this investigation were battered women residing at emergency shelters. Unlike community samples, our sample was possibly more homogeneous with regard to frequency and severity of physical abuse. Lack of variability in physical abuse scores could make it difficult to obtain significant associations between physical abuse and other variables of interest. However, as reported in Table 1, our sample appeared to be characterized by sufficient variability to detect significant relationships.

Rather than lack of variability, it is possible that our inability to obtain significant results for physical abuse was due to the focus of our measure of physical abuse. Our operationalization of physical abuse was derived by summing the product of frequency and severity of various forms of physical aggression for the year preceding shelter contact. However, women may be more likely to decide to leave their abusers, and/or suffer PTSD symptomatology, in response to the severity of the most recent violent event only and not in response to the cumulative frequency and severity of previous events. For example, a woman who has been slapped and pushed repeatedly during the preceding year and then is assaulted with objects and weapons may be more likely to take initial steps toward leaving her abuser, e.g., reside in a shelter, and may be more committed to terminating the relationship in response to this event than a woman who has been repeatedly threatened and assaulted with objects and weapons and then is slapped and pushed during the most recent violent incident. Alternatively, women may respond to changes in severity and frequency or to their own perceptions of dangerousness rather than absolute, objectively defined levels of frequency and severity.

Although our operationalization of physical abuse may have been consequential, it is also possible that our measure of PTSD symptomatology may have precluded a significant association between PTSD and physical victimization to emerge. PTSD diagnostic criteria are heterogeneous. Foa, Riggs, and Gershuny (1995) suggested that PTSD reactions can consist of three separate but related symptom clusters: numbing, arousal, and intrusion. Further, they suggested that trauma victims may have different psychological reactions characterized by different patterns of PTSD symptoms, and yet all may appropriately be diagnosed as suffering from PTSD. Symptoms of arousal and intrusion were overrepresented by our measure of PTSD symptomatology while symptoms of numbing were underrepresented. Psychological and physical abuse may be related to different pathological reactions such that symptoms from some clusters but not others would be found among survivors of psychological abuse and a different symptom pattern would be found among survivors of physical abuse. If so, additional or alternative measures that adequately assess all types of PTSD symptomatology should be employed in future research. Potential confounding effects of our operationalization of physical abuse and PTSD symptomatology may render it premature to conclude that in future samples physical victimization will not account for PTSD symptomatology or the decision to leave.

While methodological and psychometric factors may have contributed to the inability of physical abuse to predict significantly, the ability of psychological abuse to significantly and independently predict both PTSD symptomatology and intentions to terminate the relationship may reflect that, relative to physical abuse, psychological abuse exerts considerable influence on these variables. First, it is possible that women experienced psychological abuse more frequently than physical abuse. More frequent exposure to psychological abuse may allow it to have a greater impact on women's functioning than the relatively less frequent physical abuse. Unfortunately, our measures of psychological and physical abuse employ response scales of different metric prohibiting direct examination of relative frequency. Second, relative to discreet episodes of physical violence, episodes of psychological abuse may be of longer duration functionally if women internalize psychological abuse, especially emotional abuse and assaults on self-esteem and self-concept such as humiliation. That is, a physically violent episode has a beginning and an end: physically violent acts commence and cease in occurrence during a dispute. Psychological abuse, on the other hand, may be prolonged if events such as name-calling, e.g., "you're crazy/stupid," are incorporated into the self-concept, e.g., "I'm crazy/stupid." Third, psychological assaults and trauma simply may have a greater impact on psychological well-being, at least in regard to PTSD symptomatology, than physical assault. By definition, psychological abuse is psychological in nature. Its targets are affect and cognitions. The specificity and fundamental congruence between psychological abuse and psychological well-being may account for their significant association.

The results of our investigation contribute to the growing empirical base documenting the risk of PTSD among battered women. Participants' mean item score was two times greater than the recommended cutoff score for assessing for clinical levels of PTSD, with 88% of the women scoring above the recommended cutoff score. The women in our investigation completed the assessment within 2 weeks of their arrival at the shelters which, in turn, closely followed an abusive incident, i.e., trauma. The short duration of the period following the trauma (i.e., less than one month) and the absence of standardized clinical assessment do not allow determination of the extent to which women scoring high on our measure of PTSD symptomatology actually would meet DSM-IV criteria (APA, 1994) for the disorder. However, PTSD has been found to be quite prevalent among shelter residents and we would expect a significant proportion of our sample to meet criteria for the disorder as well. Treatment for PTSD symptoms and the disorder *per se* during or after shelter residence should be considered and explored as an appropriate component of intervention.

Neither perceptions of control over the partners' violence nor coping affected the probability that PTSD symptomatology would develop in abusive contexts. However, frequent and preferred use of emotion-focused strategies was predictive of PTSD symptoms. Women who were more likely to rely on ignoring the violence and focusing on less negative aspects of their lives were more likely to develop PTSD symptoms than women who focused on actions that could be taken to reduce, eliminate, or otherwise change the violence and its impact. It is not clear to what extent such action was taken, but it did appear that focusing on potential action buffered women against some of the negative effects of psychological abuse.

While they may not meet clinical criteria, women in our sample reported a high level of distress caused by PTSD symptoms. Of special note, PTSD symptomatology exerted a detrimental impact on women's responses to their victimization: high levels of PTSD symptomatology significantly attenuated the impact of physical abuse and psychological abuse on women's intentions to terminate the abusive relationship. That is, termination of the abusive relationship appeared less likely in the context of PTSD and PTSD-like reactions, apparently, no matter how badly a woman was treated by her partner. Women were able to conceive of termination of the abusive relationship as a viable option and were committed to that option in response to abuse only if they were not hampered by psychological distress. Women experiencing high levels of distress did not appear to be committed to terminating the abusive relationship and should be unlikely to attempt and succeed leaving their abusive partners.

Significant moderation of the main effects of physical and psychological abuse suggests that women's experiences of their own victimization and related decision-making processes may be more complex than we typically assume. Physical and psychological abuse frequency and severity alone did not appear to provide sufficient motivation to disengage from a dangerous situation. Rather, women's psychological well-being determined whether or not abuse was sufficient motivation. Only women who were relatively unscathed psychologically strongly intended to disengage. It may be that when abuse produces significant psychological detriments, women may feel less ready or able to terminate the relationship and attempt self-sufficiency. Interventions with battered women may have to take women's psychological well-being into account before expecting them to choose and attempt self-sufficiency. While women should not be dissuaded from attempting to leave their abusers, supportive services provided may have to vary as a function of women's psychological well-being. Future research should examine directly the extent to which psychological well-being has an impact on women's evaluation of their ability to carry out plans to terminate the relationship and their appraisal of being able to be self-sufficient.

Because of its moderating effects, it seems prudent to attempt to reduce PTSD and related symptoms. The impact of emotion-focused coping suggests that encouraging women to engage in problem-focused coping more frequently, and in preference to the use of emotion-focused strategies, may be productive. In addition to increasing or maintaining psychological distress in the context of abuse, emotion-focused coping may decrease women's ability to stay out of the abusive relationship even if they intend and do carry out plans and strategies for permanently leaving their abusive partners.[3] Continued use of emotion-focused coping may increase the risk of the development of psychological distress in response to the difficulties that may be experienced after leaving the abusive partner such as financial, employment, and housing difficulties. High levels of psychological distress, in turn, may increase the probability of returning to the abusive partner. The results of our investigation, suggesting that coping and distress have a negative impact on women's ability to terminate their abusive relationships, underscore the need for shelter stays that extend beyond the common 30-day limit. Focusing on the development of transitional housing and designing interventions that can be implemented over a longer period of time seem critical. Protective and supportive environments of longer duration would allow women to improve self-esteem, decrease psychological distress, and stabilize their improved affective and cognitive reactions enough to be able to focus on the complex task of independent living. Further, such interventions may increase the probability of maintaining constructive changes and independent living.

NOTES

[1]The overwhelming majority of women indicating "other" specified Baptist or Southern Baptist as their religious affiliations since Baptists traditionally do not consider themselves "Protestant."

[2]There were no differences in the pattern of results as a function of the type of psychological abuse, i.e., dominance/isolation versus emotional/verbal abuse. Further, each type of psychological abuse accounted for significant unique variance in PTSD symptomatology and intentions to terminate the abusive relationship. Accordingly, total PMWI scores were used as the measure of psychological abuse in all analyses.

[3]The association between the use of coping strategies in response to violence and in response to nonviolent, negative relationship events were significant: $r(64) = .72$, $p < .001$, for emotion-focused coping; $r(64) = .59$, $p < .001$, for problem-focused coping. Thus, participants appeared to react similarly to violent and nonviolent stressful events.

REFERENCES

American Psychiatric Association. (1994). *Diagnostic and statistical manual of mental disorders* (4th ed.). Washington, DC: Author.

Aguilar, R. J., & Nightingale, N. N. (1994). The impact of specific battering experiences on the self-esteem of abused women. *Journal of Family Violence, 9,* 35–45.

Arias, I., & Street, A. E. (1996, August). *Children of psychologically abused women: Effects of maternal adjustment and parenting on child outcomes.* Presented at the 8th International Conference on Personal Relationships, Banff, Canada.

Arias, I., Street, A. E., & Brody, G. H. (1996, September). *Depression and alcohol abuse: Women's responses to psychological victimization.* Presented at the American Psychological Association's National Conference on Psychosocial and Behavioral Factors in Women's Health: Research, Prevention, Treatment, and Service Delivery in Clinical and Community Settings. Washington, DC.

Astin, M. C., Lawrence, K. J., & Foy, D. W. (1993). Posttraumatic stress disorder among battered women: Risk and resiliency factors. *Violence and Victims, 8,* 17–28.

Baron, R. M., & Kenny, D. A. (1986). The moderator-mediator variable distinction in social psychological research: Conceptual, strategic, and statistical considerations. *Journal of Personality and Social Psychology, 51,* 1173–1182.

Cascardi, M., O'Leary, K. D., Lawrence, E. E., & Schlee, K. A. (1995). Characteristics of women physically abused by their spouses and who seek treatment regarding marital conflict. *Journal of Consulting and Clinical Psychology, 63,* 616–623.

Derogatis, L. R. (1977). *SCL-90 administration, scoring and procedure manual for the R(Revised) version.* Johns Hopkins University School of Medicine, Baltimore, MD.

Dutton, D. G., & Hemphill, K. J. (1992). Patterns of socially desirable responding among perpetrators and victims of wife assault. *Violence and Victims, 7,* 29–39.

Foa, E. B., Riggs, D. S., & Gershuny, B. S. (1995). Arousal, numbing, and intrusion: Symptom structure of PTSD following assault. *American Journal of Psychiatry, 152,* 116–120.

Folkman, S., & Lazarus, R. S. (1980). An analysis of coping in a middle-aged community sample. *Journal of Health and Social Behavior, 21,* 219–239.

Folkman, S., & Lazarus, R. S. (1985). If it changes it must be a process: Study of emotion and coping during three stages of a college examination. *Journal of Personality and Social Psychology, 48,* 150–170.

Follingstad, D. R., Rutledge, L. L., Berg, B. J., Hause, E. S., & Polek, D. S. (1990). The role of emotional abuse in physically abusive relationships. *Journal of Family Violence, 5,* 107–120.

Forsythe, C. J., & Compas, B. E. (1987). Interaction of cognitive appraisals of stressful events and coping: Testing the goodness of fit hypothesis. *Cognitive Therapy and Research, 11,* 473–485.

Herbert, T. B., Silver, R. C., & Ellard, J. H. (1991). Coping with an abusive relationship: How and why do women stay? *Journal of Marriage and the Family, 53,* 311–325.

Kahn, F. I., Welch, T. L., & Zillmer, E. A. (1993). MMPI-2 profiles of battered women in transition. *Journal of Personality Assessment, 60,* 100–111.

Kemp, A., Rawlings, E. I., & Green, B. L. (1991). Post-traumatic stress disorder (PTSD) in battered women. *Journal of Traumatic Stress, 4,* 137–148.

Lazarus, R. S., & Folkman, S. (1984). *Stress, appraisal, and coping.* New York: Springer Publishing Company.

Marshall, L. L. (1996). Psychological abuse of women: Six distinct clusters. *Journal of Family Violence, 11,* 379–409.

Molidor, C. E. (1995). Gender differences of psychological abuse in high school dating relationships. *Child and Adolescent Social Work Journal, 12,* 119–134.

O'Leary, K. D., & Curley, A. D. (1986). Assertion and family violence: Correlates of spouse abuse. *Journal of Marital and Family Therapy, 12,* 281–289.

Parker, B., McFarlane, J., Soeken, K., Torres, S., & Campbell, D. (1993). Physical and emotional abuse in pregnancy: A comparison of adult and teenage women. *Nursing Research, 42,* 173–178.

Ronfeldt, H. M., Bernat, J. A., Arias, I., & Calhoun, K. S. (1996, November). *Peritraumatic reactions and posttraumatic stress disorder among sexually assaulted college women.* Presented at the 30th Annual Convention of the Association for Advancement of Behavior Therapy, New York, NY.

Saunders, B. E., Arata, C. M., & Kilpatrick, D. G. (1990). Development of a crime-related posttraumatic stress disorder scale for women within the Symptom Checklist-90-Revised. *Journal of Traumatic Stress, 3,* 439–448.

Straus, M. A. (1979). Measuring intrafamily conflict and violence: The Conflict Tactics (CT) Scales. *Journal of Marriage and the Family, 41,* 75–88.

Straus, M. A. (1990). The Conflict Tactics Scales and its critics: An evaluation and new data on validity and reliability. In M. A. Straus & R. J. Gelles (Eds.), *Physical violence in American families: Risk factors and adaptations to violence in 8,145 families* (pp. 49–73). New Brunswick, NJ: Transaction Publishers.

Strube, M. J. (1988). The decision to leave an abusive relationship: Empirical evidence and theoretical issues. *Psychological Bulletin, 104,* 236–250.

Tolman, R. M. (1989). The development of a measure of psychological maltreatment of women by their male partners. *Violence and Victims, 4,* 159–177.

Vitanza, S., Vogel, L. C. M., & Marshall, L. L. (1995). Distress and symptoms of posttraumatic stress disorder in abused women. *Violence and Victims, 10,* 23–34.

Walker, L. E. (1984). *The battered woman syndrome.* New York: Springer Publishing Company.

Acknowledgments. This research was supported in part by National Institute on Alcohol Abuse and Alcoholism (NIAAA) Grant AA09224-02S1.

Offprints. Requests for offprints should be directed to Ileana Arias, Department of Psychology, The University of Georgia, Athens, GA 30602-3013.

Violence and Victims, Volume 29, Number 5, 2014

Psychological and Physical Dating Violence Perpetrated by Pregnant and Parenting Latina Adolescents

Michelle L. Toews, PhD

Texas State University

Ani Yazedjian, PhD

Illinois State University

The purpose of this study was to examine predictors of psychological and physical dating violence perpetrated by 126 pregnant and parenting Latina adolescents. We found 85.7% had perpetrated at least one act of psychological abuse and 47.6% had perpetrated at least one act of physical abuse against the father of their child in the past 3 months. When examining predictors of psychological dating violence, we found that Latina adolescents who engaged in less positive communication patterns with their parents as well as those who were both the victim and perpetrator of physical abuse within their dating relationships were more likely to perpetrate psychological abuse. When examining predictors of physical dating violence, we found that Latina adolescents who perpetrated psychological abuse against the father of their child were also more likely to perpetrate physical abuse.

Keywords: adolescent mothers; dating violence; Latinas; physical abuse; psychological abuse

According to the National Institute of Justice (2011), between 7% and 30% of adolescents experienced some form of dating violence (i.e., sexual, physical, or psychological abuse) in the last 12–18 months. Similarly, the National Center for Injury Prevention and Control reported that prevalence rates of dating violence ranged from 9% to 65%, depending on whether threats and emotional abuse were included in the definition (as cited in Howard & Wang, 2003). Previous researchers have also found higher rates of dating violence among Latino youth compared to their White counterparts (Centers for Disease Control and Prevention, 2012; Howard & Wang, 2003; Sabina, Cuevas, & Bell, 2013) as well as among pregnant and parenting adolescents (Harrykissoon, Rickert, & Wiemann, 2002; Newman & Campbell, 2011; Roberts, Auinger, & Klein, 2005). To illustrate, in their study of 73 pregnant and parenting Latina adolescents, Newman and Campbell (2011) found that nearly 84% perpetrated and 80% were victims of psychological dating violence, whereas just more than 56% perpetrated and almost 40% were victims of physical dating violence in the past 6 months. Despite these findings, little is known about what predicts dating violence among pregnant and parenting Latina adolescents (Newman & Campbell, 2011), particularly when the female is the perpetrator (Williams, Ghandour,

& Kub, 2008). This study hopes to begin filling that gap by examining predictors of both psychological and physical violence perpetrated by Latina adolescents against the father of their child.

Previous researchers have found that adolescents are ill-equipped to handle the added stressors that teen pregnancy and parenting often bring to a relationship (Ismail, Berman, & Ward-Griffin, 2007; Kulkarni, 2006; Williams et al., 2006), thus explaining the increased risk of dating violence among this population. Moreover, some adolescent mothers stayed in abusive relationships because they feared losing love or feeling rejected (Ismail et al., 2007), whereas others remained in abusive relationships because of family pressure to stay with the father of their child (Kulkarni, 2006). This might be particularly true among pregnant and parenting Latina adolescents because the cultural value of *familismo* tends to stress the importance of and loyalty to the family (Skogrand, Hatch, & Singh, 2005). It is also possible that adolescents remained in abusive relationships because they viewed behaviors such as jealousy as a sign of love (Lavoie, Robitaille, & Hébert, 2000; Sears, Byers, Whelan, Saint-Pierre, & The Dating Violence Research Team, 2006; Smith & Donnelly, 2001). This was particularly true for individuals who had witnessed interparental violence because it was within the familial environment that adolescents learned what behaviors were normal and acceptable within intimate relationships (Herrenkohl, Sousa, Tajima, Herrenkohl, & Moylan, 2008; Ismail et al., 2007; Kulkarni, 2006; Tschann et al., 2009).

To illustrate, Ismail and colleagues (2007) found that "the family environment played a significant role in shaping young women's ideas, beliefs, values, and actions related to dating violence" (p. 465). Specifically, the young women reported that if they experienced violence at the hands of their parents, they were more likely to think that it was "okay" if their partners abused them. Similarly, more than half of adolescent mothers who were victims of dating violence in Kulkarni's (2006) study reported either being victims of child maltreatment or witnessing parental violence. Tschann and colleagues (2009) also found that adolescents were more likely to be both the victim and perpetrator of dating violence when their parents had poor conflict resolution skills or resorted to psychological or physical violence when resolving conflicts. A relationship has also been found between family communication style and dating violence. Specifically, Andrews, Foster, Capaldi, and Hops (2000) found that aversive family communication patterns in adolescence predicted psychological and physical violence in young adult relationships 6 years later, suggesting that observing or experiencing aversive communication patterns in the family of origin was a precursor to dating violence not only in adolescents' current romantic relationships but also in their future relationships.

Dating violence has also been found to be more common among adolescents who lacked communication and conflict resolution skills (Foshee et al., 2008; Lavoie et al., 2000; Sears & Byers, 2010; Wolfe & Foshee, 2003). Researchers have hypothesized that adolescents who lacked these skills were more likely to resort to abusive tactics as a way of expressing their unspoken feelings, such as anger, frustration, and jealousy (Foshee, Linder, MacDougall, & Bangdiwala, 2001; Fredland et al., 2005; Sears et al., 2006; Wolfe & Foshee, 2003). These abusive tactics might start with the use of psychological abuse, such as yelling, and escalate to physical abuse. In support of this assumption, previous researchers have found that psychological abuse is a predictor of physical abuse in adolescent dating relationships (Nicodemus, Porter, & Davenport, 2011; O'Leary & Smith Slep, 2003; Sears, Byers, & Price, 2007) and adolescents report that psychological abuse frequently precedes physical abuse in their dating relationships (Sears et al., 2006). Furthermore, researchers have found a correlation between adolescents' victimization and perpetration of abusive tactics in their dating relationships (Sears et al., 2007), suggesting this relationship is bidirectional (Reeves & Orpinas, 2012).

Researchers have also found that adolescents engage in more mutual exchanges of violence (Halpern, Oslak, Young, Martin, & Kupper, 2001; Hickman, Jaycox, & Aronoff, 2004; Newman & Campbell, 2011). However, research examining gender symmetry in dating violence has been inconsistent. Specifically, although some researchers have found that adolescent males and females are equally likely to be perpetrators (Halpern et al., 2001; Hickman et al., 2004; Newman & Campbell, 2011), others have reported gender differences (Sears et al., 2006; Windle & Mrug, 2009; Wolitzky-Taylor et al., 2008). That is, some studies have found that adolescent females were more likely to perpetrate abuse (Windle & Mrug, 2009), whereas others have found that females were more likely to be victims of dating violence (Wolitzky-Taylor et al., 2008). In addition, Sears and colleagues (2006) found that adolescents believed females were more likely to perpetrate psychological abuse and males were more likely to perpetrate physical abuse. Despite these inconsistencies, what we do know is that dating violence among adolescent partners is a significant public health problem (Mulford & Giordano, 2008). Yet, little is known about potential gender differences in dating violence perpetrated by Latino/Latina adolescents who might be influenced by the cultural values of machismo and *marianismo*, which represent traditional gender roles (Lopez, Chesney-Lind, & Foley, 2012). What factors predict dating violence among adolescents also remains a relatively understudied topic (Nicodemus et al., 2011), especially among pregnant and parenting Latina adolescents (Newman & Campbell, 2011). Therefore, it is imperative to examine predictors of psychological and physical abuse among this population in an effort to develop culturally sensitive prevention and intervention programs.

THEORETICAL FRAMEWORK

To explore pregnant and parenting Latina adolescents' use of psychological and physical abuse, this study was guided by social learning theory, which posits that there are continuous and reciprocal relationships between individuals' thought processes, behaviors, and social and physical environments (Crosbie-Burnett & Lewis, 2004). When applied to abuse in adolescents' dating relationships, social learning theory would posit that individuals learn how to communicate and resolve conflicts from their observations of the strategies used and consequences experienced by those in their surrounding contexts. It is possible that some of the conflict resolution strategies observed in these contexts have included instances of psychological or physical abuse. However, because individuals have grown up observing these behaviors, they might not identify them as abusive. As a result, individuals might use similar strategies in their own conflicts, even if those strategies are not positive ones, simply because they are used by the role models to whom they have been exposed (Regan, 2009). Individuals' use of strategies might also be influenced by the reinforcement they receive from engaging in certain behaviors and the degree to which they believe they will be successful in achieving their desired outcomes. Therefore, the purpose of this study was to examine predictors of psychological and physical dating violence perpetrated by pregnant and parenting Latina adolescents against the father of their child. Specifically, we hypothesized that the communication patterns pregnant and parenting Latina adolescents used with their parents as well as the conflict tactics both they and the father of their child used in their dating relationship would predict their perpetration of both psychological and physical dating violence.

METHOD

Procedures

After obtaining approval from the university's institutional review board, we recruited pregnant and parenting adolescents enrolled in 10 school-age parenting programs to participate in a 12-week relationship education program focused on teaching communication and conflict resolution skills, characteristics of healthy relationships, how to end unhealthy relationships, and so forth. Recruitment was done via letters delivered by the program facilitators to all pregnant and parenting adolescents enrolled in the school-age parenting programs inviting them to participate in our program offered during their parenting class, if applicable, or lunch hour. Before implementing the program, adolescents provided written assent and completed a questionnaire to gather basic demographic information as well as to assess their current communication with their parents and the conflict resolution strategies they used with the father of their child. The project coordinator was present while the adolescents completed the questionnaire to offer assistance if needed.

Sample

There were 278 pregnant and parenting adolescents who participated in our program. However, because of the small number of males ($n = 62$) and non-Latinas ($n = 39$), the final sample was drawn from only Latinas. To be included in the final sample, the participants had to have completed the pretest prior to participating in the program and had to indicate they were still involved in a relationship with the father of their child (51 participants were excluded because they were not involved in a relationship with the father of their child at the time of the pretest). This resulted in a final sample of 126 pregnant or parenting Latina adolescents. The final sample ranged in age from 14 to 19 years, with an average age of 16.6, and nearly 100% qualified for free or reduced lunch. In addition, 46.0% were pregnant, and 57.9% had a child at the time of the pretest.

Instruments

Communication with parents was measured using McCubbin, McCubbin, and Thompson's (1996) 10-item Family Problem Solving Communication (FPSC) scale. Selected for its psychometric properties, the FPSC measures both positive (affirming) and negative (incendiary) patterns of communication in families (McCubbin et al., 1996). Items are scored on a 4-point Likert-type scale ranging from 1 (*false*) to 4 (*true*). Sample items from the affirming subscale included respecting each other's feelings, talking things through, and taking time to listen. Sample items from the incendiary subscale included yelling and screaming, walking away from conflicts without much satisfaction, and making matters more difficult by fighting and bringing up the past. A mean of the responses for the total scale was used in the analyses, with higher values indicative of more positive communication patterns. Cronbach's coefficient alpha for this sample was .75 for the total scale.

Psychological and physical abuse was measured using Straus, Hamby, Boney-McCoy, and Sugarman's (1996) Revised Conflict Tactics Scale (CTS2). The CTS2 has been widely used with diverse participants (including low-income individuals, Latinos, and adolescents), and several studies have noted its high degree of validity and reliability (see Straus, 2004). For the purposes of our study, the pregnant and parenting Latina adolescents were asked to report how frequently (0 = *never* to 6 = *more than 20 times*) both they and their partner used various strategies when resolving conflict over the past 3 months. Sample items from the 8-item psychological aggression subscale included name calling, shouting or yelling, insulting or swearing, threatening, or stomping out of the room. The 11-item physical assault subscale included items such as kicking, slapping, grabbing, pushing, or throwing items. A mean of the responses was used in the analyses, with higher values indicative of more frequent abusive tactics. Cronbach's coefficient alphas for this sample ranged from .79 to .82 for the psychological subscale and .71 to .86 for the physical abuse subscale.

ANALYSIS AND RESULTS

We first ran frequencies to determine how many Latina adolescents reported they or their partner perpetrated at least one abusive tactic in their relationship. Based on their responses, we found that 85.7% had perpetrated at least one act of psychological abuse and 47.6% had perpetrated at least one act of physical abuse against the father of their child in the past 3 months. In addition, 70.6% reported they had been the victim of at least one act of psychological abuse and 16.7% had been the victim of at least one act of physical abuse by the father of their child in the past 3 months.

A correlational analysis was then conducted to determine relationships between the study variables. A probability level of $p < .05$ was used to test the correlational analysis. As can be seen in Table 1, perpetration of psychological abuse was inversely related to

TABLE 1. Means, Standard Deviations, and Correlations for Study Variables

Variables	1	2	3	4	5
1. Communication with parents	—				
2. Perpetrated psychological dating violence	−.50***	—			
3. Victim of psychological dating violence	−.36***	.78***	—		
4. Perpetrated physical dating violence	−.29**	.72***	.44***	—	
5. Victim of physical dating violence	−.18*	.47***	.63***	.34***	—
M	3.07	0.94	0.67	0.23	0.10
SD	0.53	0.94	0.89	0.39	0.36
α	.75	.79	.82	.71	.86

*$p < .05$. **$p < .01$. ***$p < .001$.

TABLE 2. Regression Analysis Predicting Latina Adolescents' (*n* = 126) Perpetration of Psychological Dating Violence

Variable	Model 1			Model 2		
	B	*SE B*	β	*B*	*SE B*	β
Communication with parents	−0.88***	.14	−.50	−0.52***	.10	−.29
Perpetrated physical dating violence				1.32***	.14	.55
Victim of physical dating violence				0.61***	.15	.23
R^2		.25			.65	
F for change in R^2		40.75***			71.86***	

***$p < .001$.

communication with parents ($r = -.50$, $p < .001$) and positively related to being the victim of psychological abuse ($r = .78$, $p < .001$) and being the perpetrator and victim of physical abuse ($r = .72$, $p < .001$ and $r = .47$, $p < .001$, respectively). Perpetration of physical abuse was inversely related to communication with parents ($r = -.29$, $p < .01$) and positively related to being the perpetrator and victim of psychological abuse ($r = .72$, $p < .001$ and $r = .44$, $p < .001$, respectively) and being the victim of physical abuse ($r = .34$, $p < .001$).

Next, we used two hierarchical regression models to determine if two clusters of variables were predictive of Latina adolescents' perpetration of psychological and physical dating violence. The two clusters used in the regression models were (a) communication with their parents and (b) their and their partners' perpetration of psychologically and physically abusive tactics. Only the variables that were correlated with the outcome variable were included in the analyses. In addition, partners' perpetration of psychological abuse was excluded from the analyses because of multicollinearity. As can be seen in Table 2, communication with their parents contributed to a significant amount of the variance in Latina adolescents' perpetration of psychological abuse ($F = 40.75$, $p < .001$, $R^2 = .25$). Latina adolescents who engaged in more negative communication patterns with their parents were more likely to perpetrate psychologically abusive tactics against the father of their child. The second cluster also contributed to a significant amount of the variance in Latina adolescents' perpetration of psychological abuse ($F = 71.86$, $p < .001$, $R^2 = .65$). Examination of the individual variables revealed that negative communication patterns with parents, perpetration of physical abuse against the father of their child, and being the victim of physical abuse at the hands of their partners were all significant predictors of perpetrating psychological dating violence.

As depicted in Table 3, communication with their parents contributed to a significant amount of the variance in Latina adolescents' perpetration of physical abuse ($F = 11.57$, $p < .01$, $R^2 = .09$). Latina adolescents who engaged in more negative communication patterns with their parents were more likely to perpetrate physically abusive tactics against the father of their child. The second cluster also contributed to a significant amount of the

TABLE 3. Regression Analysis Predicting Latina Adolescents' ($n = 126$) Perpetration of Physical Dating Violence

Variable	Model 1			Model 2		
	B	$SE\ B$	β	B	$SE\ B$	β
Communication with parents	−0.22**	.06	−.29	0.07	.05	.09
Perpetrated psychological dating violence				0.32***	.03	.77
Victim of physical dating violence				−0.01	.08	−.01
R^2		.09			.52	
F for change in R^2		11.57**			55.64***	

**$p < .01$. ***$p < .001$.

variance in Latina adolescents' use of physical abuse ($F = 55.64$, $p < .001$, $R^2 = .52$). However, perpetration of psychological abuse against their partners was the only significant predictor of perpetrating physical dating violence.

DISCUSSION

The purpose of this study was to extend previous research by focusing on predictors of psychological and physical dating violence perpetrated by pregnant and parenting Latina adolescents. This is an important area of research because this group is at greater risk for experiencing and using psychologically and physically abusive tactics (Harrykissoon et al., 2002; Newman & Campbell, 2011; Roberts et al., 2005) and they have the highest birth rate among adolescents (National Campaign to Prevent Teen and Unplanned Pregnancy, 2013); yet, we know very little about what predicts dating violence among this population. Supporting the fact that prevalence rates are higher among Latino youth (Centers for Disease Control and Prevention, 2012; Howard & Wang, 2003; Sabina et al., 2013) as well as among pregnant and parenting adolescents (Harrykissoon et al., 2002; Newman & Campbell, 2011; Roberts et al., 2005), the Latina adolescents in our study reported higher frequencies of both psychological and physical abuse compared to the percentages reported in previous studies (Howard & Wang, 2003; National Institute of Justice, 2011). Also in support of previous research, we found, for the most part, that the Latina adolescents reported engaging in mutual exchanges of violence with their partners (Halpern et al., 2001; Hickman et al., 2004; Newman & Campbell, 2011). Interestingly, however, similar to Windle and Mrug's (2009) findings, the Latina adolescents in our study were more likely to perpetrate both psychologically and physically abusive tactics than their partners.

Also in line with previous research, we found the Latina adolescents in our study were more likely to perpetrate psychologically abusive tactics with their partners if they engaged in more negative communication with their parents (Andrews et al., 2000). This finding also provides support for the social learning explanation of dating violence. Specifically, the fact that negative communication patterns with one's parents was related to Latina adolescents' perpetration of psychologically abusive tactics in their dating relationships provides support for the idea that they learned how to resolve conflicts with their partners by mimicking the strategies employed by their parents (Crosbie-Burnett & Lewis, 2004; Regan, 2009; Toews, Yazedjian, & Jorgensen, 2011; Tschann et al., 2009).

Our findings also support the idea that perpetration and victimization of abuse in Latina adolescents' dating relationships is bidirectional (Reeves & Orpinas, 2012). Similar to previous research, we found that pregnant and parenting Latina adolescents who were both the victim and perpetrator of physically abusive tactics with the father of their child were more likely to use psychologically abusive tactics in their dating relationships (Sears et al., 2007). We also found that Latina adolescents who perpetrated psychologically abusive tactics with the father of their child were more likely to perpetrate physically abusive tactics as well (Nicodemus et al., 2011; O'Leary & Smith Slep, 2003; Sears et al., 2007). This finding supports the idea that adolescents who lack effective communication and conflict resolution skills are more likely to resort to abusive tactics (Foshee et al., 2008; Fredland et al., 2005; Sears & Byers, 2010; Wolfe & Foshee, 2003).

As this discussion demonstrates, our findings can be usefully framed with the interpretations offered by social learning theory as well as by the findings of extant research. At the same time, a few of our hypothesized relationships did not find support in this research. First, the communication pattern Latina adolescents engaged in with their parents was not predictive of their perpetration of physical abuse once their perpetration of psychologically abusive tactics was added to the model. Although social learning theory argues that individuals learn interactional skills through observing the behaviors of those around them (Crosbie-Burnett & Lewis, 2004), based on the findings of our research, it seems that the communication patterns Latina adolescents used in their family of origin predicted their perpetration of psychologically abusive tactics, which, in turn, predicted their perpetration of physical abuse. Perhaps a better predictor of physical abuse would be whether the pregnant and parenting Latina adolescents witnessed interparental violence and/or experienced physical violence at the hands of their parents (Ismail et al., 2007; Kulkarni, 2006). In other words, negative communication patterns might be a better predictor of psychological abuse (an extremely negative way of communicating), whereas witnessing or experiencing violence better predicts whether one will perpetrate physical abuse.

Second, contrary to previous research, being the victim of physical abuse by the father of their child was not predictive of Latina adolescents' perpetration of physical abuse (Nicodemus et al., 2011; O'Leary & Smith Slep, 2003; Sears et al., 2007). However, the two variables were correlated. This finding, combined with the fact that their perpetration of psychologically abusive tactics was the only variable predictive of their perpetration of physical abuse, suggests that Latina adolescents' own ineffective conflict resolution strategies are better predictors of physical abuse than their partner's conflict resolution skills.

LIMITATIONS AND IMPLICATIONS

Although our study is one of the first to examine predictors of psychological and physical dating violence perpetrated by pregnant and parenting Latina adolescents, the results of this study must be interpreted with some caution because of several methodological limitations. First, we cannot generalize our findings across groups because our participants were of Latino origin and most were low-income. Second, although no names were associated with the data collected, because of the sensitive nature of the questions, social desirability bias might have influenced our findings. Last, because the data were correlational in nature, no causal interpretations can be made.

Despite these limitations, this study has many implications. First, because we found pregnant and parenting Latina adolescents who perpetrated psychological abuse were also more likely to perpetrate physical abuse, skills-based programs that teach effective communication and conflict resolution skills are critical for this high-risk population. For example, most of our sample had insulted or yelled at the father of their child and/ or stomped out of the room during a disagreement at least once in the last 3 months. By offering programs that teach how to communicate more effectively and resolve conflict, adolescents will be better able to express their feelings without resorting to abusive tactics (Adler-Baeder, Kerpelman, Schramm, Higginbotham, & Paulk, 2007; Gardner, 2001; Gardner, Giese, & Parrot, 2004; Toews & Yazedjian, 2010). This will benefit not only their relationship but their children's future relationships as well because previous research has found that adolescents were more likely to be both the victim and perpetrator of dating violence when their parents had poor conflict resolution skills (Tschann et al., 2009).

Second, because of the cultural value of *familismo*, it is recommended that these skills-based programs involve the entire family (Skogrand et al., 2005). This is particularly relevant for the Latina adolescents in this sample because we found that the negative communication patterns they engaged in with their parents predicted their perpetration of abusive tactics with the father of their child. Given that nearly 40% of our participants reported that they and their parents yelled and screamed at each other and almost half reported that they walked away from conflict with their parents without much satisfaction and/or believed they and their parents made matters more difficult by fighting and bringing up the past, such programs could focus on how to effectively resolve conflict in an effort to improve their familial relationships and positively impact adolescent parents' romantic relationships.

It is also important for educators to encourage both adolescent males and females to participate in skills-based relationship education programs because the Latina adolescents in our study reported engaging in mutual exchanges of violence with the father of their child. By involving the couple, both partners will have the opportunity to practice the skills they are learning in a safe environment. However, getting fathers to participate can be particularly challenging because many fathers tend to either be older than adolescent mothers or not enrolled in school (Bunting & McAuley, 2004). As a result, it is important to offer programs in the evenings and weekends to accommodate the schedules of working fathers.

In addition, the findings from this study have implications for future research. Because our sample included only Latinas, we were unable to determine the relationship between culture and the use of violence in dating relationships. Future research should explore differences across ethnic groups, taking into account both the role of culture and gender, because previous research has suggested differences in psychological and physical abuse by race (Foshee et al., 2008; Halpern et al., 2001; Nicodemus et al., 2011). From a social learning perspective, it is possible that ethnic groups might vary not only in their definitions and acceptance of violence in dating relationships but also in their expectations of males and females' behaviors in such circumstances. Exploring these differences across groups would be useful in developing culturally relevant prevention and intervention programs. Such programs are greatly needed for pregnant and parenting Latina adolescents given there are no programs specifically developed for this population. In addition, studies should examine the relationship between violence and the duration of the relationship noting at what stage violence tends to begin. These findings would be helpful because defining what constitutes a romantic relationship during adolescence can be particularly complicated.

Future studies should also compare experiences with dating violence between those who are pregnant and those who are already parenting. Ideally, longitudinal studies that examine relationships from pregnancy through parenting should be conducted to gain a more thorough understanding of the etiology and causal sequence of abusive behaviors. In addition, qualitative studies could explore the topics that provoke arguments among adolescent parents (e.g., child-rearing responsibilities, gender role expectations, interactions with opposite sex peers, jealousy) and which topics are more likely to lead to violent confrontations, paying particular attention to whether different topics incite violence for males and females. These kinds of detailed narratives can provide greater insight into the ways in which the context of violence can change according to adolescents' circumstances. These results would be particularly useful in developing different kinds of intervention or prevention programs, which are delivered separately to males or females or specifically tailored to the stage of parenthood adolescents are currently experiencing. The data could also be used to further develop measures of dating violence that assess not only the actual abusive tactics and frequency of abuse but also the sequence of abuse and the motivation or intent behind those abusive behaviors.

REFERENCES

Adler-Baeder, F., Kerpelman, J. L., Schramm, D. G., Higginbotham, B., & Paulk, A. (2007). The impact of relationship education on adolescents of diverse backgrounds. *Family Relations, 56*, 291–303. http://dx.doi.org/10.1111/j.1741-3729.2007.00460.x

Andrews, J. A., Foster, S. L., Capaldi, D., & Hops, H. (2000). Adolescent and family predictors of physical aggression, communication, and satisfaction in young adult couples: A prospective analysis. *Journal of Consulting and Clinical Psychology, 68*(2), 195–208. http://dx.doi.org/10.1037/0022-006X.68.2.195

Bunting, L., & McAuley, C. (2004). Research review: Teenage pregnancy and parenthood: The role of fathers. *Child and Family Social Work, 9*, 295–303. http://dx.doi/org/10.1111/j.1365-2206.2004.00335.x

Centers for Disease Control and Prevention. (2012). Youth risk behavior surveillance—United States, 2011. *Morbidity and Mortality Weekly Report, 61*(4), 1–168.

Crosbie-Burnett, M., & Lewis, E. A. (2004). Theoretical contributions from social– and cognitive–behavioral psychology. In P. G. Boss, W. J. Doherty, R. LaRossa, W. R. Schumm, & S. K. Steinmetz (Eds.), *Sourcebook of family theories and methods: A contextual approach* (pp. 531–558). New York, NY: Springer.

Foshee, V. A., Karriker-Jaffe, K. J., Reyes, H. L. M., Ennett, S. T., Suchindran, C., Bauman, K. E., & Benefield, T. S. (2008). What accounts for demographic differences in trajectories of adolescent dating violence? An examination of intrapersonal and contextual mediators. *Journal of Adolescent Health, 42*(6), 596–604. http://dx.doi.org/10.1016/j.jadohealth.2007.11.005

Foshee, V. A., Linder, F., MacDougall, J. E., & Bangdiwala, S. (2001). Gender differences in the longitudinal predictors of adolescent dating violence. *Preventative Medicine, 32*, 128–141. http://dx.doi.org/10.1006/pmed.2000.0793

Fredland, N. M., Ricardo, I. B., Campbell, J. C., Sharps, P. W., Kub, J. K., & Yonas, M. (2005). The meaning of dating violence in the lives of middle school adolescents: A report of a focus group study. *Journal of School Violence, 4*(2), 95–114. http://dx.doi.org/10.1300/J202v04n02_06

Gardner, S. (2001). Evaluation of the "Connections: Relationships and Marriage" curriculum. *Journal of Family and Consumer Sciences Education, 19*, 1–14.

Gardner, S., Giese, K., & Parrot, S. (2004). Evaluation of the "Connections: Relationships and Marriage" curriculum. *Family Relations, 53*, 521–527. http://dx.doi.org/10.1111/j.0197-6664.2004.00061.x

Halpern, C. T., Oslak, S. G., Young, M. L., Martin, S. L., & Kupper, L. L. (2001). Partner violence among adolescents in opposite-sex romantic relationships: Findings from the National Longitudinal Study of Adolescent Health. *American Journal of Public Health, 91*(10), 1679–1685. http://dx.doi.org/10.2105/AJPH.91.10.1679

Harrykissoon, S. D., Rickert, V. I., & Wiemann, C. M. (2002). Prevalence and patterns of intimate partner violence among adolescent mothers during the postpartum period. *Archives of Pediatrics and Adolescent Medicine, 156*, 325–330. http://dx.doi.org/10.1001/archpedi.156.4.325

Herrenkohl, T. I., Sousa, C., Tajima, E. A., Herrenkohl, R. C., & Moylan, C. A. (2008). Intersection of child abuse and children's exposure to domestic violence. *Trauma, Violence & Abuse, 9*(2), 84–99. http://dx.doi.org/10.1177/1524838008314797

Hickman, L. J., Jaycox, L. H., & Aronoff, J. (2004). Dating violence among adolescents: Prevalence, gender distribution, and prevention program effectiveness. *Trauma, Violence & Abuse, 5*(2), 123–142. http://dx.doi.org/10.1177/1524838003262332

Howard, D. E., & Wang, M. Q. (2003). Risk profiles of adolescent girls who were victims of dating violence. *Adolescence, 38*, 1–14.

Ismail, F., Berman, H., & Ward-Griffin, C. (2007). Dating violence and the health of young women: A feminist narrative study. *Health Care for Women International, 28*, 453–477. http://dx.doi.org/10.1080/07399330701226438

Kulkarni, S. (2006). Interpersonal violence at the crossroads between adolescence and adulthood: Learning about partner violence from young mothers. *Violence Against Women, 12*, 187–207. http://dx.doi.org/10.1177/1077801205280933

Lavoie, F., Robitaille, L., & Hébert, M. (2000). Teen dating relationships and aggression. *Violence Against Women, 6*, 6–36. http://dx.doi.org/10.1177/10778010022181688

Lopez, V., Chesney-Lind, M., & Foley, J. (2012). Relationship power, control, and dating violence among Latina girls. *Violence Against Women, 18*, 681–690. http://dx.doi.org/10.1177/1077801212454112

McCubbin, M. A., McCubbin, H. I., & Thompson, A. I. (1996). Family Problem Solving Communication Scale. In H. I. McCubbin, A. I. Thompson, & M. A. McCubbin (Eds.), *Family assessment: Resiliency, coping, and adaptation—Inventories for research and practice.* Madison, WI: University of Wisconsin System.

Mulford, C., & Giordano, P. C. (2008). Teen dating violence: A closer look at adolescent romantic relationships. *NIJ Journal, 261*, 34–40. Retrieved from https://www.ncjrs.gov/pdffiles1/nij/224089.pdf

National Campaign to Prevent Teen and Unplanned Pregnancy. (2013). *Fast facts: Teen pregnancy and childbearing among Latina teens.* Retrieved from http://www.thenationalcampaign.org/resources/pdf/FastFacts_TPChildbearing_Latinos.pdf

National Institute of Justice. (2011). *Prevalence of teen dating violence.* Retrieved from http://www.nij.gov/nij/topics/crime/intimate-partner-violence/teen-dating-violence/prevalence.htm

Newman, B. S., & Campbell, C. (2011). Intimate partner violence among pregnant and parenting Latina adolescents. *Journal of Interpersonal Violence, 26*(13), 2635–3657. http://dx.doi.org/10.1177/0886260510388281

Nicodemus, P. D., Porter, J. A., & Davenport, P. A. (2011). Predictors of perpetrating physical date violence among adolescents. *North American Journal of Psychology, 13*(1), 123–132.

O'Leary, K. D., & Smith Slep, A. M. (2003). A dyadic longitudinal model of adolescent dating aggression. *Journal of Clinical Child & Adolescent Psychology, 32*(3), 314–327. http://dx.doi.org/10.1207/S15374424JCCP3203_01

Reeves, P. M., & Orpinas, P. (2012). Dating norms and dating violence among ninth graders in Northeast Georgia: Reports from student surveys and focus groups. *Journal of Interpersonal Violence, 27*(9), 1677–1698. http://dx.doi.org/10.1177/0886260511430386

Regan, M. E. (2009). Implementation and evaluation of a youth violence prevention program for adolescents. *The Journal of School Nursing, 25*(1), 27–33. http://dx.doi .org/10.1177/1059840508329300

Roberts, T. A., Auinger, P., & Klein, J. (2005). Intimate partner abuse and the reproductive health of sexually active female adolescents. *Journal of Adolescent Health, 36*, 380–385. http://dx.doi .org/10.1016/j.jadohealth.2004.06.005

Sabina, C., Cuevas, C. A., & Bell, K. A. (2013). *Dating violence among Latino adolescents (DAVILA) study* (Document No. 242775). Retrieved from https://ncjrs.gov/pdffiles1/nij/grants/242775.pdf

Sears, H. A., & Byers, E. S. (2010). Adolescent girls' and boys' experiences of psychologically, physically, and sexually aggressive behaviors in their dating relationships: Co-occurrence and emotional reaction. *Journal of Aggression, Maltreatment & Trauma, 19*, 517–539. http://dx.doi .org/10.1080/10926771.2010.495035

Sears, H. A., Byers, E. S., & Price, E. L. (2007). The co-occurrence of adolescent boys' and girls' use of psychologically, physically, and sexually abusive behaviors in their dating relationships. *Journal of Adolescence, 30*, 487–504. http://dx.doi.org/10.1016/j.adolescence.2006.05.002

Sears, H. A., Byers, E. S., Whelan, J. J., Saint-Pierre, M., & The Dating Violence Research Team. (2006). "If it hurts you, then it is not a joke": Adolescents' ideas about girls' and boys' use and experience of abusive behavior in dating relationships. *Journal of Interpersonal Violence, 21*, 1191–1207. http://dx.doi.org/10.1177/0886260506290423

Skogrand, L., Hatch, D., & Singh, A. (2005). *Understanding Latino families, implications for family life education.* Retrieved from http://extension.usu.edu/files/publications/publication/ FR_Family_2005-02.pdf

Smith, D. M., & Donnelly, J. (2001). Adolescent dating violence: A multi-systemic approach of enhancing awareness in educators, parents, and society. *Journal of Prevention & Intervention in the Community, 21*, 53–64. http://dx.doi.org/10.1300/J005v21n01_04

Straus, M. A. (2004). Cross-cultural reliability and validity of the Revised Conflict Tactics Scale: Reliability study of university student dating couples in 17 nations. *Cross-Cultural Research, 38*(4), 407–432. http://dx.doi.org/10.1177/1069397104269543

Straus, M. A., Hamby, S. L., Boney-McCoy, S., & Sugarman, D. B. (1996). The Revised Conflict Tactics Scale (CTS2): Development and preliminary psychometric data. *Journal of Family Issues, 17*, 283–316.

Toews, M. L., & Yazedjian, A. (2010). "I learned the bad things I'm doing:" Adolescent mothers' perceptions of a relationship education program. *Marriage and Family Review, 46*, 207–223.

Toews, M. L., Yazedjian, A., & Jorgensen, D. (2011). "I haven't done nothin' crazy lately:" Conflict resolution strategies in adolescent mothers' dating relationships. *Children and Youth Services Review, 33*, 180–186.

Tschann, J. M., Pasch, L. A., Flores, E., VanOss Marin, B., Baisch, E. M., & Wibbelsman, C. J. (2009). Nonviolent aspects of interparental conflict and dating violence among adolescents. *Journal of Family Issues, 30*(3), 295–319. http://dx.doi.org/10.1177/0192513X08325010

Williams, J. R., Ghandour, R. M., & Kub, J. E. (2008). Female perpetration of violence in heterosexual intimate relationships: Adolescence through adulthood. *Trauma, Violence & Abuse, 9*(4), 227–249. http://dx.doi.org/10.1177/1524838008324418

Williams, L., Morrow, B., Shulman, H., Stephens, R., D'Angelo, D., & Fowler, C. I. (2006). *PRAMS 2002 surveillance report.* Atlanta, GA: Division of Reproductive Health, National Center for Chronic Disease Prevention and Health Promotion, Centers for Disease Control and Prevention.

Windle, M., & Mrug, S. (2009). Cross-gender violence perpetration and victimization among early adolescents and associations with attitudes toward dating conflict. *Journal of Youth and Adolescence, 38*, 429–439. http://dx.doi.org/10.1007/s10964-008-9328-1

Wolfe, K. A., & Foshee, V. A. (2003). Family violence, anger expression styles, and adolescent dating violence. *Journal of Family Violence, 18*(6), 309–316. http://dx.doi. org/10.1023/A:1026237914406

Wolitzky-Taylor, K. B., Ruggiero, K. J., Danielson, C. K., Resnick, H. S., Hanson, R. F., Smith, D. W., . . . Kilpatrick, D. G. (2008). Prevalence and correlates of dating violence in a national sample of adolescents. *Journal of the American Academy of Child and Adolescent Psychiatry*, *47*(7), 755–762. http://dx.doi.org/10.1097/CHI.0b013e318172ef5f

Acknowledgments. Funding for this research was provided by the U.S. Department of Health and Human Services, Administration for Children and Families (Grant: HHS-2006-ACF-OFA-FE-0033). Any opinions, findings, and conclusions or recommendations expressed in this article are those of the authors and do not necessarily reflect the views of the U.S. Department of Health and Human Services, Administration for Children and Families.

Correspondence regarding this article should be directed to Michelle Toews, PhD, Texas State University, School of Family and Consumer Sciences, 601 University Drive, San Marcos, TX 78666. E-mail: mtoews@txstate.edu

Interpersonal and Systemic Aspects of Emotional Abuse at Work: The Target's Perspective

Loraleigh Keashly

Wayne State University

The most frequent form of workplace aggression is not physical, it is emotional and psychological in nature. Known by many names, emotional abuse at work is rapidly becoming recognized as pervasive and costly both in individual and organizational terms. Most of the research to date on emotional abuse at work has utilized survey and other quantitative methodologies in an effort to document the presence, prevalence, and impact of these behaviors. However, these methodologies are based on researchers' definitions and theories of what constitutes emotional abuse rather than on the meaning given to these experiences by the targets of these behaviors. A thorough understanding of this phenomenon requires a scholarly appreciation of the target's experience. Taking "feeling abused" as the criterion variable, this study examined target's experiences based on interviews with people who self-identified as having experienced difficulties with a boss, coworker, or subordinate. The interpersonal aspects of emotional abuse focused on the nature of behaviors exhibited and the respondents' labeling of their experience. Consistent with elements of researchers' definitions, behaviors were defined as abusive when they were repetitive, resulted in injury or harm to target, and were experienced as a lack of recognition of the individual's integrity. Judgments of violation of standards of conduct and unsolicited nature of the behaviors were also related to respondents' experiences. Relative power differential was also an important element. However, contrary to researchers' definitions, actor intent was not central in defining the experience as abusive. The systemic aspect of emotional abuse was illustrated in the nature of organizational responding to concerns raised by respondents. These responses were of critical importance in respondents' labeling of their experiences as abusive. The focus on the meaning of the behaviors for the respondents provides an enriched picture of key definitional elements. Implications of the findings for future research are discussed.

W orkplace violence is a growing public concern. The more dramatic examples of assault and homicide have riveted research and public attention on understanding and ameliorating hostilities in the workplace. Contrary to popular belief, these extreme forms of physical violence are quite rare in workplaces. In fact, the more frequently occurring forms of violence tend to be psychological in nature (e.g., Neuman & Baron, 1997; Richman et al., 1999). In their nationwide survey of American full-time workers, Northwestern National Life Insurance (1993) found that being "harassed" was three times more likely than being threatened with physical harm and six times more likely than being physically attacked. They found that the effects of psychological forms of violence are as dramatic and extensive as physical violence. Those who have been

---

harassed report higher rates of psychological distress (e.g., anger, fear, stress, depression), disruption in work life (including leaving or changing jobs, lowered productivity, or interpersonal problems) and similar rates of physical illness as physical attack victims. In addition, physical and psychological violence tend to be perpetrated by different persons. Physical violence is more likely to be perpetrated by organizational outsiders (e.g., consumers, clients) while psychological violence is more likely to be committed by organizational insiders, people with whom the target has an ongoing relationship, that is, bosses, coworkers, and subordinates (Barling, 1996; Bassman, 1992; Neuman & Baron, 1997). Yet despite such evidence, psychological violence has received far less attention than physical violence. In an effort to draw attention to this growing problem, the International Labor Organization 1998 report on workplace violence as a global problem concluded that psychological forms of violence are of increasing concern, have significant negative effects and warrant as much attention as physical violence.

Some forms of psychological violence such as sexual harassment (e.g., Fitzgerald & Shullman, 1993) and to a lesser degree racial harassment (e.g., Clayton, 1992) have received more attention. However, there is a form of psychological violence that is not uniquely associated with group-based membership that is only now gaining research and public attention. Recent evidence suggests that at least in North American workplaces, it is the more frequent form of psychological violence (Richman et al, 1999; Rogers, 1998). This "generalized" or "status-blind" form of psychological violence is known by many names. In Europe where it has been the subject of a significant amount of research and has been reflected in legal, social and workplace policies, it is referred to as bullying (e.g., Einarsen, 1999; Hoel, Rayner, & Cooper, 1999), mobbing (Leymann, 1990; 1996) or workplace harassment (e.g., Bjorkqvist, Osterman, & Hjelt-Back, 1994). In North America, particularly the U.S., which until recently has paid little public and research attention to this form of psychological aggression and violence, it has been referred to as workplace mistreatment (Price Spratlen, 1995), verbal abuse (e.g., Cox, 1991; Rosenberg & Silver, 1984), psychological abuse (Sheehan et al., 1990), emotional abuse (Keashly, Trott, & McLean, 1994; Nicarthy, Gottlieb, & Coffman, 1993), generalized workplace harassment (Richman et al., 1997) or simply abuse (Bassman, 1992, Ryan & Ostreich, 1991). While there is variability in the definitions associated with each of these terms (Hoel et al., 1999; Einarsen, 1999; Keashly, 1998), in essence, they describe interactions between organizational members that are characterized by repeated hostile verbal and nonverbal, often nonphysical behaviors directed at a person(s) such that the targets' sense of him/herself as a competent worker and person is negatively affected. Some examples of hostile behaviors considered as "psychological" in nature include using derogatory names, engaging in explosive outbursts (e.g., yelling or screaming at someone for disagreeing), intimidating by use of threats of job loss, withholding needed information, aggressive eye contact, "the silent treatment," isolating from others, obscene or hostile gestures, and humiliating or ridiculing someone in front of others. The term emotional abuse will be used in this article to refer to this more generalized form of psychological violence.

EXAMINING EMOTIONAL ABUSE

Operationalizing emotional abuse has occurred in primarily two ways. One way involves providing people with a checklist of behaviors and having them indicate the frequency of their occurrence. Frequency of occurrence and often duration of exposure are treated by researchers as indicators of the degree to which respondents have been treated abusively; the more frequent and the longer the period of time, the more abusive the treatment (Hoel et al., 1999; Einarsen, 1999). Alternatively, specific definitions of emotional abuse (or bullying, workplace mistreatment, workplace harassment or whatever the chosen term) are provided and the respondents are asked whether they would characterize their experience in that way. The challenge is that both approaches assume a one-to-one relationship between behavior endorsement or endorsement of definition and the targets' actual experience of being "abused" or "bullied" or "harassed" or "mistreated" (Liefooghe & Olafsson, 1999). It is often simply assumed that people will experience these behaviors as abusive because the behaviors were selected to reflect emotional abuse. While many studies are able to report notable frequencies for these types of behaviors (see Einarsen, 1999; Hoel et al., 1999), few address whether such frequency is in fact related to these behaviors being experienced as more or less abusive.

A cursory examination of behaviors captured under the rubric of emotional abuse shows that some of these behaviors are ambiguous (e.g., showing up late for meetings with the target; glaring). In fact, much of the behavior captured under the rubric of emotional abuse is passive (acts of omission) and/or indirect (directed at persons or objects important to the target; Neuman & Baron, 1997), making it difficult for either the researcher or the target to readily identify the behavior as abusive. In earlier research (Keashly et al., 1994; Jagatic & Keashly, 1998), we found that even though people endorsed the same behaviors, there was variability in the impact of the behavior on them. Thus, while some of the behaviors (e.g., putting someone down in public; swearing in a hostile manner) may be "inherently" abusive or harassing according to social consensus (Liefooghe & Olafsson, 1999; Keashly et al., 1996; O'Leary-Kelly, Griffin, & Grew, 1996; Richman et al., 1997), and could be expected to be experienced as abusive by most people; other behaviors are not, often occurring frequently in "normal" daily interactions (Leymann, 1990). It is these latter behaviors that draw our attention to the pivotal role of the subjective appraisal and interpretation of those in the situation. To date, the majority of research has utilized definitions (i.e., interpretations) of emotional abuse or what Brodsky (1976) calls "objective harassment." "Subjective harassment" or the subjective appraisal of these behaviors and interactions by the target has not been explored in much detail (ex. Lewis, 1999; Liefooghe & Olafsson, 1999; Rogers, 1998). This is a critical step as demonstrated by work in the related area of sexual harassment. A key definitional element in sexual harassment research and policy is that the target "feels" harassed (e.g., Magley, Hulin, Fitzgerald, & DeNardo, 1999). Thus, an important way to operationalize emotional abuse in research would be respondents' feelings of being abused, victimized, bullied, harassed, and so forth. The focus would then be on identifying what features of the situation are important to targets in formulating these subjective appraisals and experiences (Einarsen, 1999).

ELEMENTS OF TARGETS' EXPERIENCE

Interpersonal Features. Reviews of abusive workplace behaviors have identified a number of interpersonal elements that are important in researchers' and other observers' conceptualization of emotional abuse (e.g., Hoel et al., 1999; Einarsen, 1999; Fitzgerald &

Shullman, 1993; Keashly, 1998). In brief, from the perspective of the observer, verbal and nonverbal behaviors would be defined as emotionally abusive when:

1. They are of a repeated nature or part of a pattern of behaviors;
2. They are unwelcome and unsolicited by the target;
3. They violate a standard of appropriate conduct toward others;
4. They result in harm or injury to the target;
5. The actor intended to harm the target or when the actor could have controlled the behavior itself, and
6. When the actor is in a more powerful position relative to the target.

While these elements are influential in observers' conceptualizations, an important question is whether these various features figure prominently in the understanding of those on the receiving end of these behaviors. Some initial support for some of these features comes from our earlier research (Keashly, Welstead, & Delaney, 1996). We found that prior history with the actor (repeated behavior), intent, and degree of negative emotional impact (harm) but not organizational position (relative power) were related to employees' perception of the interaction as abusive. Specifically, we presented employees with hypothetical scenarios of hostile behavior that varied in their rated severity as well as in the information regarding the actor, particularly organizational position and history of behavior. Employees were then asked to imagine themselves as the target of these behaviors. Perceptions of severe hostile behaviors (swearing; public putdowns) were found to be unaffected by this additional information; they were perceived as abusive regardless of who did it and how often. More ambiguous behaviors such as forgetting to inform of a meeting or not acknowledging possession of a critical document were affected by prior experience with the actor. If the actor had done these types of behaviors before, then employees were more likely to see the behavior as abusive. Perceived intent and degree of negative emotional impact the respondent would experience as a result were found to mediate the relationship between prior history and perceptions of abusiveness. Interestingly, we found that the actor's position (boss, coworker, subordinate) was not related to perceptions of abusiveness. This is contrary to research on sexual harassment and researchers' definitions of emotional abuse (Fitzgerald & Shullman, 1993; Keashly, 1998). It is likely that operationalizing power differential in terms of organizational position is too limiting as power can be derived from a variety of sources such as interdependence of tasks or relationships with powerful others (Cleveland & Kerst, 1993; Thacker & Ferris, 1991).

The element of solicitation by the target has been found to be significantly related to observers' judgments of sexual harassment on the part of the actor (Fizgerald & Shullman, 1993). To the extent the victim is viewed as complicitous in any way to the situation, observers are less likely to evaluate the actor's behavior as sexually harassing. The notion of a "provocative victim" is beginning to be discussed in the emotional abuse literature (e.g., Einarsen et al., 1994) yet to date there is little systematic research examining how target behavior would relate to perceptions of abusiveness. While target behavior may be an important determinant of observer judgments, it may not be for the targets themselves (Baumeister et al., 1990). This relationship has not been directly examined as yet. The challenge with research focused on perceptions of abusiveness or sexually harassing is that it is based on hypothetical and somewhat artificial scenarios. It is unclear how relevant these factors would be in people's actual experiences.

Finally, the element of violation of standards of conduct is a critical part of much writing on emotional abuse. For example, Harvey Hornstein (1996) talks about "brutal boss" behavior as violating the norms of a "civil" society without defining those norms. Folger (1993) has argued that a key obligation of employers is to treat the employee in such a way as to respect his/her dignity as a human being without defining what that treatment is. While it may seem "clear" that many of the behaviors examined under the rubric of emotional abuse violate such standards, there is no systematic evidence to support this nor to support the idea that such violations would be associated with the experience of feeling abused (Keashly, 1998). In this study, then, the key question was what features targets spontaneously report as being influential in their experience of feeling "abused."

Systemic Aspects. One of the very consistent findings in the workplace abuse literature is that the majority of people who indicate they have been exposed to emotionally abusive behaviors at the hands of a fellow organizational member indicate that they chose to do nothing (e.g., Cox, 1991; Fitzgerald & Shullman, 1993; Keashly et al., 1994). The rationale frequently given is that either nothing would be done by the organization or the target would be subjected to retaliation by the actor or others. In essence, the targets believe that the organization would not support them through the complaint process either because there were no resources via the organization to respond or there were organizational barriers to their own responding (Rogers, 1998). An important element in people's appraisals of a situation as stressful is whether they perceive they have the resources to cope and respond to what is happening, that is, secondary appraisal (Folkman & Lazarus, 1984). These resources can be construed in two broad categories:

1. Personal resources such as high self-esteem, self-determination, and conflict management skill and
2. Organizational resources such as coworker and supervisory support, relevant workplace policy, and effective implementation of policy.

Regarding organizational resources, a powerful way in which an organization communicates its standards of conduct is through the actual handling of complaints regarding such behavior (Brodsky, 1976; Lind, 1997). In addition to the presence of formal written policies, if the organization or its representatives is viewed as not treating targets' experiences seriously or dealing with the offensive behavior(s) promptly and appropriately, then the organization will likely be viewed as tolerant of these behaviors and essentially in collusion with the actors to maintain these behaviors (Bies & Moag, 1986). Thus, the target may perceive that little if any support and resources will come from the organization to help them cope and respond. This inability to respond and thus, defend themselves (Einarsen, 1999) suggests that the situation will be experienced as stressful and strain will result. Extending this to feelings of being abused, to the extent targets perceive lack of support from the organization or indeed a tolerance on the part of the organization, their feelings of being abused will be enhanced. Thus, it is hypothesized that organizational response to targets' complaints will figure prominently in targets' experience of feeling abused.

THE CURRENT STUDY

In addressing the question of subjective meaning of hostile interactions, methodology is a critical aspect. In contrast to the quantitative approach in which the researcher defines the variables and permitted responses, a qualitative approach allows the respondents to speak for themselves and thus, unexpected (from the researcher's perspective) factors and responses may be revealed (Lewis, 1999). In addition, such an approach permits an exploration of how these factors or elements are woven together by the respondent in an effort to understand what they are experiencing. Thus, for this study we chose to interview people who self-identified as having "interpersonal difficulties" with someone at work about their experiences. To address the questions concerning what elements are influential in their experiences of feeling abuse, respondents were asked to describe in as much detail as possible the specific behaviors and events, what they called this experience, who was involved, what the effects were on them and how they dealt with the situation.

METHOD

Respondents

In response to newspaper ads, 35 people agreed to be interviewed about their experiences of "interpersonal difficulties" with a boss, subordinate, or coworker. The wording "interpersonal difficulties" was chosen because we wanted a phrase that people were familiar with yet was sufficiently vague that they would be able to talk freely about what they labeled their experience (Liefooghe & Olafsson, 1999).

Due to equipment problems, language difficulties, or inability to describe specific incidents, six of the interviews were unusable for this study. Of the remaining 29, 22 were women. Respondents ranged in age from 22 to 69 years. Length of time on the job ranged from 4 months to 26 years. All but one respondent were full-time employees in a variety of occupations ranging from unskilled (e.g., box packers) to semiskilled (e.g., building painter) to skilled (e.g., secretary, emergency dispatch technician) to professional (e.g., nurse). Thirty-four relationships were described (some respondents reported on more than one relationship): 22 boss-subordinate; 9 coworker-coworker; and 3 organizational group-employee. The latter category involves difficulties with boards of directors and with management during a strike. No one spoke as a boss having difficulties with a subordinate.

Instrument

A semistructured interview protocol was developed and questions and probes covered seven areas: self as worker; abusive events; actor and attributions; reactions to behaviors; impact on life; coping and support; and current state of affairs. After describing the events and behaviors they experienced, respondents were asked what they would call what they had been experiencing. Once they had labeled their experience (if they could), we asked them to rate the behaviors on a number of semantic differential scales utilized in previous scenario studies (Keashly et al., 1996) which included items of abusive/not abusive and harassing/not harassing. Depending upon the rating given to either of these scales, we asked the respondents what "made" the behaviors (not) abusive or (not) harassing.

All interviews were audiotaped and then transcribed verbatim.

Analytical Approach

An initial broad set of categories reflecting the seven areas of questioning was utilized in the first reading of the transcripts. As sections were coded, more refined categories and new category codes were developed. For example, "effects of abusive behaviors" was broken down into physical health, psychological well-being, and job-related outcomes. New category codes included expectations of how people should be treated at work and analogies describing respondents' experience of abuse.

The coding scheme was then revised and transcripts were read through and coded again. Quotations associated with each code were gathered together and themes or dimensions for each code category were identified, that is, a further refinement of the coding category.

For this article, the following category codes were focused upon: specific behaviors, definitions of abuse and harassment, behavioral qualities, analogies, organizational handling, expectations, and violations.

RESULTS

In this section, the specific behaviors respondents related are summarized into descriptive categories based on mode (verbal, nonverbal) and directness (direct, indirect). The ways in which the respondents defined and labeled the behaviors they were experiencing are then discussed. Finally, the respondents' sense of the role of the organization in the occurrence of these behaviors and how that relates to their experience of being treated abusively is presented. But first, it is important to talk about the unique features of emotional abuse that pose challenges for those doing research or intervention work.

Describing the Indescribable

"It doesn't sound like much when you put it into words, but it is" (Carolyn, lines 673–674). After relating her experiences with a female coworker, Carolyn succinctly identifies the major challenge with abusive workplace behavior: it is hard to describe. This is a theme that ran through many of our respondents' interviews. This challenge is not only formidable for the targets who must convince others (including themselves) of the seriousness and harm in the situation but also for researchers, practitioners and concerned organizational members who want to document and characterize the phenomenon and develop ways to deal with these situations. Indeed, unlike the more observable physical violence, the "proof" of such treatment rests with the targets. The experience of being "hard to describe" was captured in at least two ways in respondents' comments:

1. References to the subtle or hidden nature of the behaviors and
2. Statements that no one would truly understand until they had experienced it themselves.

Subtle, Hidden Qualities.

Very manipulative, extremely manipulative. (I: sounds like he harasses people in a very subtle way.) He does. In a very, very very subtle way, yes. A very subtle way, like you don't know what's happening to you. (Brenda re. male boss, lines 2310–2320)

She doesn't just pick on you. I mean if she just picked on you because you were just stupid and kept calling you stupid well, that's one thing but that's too obvious. It's hidden amongst everything that you can be put down on. Whether it's your work, the way you look, your family . . . (Gina re. female manager, lines 1638–1645)

Respondents suggested that the actors were aware of what they were doing by very closely controlling their choice of behavior and keeping it "not obvious" to others. This ability is often characterized as cleverness on the part of the actor.

. . . he would tend to take it out on whoever screwed up. (I: And how does he take it out?). He's very rude. He can be very rude. (I: What would he say that's rude?) It's hard to give, he's very good at it, okay, in the sense that he doesn't, he won't go overboard. (Max, lines 232–245)

. . . he intimidates up, too and I think also he is very clever at what he does. He's a genius at what he does actually because it's all well thought out and he can do it so that nobody would question him. (Marnie, lines 451–456)

(I: So he tried to humiliate you?) Exactly. Very much so. Very much so, but in a very nice way that cannot, you can't get your finger on it. A patient wouldn't notice it. (Brenda, lines 840–846)

Even Debbie's attempts to pin her principal down by having her specifically identify the "problems" she indicated Debbie was having in her class were unsuccessful.

The answer I got was that there was not enough conversation, that there was too much activity, and she wanted them on curriculum. I said 'Does that mean that is no?' That is, what I mean by everything is you know, and she is very careful, she will justify and cover herself as well if she can. So you can't ever say that she is doing x, y, and z wrong, (lines 1012–1021)

Thus, respondents' interpretation appears to be that the actor is able to control his or her behaviors to avoid detection or documentation by either the target or someone observing. This perception of controllability of behavior by the actor is also a discerning element in researchers' conceptualization of emotional abuse.

The effect of this subtlety, of not knowing what is happening, is a disturbance in or undermining of the targets' certainty of and trust in their own senses which is necessary for them to relate their experience to others who are in a position to support them or to respond to the situation.

It's hard to describe but you can attack someone's mental well-being. In a sense that's what she's doing. (Gina, lines 1665–1668)

. . . it's sort of picking away at your mind, and you don't feel pain in that sense. You know, you just feel self-doubt and you feel humiliation. You, you feel a little unsure about things, and it just kind of builds up. (Peter, lines 1763–1769)

. . . it's really quite difficult 'cause these things are so insidious that it's difficult to remember everything on an ongoing basis. (Ioan, lines 278–282)

Thus, the subtle or hidden nature of these behaviors not only makes them difficult to describe specifically to others but also undermines the targets' own abilities to discern exactly what has been going on. It could be argued that the behaviors become unidentifiable and likely not punishable.

Not Until You've Been There. In their frustration of trying to describe the indescribable, several respondents would summarize their descriptions by arguing that it was not possible for others (including the researchers) to truly understand until it had happened to them.

. . . unless you live it, you don't understand it, you just don't understand it. (Carolyn, lines 1211–1213)

Both Gina and Greta describe situations where support from others was contingent on these people having had similar experiences.

> You're only supported by other people who are sympathetic to your situation because they've been there themselves. (Gina, lines 2151–2153)

> But she (her friend) had to go through some of that (same treatment that Greta received) to realize what I was going through and I was glad that I was able to say that she didn't deserve it and she was better than that instead of the same kind of stuff she told me (that Greta deserved the problems she had with her coworker). (Greta, lines 1685–1691)

Samantha suggests that it is not simply not having similar experiences that prevents others from understanding.

> Lots of people don't really know . . . nobody wants to . . . because nobody wants to . . . (lines 1237–1239)

Indeed, in a recent note I received after a presentation on emotional abuse at work, one woman reflected on her own experience and the frustration she felt at trying to describe what was happening to others.

> It's amazing when you try to talk about the abuse, people seem to make you feel, it is not as bad as you think. You're made to feel like your just a complainer and troublemaker, and people really don't want to believe you. I understand why children often keep quiet about abuse. It's bad enough to deal with as an adult, I can't imagine trying to deal with all the stigma as a child. (Shirley, personal communication 1996)

Thus, what is "indescribable" may not simply be an inherent feature of the often covert, hidden nature of the behaviors and the resultant difficulty in identifying such behaviors. It may also reflect others' willingness to listen and understand the experience from the perspective of the target, that is, denial (Wyatt & Hare, 1997).

Abusive Behaviors

As can be seen in Table 1, the range of behaviors that respondents were exposed to is quite broad ranging from behaviors easy to identify as inappropriate and hostile such as swearing and yelling to the more subtle and ambiguous (indescribable) behaviors such as discounting and inaccessibility of needed resources. Of the 21 categories identified, only 4 involve a physical component (nonverbal innuendo, physical gestures, discount, denial of resources). This contradicts the popular perception that physical attack and threat are the more frequent type of workplace violence (Neuman & Baron, 1997). In addition, the majority (14) of categories involve direct behaviors and only three of the identified categories contain passive elements: discount, quality of communication, and denial of resources. This is contrary to Baron and Neuman's (1996) research on workplace aggression which found that indirect and passive behaviors were more frequent than direct and active ones.

Earlier it was argued that some behaviors can be clearly labeled as abusive while others are more ambiguous requiring additional information. The respondents themselves provided evidence in support of this argument by identifying behaviors they thought were definitely abusive and contrasting these with some of the behaviors they had experienced. For example, swearing, yelling, and public putdowns were explicitly identified as being abusive and inappropriately hostile for a workplace.

TABLE 1. Categories of Actor's Behaviors

Category	Illustrative quotes
Personal criticism—criticizing the person on nonwork-related issues	"'This went on for two hours.... She just pulled me down from top to bottom. Everything about me. My make-up. My hair. My clothes. My kids. My husband. She just went so far beyond the normal limits of what, it was nothing to do with work but it was spite." (Jackie re. female manager, 6:25) "... the fact that I'm a university student, you know, he'd be taking pot shots at my ambition for a degree. I mean where's this going to get you? You know, I mean guys like me are the movers and shakes of the world, you know.... Where are the guys keeping the economy going? You people are parasites, you know. You just sit there and read your books all day long" (Peter re male supervisor on a summer job; 21:29)
Work criticism—excessively harsh, trivial, destructive comments on work	"It was starting about November. Well, why isn't this done? You don't seem to be organized? Why isn't your filing up to date? Well, we were very busy. We have an annual conference and things had not changed but anyway, every day it was well, why aren't you doing this? Why aren't you doing this? Why aren't you doing this?" (Barb re. female executive director, 7:6) "If I made a small mistake, she makes it out to be great, a terrible thing and a bigger mistake than what it is when all day long she won't complain about anybody else."(Catherine re female coworker; 18:12)
Angry displays —yelling	"W (the inspector) yelled and told me me if I didn't like my job to leave and find something else. Now this man is screaming." (Eva) 20:35 "I was in the back and I was doing my job and he came up and started ranting at me about something I had done or hadn't done ... Whatever it was nothing ... talking to me in his raised voice." (Brenda re. male boss, 30:15).
—swearing, name calling	"the executive director would pull him aside and say 'what the fuck do you want? You want the fucking job, you fucking idiot?" (Donna re. male executive director, 13:20) "when she went and disconnected the phone, she started ranting and raving, pacing around the floor behind me, 'I can't believe you, I just can't, you stupid bitch." (Samantha re. female coworker, 17:65)
—physical gestures —no contact	"he'll think nothing of just getting a file and throwing it, ramming it down on the floor to make a point. But at this particular one, he had one of those massage your hands, he plays a lot of golf and he chucked that on the floor a couple of times because we were discussing issues amongst ourselves" (Mamie re. male boss, 11:49) "He called me into his office. He proceeds to shout, lean across his desk, point his finger in my face, pound the desk ..." (Joan re. male manager, 2:35)

(Continued)

TABLE 1. Categories of Actor's Behaviors (Continued)

Category	Illustrative quotes
Threaten	"And Dr. Z said to me 'well things are going to change' and he didn't say 'Or else' but it was implied. I mean, I'm not stupid, that I don't know what 'or else means'" (Ron re. male dept. chair, 26:36). "she just said 'well, I'll get to the boss and you know who he'll believe, don't you? And I said, 'but you know it's a lie.' She said, it doesn't matter, you know who he'll believe don't you ... It was a threat. It wasn't anything else and cannot be perceived as anything but a threat." (Carolyn re. female coworker, 23:16,55)
Retaliation —punishes target for complaining or confronting	"Because the partition has been put up she has had the lighting in my area turned off. Hers is always turned off in her area 'cause now the light bothers her. Mind you, before I stopped talking to her, there was no problem with the lights" (Greta re. her female coworker, 5:20) "Like I say, I didn't bring this to anybody's attention because of the fact that, you ever hear of being black-balled? Well, I would have been. Absolutely and totally black-balled." (Don re. his male supervisor, 3:11).
Dishonesty —misrepresenting facts or opinions; backstabbing (nice to face; nasty behind back)	"I brought this to her attention and said if I have some time why can't I go and help the purchaser.... I asked again about it and it was 'well, the purchaser doesn't want you to work with you.' (I: was that true?) No, the purchaser didn't even know that I'd inquired about helping her (Gina re. female manager, 9:23). "in one-on-one meetings with him, I'll hear it 'you know, that Mike is such a jerk, he doesn't know what the heck he is doing...' and you know go on the floor 'Mike, fantastic job. Keep up the good work.'" "(Rod re. male manager, 24:30)
Gossip, rumor—telling stories, usually untrue about the other person	"Her husband's an ambulance attendant in another city and after a while, this stuff was going on, it dawned on me, that some of the ambulance attendants in that branch have knowledge of her opinion towards me. And some of them were rude towards me, and others were knowing ..." (Samantha re. female coworker, 17:32) "she spoke of an incident where she was in the company of the secretary and the president and they were both talking about me, how much they hated me. To the point she was giving exact quotes and stuff." (Donna re. board of directors)
"Others think" —hiding own opinion by saying others agree or think the same thing	"He would come to me and say, you know, I've been talking to somebody, and, and we think that you're becoming increasingly difficult and hard to work with." (Pam re. male coworker, 14:21) "He said 'well, you don't work effectively with the other staff. I said 'what other staff?' He said 'well, just in general.' I said 'no, you can't be general. You have to have specifics." (Joan re. male manager, 2:49)

(Continued)

TABLE 1. Categories of Actor's Behaviors (Continued)

Category	Illustrative quotes
Breach of confidentiality —reveal info told in private	"But no matter what I said to this man, everybody else knew it and anything I said in front of these people, he knew it so it was a no win situation." (Don re. male supervisor, 3:52) "The girl that was driving me, she told me after that ... M had told her everything that I had said in confidence." (Barb re. female executive director, 7:14)
Differential/unfair treatment —treat differently from other employees, primarily negative	"I was just meeting the standards of the department and so when I was criticized for it, I started doing it but it's not that I wasn't the only one doing it, it was just general." (Marnie re. male boss, 11:61) ". . . the other girls were wearing their jeans and I hadn't been wearing my jeans. So I started wearing them ... I got questioned why I was wearing them by M (immediate supervisor) I says 'I thought the rules had changed. She's "what do you mean?' I's "cause the other girls are wearing them. She says 'No, don't YOU wear them.'" (Eva re. female supervisor, 20:28, 31)
Shifted responsibility —takes credit for good, blames for bad	"She, of course, will blame it on... if someone gets mad at her and chews her out for something, she says, her instant reply to that is PMS. She always uses that." (Catherine re. female coworker, (18:34) "there are certain ways of making a plant productive, you have to reduce waste, things like that and other people may have good ideas, but he'll turn it into his idea type of thing, and he won't share the glory. It's not a team effort." (Rod re. male manager, 24:26)
Lack of support —not caring, lack of encouragement or constructive feedback	"... we all really wanted to make it work. But if you don't have the encouragement or the means to do it, then it's very, very difficult. So it was extremely frustrating." (Anna re. Board of Directors, (22:20) "But no one will ever come and rant and rave and say 'oh, you've done a good job' or nobody's ever really complimented me." (Eva re. male supervisor & the company, 20:109)
Game-playing —manipulate other's behavior; set other person up for failure	"if you're my friend, I'll do things for you, type of attitude. Like if you keep me happy, I'll be nice and let you do this or I'll give you credit for that or I like you better than I like her today so I'm going to be extra special nice to you but I'm going to stay on you." (Joan re. male manager, (2:13) "he's told me with one of the ... women that he hired, he's said to me, I did that, he told her to get this and this and this done by a certain amount of time and all that and he started sort of getting on her case because it wasn't done and later he said to me, he says 'ya, I did that cause I kind of wanted to see what she was made of, see how far I could go." (Max re. male boss, 27:94)

(Continued)

TABLE 1. Categories of Actor's Behaviors (Continued)

Category	Illustrative quotes
Inappropriate authority —acts as if in a position of authority when not	"As soon as he was gone, S (a coworker) came flying up the stairs and on to the porch. 'You look out, girlie. I'll ask whatever questions I want. You have to answer to me. I'm the boss up here.'" (Sheena re. male coworker, 8:14) ". . . this woman (the owner) kept interfering in the way I was doing my job ... I was a broker, I was not her employee ... I was dispatched to her, I paid her commission on the parcels, she got her money before I even got mine ... I should have been allowed, and so should all brokers be allowed to do the job as they see fit because we're professionals." (Roger re. female owner of courier service, 25:32)
Pulling rank —asserts position regardless of the issue	"It was just another harassment to take the car phone in the first place without discussion, the way he did it, the fact that there was no negotiation ... It's a done deal. Don't question me. I made the decision. I'm the boss." (Marnie re. male boss, 11:26) "I didn't feel that when I went to her with a particular case that she would kind of either see my side of it or want to see that I'd made a certain decision in the case,... if I wanted to discharge a case, or not discharge a case, she seemed to find reason to say that it shouldn't happen ... it was almost like it was just 'you can't do it because I said so.'" (Susan re. female supervisor, 34:25)
Discounting —ignore, dismiss, or fail to acknowledge or recognize the others or their contribution	"just her general attitude was like, like she never saw you. She never knew you existed, she never, you know, you weren't there. You were just a student. (I: So she just ignored you most of the time?) Yeah, she just ignored you. She wasn't really rude. You weren't there." (Kathy re. female director, 10:59) "(I:did you ever explain that to her?) I tried to, but she just told me that I was, I was not seeing it in the way I should be seeing it, and in her opinion, I was wrong and she was right." (Samantha re. female coworker, 17:51)
Quality of communication —no discussion, not listen, indirect, thru others or memos	"lots of memos, like my file is this thick, never one-to-one situation or if it was, it was very rare. It was mostly memos sitting on your desk when you got in."(Marnie re. male manager, (11:23) "It was the fact that he shouts and is not willing to listen to the questions he's asking. He's not willing to listen to the answers and he's not interested in them. It's like a rhetorical question." (Sheena re. male coworker, 8:61)
Denial of resources or opportunities —not providing needed info, materials, or opportunities for completing tasks	"Cause she ws always owning it, she was always asking them, she was never allowing them to do anything" (Kathy re. female director, (10:34) "Since September, I have found that access to the things I need to do my job has been denied, and I'm talking about basic workbooks here, basic resources that I need to do my job properly . . . she either refuses to purchase them or just ignores me when I got to speak to her ..." (Debbie re. female principal, (19:5)

(Continued)

TABLE 1. Categories of Actor's Behaviors (Continued)

	"I never got my phone messages, whether they were personal or across campus. It didn't matter who called. If they were for me, I never got the message. If they were for ... anybody else, it was a neatly written message but not me." (Carolyn re. female coworker, 23:49)
	"he knows it was something that I liked to do because it was my assistance in helping the patient ... I had a couple of them say they only wanted their color choice if I was there. These were his friends but he won't give me that satisfaction." (Brenda re. male boss, 30:34)
	"we were having a luncheon for someone, she'd go in there and say, 'well, I just think these luncheons are taking far too long, and taking far too much time away from your work' and she's basically try to undermine them ... people started feeling uncomfortable about doing things around the office, and she was trying to destroy that." (Susan re. female supervisor, 34:70)
Nonverbal innuendo —body language, eye contact, sighs, silence that suggest disapproval	"at a meeting, for example, he will do things like snort at a comment made or an opinion presented ... he reads newspapers while sitting at the meeting, the look ... there's a look that feels like it could kill, in the sense of very, very aggressive look ... staring you down." (Pat re. male coworker, (14:35).
	"He'll walk around with a gruff face and it's to the point where if I have a problem with something I won't go to him anymore because I don't want to be talked to in the tone of voice that he'll talk to me just with the insinuations of, in his tone, of, you know, you're screwing up or you should know this by now." (Max re. male manager, 27:47)
Unreasonable expectations —requests that are difficult to meet and considered atypical	"I was working by myself and he expected me to do this job in approximately 6 hours, one man. Like, even if I'd continuously, never even stopped to, even if I had somebody else driving the loader, we'd never have it done by noon and this is another part of the pressure." (Don re. male supervisor, 3:88)
	"There I was 8.5 months pregnant. I really wasn't in great shape and it was hot. I remember being very hot and just thinking that it was cruel, almost cruel of her to make me go out, it's like about 5:30 on a Thursday night ... I just thought it was really unusual." (Susan re. female supervisor, (34:32)

(I: So when you think of abuse you think of people swearing at you?) Yes. Mind you, in a way I guess it was sort of verbal abuse when you say to somebody 'Don't you have the confidence to do this?' and 'Don't you have a better life to do?'. I mean you can put someone down pretty hard by choice words, too. I don't think She ever. . . she didn't ever really swear at me. (Barb, lines 1132–1141)

. . . (he) doesn't go all the way to the other end. I mean he's never called, you know, called me, well, you stupid bitch. (Pat, lines 2662–2666)

Well, I guess it's more on the level of verbal abuse. Um, you don't mind harsh language, do you? . . . And he says "Will you quit your fucking around and, you know, just park way over there not behind me here. You fuck off." (Peter, lines 312–339)

(I: So she yelled at you, right in front of a bunch of people.) Yea, yea. That was, that was, that was abusive . . . (Eleanor, lines 1112–1116)

She was abusive in that she made you feel, she could make you feel horrible. That she could make you feel incompetent. But it wasn't she never really stood there and screamed . . . I guess it is abusive in that it wasn't nice but . . . she didn't stand there and scream and threaten to take you all over, you know, threaten to take you to court or . . . you didn't have to worry about her pulling out a knife and stabbing you. (Kathy, lines 1980–2016)

Thus, the more active and direct verbal/physical behaviors were seen as clearly abusive and used to assess to what degree other behaviors our respondents were experiencing were also abusive. This discussion of the behaviors they considered abusive highlights a dimension that is not explicitly present in researchers' definitions of abuse, that is, that of subtlety or indirect and passive (Baron & Neuman, 1996).

Lay Definitions of Abusive Treatment

The most frequently chosen label for their experience was harassment followed by references to various forms of abuse such as verbal, emotional, and mental. Once respondents had chosen a label for their experiences, they were asked what it was about the behaviors and interactions that made them "abusive" or "harassing." The responses were characterized by three themes:

1. past history with the actor;
2. effects on the respondent; and
3. qualities of the behavior.

Past History. A central feature of many respondents' descriptions was the continual or recurring nature of the behaviors they were exposed to. For example:

The constant putdown, the going into his office and seeing memos on his desk about my work. Like when I would go in if I was putting something on his desk and I'd see these memos and I know that he was coming at me again and this is really unnerving. (Mamie re. male manager, 776–783)

. . . just the fact that when he turned me out on a job, this guy was constantly there watching. Like one way or other, he was there watching. (Don re. male boss, 469–473)

Continual undermining, I guess . . . to continually tell me that I earn peanuts. To continually interject when I am speaking to someone else. (Greta re. female coworker, lines 1117–1132)

Susan, a visiting nurse, when speaking of interactions with her supervisor, noted that the behaviors she experienced were abusive not so much because they occurred often but rather because she carried the belief that her supervisor was always there in her mind.

Because it left that feeling all the time. It wasn't that I had to listen to it everyday, but I felt that way all the time, so whether she was there or I saw her, in the back of my mind, she was watching me, so it, it was with me all the time, (lines 1688–1694)

Thus, for these respondents, behaviors experienced as abusive or harassing have an element of repetition to them.

Another element of past history with the actor concerns whether others have been treated similarly by the actor, that is, distinctiveness (Kelley et al., 1973). A number of respondents noted that knowing that others were treated that way helped them realize the behavior was not due to something they had done but rather due to the actor him/herself.

> And when you realize that you're not the only one. It's happened to umpteen people before you and people since you've worked there. . . she has a history of it. (Gina re. female manager, 1796–1805)

> . . . if it was just me, then maybe I would have to step back and take a look and say, ok, what is going on here. But it isn't just me. I'm not the only one being abused. (Debbie re. female principal, lines 2101–2105)

Brenda relays a story of how her boss, a dentist who was a former lover, did similar things to another woman in the office who quit her job as a result. She notes:

> He was certainly unreasonable but that's the way he is with everybody he wants to get rid of. (lines 2294–2297)

Again, having evidence of past behavior either with respect to being exposed to these behaviors repeatedly themselves or knowing that others have experienced it is important in perceiving the behaviors as abusive. These features are consistent with the researcher-identified element of abusive behaviors involving a pattern of behavior. However, our interviews reveal that a pattern may be the result of keeping the behavior alive in memory rather than of actual repetitious performance of the behavior on an ongoing basis by the actor.

Effects on the Respondents. Many respondents noted that they defined the behaviors as abusive by the effects it had on them. Jackie, a purchaser for a manufacturing firm, referring to her manager's ongoing criticism of her, noted:

> If you feel abused then it's abusive behavior . . . I was an abused child (by her mother) and it brought back these exact same feelings . . . (lines 1119–1124)

Other respondents described more specific effects on them ranging from physical illness to feelings of incompetency and inadequacy to decreased work productivity.

> I find it very abusive because I'm finding that my self-esteem is being lowered. I don't know. All the qualities that make me who I am I think they are belittled by him and as a result I feel like I'm abused almost every day at work. (Rod re. male manager who was a former subordinate, lines 1297–1304)

> I tend to classify harassing behavior as that which causes a degree of irritation or concern that causes you to either not be as productive as you can or not to be able to function to your fullest extent and I think that is what his behavior is. (Joan re. male manager, lines 1132–1140)

> I really think it becomes abusive because you walk way there, I mean if it gets to a point where you're nervous about coming to work. You're nervous about doing your job right. You hate your job. (Gina re. female manager, lines 1784–1789)

Peter, a summer student working for a man doing pool maintenance, clearly articulates the mechanism through which his boss's behavior has its effect on him. He does this by contrasting his experience with a physical attack.

. . . if the guy was to physically assault me, it would be clear in my mind what course of action to take too. And that would be it. But here it's sort of picking away at your mind, and you don't feel pain in that sense. . . you just feel self-doubt and you feel humiliation. You feel unsure about things and it just kind of builds up. So it's abusive in a way that destabilizes or depletes the very resources that it takes to do well . . . you don't feel like a man anymore, a grown man who can take care of himself, (lines 1758–1781)

Peter identifies a possible mechanism through which these hostile behaviors affect the individual, that is, by overwhelming one's ability to do well or to cope. From Peter's perspective, the behaviors themselves undermine or deplete the resources he would require to cope with the actor, leaving him open to harm. Essentially, these behaviors disable the target.

Respondents' discussion of the nature of the organizational relationship they had with the actor reveals that the relative power differential also affected respondents' ability to cope or respond and hence, the degree of injury or harm they experienced. Brenda and Kathy noted that the nature of the actor's behavior toward them was experienced as more threatening and intense because the actors could fire them.

Threatening, it's only threatening in that, you know, you always fear you're going to lose the job and then I know the only reason I've got it is because he feels he can't get rid of me. (Brenda, lines 2106–2111)

She gets irrational with everybody, but, I don't think she would have lost it as much, if I had been a regular staff. Because more of the regular staff has been there for like, 8 or 9, 10 years. And there's no way she could get rid of them. And you know, whereas I was just a student and I was going, and what could I do to her. (Kathy, lines 1091–1100)

While Sheena's actor was a coworker, she defined his behaviors toward her as abusive because she had been concerned that he could influence her employer's evaluation of her.

I definitely call it abuse. Emotional abuse. What if I did work under him? What if I did have to be subject to that kind of harassment. Fortunately, the B's hire me outside of him and Mrs. B. has already asked me if I could come back next year. She is not concerned with his opinion of me. But what if she was? So I definitely consider it emotional abuse, (lines 852–862)

In her definition of abusive behavior, Joan explicitly identifies the actor's relative power in terms of the capacity to disable the targets' ability to respond effectively to the behaviors:

. . . any behavior toward another person that is unacceptable to that person, that they have to take it to a certain degree because of the other person's more powerful position is abusive. (lines 1178–1183)

Indeed, several respondents explicitly stated that their ability to respond to the behaviors they were experiencing was severely limited by the fact the actor was in a more powerful position to them.

. . . if this was just a personal relationship, I can walk! You know, I don't need to be here. But this is, this is, he's my employer. He knows I'm a student. (Peter, lines 1728–1732)

. . . it's not in my nature to be aggressive in the sense, especially with someone who is my superior. (Max, lines 1131–1134)

Barb describes how she has handled verbal abuse from the public but that she could not do the same thing with her executive director.

> . . . a lot of times people phoning and it was verbal abuse and I would just say "I'm not listening to this. When you can call back in a calm voice, you do that" and I would hang up but when it was a different relationship with her . . . (lines 1070–1076)

> I suppose the thing was they really wouldn't have the power to have you fired and I think, you see, this is the power that she would have held over me and I think it would have been, if you've ever been fired, I mean which I never have, but I think that would be very devastating. . . it was easier, probably that was the easy way out, was to quit, (lines 1150–1164)

Once Gina switched to a new department, her style of handling her former manager changed to one that was more active and direct, illustrating how the actor's relative power can influence target responding.

> . . . I'm in another department now and if you come to me and don't like the way I've done something, I can talk back to you because you're not my boss any more and I'm not going to suffer any more repercussions because I do defend myself . . . so right there, you have a security. You feel secure and safe. (Unes 2205–2218)

Thus, as with researcher definitions, a critical element that makes the behavior abusive is that it results in harm for the person toward whom it is directed, possibly by disabling the individual's personal resources to cope. Also, consistent with researcher definitions, actor power was an important element in experiences of abusive behavior. However, respondents' discussion of relative power reveals that the power differential has its effects primarily by making the target more vulnerable (and the effects greater) by restricting their options for responding and coping.

Behavioral Qualities. Respondents characterized abusive behaviors as possessing certain qualities. These included being unwanted, unacceptable, hostile, controlling, demeaning, humiliating, unfounded or unreasonable, or disrespectful of a person's integrity. In a thorough description of why she considers her manager's behavior abusive, Jackie notes a number of these qualities:

> I think it's a form of harassment because her comments are often of a personal nature. They're often of a very hostile nature. They're always unwanted. They're never requested and yet you' re deluged with them all the time . . . it's constant, it's belittling, and it's untrue, (lines 1095–1115)

A number of respondents noted that these behaviors lack respect and consideration for the individual person and their boundaries. Indeed, some respondents spoke of these behaviors as violations of themselves.

> When someone infringes on someone else's rights, that's abuse. (Sheena re. male coworker, lines 1811–1813)

> It's intimidating and abusive because it has absolutely no respect for people as an individual . . . It's total disrespect for the individual whether it's me or someone else and it still goes on, you know. For your own, as an individual, for your privacy and just total. (Carolyn re. female coworker, lines 866–894)

> . . . when he's doing it, he doesn't care about what's happening or what he, what kind of emotional trauma he's putting on people. So he has no consideration for your feelings. When he's in one of those moods, no. (Max re. male manager, lines 980–984)

Analogies to being treated as a small child rather than as an adult illustrate the degree of diminishment respondents felt when dealt with by the actors.

> Not giving you autonomy. It was just as if you're a 3-year old. (Kathy re. female executive director, lines 2056–2058)

> I'm not an infant, I can think for myself. I can run a classroom. I can do my job. (Debbie re. female principal, lines 2013–2015)

> . . . what upset me most. A sense of feeling like a kid. That was my memory of it. I felt like a kid. It's hard to qualify, 'cause when I was a kid, I had pretty positive experiences but, in a sense of feeling, like you're not a man anymore. (Peter re. male boss, lines 946–952)

Anna, an executive director of a housing cooperative, described the board of director's behavior toward her as ignoring her adult status and abilities.

> It's like I'm a grown adult, with being a grown adult, able to make my own decisions and function in the work and being given a whole bunch of responsibilities in my job. And then suddenly turning around and saying well, you can't carry out those responsibilities. Or you're not capable of making decisions to decide whether you are capable of carrying out those decisions. It's like you go for an interview for a job and the interviewer says . . . I don't think you can do this job even though you have all the qualifications . . . it would be a personal thing. My sense of integrity, my sense of sincerity, my sense of doing the best job I possibly could, (lines 1025–1048)

Anna's response indicates the contradiction that is experienced when hired to do a particular job that requires an adult with responsibilities and then not treated as capable of doing the job, that is, of being adult enough to make the decisions. The confusion from the "mixed messages" that results is experienced as a violation of her sense of self as a competent person. Thus, negative behaviors are experienced as abusive when they contravene, undermine, or appear to ignore the integrity and competency of the target. This is related in some degree to the harm, the unwelcome/unsolicited, and the standard dimensions identified from researchers' definitions of abusive workplace behavior.

Intent. Interestingly, the dimension of intent received little support from respondents' experiences of behaviors as abusive. Only two respondents explicitly mentioned actor intent as critical in their definition of the experience as abusive. In response to the question of what makes the behavior they described as abusive or harassing, Samantha and Brenda noted perceived intent to harm them on the part of the actor.

> . . . ongoing with intent to make the person feel uncomfortable; to destroy a person's character. (Samantha, lines 880–888)

> I was thinking of emotionally harassing. Okay? Physical harassing is when somebody intentionally hurts you and that's what he's intentionally doing that to me . . . So it's harassing.

> It is harassment, and you know, it's emotionally and it's abusive and it's harassment. (Brenda, lines 2192–2206)

When intent was not mentioned spontaneously, we asked respondents explicitly about their attributions regarding the behavior. Half (15) of the respondents felt that the actor was deliberate in his behavior. For example,

He knew as far as I'm concerned, he knew what he was doing. (Don, lines 80–82)

It was almost as if it was planned. (T: So you think that she was quite deliberate in her treatment of you?) Yes. Absolutely, because she knew the type of person that I was. She knew I could not handle, not well, stress . . . she knew that I was, I had a weakness like that. (Barb, lines 1054–1066)

The plant manager's office is right beside the reception area so she did her, she did what she aimed to do. . . she said it herself to the plant manager. I want these people to be scared of me. (Gina, lines 883–889; 1040–1041)

The other respondents attributed the actor's behavior to other factors such as frustration, egocentrism or lack of awareness.

. . . he was really quite a self-absorbed man. So to deliberately intend to have an impact on someone's life that way, I don't think even occurred to him. . . I think that was just normal to him. (Peter, lines 1485–1496)

. . . I don't think he really intended to hurt me . . . Like he thought it was a good thing, is that it? Yah, he thought that was good for both of us. (Kerry, lines 725–736)

It (derogatory slur) wasn't intended sexually though he was just, at least I hope not, he was just frustrated . . . (Sheena, lines 509–512)

While it is clear that respondents make attributions regarding the intentionality of actor's behavior and many indicated they believe the actor could have controlled their behavior as noted in the discussion of indescribability, the prominence of these attributions in defining their experience as abusive is unclear.

Summary. Consistent with the elements of researchers' definitions, verbal and nonverbal behaviors were defined as abusive by our respondents when they: (a) had recurred to them or had happened to others; (b) resulted in injury or harm to the target by undermining the ability to cope or respond; and (c) were experienced as a lack of recognition of the integrity of the individual. Respondents' experience also involved judgments of some kind of standards being violated and the behaviors being unwelcome and unsolicted. Relative power differential was also an important element for respondents in this study, primarily through diminishment of the targets' ability to respond or cope with the actor's behavior.

Organizational Norms and Support

The respondents' discussion of their organization's response to their experience draws out the centrality of this response to their overall definition of their experience at the hands of the actor as abusive.

The majority of the respondents let someone in a position of authority know about their experiences with varying degrees of success. Four chose not to let the organization know because they believed that there was no one to whom they could complain or that when they did, nothing would be done. Barb left her job because of her boss's treatment of her.

. . . it was almost harassment really but I had nowhere to go, nowhere to go and I just thought rather than running her name down . . . Who could I have gone to? Where could I have gone? (Barb, lines 1271–1281)

Anna's struggles involved her board of directors not providing her with sufficient resources to do her job and then berating her for not completing her tasks. When asked if she had complained to anyone higher up, Anna replied "There's none higher."

Catherine did have a supervisor to whom she could complain but chose not to for a number of reasons.

> I'm not a squealer, I don't go running to the supervisor. This time I can't go to a supervisor 'cause she's much like myself . . . she's very passive, very laid back and to me she's not about to do anything for me anyhow . . . she's not really involved, you know, my supervisor. It's not fair to let her know what's going on. (lines 397–416)

Although she argues that it is not her supervisor's job to deal with the problem, Catherine later changes her position and indicates that it is her supervisor's responsibility to handle the difficult coworker, not Catherine's.

> I don't think it is for me. I feel it's for my supervisor. She is there . . . she sees what goes on and she knows. She is not stupid. She can sense. I can imagine there have been other girls that have spoken to her about this person. She knows. I know she knows, (lines 1694–1703)

So even though Catherine refuses to complain to her supervisor, she assumes her supervisor knows and therefore should do something about it and knows she likely will not.

Kathy, a summer student in a federal agency, found that while her immediate supervisor and her coworkers were fine, the director of the unit was a problem. While Kathy went into great detail about what this woman did to others and sometimes to her, she never discussed it with her supervisor or coworkers. When asked why, she indicated that the unit director was a friend of the agency director and so any complaint would be ignored.

> J's and M's (another director) butts have been saved by L(agency director) so far. (lines 2140–2142)

The rationale of these respondents is consistent with that given by respondents in other studies where by far the majority of respondents did not let their concerns be known to the organization (see Keashly, 1998). Unfortunately, the assumption that nothing effective would happen appears to be supported by the experiences of many of the respondents who did complain to higher ups. Thus, the decision not to complain may indeed have some basis in fact.

Interestingly, for all respondents, there was no evidence that any organization or its representatives ever "doubted" or denied that the actors had behaved as respondents said they had. That is, there was an acceptance that the behaviors existed. What did vary is how they chose to deal with the situation. This "decision" appeared to be based on an assessment of whose responsibility it was to deal with the problem presented, that is, the organization or the target (see Table 2 for examples). Responses that related to the organization taking responsibility for handling the concerns included working around the problem, taking action with no discernible outcome, and direct action with respect to the actor. The responses that seemed to leave the problem with the target included taking no action, minimizing target complaints, attributing the problem to personalities, and blaming or retaliating against the target. In all cases, organizations or their representatives were described as using more than one response.

TABLE 2.   Types of Organizational Responses to Targets' Complaints

Organization's Responsibility:

1. Working around the problem

"The plant manager said (to Human Resources) 'give it to her because she deserves to get out of that manager's domain,' which is basically admitting that this is a problem manager but he won't do anything about it." (Gina, 1263–1258)

"I have been told that this girl had other encounters with other people and management gave me examples of situations that they've had . . . that was one of four or five people that had left because of her. And management asked me to try to stick it out, to not give up." (Samantha, 531–543)

2. Promised action with no discernable outcome

". . . (after a morale survey initiated in response to Joan's complaint) I got a call from our Human Resources Vice-President to tell me that they were absolutely appalled at the comments that associates had made about their managers, about the way they were treated, about the circumstances they found themselves in. At that point, he told me that the company was going to ensure that all the managers would have retraining and they would be helped to deal more effectively withstaff and interact on more positive terms. That's a year ago, I think. We haven't seen anything. "(Joan, 664–680)

"I had an interview with the personnel department and they said they would speak to the people and get back to me which they never did . . ." (Marnie, 185–188)

"There's all kinds of letters from all over the department (about her behavior) put in a separate file, not in her personnel file because nobody will step on her. and so she keeps getting away with it." (Carolyn, 502–511)

3. Direct action with respect to the actor

"I don't know how many times she's been in the manager's office. At least since I've been there, she must have been in two or three times because I've complained, the purchaser (Jackie) complained, other managers have complained and I'm sure she has been told but she's still working there. Now if you've been with a company seven or nine years, you've done these things, you've been in the plant manager's office, I don't think they're going to get rid of you and I think she, in a sense, realizes it. "(Gina, lines 1151–1164)

". . . what happened was I was pulled off the shift and I wrote up a formal complaint, gave it to management. I was under the opinion management would deal with it directly. When management read it, they were concerned and they had to sent it up to the regional office. When the regional office read it, they were alarmed and they read it and decided a formal investigation should take place . . . so the way I felt in the process was that I gave the bullet, someone else shot the gun." (Samantha, lines 1087–1100) Target responsibility

1. No action taken

"Him (A) and the big boss were buddies. There was just, A was his like, A was his god. There was nobody better than A.. . . (I: So did the big boss treat women in the same way?) No, no. He was, no, no, he was pretty good until the end. (I: So he just ignored A's thing?) Oh, ya. He just let him do what he wanted. "(Leslie, lines 208–237)

". . . the boss that retired told me he was intimidated by him. He said 'I should have done something about it.'" (Marnie, lines 352–354)

2. Minimizing target's complaint

". . . the chief, his supervisor, constantly minimizes, constantly tries to really play up the good things that he might have done, to totally wipe out these other things that are happening. Doesn't look at it as a total package, you know." (Pat, lines 1306–1312)

"I basically got told, well, we can't really get rid of this person and we could do worse and I don't know how. I don't know how they could do worse." (Gina, lines 806–810)

TABLE 2. Types of Organizational Responses to Targets' Complaints (Continued)

3. Attributions to personality

"I told my boss and he said, well, you know, different personalities, you know. You've got to be accommodating and I thought well, I am accepting, accommodating and I tolerate so much." (Greta, lines 155–160)

". . . there was no support from them (actor's supervisor and Carolyn's boss). As far as they were concerned the difficulty lay between, it was as much my fault as hers." (Carolyn, lines 425–429)

"And that's what her supervisor would say even though he'd sit there and watch. 'It's just between the two of you. Just keep it there.'" (lines 1266–1270)

4. Blaming of or retaliation against the target

"So when I got back to work, he (the senior supervisor) called me in the office. He wanted to talk to me and he had this guy (Don's supervisor) sitting right beside him. So he wanted to sit down so we could talk and we started off very pleasant. Then all of a sudden, both of them, both of them sat there and picked things I did wrong, just this and this and this and this and I felt so humiliated, so degraded . . . like simple things. He didn't want me going to use the bathroom during the working hours." (Don, lines 1032–1052)

". . . when I went to his new boss, I didn't get any support whatsoever so I went through the system that the bank has, like the grievance procedure through the bank and it did nothing for me. What they did was they concentrated on an area that I was not strong in and it was paperwork and so they just zeroed in on this particular area." (Mamie, lines 167–176)

1. Company Responsibility

Working Around the Problem. This category captures responses that never dealt directly with the actor or situation but rather focused their efforts on helping the target adjust or survive. In essence, the respondents' concerns are heard and acknowledged indicating the company has taken responsibility for some kind of response. The response, however, is directed more at helping the target become more resistant than in dealing with the source of the stress, that is, the actor (Kahn & Byosiere, 1992).

Promised Action With No Discernible Outcome. This category of responding refers to the respondents' awareness that the company either promised or had taken some action but that they could not discern what the ultimate outcome of that had been. The organization appears then to be taking the situation seriously, yet the lack of continued action and particularly the lack of overt resolution suggests to respondents that nothing will in fact occur.

Direct Action With Respect to the Actor. This category refers to situations in which the organization took discernible and direct action with respect to the actor ranging from speaking with the person to in one case firing the individual. While direct action was appreciated by the respondents, the impact of the action was mixed, rarely creating a noticeable improvement in the situation between the actor and the target. For example, some respondents reported that while the actors had been told about the complaints and asked to stop their behavior, the actors often showed little remorse and did not desist from the behavior.

2. Target's Responsibility

No Action Taken. As had been expressed by those respondents who chose not to complain, several respondents found that despite letting more senior people know about their concerns, there was little evidence that anything had in fact been done regarding the actor or the situation with the target. In some situations, the relationship between the actor and a more senior person worked against any action being taken. For example, personal relations between the actor and the senior person appeared to prevent any action being taken. Even when there were no complications due to the senior person's relationship to the actor, action was often not taken. By not taking action in response to the respondents' complaints about behaviors of which management was aware, the organization effectively left the problem with the target.

Minimizing Target's Complaint. This response involved not focusing on the target's complaint by either highlighting the actor's strengths and abilities or pointing out that "it could be worse." It appears that the organization reframes the situation such that the actor's strengths or resources are highlighted and defined as "doing the job," implying that the behaviors complained about are not relevant. The behaviors of concern were not denied; they were simply de-emphasized. The effect, though, is to trivialize the target's concerns and experience. An interesting benefit of this response is that the organization or its representative does not have to "do" anything with respect to the actor. This leaves the responsibility for the quality of the interaction with the target, perhaps implying they are "making too much out of it."

Attributions to Personalities. The infamous "personality conflict" was used by some organizations to describe a target's complaint of abusive interactions with the actor (Gwartney-Gibbs & Lach, 1993). By attributing the problem to "personalities," the organization could legitimately place responsibility on the shoulders of the parties and instruct them to work it out. Jackie challenged her plant manager's interpretation:

> I mean, how many other people do I fight with around here and how many people does she fight with? You've got to see that it's not just a personality conflict but you are saying it is. Well, he clarified that a little in terms of I'm more sort of easy-going. I'm not pouncing on details the way she is so in that way your personality bothers hers and she bothers you because she is so heavy handed. (Jackie, lines 433–444)

By focusing on personalities, he effectively ignores Jackie's comments of the actor's history of similar situations with other workers, the resultant attribution to the actor, and the call to action it would entail. Thus, this response frees the organization from having to take any direct action.

Blaming of or Retaliation Against the Target. For several of the respondents, the organization responded to their complaints by reframing the problem to blame the target for the situation or by undercutting the respondents' credibility by attacking their work performance. For example, when Eleanor, a nurse, complained about her supervisor's behavior toward her to the nursing manager and her coworkers, nothing was done. When asked how she thought management saw the problem, Eleanor indicated "I am the troublemaker" (line 807). By blaming the target for the situation or attacking the target's credibility, the organization manages to remove themselves from taking responsibility for dealing with the situation. After all, if the target created the situation or cannot be believed, then what is an organization to do.

In sum, there are a variety of ways in which the respondents' organizations responded to the complaints as they were presented. Some responses reflected the organization's sense of responsibility that they needed to respond while others suggested that the organization left the responsibility with the target, essentially freeing the organization from having to deal with a difficult situation. None of the respondents expressed satisfaction with their organization's handling of the situation.

Implications of Organizational Responding

The organization's response (or lack thereof) had tremendous implications for how the respondents viewed their organizations and their place in them as employees. Several respondents explicitly stated that they felt the lack of response or the limited response of the organization effectively supported the actor's behavior. Joan was told by the Human Resources Vice President that retraining of managers would occur. It has been a year since this comment was made and there had been no subsequent action taken. Joan interpreted this in the following way:

> I feel that with me putting forward to the company the situation and making them aware of his behavior, something should have been done about him by now. If he is fired or let go it's only because he's of no further use in the reorganization not because his behavior warrants it. (lines 914–923)

> If my manager for instance had a good manager with a good handle on how people should be treated and how to get the best from them, his behavior would have been better because it would not have been allowed to be as it is. . . I think it's the organization's fault. Yes . . . they are not demanding the standards of behavior be expected from their management people as they should be. (lines 782–802)

Pam also notes that the organization's dealing with her male coworker over time has supported the problem.

> The really big, big problem in this one is that you have a situation where for, for well 23, actually this person's been here for more than 23 years . . . these behaviors have been condoned by whomever is his supervisor, (lines 1411–1417)

In Greta's situation, the organization has indicated they are aware that her female coworker is difficult to deal with yet chose not to confront her about it. As a result,

> I told the director. I said you've created this monster, you know, and you're stuck with her. (lines 635–638)

> But if I quit, in my resignation letter they are going to know why I'm quitting. It won't be because of her, it will be because they can't deal with her. (lines 1311–1315)

Gina implies that the organization is responsible on some level for the ongoing behavior of her manager.

> . . . in any other company so many complaints about one person would have been seriously looked at . . . when you have almost every manager with a complaint and even before I came, she was close to being fired but that plant manager passed on and then the new plant manager came in and he's not the firing kind . . . It's almost like the plant manager would love somebody else to do it for him. (lines 2021–2045)

> Now, if you've been with a company seven or nine years, you've done these things, you've been in the plant manager's office, I don't think they're going to get rid of you and I think she, in a sense, realizes it. (lines 1159–1164)

Ron is even more explicit about why the company is willing to put up with his coworker's behavior:

> . . . they're going to tolerate whatever they have to tolerate in order to get the money (his coworker's institute brings in), (lines 1216–1219)

In addition, from their experiences with the organization over the specific situations with the actors, respondents identified that the main lesson they had learned from the experience was that speaking out about similar problems was not wanted.

> . . . again the company has not acted on any of the justifiable concerns we've put forward so there isn't a lot of positive feedback to reinforce the fact the you know, you're right in speaking out when you see something is wrong and that's kind of unfortunate. (Joan, lines 1550–1558)

> . . . even confrontation is alright if you have to be on the defense but if you're trying to point out something that this manager had done wrong, it's almost, what's the point. Nothing will come of it. (Gina, lines 1882–1888)

> You know, like sometimes you feel that you're in a surrounding where you don't want, where they don't want anything to upset the apple cart. That you tow the line and let things go on as they are. Even if you see things are wrong. Because they just don't want to upset the apple cart. (Ron, lines 2230–2239)

Implicit in these messages is the idea that individual employees do not matter to the organization for if they did, the employees could feel that they could speak out about what they see and they would be taken seriously. The costs of these experiences were feelings of decreased commitment and loyalty to their organization and doing the minimum work to get by.

> If you're to have an hour for lunch, I'm going to be gone. I'm gone from the office and I don't care if the phone rings off the hook, I just don't care anymore which I think is sad. (Barb, lines 1496–1501)

> . . . after five years, you get a pin with a sapphire in it and after ten you get two and so on and so forth and I got my five-year pin and I just took it home and threw it in the drawer 'cause I just lost all sort of loyalty to the company and at the same time, I don't like that. (Mamie, lines 1332–1339)

For our sample, then, there was little evidence and, hence, faith that intervention by the organization would either be undertaken or would even be effective and that the organization essentially colluded in keeping the situation as it is.

Standards of Behavior: The Principled Workplace

What became clear as people spoke of their experiences and the organizations' response to them is that they had some implicit and explicit expectations about how they felt they should be treated in the workplace and how such problems should be handled. The term "principled workplace" seems to capture the sense of clarity the respondents felt when they spoke of why the behaviors and the organizations' responses were a problem. Three principles seem to arise repeatedly in respondents' comments. The first two principles or standards appear to have been part of discerning whether and how the actor's behavior may have been abusive while the third standard speaks more directly to the organization's role in the experience.

1. Work criticism should be legitimate and constructive. Criticism was proposed to be most effective when it was collaborative, clear, supportive, balanced and ongoing.
2. There needs to be acknowledgment and recognition of the workers as full and complete adult persons who have skills, and abilities, as well as personal needs for fulfillment and life outside the organization. A term used often was of the actor or the organization "not caring" about the workers.

3. Disputes and grievances over problems need to be handled internally and in the following manner: (a) discuss concerns with the person who is complaining; (b) deal directly with the issues; (c) act on complaints by gathering information; (d) give timely feedback re the status of the situation; (e) there must be resolution to the situation; (f) protect the complainant.

A list of more specific ways in which the respondents felt they should be treated as workers included a reasonable workload, encouragement, sufficient resources to do the job, facilitating appropriate autonomy or authority on the part of the worker, reciprocity instead of exclusion, clear definition of discipline, clear guidance of what is expected and required. They also requested that they be listened to as opposed to talked at. Focusing on more specific behaviors, respondents were also very specific that there be no abusive language (yelling, screaming, derogatory putdowns), criticism of personal life, nor blaming for something one did not do; examples of "inherently" abusive behaviors.

DISCUSSION

By focusing on the actual experience of targets and their feelings of being abused, this study has enriched our understanding of what constitutes emotionally abusive behavior. Descriptively, the behaviors noted were primarily verbal and nonphysical, active and direct. Interestingly and not surprisingly, these behaviors were not physical in nature as the media and research would suggest. The predominance of verbal and nonverbal/nonphysical behaviors in our respondents' experience is consistent with more recent research that finds that psychological forms of violence are more frequent than physical violence (e.g., Greenberg & Barling, 1998; Neuman & Baron, 1997; NNLI, 1993; Richman et al., 1999; Rogers, 1998). However, the active and direct nature of these behaviors is contrary to Neuman and Baron's (1997) profile of aggressive behaviors in the workplace which notes the most frequent behaviors as primarily passive and often indirect.

One possible explanation is that these behaviors are the easiest ones for the respondents to describe. As suggested in the section on indescribability of behaviors, the respondents may have felt the need to convince us of what was happening to them and chose the more "obvious" examples. This ties directly to the argument that some behaviors by social consensus would be viewed as abusive while other behaviors require additional information before the majority of people would make such a judgment (O'Leary-Kelly et al., 1996; Richman et al., 1997). Normative information on people's evaluations of different behaviors would be important in order to assess the validity of this argument.

Another explanation is that the described events are the most salient or memorable and thus, more accessible for the recall required by the interview (Rogers, 1998). This explanation points up a limitation of the interview method for developing a comprehensive picture of the behaviors directed at the respondents. Lack of salience of the more passive and indirect behaviors as well as concerns about "making the case" for their experience may lead to underreporting of these behaviors. Neuman and Baron's (1997) application of Buss's (1961) framework of human aggression to the development of comprehensive behavioral checklist increases the likelihood of getting a more "accurate" picture of the range of behaviors that people experience. The limitation of that approach as noted earlier is that the more ambiguous behaviors which are passive and more indirect are not consistently experienced as abusive.

Another possible explanation for our findings is that the described behaviors are to some degree acceptable and tolerable within organizations so there is less need to be "secretive" or subtle. This interpretation is consistent with the hypothesis that one source of workplace emotional abuse is that actors are conforming to organizational expectations for behavior, that is, this is how we do business (Archer, 1999). Evidence on sexual harassment has found that organizational tolerance of sexual harassing behaviors is associated with greater occurrence of these behaviors (Fitzgerald & Shullman, 1993; Pryor, LaVite, & Stoller, 1993). This explanation is less likely for our sample because our respondents came from a variety of organizations and it is unlikely that all of these organizations shared the same management or work philosophy. However, this argument was not directly addressed in this study and is still an empirical question.

Feeling Abused

Many of the elements identified as critical in researchers' definition of emotional abuse were also spontaneously identified by the respondents. Experientially, respondents identified behaviors as abusive when there was past history with the actor behaving in this way, when harm was experienced by the target and when the boundaries or the integrity of the target had been perceived to have been violated by the actions. Relative power differential was also relevant in respondents' experiences. Unlike researchers' conceptualization, attributions of the actor's hostile intent was not a critical element in respondents' labeling of their experience as abusive. Of particular note, though, is that by examining how targets themselves make sense of their experience, a more complex picture of these elements is revealed.

Pattern of Behavior. Most research on emotional abuse has operationalized emotional abuse as repetitive behavior as defined by frequency and duration of occurrence (Einarsen, 1999; Hoel et al., 1999). When such information is gathered by behavioral checklists, the assumption is that the respondent has experienced these behaviors directly, that is, that a particular actor behaves toward him/her this way frequently. While this assumption was true for all of our respondents, two additional features were revealed. First, frequency of occurrence may not necessarily be in terms of actual conduct but in terms of reliving previous interactions in the respondent's mind. Thus, while a particular event such as being put down in front of others may have only happened once, the target may relive that event frequently. Indeed, a particular actor may appreciate the value of a particular performance for influencing others' behavior over the long term, that is, aggressive behavior as social control (Barling, 1996). Current definitions of frequency do not incorporate this particular mode and need to consider ways in which this can be assessed.

The second way in which frequency of occurrence was discerned by respondents was in terms of witnessing others' abusive treatment, that is, distinctiveness (Kelley et al., 1973). Having seen others treated in a hostile manner was interpreted as evidence of patterned behavior which was associated with the experience of feeling abused. While little research has examined how observing others' experiences relates to a person's own experience of feeling abused, more research is now addressing the issue of the impact of being a witness on the witness's well-being (e.g., Barling, 1996; Bjorkqvist et al., 1994). In essence, those who witness abusive treatment of others report similar signs of strain such as anxiety, depression, and so forth. The findings of the current study not only support this trend to consider witnesses as victims but also suggest the importance of examining how one (or more) worker's experiences with an actor(s) influence how another worker may experience behavior by the same actor(s). In addition, the findings point out a possible way in which coworkers may facilitate the labeling of a target's experience by sharing with the person stories of their own experiences with the actor(s). For example, Pam, one of the respondents, explicitly noted that she made a point of talking about her experiences to others to help them see that how her coworker was treating them was wrong and abusive. This draws our attention to the role of coworkers as a source of social support and what support it is that they offer which will be discussed shortly.

Harm to the Target and Coping. All respondents noted that the degree of negative effects they experienced was important information to them in labeling their experiences as abusive. Often, the effects had to be notably severe and a change from an earlier time on the job such as illness requiring sick leave, anxiety and nervousness, hating a job they once loved, before they decided they were being treated abusively. While respondents identified a number of negative effects that are consistent with the extant literature on workplace emotional abuse (Einarsen, 1999; Hoel et al., 1999; Keashly, 1998), their discussions revealed that the behaviors had these effects because of their potential to disable the target's ability to respond or cope effectively. That coping is a key mediator in people's experience of stress and strain is well documented (e.g., Kahn & Byosiere, 1992). What is particularly interesting here is that the most frequently reported psychological effects of abusive treatment, decreased self-esteem and self-confidence (e.g, Brodsky, 1976; Einarsen, 1999; Rosenberg & Silver, 1984) are also examples of the personal resources that are important in coping with perceived threatening situations. To the extent that these resources are directly undermined by the behaviors of the actor, the target's ability to cope and hence reduce other negative impact is diminished further, making them increasingly vulnerable to attack. The findings of the current study draw attention to the need to explore the ways in which personal/psychological resources are affected by the behaviors defined as abusive.

Power and Coping. The respondents' discussion of the influence of relative power of the actor in their experiences of feeling abused highlights at least two interesting aspects of power. First, the "tale of power" included but was not limited to the formal organizational position of the actor, as attested to by the experiences of abusive treatment by coworkers. Indeed, peers and subordinates have also been identified as sources of abuse in other research (e.g., Bjorkqvist et al., 1994; Keashly et al., 1997; Price Spratlen, 1995). Neuman and Baron (1997), for example, found that the majority of actors are coworkers. Yet power was clearly an aspect of all the respondents' experiences as captured by analogies to feeling treated as a child or feeling diminished or discounted. These are characteristic feelings and features of dominant-subordinate relationships. Thus, other ways of understanding relative power are needed. For example, Cleveland and Kerst (1993) in discussing sexual harassment suggest the need to consider other sources of power. Even equal power (coworkers) and less powerful (subordinates) actors can derive power from informal networks, inter-dependency of tasks, support from supervisors or groups such as unions. In essence, worker dependency on others creates a situation for power to become an issue. Consistent with this line of argument, Hoel and associates (1999) in their review of workplace bullying literature suggest that "bullying exists when someone establishes power over someone else and is perceived to reinforce their superiority unnecessarily" (p. 197).

A second finding about relative power is that it is key in respondents ' experience because of its relationship to their ability to respond and cope. The relative power of the actor limited the options the target had for responding. For example, directly confronting the actor can have tremendous negative implications, for example, loss of job, write-up for discipline, open self up to a tirade, sabotage, gossip. This is a particularly interesting example as it is the choice often suggested by outsiders as to how the target should deal with the actor. As a respondent's range of choices becomes limited, her ability to miti-gate the impact of the behaviors on herself is reduced. Einarsen and Skogstad (1996) are among the few researchers who explictly make the connection between power and ability to defend by arguing that a hostile, aggressive situation is bullying when one party can not defend herself but it is a conflict when the parties are of "equal" strength.

Intent. While respondents spoke of making attributions regarding the actor's intention and initially spoke of the controllable nature of the behavior, these assessments did not appear to figure prominently in their discussions of how they labeled their experience. This is interesting because a critical component of many researchers' definition of emotional abuse is that the behavior was or is perceived to be intentional on the part of the actor (e.g., Baron & Neuman, 1996; Einarsen, 1999).

In a recent review of the workplace bullying literature, Hoel, Rayner, and Cooper (1999) argue that while intent is inferred by researchers, it is rarely established by check-ing with the perpetrator and thus is of little significance. This criticism is relevant if the interest is in actor's actual intent. In fact, some researchers get around this issue by including intent as either actual or perceived (see Einarsen, 1999). In this study, we are clearly concerned with perceived intent. One possible explanation for the apparent lack of cen-trality of perceived intent in respondents' labelling of their experience may be that a number of the other elements that figured prominently may have their influence through these attributions. For example, prior history with the actor provides information on the consistency and distinctiveness of the actor's behaviors, factors that are related to attribu-tions for behavior (Kelley et al., 1973). People are more likely to attribute a behavior to something about the actor if the behavior has been shown consistently in the past and it is distinctive in terms of the target. Indeed, our earlier research (Keashly et al., 1996) suggested that intent along with impact mediated the relationship of prior history with perceptions of abusive-ness. Thus, while judgments of intention were made and reported, the antecedent condition of prior history may have been more salient in their minds. In fact, the structure of the interview as a temporal sequence may have contributed to this. In essence, what is being argued is that attributions of intention may indeed be an important aspect of targets' experience but that the various elements are interwoven with the presence of some informing the assessment of others.

In a related vein, it is not clear from this study nor other research in workplace abuse as to whether all the elements identified in this study and in research definitions are necessary and/or sufficient for labelling the experience as abusive (Keashly, 1998). For example, vio-lating standards of behavior may be a necessary and sufficient criteria for behaviors such as swearing in a hostile manner to be labeled as abusive while more ambiguous behaviors like glaring, not showing up for meetings may require elements of repetition, harm and intent before they are perceived as abusive. Determining the combinations of and inter-relationships among the elements could be examined more directly using scenario studies in which relevant information is varied.

Organizational Responding. Two types of organizational responses were identified based on primary responsibility for dealing with the situation: the organization or the target.

The nature of the organization's response to the target's concerns functioned in at least one of two ways:

1. Communicating availability of resources to help the target to respond and
2. As abusive behavior itself.

Regarding resources, to the extent the organization's response was viewed as ineffective, organizational resources for coping were viewed as nonexistent. Thus, with limited personal resources (due to the treatment) and limited if any organizational resources, the stress-appraisal framework would suggest that the respondents would feel strain, that is, feel abused. One argument is that the nature of the behavior and the other factors are related to primary appraisal while the ability to defend is a secondary appraisal assessment. Thus, there is an opportunity for the experience to not be abusive to the extent the respondent or potential target can defend themselves. However, it appears that the nature of the behavior and the various contextual elements effectively create a situation of disabling the person's own resources to cope. Similarly, organizational responding can facilitate or disable the target's ability to respond and hence can mitigate or enhance the harm to the target. The organization has an opportunity to shore up those resources by having and instituting timely and effective responses to expressed concerns. For most of our respondents, the organizational resources were perceived as extremely limited and in that way facilitated their experience of feeling abused. In terms of organizational response as abusive behavior itself, the particular response of blaming or retaliating against the target is a vivid example of active and direct behavior focused on disabling the person with the complaint.

The organization's response to the respondents' complaints was also interpreted by the respondents as an indicator of the organization's perception of their worth as a worker (Folger, 1993). To the extent they perceived the organization did not value them, respondents' commitment to, and quality of, productivity were reportedly reduced. Several of our respondents noted that they felt less committed to the organization as a result of the response and would simply do their jobs and nothing more. In some cases, some chose to change positions or leave the organization, which is another frequent response to abusive treatment (Hoel et al., 1999; Keashly, 1998).

Another response of our respondents was to perceive that the organization did not want to hear about problems and they had learned not to "speak up." Fear of speaking up has been identified as a critical aspect of many employees' organizational experience. In an extensive interview study with over 250 workers, Ryan and Oestreich (1991) found that fear of speaking up was associated with abrasive and abusive conduct on the part of managers. Harvey (1995) empirically examined the role of the "fear of speaking up" in the effects of bosses' negative interpersonal behavior on employees' experiences of stress and strain. He found that fear of speaking up mediated the relationship between bosses' behaviors and job tension, job satisfaction, and general well-being. Thus, to the extent that respondents were not afraid to speak up, the effects of their bosses ' behaviors on them were reduced. Our study suggests that one way to reduce employees' fear of speaking up is to respond quickly and effectively to their grievances.

While none of our respondents indicated more than disaffection and disconnection from the organization, other research suggests that employees may express their dissatisfaction and frustration with hostile behaviors of their own such as sabotage, theft, lying, and emotionally abusive behaviors (Neuman & Baron, 1997) or suing the organization for mistreatment (Lind, 1997).

Standards of Behavior. While it has been explicitly stated and implicitly agreed that abusive and aggressive behaviors in the workplace violate the standards of a civil society such as respect, fairness, and safety, there has been surprisingly little articulation of exactly what these standards are. Some possible standards were gleaned from looking at respondents' discussions of their experiences on the whole and are not "surprising" in any real or theoretical sense. Constructive criticism (specific, timely, considerate in tone, no attributions to personality) has long been touted and indeed demonstrated to have a significant impact on how employees feel toward their supervisor, their work, and their own abilities (e.g., Baron, 1988). The ways to manage conflict constructively as derived from respondents' discussion are clearly described in the burgeoning conflict management literature (e.g., Ury, Brett, & Goldberg, 1988). And the principle of workers as full, autonomous beings with rich and complex lives is consistent with a growth-oriented model of human development. While suggestive of possible standards, there is still no systematic evidence that the specific behaviors denoted in workplace abuse research would indeed violate these standards. And while the current study's findings suggest that violation of standards is associated with feeling abused, neither this nor other available research conclusively supports this. In order to do so, future research would need to identify specific standards of conduct, select behaviors that would be hypothesized to violate these standards, and then examine potential targets' perceptions of these behaviors. Research focusing on standards of conduct would also be useful as a basis for development of workplace policies on abusive behaviors.

Target Response and Coping. As is clear from the preceding discussion, the target's ability to respond and cope played a significant role in the feeling of being abused. These conclusions are consistent with a stress-coping framework (e.g., Folkman & Lazarus, 1984). Yet, to date, there has been very little research on not only how targets respond but also on the dynamics of that coping, including the role of personal and organizational resources.

As noted earlier, the most frequently reported response to abusive interactions is to "do nothing," (e.g., Fitzgerald & Shullman, 1993; Keashly, 1998). Our respondents were atypical in that the majority of them formally reported the behavior. This likely reflects the self-selected nature of the sample as people who had already identified themselves as "feeling" abused. This would be in contrast to respondents in other studies where emotional abuse is defined by frequency of behaviors from a checklist and who may not have identified themselves as "abused." This interpretation is based on the assumption that labeling the experience will affect people's responding and the effects of the abusive behaviors; an assumption that has yet to be empirically demonstrated. Indeed, recent research on sexual harassment indicates that simply being exposed to the behavior is sufficient to create negative effects; labelling is irrelevant (Magley et al., 1999). Returning to coping responses, many of the responses reported in the literature appear to be generated because they seemed reasonable rather than having any conceptual tie to the behavior, the actor, the target or other situational aspects. A possible conceptual framework for classification is provided by Fitzgerald and her colleagues in their work on an inventory to assess strategies for dealing with sexual harassment (Fitzgerald & Shullman, 1993). The framework consists of strategies characterized as either internally (emotion) focused (e.g., endurance, denial, detachment, relabeling, illusory control) or externally (problem) focused (e.g., avoidance, appeasement, assertion, reporting, seeking social support). The advantage of an inventory is that it provides consistent information across a variety of studies and permits the examination of the relationship of type of response to a variety of other factors.

In terms of the dynamics of coping, research is needed to identify and examine the factors that will influence target's responding. In the current study and consistent with a stress-appraisal framework like Folkman and Lazarus's (1984) work, it appears that the availability of personal and organizational resources is a critical influence. Thacker (1992) in her work on coping with sexual harassment has argued that perceived control to alter the situation mediates target choice and that attribution for the event and access to resources affect perceived control. In essence, targets will perceive limited ability to control the situation when they do not attribute the cause of the behavior to the actor and/or have few resources available to respond. With little perceived control they are more likely to acquiesce. They are more likely to be active and direct when they attribute the behavior to the actor and/or have resources to respond. While the current study is suggestive of the resource link to responding, this relationship needs to be examined more systematically, initially through scenario studies and manipulation of key factors.

It is relevant in this discussion of coping and resources to highlight the need to focus research attention on the role of coworkers and other organizational members in target's experiences. As noted in this study, knowing of others' experiences with a particular actor as well as experiencing the response of the organization's representatives to the target's concerns were connected to their overall experience of feeling abused. While this study identified some possible responses on the part of the organization to concerns, details of what coworkers did or did not do that were important in the respondents' experiences and were not provided. As mentioned earlier, coworkers may be important in helping frame the interactions with the actor for the target by providing alternate explanations. Notable rates of witnessing of abusive interactions and evidence that witnesses experience negative effects from this experience (e.g., Rayner, 1999) emphasize the importance of considering coworkers in the overall experience of emotional abuse at work. To date, there has been only limited research on this group.

LIMITATIONS

The limitations of any study methodology are intimately connected to the purported research questions. It can be argued that the self-report and retrospective nature of this study is inherently problematic in terms of whether the reports provided are accurate (i.e., confirmed by observers). The self-report nature is actually a key strength for this study which focused on targets' understanding of what they were experiencing, that is, subjective harassment (Brodsky, 1976). The retrospective nature is a limitation in that the description is being developed post hoc and any apparent interconnections among the elements identified may be an artifact of weaving a consistent story. A prospective study in which diaries of experiences over a period of months for new employees would allow insight into both the temporal and interactive components of the experience.

Another possible limitation is the nature of the sample. It is definitely self-selected as it focuses on those who have identified themselves as experiencing "interpersonal difficulties" at work. Thus, the respondents' discussion of their experience can not and should not be generalized to those who may have indeed been exposed to similar behaviors but have not labeled that experience as difficult or abusive or bullying. Yet in relationship to the key question of what factors are relevant in targets' understanding of their experience, it is completely appropriate. A key question is whether the elements identified and the proposed interconnections would be "validated" with another sample. This validation is an important step in terms of generalizing that the elements as identified and described have the same meaning and the purportedly similar relationships as the analysis of these respondents suggests.

Qualitative analysis often comes under scrutiny because of the reliance on the author's interpretation. Indeed, it is often argued that a different researcher may have provided a different interpretation. This is also true for quantitative analysis. That is why in this study and others the data as they were used are reported to allow the readers to make their own connections and stimulate questions for future consideration.

Conclusion

That there is violence in workplaces is now unquestionable. Our awareness, though, of the nature and extent of that violence is changing. Psychological forms of violence are receiving much needed attention. Emotional abuse as a psychological form of violence is increasingly the focus of research around the world (see Einarsen, 1999; Hoel et al., 1999; Keashly, 1998). As with sexual harassment work, the challenge of the objective versus subjective nature of emotional abuse is alive in the workplace abuse literature. In the current study, the focus was on the subjective phenomenon of feeling harassed and the factors related to these experiences. It was found that elements important in researchers' and other observers' definition and labeling of emotional abuse were similar. The use of a qualitative approach has allowed insight into how these various discrete elements as operationalized in more quantitative experimental work are experienced, interpreted and interconnected in targets' own stories of their experiences. These findings provide the basis for further work focused on documenting some of the proposed connections more directly.

A final contribution of this study concerns systemic features of emotional abuse at work, that is, the organization's role. What becomes clear in respondents' descriptions of their experiences with the actor and their organization is that work is a critical source of achievement and self-esteem and that workers expect the workplace to be supportive and challenging for their development. They also expected that just as they give to the organization, the organization needed to give to them in terms of acknowledgement and encouragement to continue to develop. Experiences with the actor(s) and subsequent responses of the organizations appears for the respondents to have violated these requirements that were fundamental to their well being and contributed to their sense of being abused. It is likely that these experiences will have a profound impact on their ties to and efforts for the organization. Thus, research and organizational attention needs to be focused on identifying and clarifying the roles the organization plays in emotional abuse at work.

REFERENCES

Archer, D. (1999). Exploring "bullying" culture in the para-military organization. *International Journal of Manpower,* 20(1/2), 94–105.

Ashforth, B. (1994). Petty tyranny in organizations. *Human Relations, 47,* 755–778.

Barling, J. (1996). The prediction, experience, and consequences of workplace violence.In G. R. VandenBos and E. Q. Bulatao (Eds). *Violence on the job* (pp. 29–50). Washington, DC: American Psychological Association.

Baron, R. A. (1988). Negative effects of destructive criticism: Impact on conflict, self-efficacy, and task performance. *Journal of Applied Psychology,* 73(2), 199–207.

Baron, R. A., & Neuman, J. H. (1996). Workplace violence and workplace aggression: Evidence on their relative frequency and potential causes. *Aggressive Behavior, 22,* 161–173.

Bassman, E. S. (1992). *Abuse in the workplace.* Westport, CT: Quorum Books.

Baumeister, R. F., Stillwell, A., & Wotman, S. R. (1990). Victim and perpetrator accounts of interpersonal conflict. *Journal of Personality & Social Psychology, 59,* 994–1005.

Bjorkqvist, K., Osterman, K., & Hjelt-Back, M. (1994). Aggression among university employees. *Aggressive Behavior, 20,* 173–184.

Bies, R. J., & Moag, J. S. (1986). Interactional justice: Communications criteria of fairness. In R. Lewicki and B. Sheppard (Eds.), *Research in negotiation in organizations,* (Vol. 1, pp. 43–55). Greenwich, CT: JAI Press.

Brodsky, C. M. (1976). *The harassed worker.* Lexington, MA: Lexington Books.

Buss, A. H. (1961). *The psychology of aggression.* New York: John Wiley & Sons, Ltd.

Clayton, S. D. (1992). Remedies for discrimination: Race, sex, and affirmative action. *Behavioral Sciences and the Law, 10*(2), 245–257.

Cleveland, J. N., & Kerst, M. E. (1993). Sexual harassment and perceptions of power: An unarticulated relationship. *Journal of Vocational Behavior, 42,* 49–67.

Cox, H. (1991). Verbal abuse nationwide, Part II: Impact and modifications. *Nursing Management, 22,* 66–69.

Einarsen, S. (1999). The nature and causes of bullying at work. *International Journal of Manpower, 20*(1/2), 16–27.

Einarsen, S., Raknes, B. I., & Matthiesen, S. M. (1994). Bullying and harassment at work and their relationships to work environment quality: An exploratory study. *European Work and Organizational Psychologist, 4,* 381–401.

Einarsen, S., & Skogstad, A. (1996). Bullying at work: Epidemiological findings in public and private organizations. *European Journal of Work and Organizational Psychology, 5,* 185–202.

Fitzgerald, L. E, & Schullman, S. L. (1993). Sexual harassment: A research analysis and agenda for the 1990s. *Journal of Vocational Behavior, 42,* 97–109.

Folger, R. (1993). Reactions to mistreatment at work. In J. K. Murnighan (Ed.), *Social psychology of organizations* (pp. 161–183). Englewood Cliffs, NJ: Prentice-Hall.

Folkman, S., &Lazarus, R. S. (1984). If it changes, it must be process: Study of emotional and coping during three stages of a college examination. *Journal of Personality and Social Psychology, 48*(1), 150–170.

Greenberg, L., & Barling, J. (1998). Predicting employee aggression against coworkers, subordinates, and supervisors: The roles of person behaviors and pearceived workplace factors. *Journal of Organizational Behaviour, 20,* 897–913.

Gwartney-Gibbs, P. A., & Lach, D. H. (1993, June). *Defining disputes in the workplace: The role of gender.* Paper presented at the 5th NCPCR conference, Portland, OR.

Harvey, S. R. (1995). *Bosses' negative interpersonal behaviors: A latent variable test of personal and organizational outcomes.* Unpublished doctoral dissertation, University of Guelph, Ontario.

Hoel, H., Rayner, C., & Cooper, C. L. (1999). Workplace bullying. In C. L. Cooper & I. T. Robertson (Eds)., *International Review of Industrial and Organizational Psychology, 14,* 195–230.

Hornstein, H. A. (1996). *Brutal bosses and their prey: How to identify and overcome abuse in the workplace.* New York: Riverhead Books.

Jagatic, K., & Keashly, L. (1998). *The nature of graduate student-faculty relationships.* Unpublished manuscript, Wayne State University, Detroit, MI.

Kahn, R. L., & Byosiere, P. (1992). Stress in organizations. In M. D. Dunnette & L. M.Hough (Eds.), *Handbook of industrial and organizational psychology* (Vol. 3, pp. 242–298). Palo Alto, CA: Consulting Psychologists Press.

Keashly, L. (1998). Emotional abuse in the workplace: Conceptual and empirical issues. *Journal of Emotional Abuse, 1*(1), 85–115.

Keashly, L., Trott, V., & MacLean, L. M. (1994). Abusive behavior in the workplace: A preliminary investigation. *Violence and Victims, 9*(4), 125–141.

Keashly, L., Welstead, S., & Delaney, C. (1996). *Perceptions of abusive behaviors in the workplace: Role of history, emotional impact, and intent.* Unpublished manuscript, University of Guelph, Ontario.

Keashly, L., Harvey, S. R., & Hunter, S. (1997). Abusive interaction and role state stressors: Relative impact on student residence assistant stress and work attitudes. *Work & Stress, 11*(2), 175–185.

Kelley, H. H., (1973). The processes of causal attribution. *American Psychologist, 28,* 107–128.

Lewis, D. (1999). Workplace bullying: Interim findings of a study in further education and higher education in Wales. *International Journal of Manpower, 20*(1/2), 106–118.

Leymann, H. (1990). Mobbing and psychological terror at workplaces. *Violence and Victims,* 5(2), 119–126.

Leymann, H. (1996). The content and development of mobbing at work. *European Work & Organizational Psychology, 5,* 165–184.

Liefooghe, A. P. D., & Olafsson, R. (1999). "Scientists" and "amateurs": Mapping the bullying domain. *International Journal of Manpower, 20*(1/2), 39–49.

Lind, E. A. (1997). Litigation and claiming in organizations: Antisocial behavior or quest for justice? In R. A. Giacalone & J. Greenberg (Eds.). *Antisocial behaviors in organizations* (pp. 150–171). Thousand Oaks, CA: Sage.

Magley, V. J., Hulin, C. L., Fitzgerald, L., & DeNardo. (1999). Outcomes of self-labeling sexual harassment. *Journal of Applied Psychology, 84,* 390–402.

Neuman, J. H., & Baron, R. A. (1997). Aggression in the workplace. In R. A. Giacalone & J. Greenberg (Eds.), *Antisocial behaviors in organizations* (pp. 37–67). Thousand Oaks, CA: Sage.

NiCarthy, G., Gottlieb, N., & Coffman, S. (1993). *You just don't have to take it: A woman's guide to confronting emotional abuse at work.* Seattle, WA: Seal Press.

Northwestern National Life Insurance Company. (1993). *Fear and violence in the workplace.* Minneapolis, MN: Northwestern National Life Insurance Company.

O'Leary-Kelly, A. M., Griffin, R. W., & Glew, D. J. (1996). Organization-motivated aggression: A research framework. *Academy of Management Review, 21*(1), 225–253.

Price Spratlen, L. (1995). Interpersonal conflict which includes mistreatment in a university workplace. *Violence and Victims, 10,* 285–297.

Pryor, J. B., LaVite, C. M., & Stoller, L. M. (1993). Asocial psychological analysis of sexual harassment: The person/situation interaction. *Journal of Vocational Behavior, 42,* 68–83.

Rayner, C. (1999). From research to implementation: Finding leverage for prevention. *International Journal of Manpower, 20*(1/2), 28–38.

Richman, J. A., Rospenda, K. M., Nawyn, S. J., & Flaherty, J. A. (1997). Workplace harassment and self-medication of distress: A conceptual model and case illustrations. *Contemporary Drug Problems, 24,* 179–199.

Richman, J. A., Rospenda, K. M., Nawyn, S. J., Flaherty, J. A., Fendrich, M., Drum, M. L., & Johnson, T. P. (1999). Sexual harassment and generalized workplace abuse among university employees: Prevalence and mental health correlates. *American Journal of Public Health, 89,* 358–363.

Rogers, K. (1998). *Toward an integrative understanding of workplace mistreatment.* Unpublished Doctoral dissertation, University of Guelph, Guelph, Ontario.

Rosenberg, D. A., & Silver, H. K. (1984). Medical student abuse: An unnecessary and preventable cause of stress. *The Journal of the American Medical Association, 251*(6), 739–742.

Ryan, K. D. & Oestreich, D. K. (1991). *Driving fear out of the workplace.* San Francisco: Jossey-Bass Inc.

Sheehan, K. H., Sheehan, D. V., White, K., Leibowitz, A., & Baldwin, D. C. (1990). Apilot study of medical student "abuse": Student percpetions of mistreatment and misconduct in medical school. *The Journal of the American Medical Association, 263,* 533–537.

Thacker, R. A., & Ferris, G. R. (1991). Understanding sexual harassment in the workplace: The influence of power and politics within the dyadic interaction of harasser and target. *Human Resources Management Review, 1*(1), 23–27.

Thacker, R. A. (1992). A descriptive study of behavioral responses of sexual harassment targets: Implications for control Theory. *Employee Responsibilities and Rights Journal, 5*(2), 155–170.

Ury, W. L., Brett, J. M., & Goldberg, S. B. (1988). *Getting disputes resolved.* San Francisco: Jossey-Bass.

Offprints. Requests for offprints should be directed to Loraleigh Keashly, PhD, College of Urban Labor, and Metropolitan Affairs, Wayne State University, 3261 Faculty/Administration Building, Detroit MI 48202.

CPSIA information can be obtained
at www.ICGtesting.com
Printed in the USA

9 780826 194657